MW00856614

READY READER ONE

READY READER ONE

The Stories We Tell With, About, and Around Videogames

EDITED BY
MEGAN AMBER CONDIS
AND MIKE SELL

Louisiana State University Press
Baton Rouge

Published by Louisiana State University Press
lsupress.org

Designer: Michelle A. Neustrom
Typefaces: Whitman, text; Big Chub and Metropolis, display

Cover illustration courtesy Adobe Stock/Two Pixel.

Library of Congress Cataloging-in-Publication Data
Names: Condis, Megan, 1984– editor. | Sell, Mike, 1967– editor.
Title: Ready reader one : the stories we tell with, about, and around videogames /
    edited by Megan Amber Condis and Mike Sell.
Description: Baton Rouge : Louisiana State University Press, 2024. | Includes index.
Identifiers: LCCN 2023045636 (print) | LCCN 2023045637 (ebook) | ISBN
    978-0-8071-8089-1 (cloth) | ISBN 978-0-8071-8230-7 (paperback) | ISBN
    978-0-8071-8227-7 (epub) | ISBN 978-0-8071-8229-1 (pdf)
Subjects: LCSH: Video games in literature. | Video gamers in literature.
Classification: LCC PN56.V48 R643 2024 (print) | LCC PN56.V48 (ebook) |
    DDC 080.01—dc23/eng/20240117
LC record available at https://lccn.loc.gov/2023045636
LC ebook record available at https://lccn.loc.gov/2023045637

CONTENTS

ACKNOWLEDGMENTS

I would like to thank my partner, Brian Duhan, for always being my place of safety and strength. Thank you to Amy and Bill Davis for indulging me in my love for videogames back in the late '80s and early '90s. I wouldn't be where I am now if not for you! Thank you to Zack and Ericka Davis for being my sounding boards and for being amazing traveling partners. Thank you to Bobby and Meg Schweizer, Narissra Punyanunt-Carter, Katie Langford, Asheley Landrum, Melissa Gotlieb, Brian McLaughlin, and Ioana Coman for your friendship and support. Thank you to David Perlmutter, Mark Gring, and Rob Peaslee for being the best admins an assistant prof could hope for. And thank you to Mike Sell for being an amazing research partner and friend.

—MEGAN AMBER CONDIS

First, thanks go to Megan for being an exemplary coeditor. The editorial process is inevitably arduous, but given the nascent status of our topic and the challenges of sustaining the project across the COVID lockdown, a reliable and resilient partner has made all the difference. Academic writing is a team sport, and our contributors have been patient, assiduous, and resolute. As a faculty member of the Department of English and the Graduate Program in Literature & Criticism at Indiana University of Pennsylvania, I have the privilege of embodying the scholar-teacher model. The undergraduate and graduate students in my courses on videogames and playful literature have provided both affirmation and motive force for my research, particularly Jeff Ambrose, Brandi Bilotte, Shepard Maderer, Bradley Markle, Pope, and Zeeshan Siddique.

—MIKE SELL

And finally, from both of us, our thanks to Jenny Keegan, the staff of Louisiana State University Press, and our anonymous reviewers.

READY READER ONE

Introduction

The Stories We Tell With, About, and Around Videogames

MIKE SELL

Where Is the Literature in Gaming Literacy?

In his 2013 "Manifesto for a Ludic Century," game designer Eric Zimmerman argues that one of the most empowering knowledge sets for the twenty-first century is gaming literacy. Why? A good guess would be the explosive growth of the games industry. Videogames generated nearly $180 billion in revenue during 2021, and livestreamed games grew their audience to more than 700 million (Takhashi, "Game Livestreaming," "Global Game Market"). In 2020, the game and puzzle market was valued at more than $12 billion (Jarvis). Those playful markets pale in comparison to sports and gambling, the former topping $600 billion in 2022 ("Sports"), the latter $516 billion ("Global Gambling Market 2021"). In sum, countless people practice gaming literacy around kitchen tables and televisions, on phones and videogame consoles, at hobby stores, slot machines, and soccer fields. They don't always do it well. All too often, they do it in ways that are thoughtless and cruel.

But gaming literacy matters not simply because of the size of the gaming market. For one, games are a representational medium built out of systems: rules, procedures for enacting and enforcing rules, semiotic systems signifying the state of play. A game represents, according to Zimmerman, the world as "a set of parts that interrelates to form a whole." So it makes sense that we should understand how the medium shapes and is shaped by what it renders into image, sound, feeling, tone, and story—exactly as we should with any representational medium. Of course, playing a game is different than contemplating a painting or watching a dance. When we play, we're an active collaborator and cocreator. Gaming literacy is, in part, about understanding that activity. Zimmerman explains that, with the rise of powerful computers and digital networks, information itself "has been put at play. Our information networks no longer take the form of vast card catalogs or webs of pneumatic tubes. Digital networks are flexible and organic." These networks are increasingly ubiquitous, as are obligations to play.

This is partly the consequence of "gamification," the application of game design principles to nongaming environments and activities. In *The Gameful World*, Steffen P. Walz and Sebastian Deterding describe a multi-billion-dollar gamification market whose proponents advocate, in a tone that "is nothing if not evangelical," the use of points, badges, and leaderboards to promote everything from beer and chicken wings to the wellness routines that work off the effects of the same (3–4). The gamification of education is increasingly popular, too—as in, for example, classroom apps like *Kahoot!*, which enables teachers to design quizzes as game show–style group activities.

For proponents of gamification, the incorporation of games and game design strategies promotes choice, agency, and engagement. However, it also provides opportunities for exploitation and surveillance, a trend explored by Nicholas Bowman and my coeditor, Megan A. Condis. While acknowledging the benefits, they also describe how "gamification efforts de facto convert employees' personal leisure time into productive time," a trend that is all the more troubling when play is mandated (197). In 2001, performance theorist Jon McKenzie argued that shifts in the organizational structures and management strategies of capital were obliging us all to "Perform—or else!" Whether understood as "organizational efficiency," annual "performance reviews," or the "embodied enactment of cultural forces," our lives are increasingly analyzed in terms of the quality of our performance (7–8). What McKenzie didn't notice was that all of this could be kind of, well, fun.

The order of our day? Play—or else!

As Walz and Deterding note, when it comes to gamification, "we are dearly lacking solid description, analysis, and reflection of just *what is happening now* and just *how it will affect us, the people*." They argue for an interdisciplinary approach that combines "philosophy, game studies, human–computer interaction, psychology, sociology, economics, anthropology, and other disciplines" (9). However, while expert analysis is necessary, it's not sufficient. To fully understand "how playing, understanding, and designing games all embody crucial ways of looking at and being in the world" (Zimmerman), we need to put the perspectives of experts into dialogue with the "on-the-ground" literacies of those who play.

Brian Street, one of the leaders of the New Literacy Studies movement, makes a distinction between "autonomous" and "ideological" models of literacy. Yes, literacy is a set of skills that enable a person to do useful things—skills that are functionally "autonomous" from the contexts in which they are deployed. But literacy is also "a social practice . . . always embedded in socially constructed epistemological principles." Literacy practices are "rooted in conceptions of knowledge, identity, and being. They are also always embedded in social practices" (77–78). If conceptions of literacy are necessarily ideological, how do current understandings of gaming literacy address its ideological nature? Frankly, not as well as they should, which is precisely where the question of storytelling—and the mission of this anthology—comes into play.

Consider, for example, the question of fun. Games are fun, games are beautiful, and as Zimmerman writes, "Appreciating the aesthetics of games—how dynamic interactive systems create beauty and meaning—is one of the delightful and daunting challenges we face in this dawning Ludic Century." But for many, games often are neither beautiful nor fun. Consider the question of failure. Unlike most aesthetic experiences, where failure to succeed can be disappointing or frustrating, failing in a game is typically a spur to try again. Colleen Macklin and Bonnie Ruberg (qtd. in Clark and Kopas) argue that this is an especially significant experience for the queer player: playing a game "provides a safe space for failure—and indeed, many games emphasize repeated failure as part of a learning process." Naomi Clark and Merritt Kopas (now merritt k) question this assumption. "If games provide a safe space for failure," they ask, "and that space makes them inherently queer, then why is it that so many women, so many queers, simply fall out of wanting to play games at some point while growing up?" For those "made to feel incapable in other realms . . . adulthood—with the promise of leaving play—is the real escape. How many of us looked forward with desperate anticipation to the day we'd never have to take another gym class or play another game of Friday-night *Scrabble* with our families?" Those are stories that aren't often told by theorists of gaming literacy.

Where do stories of bullying, misogyny, and queerphobia fit into our theories of gaming literacy? The cultures of gaming are rife with thoughtlessness, prejudice, and willful cruelty—and so is the games industry, as evident in the 2021 suit filed by the California Department of Fair Employment against Activision Blizzard for a "frat boy" workplace culture that promoted harassment and abuse of women employees. This comes as no surprise. As Condis argues in her book *Gaming Masculinity*, toxic masculinity is a logical consequence of the performative, collaborative, communicative, and competitive culture surrounding games. The trolls who engineered the vitriol and violence of Gamergate, for example, merely weaponized "the normative rhetorical practices of hardcore online gamers, a blown-up version of their complex and contradictory views regarding the politics of embodiment and identity" (3). In other words, toxic masculinity is a gaming literacy. But it's also a *story*, a story told by violent, intolerant men about "feminist spoilsports" and "social justice warriors" and "ethics in games journalism." And if we turn our attention to the ways those stories are told and distributed—on social media platforms like Reddit, Twitter, Facebook, and 4Chan; on blogs and in the comment sections of YouTube; in the customer review sections of gaming platforms like Steam—we can take a step further and designate toxic masculinity as, quite literally, a *literature*.

To fight the trolls, we need to tell a different kind of story about games and play.

The Literature of Games Literacy

Scholars have long recognized the importance of the stories we tell about literacy. In their 1992 essay "Reading Literacy Narratives," Janet Cary Eldred and Peter Mortensen call for the study of texts that tell the story of talking, reading, and writing. George Bernard Shaw's 1912 play *Pygmalion*, for example, raises "questions about the nature of literacy education, about whether literacy can be acquired without institutional training, about the relationship between literacy and socialization, employment, and mobility, about the continuities and tensions between speech and writing, about the influence of popular and literary genres on literacy formation, and about the role of gender in the acquisition of schooled language" (513).

The "romance of literacy" is an enduring and widespread trope (529). This is particularly true for those denied access to literacy. In *Figures in Black* (1987), Henry Louis Gates Jr. explores the romance of literacy in Black American slave narratives. He writes, "Learning to read, the slave narratives repeat again and again, was a decisive political act; learning to write . . . was an irreversible step away from the cotton field toward a freedom larger even than physical manumission." Literacy for the Black American, particularly its "ideological" value (to recall Street), "became the central, indeed controlling, metaphors (if not mythical matrices) in Afro-American narrative" (Gates 4). The stories we tell about literacy matter—and they matter because they show us what literacy is and why it matters.

While the stakes of gaming literacy are typically not as high for players of games as reading and writing were for the impoverished female Londoner or the enslaved Black American, they are occasionally a matter of life and death. In his essay in this collection, Rob Gallagher examines three "ludobiographies," a subgenre of life-writing in which writers explore the roles gaming plays in their lives. Zoë Quinn's *Crash Override* (2017), for example, tells the harrowing story of Quinn's victimization by the trolls of Gamergate who refused to accept that there were other tales to tell both with and about videogames. Florencia Rumpel Rodriguez's zine *In the beginning we all played Family* (2019) tells the story of players in Argentina who lack the wealth required to play present-generation videogame consoles. Hers is a story of pirated hardware, inadequately localized software, and bootlegged software. But most importantly, it's a story of a child playing games with her father. Videogame speedrunner Narcissa Wright's "all the categories are arbitrary" is a poem that explores Wright's gender transitioning in light of her experience speedrunning *The Legend of Zelda: Ocarina of Time*. Gallagher sees in Wright's speedrunning and in her poem "a form of metagaming that pushes the limits of the game, but also of the embodied player."

If, as Gallagher argues, ludobiographies "post a subtle but salutary challenge to hegemonic understandings of gaming" by "reveal[ing] how and by whom games were *actually* played," Francis Butterworth-Parr's essay here demonstrates how videogame stories can serve as "valuable discursive touchstones for rendering and interrogating videogame controversies." In Michael W. Clune's *Gamelife: A Memoir* (2015), that controversy concerns what the World Health Organization calls "gaming disorder," more popularly known as "videogame addiction." Recalling the distinction between top-down and on-the-ground literacies, Butterworth-Parr argues that the lack of consensus concerning videogame addiction is all the more problematic because the "conversation occurs without the voice of those for whom videogames are a formative medium." Ultimately, Butterworth-Parr says, gaming literacy narratives open a space for alternative perspectives and useful vocabulary. In sum, if we want to understand what and how games "mean," then we need to read the stories players tell about them and be alert to the values that those stories reinforce or challenge.

Consider Ernest Cline's novel *Ready Player One* (2011), perhaps the single most popular story about videogames ever told, with 1.7 million copies in print, a 2018 film adaptation directed by Steven Spielberg, and a best-selling sequel (Juris). Megan and I have spent many hours and thousands of words pondering Cline's exasperatingly slippery story about videogames and the people who play them. Megan's essay in this collection is her second to date, and the title of this anthology is our own little Easter egg for the "gunters" in our audience. We remain fascinated by Cline's story of a near-future society in which most of the world spends most of its time in a full-body virtual reality videogame known as the OASIS. Indeed, this anthology would not exist without Cline's book. I first encountered Megan when I read her essay "Playing the Game of Literature: *Ready Player One*, the Ludic Novel, and the Geeky 'Canon' of White Masculinity." I was taken by her analysis of the way the novel affirms the importance of fan culture and insists that the on-the-ground literacies of videogame players matter, even if the "geeky canon" narrated by Cline affirms a breathtakingly narrow vision of those literacies.

While it's clear *what* Cline is doing when he imagines that canon, it's less clear *why*. Is that straight, white, Midwestern, male slice of gaming literacy meant to strike the reader as narrow? It's hard to say. Consider the way the text treats personal and historical trauma. The creator of the OASIS, James Halliday, was the child of an abusive, alcoholic father and an untreated manic-depressive mother. That personal trauma was compounded by larger historical trauma. Halliday grew up working-poor in Middletown, Ohio, one of those rust belt towns that collapsed in the 1980s under the weight of global economic shifts in manufacturing and the corrosive spread of methamphetamine addiction. The novel's hero, Wade/Parzival, suffers similarly, losing his father to violence, his mother to a drug overdose, and the promise of a better future to the slow-motion apocalypse cascading around him.

But it's not just the characters and their world that are traumatized. The puzzle that Halliday creates to pass on his vast wealth gamifies that trauma. To solve it, the player must relive Halliday's trauma and his strategies for managing it, most obviously when they visit Planet Middletown. Designed personally by Halliday, its surface is punctuated by "256 identical copies" of his hometown, "spread out evenly across the planet's surface" (101). Each of the copies is an idealized representation of 1980s Midwestern life: its residents friendly, its skies clear, its future bright. In each of those Middletowns is a simulacrum of

Halliday's childhood home. But it's missing something. Literalizing the representational gap that is common to traumatic experience, Wade tells us, "For whatever reason, Halliday had decided not to place NPC [nonplayer character] re-creations of himself or his deceased parents here" (103). As I've written elsewhere, "In its planetary scale and monomaniacal attention to detail, Planet Middletown crystallizes the loneliness, immobility, and passive-aggressive egotism that enabled James Halliday to turn misery into triumph (Sell, "A Defense"). But even as it presents the personal and systemic trauma suffered by white men and the ways they use videogames to protect themselves from that trauma, Cline nevertheless affirms the rugged, libertarian individualism that helped to create that trauma in the first place.

In vivid contrast to *Ready Player One*'s libertarian, white-boy virtual reality mod of Joseph Campbell's monomyth, we have Cory Doctorow's 2010 novel *For the Win*. As Condis argues in her essay here, Doctorow's novel tells a very different kind of story about videogames and those who play them. It concerns an unlikely alliance among videogame players, gold farmers, and other digital laborers who "use their superior gaming skills to negotiate with both their bosses in the real world and the game designers who built the virtual worlds in which they work." What Doctorow achieves, Condis concludes, is not just a different story about videogames, but a different way of conceiving a *videogamer*, defining them "not as someone who can achieve success in a game whose rules have been written to benefit powerful institutions but rather as someone who can find unexpected ways to rewrite that game's rules towards radical ends." In sum, there is more than one story to tell about videogames, videogame players, and videogame cultures.

This anthology affirms and celebrates the idea that videogames are always already wrapped up in storytelling, whether by the games themselves or by the people who make and play them. As Thomas Apperly argues, "The digital game ecology is shaped through myriad and plural local situations that collectively enact the global" (13), and those myriad situations require us to recognize not only what Philip Penix-Tadsen describes as "the myriad ways culture is incorporated into game mechanics" but also the way games and gaming practices are "embedded and situated in the material and mundane everyday" (6). The essays Megan and I have curated explore a rich variety of gaming literacies and literacy stories and are examples of how scholars can make use of both the expert perspective and the on-the-ground playful experience.

Defining the Genre

We define videogame literature as written works about videogames, videogame players, and videogame culture. Why only written works? Because scholars haven't paid enough attention to them. For those interested in movies, there is a fairly extensive body of work to consult, including Geoff King and Tanya Krzywinska's *ScreenPlay: Cinema/Videogames/Interfaces* (2002), Gretchen Papazian and Joseph Michael Sommers's *Game On, Hollywood!: Essays on the Intersection of Videogames and Cinema* (2013), Marie-Laure Ryan's monographs and edited anthologies on cross-media adaptations and storyworlds, Jasmina Kallay's *Gaming Film: How Games are Reshaping Contemporary Cinema* (2013), and the 2020 issue of *Arts* magazine edited by Christian Thomas (which includes my essay "What Is a Videogame Movie?"). These have established key concerns for the study of videogame adaptation, including the differential nature of interactivity, the productive tension between adaptation and remediation, the role of global corporations in the propagation of what Henry Jenkins calls "transmedia storytelling," the growth of fan communities as critics and creators, the persistence of negative stereotypes, and the distinct ways in which videogames and films construct narratives and storyworlds.

These concerns pertain to videogame literature, as our contributors demonstrate. In her essay on adaptations of Lewis Carroll's *Alice's Adventures in Wonderland* and *Through the Looking-Glass*, Kristen Starkowski surveys "the longer historical and broader ludological character of videogame literature," mapping a transmedia tradition of playful texts that encompasses the wider Victorian culture of word-based games in which Carroll's books were created and received.

Andrew Bailey explores metatextual narrative references in *Kentucky Route Zero* and *Disco Elysium,* two videogames that literally play with the canon of twentieth-century literature. Bailey highlights the way those games articulate the realist and postrealist literary traditions with digital technologies and digital games, the latter comprising something like the technological unconscious of modern literature.

Chloe Anna Milligan explores embodiment in videogame literature. Against conventional wisdom, she insists that reading digital game texts is a form of play "with material registers and ramifications." Milligan makes her case by mapping a genealogy of playful texts across historical and media boundaries, including the "feelies" packaged with the text-based adventures published by Infocom in the 1980s, the crime dossiers created by Dennis Wheatley and J. G. Links in the 1930s, and Aldous Huxley's *Brave New World* (1932).

Niels 't Hooft tells the story of an emerging global community of readers, players, game designers, and writers who share a common taste culture, the exemplum of which is the novels of Haruki Murakami. Hooft shows how Murakami influenced videogame designers and vice versa, and in a ludobiographical turn of his own, discusses how that community enabled his own career as a writer.

Finally, José Blázquez examines the ways in which storytelling informs the participatory culture around videogames; specifically, players remediating videogame narratives, bugs, exploits, and mods. As he notes, the machinima, photography, and "gamics" that players create are in turn shared in social media spaces, becoming, in due course, spurs to even more storytelling.

Thus, our decision to limit the scope of this anthology to written works should not suggest that they don't share formal, thematic, social, economic, and cultural characteristics with other media. Nevertheless, written works about videogames are distinct, as are the questions that can be asked about them, which is why the dearth of scholarly works on them is so odd. One exception is Jason Barr's *Video Gaming in Science Fiction: A Critical Study* (2018). Though his focus is narrower than ours, he shares our interest in how writers embrace videogames as subject matter, how scholars can utilize videogame theory to read videogame literature, and how the stories we tell about videogames both depict and constitute videogames as a cultural phenomenon (5, 10).

A second and especially insightful exception is Mia Consalvo's *Cheating: Gaining Advantage in Videogames*. Though her focus is the production of the videogame player as a cultural and ethical subject, that subject's emergence can be traced to the videogame magazines and strategy guides. As Consalvo demonstrates, game magazines like *Nintendo Power* and *Electronic Gaming Monthly* "helped contribute to a growing culture of gaming, creating a space for game players to learn about upcoming titles, read reviews, and gain strategy tips and hints for the games they had just bought" (23). As the culture of videogames evolved, the magazines evolved too, their emphasis shifting from tips and tricks to "profiling the development of particular games, multireviews of games, and entertaining information about the game industry and its personalities" (35). For the "power gamer," access to and understanding of the textual production surrounding games and play became increasingly "indistinguishable from actual game-playing ability" (38).

For our present concerns, we would note that the power gamer was also a power *reader*, not only a consumer of games but also a canny negotiator of a network of *paratexts*, defined by Gérard Genette, as all of the matter that surrounds the core experience of a text. The paratext, he writes, functions as "a zone between text and off-text, a zone not only of transition but also of *transaction*: a privileged place of a pragmatics and a strategy, of an influence on the public, an influence that—whether well or poorly understood and achieved—is at the service of a better reception for the text and a more pertinent reading of it" (2). Given her otherwise comprehensive account of the rise of the videogame's paratextual economy, it's odd that Consalvo doesn't include the *literary* literature of videogames—the vast body of short fiction, life-writing, poetry, television series, movies, histories, and novels about videogames, videogame players and designers, and the cultures of videogame play that emerged simultaneously with videogame magazines and guides and remain popular.

Our contributors explore these issues explicitly. In their essays, Condis compares representations of the "gamer" in *Ready Player One* and *For the Win*, and Butterworth-Parr deconstructs the stereotype of the videogame addict by counterposing the popular and medical discourses on the subject with the obsessive, perhaps dependent player in *Gamelife*.

In his essay, Jarrel de Matas explores the trope of retrogaming in D. B. Weiss's *Lucky Wander Boy* (2003), centering the protagonist's obsession with old games to highlight the book's acidly self-indulgent vision of posthuman society.

Riziki Millanzi delves into Brittney Morris's young adult novel *SLAY* (2019) and its bracing vision of young Black women as designers and players. *SLAY* confronts the wider spectrum of Black stereotypes, utilizing the tropes of videogames to contextualize, complicate, and cancel them.

That focus on community is shared by "Reading Fans Reading," in which Craig Carey unpacks Davey Wreden's *The Beginner's Guide* (2015) and its representation of a curious breed of videogame writer: the fan theorist.

In their essays, Holly Parker and Aaron Heinrich explore how videogames mediate personal relationships and difficult emotional experiences. Parker focuses on Keith Stuart's 2016 novel *A Boy Made of Blocks*, helping us understand how Stuart uses *Minecraft* to capture both a neurotypical parent's struggle to connect with his autistic child and neoliberal pressures to sustain the family as a site of economic and ideological productivity. Heinrich compares two novels about grieving parents, Dennis Cooper's *God Jr.* (2005) and Jeanette Winterson's *The Gap of Time* (2015). He shows how they remediate the videogame avatar and the "communal healing" possibilities of playful temporality to defamiliarize the labor of mourning.

These essays fulfill our mission to modify how we think about videogames, videogame players, and the cultures of videogame play.

But we also need to understand the role those stories play as material, ideological, and economic artifacts. Another exception to the absence of scholarly works on videogame literature is Tamer Thabet and Tim Lanzendörfer's essay "The Video Game Novel: StoryWorld Narratives, Novelization, and the Contemporary Novel-Network." By way of a detailed analysis of the publication and reception of *Halo: The Fall of Reach* (a novel by Eric C. Nylund that tells the backstory of the game's protagonist, Master Chief), they untangle a knot of material, social, and economic factors shaping not just the videogame novel (one of the most popular novel genres in the world) but also the contemporary novel more generally.

Our contributors explore similar territory. Michelle Shea digs into the multi-million-dollar market for videogame literature intended for young readers. Publishers, she argues, want to take advantage of the huge profit margins and built-in audiences represented by the gaming community, but there is also opportunity for great communication and collaboration as a result of the increasingly indistinct line between "readers" and "gamers."

Michał Dawid Żmuda explores paratexts and storyworld creation in digital games, highlighting the variety of written texts that serve as "experiential thresholds" for videogames. These include mundane texts such as cover blurbs but also more elaborate creations like letters and maps, fictional diaries, and novels. Żmuda argues that, if we're going to talk about "videogame literature," we need to define it so that it encompasses far more than novels, short fiction, poetry, and drama.

This includes game guides, walkthroughs, and Frequently Asked Questions sections (FAQs). In his book *Playing with Videogames*, James Newman identifies these texts as critical for understanding "the meanings of videogames to players and the myriad ways in which they make use of them besides just playing them—playing *with* them." Further, they "reveal much of the videogame fan's understanding of the processes of commercial media production, including the tensions between creative vision, budgetary constraints, deadlines, and technical limitations." They also provide useful perspectives on the gaming community, a community for whom "play is always and already situated within a shared experience" (vii–viii).

The texts presented here comprise by far the largest corpus of videogame literature and arguably are the most acute lens into the on-the-ground literacies of videogame players. Readers interested in this dimension of videogame literature will find illuminating the essays by Carey on fan theories, Jesika Brooks on the rhetoric of boss battle walkthroughs, and Christopher Lovins on the critical discourse surrounding videogame novelizations.

Brooks argues that because videogames combine gameplay, narrative, and intense personal and social experience, they inspire those who play them to invent new forms of storytelling. Boss battle walkthroughs are fascinating texts, as they veer from one rhetorical mode to the next (from technical writing to personal narrative to critical reflection) and are rarely read from start to finish.

In his essay, Lovins writes about fans of the best-selling *Mass Effect* tetralogy. In addition to helping us understand the commercial and creative challenges shaping videogame novelizations, Lovins tells the tale of an active and increasingly powerful fan culture. Criticisms of the fourth novel compelled BioWare, the company that produced the game and its novels, to apologize and promise better products in the future. For those of us who have lived through the controversies surrounding all-female *Ghostbusters*, Asian American *Star Wars* characters, and the Snyder Cut, the tale that Lovins tells feels portentous.

Opening the Umbrella

Given this diversity, it behooves us to refine our definition of videogame literature so that it's more than simply "written works about videogames." But that's easier said than done. Novels like *Ready Player One* and *For the Win* are obviously videogame literature. Both are set in the world of videogames and feature videogame players, designers, and other fans and industry-associated folk as characters. Both are clearly *about* videogames. This is also true of Neal Stephenson's *Reamde* (2011), whose protagonists include the makers and players of a massively multiplayer online roleplaying game similar to *World of Warcraft*. True, too, of Jennifer Haley's play *Neighborhood 3: Requisition of Doom* (2009), part of which takes place in an augmented reality zombie hunter game. Many of our contributors write about these kinds of stories: Butterworth-Parr on *Gamelife,* Condis on *Ready Player One* and *For the Win*, De Matas on *Lucky Wander Boy,* Heinrich on *God Jr.* and *The Gap of Time*, Millanzi on *SLAY*, Parker on *A Boy Made of Blocks,* and Gallagher on *Crash Override, In the beginning we all played Family,* and "all the categories are arbitrary." Similarly, novelizations of videogames like *World of Warcraft* and *Minecraft* would fill our literary-critical bill of lading. Shea's essay on novelizations as a powerful driver of youth literacy and Lovins's on the fan culture surrounding the *Mass Effect* novels demonstrate the value of these texts to our understanding of videogames.

But what about Alex Gino's young adult novel *George* (2015)? Though not focused on videogames, it includes a poignant interlude in which the protagonist plays *Mario Kart* with her brother. In a 2016 article for *Kill Screen*, Bryan Cebulski reads the moment "as a device to show the unspoken affections shared between the two," Scott and George, the latter of whom is preparing to come out as trans. But the way Scott and George play is also meaningful to Cebulski. The characters' choice of in-game characters (Scott choosing "the bulky, brusque and evil Bowser," George selecting the minuscule Toad) "further enforce[s] the dichotomy between the two characters" when it comes to gender identification.

A similar use of videogames can be found in Raven Leilani's *Luster* (2020). Edie, a twenty-three-year-old Black woman, plays all sorts of videogames with Akila, the adopted Black preteen daughter of the wealthy, older white couple with whom Edie gets emotionally and sexually involved. These include "a turn-based RPG [roleplaying game] where the protagonist is an army mail clerk with amnesia" and in which a vibration of the controller "indicates the genesis of a new memory" (115), "a collaborative multiplayer where we have to prepare burgers for a ravenous fast-food crowd" (159), and others. In an interview with Kendra Winchester, Leilani explains that these moments celebrate "two Black women engaged in a joyful experience." But they also show how videogames can be used as vehicles for social criticism. Leilani tells Winchester that "when Edie and Akela are drawing nearer to each other, they are doing it through this medium. They're doing it through these avatars . . . relating to each other in a digital context where they are still kind of disembodied in the way that a lot of Black women have to be as they move through the world."

Though videogames do not occupy the center of attention in *George* and *Luster*, they do important narrative work. They provide, in Tom Boellstorf's words, "clearer insight into the way gaming affects our daily activities, including the lives of those who do not play games or participate in new media practices" (Roig et al., 90). We should be alert to the presence of videogames in the texts we read and watch. Watching someone play can be a rich source of information.

If videogame literature enables us to be more attentive to the ways in which videogames, videogame players, and videogame cultures are represented, then it follows that we should be just as attentive to what counts as a videogame in the first place. In my essay "What Is a Videogame Movie?" (2021), I argue that whether we consider something a videogame movie depends on assumptions about "the technology that comprises the videogame as medium," "the diverse histories and play cultures of and around videogames, many of them yet to be brought into the fold of scholarship," the tendency to focus only on "big-budget games produced by multinational corporations," and "the heteronormative, nationalist, and ethnocentric ideologies that shape not just what videogames are made, but the play cultures and game literacies that are affirmed or marginalized by those ideologies." In contrast, art historian Lana Polanski writes, we might explore a "lesser-known history . . . a more intimate account composed of a long heritage of games deliberately concerned with the artistic, political and personal." That's a story not about next-generation consoles and multibillion-dollar intellectual properties but about bulletin board systems, little-known designers, and outmoded technologies. By excavating the past for "its most intriguing contributions," we can, "hopefully, point to a better alternative reality."

Chloe Anna Milligan's essay here on feelies does precisely that. She compares three older examples of interactive media, two of them predigital. First, there are the feelies described in Aldous Huxley's 1932 dystopian novel *Brave New World*, which provide its audiences "an almost intolerable galvanic pleasure" (167–68). Second, there are the fictional crime dossiers of Dennis Wheatley and J. G. Links, which included clues like cigarette butts, locks of hair, crime scene photographs, and so on. Third, there are the material objects packaged with the digital text adventures produced by Infocom between 1984 and 1989. These three texts suggest a genealogy of interactive narratives that is incompletely understood and still very much in play, as is evident from the multimillion-dollar market in videogame replica props and the worldwide passion for cosplay. Milligan's suggestion that *Brave New World* and *Murder off Miami* should be historically retrofitted as a work of "videogame literature" aligns with Steve Keane's argument that older sci-fi films like Brett Leonard's *The Lawnmower Man* (1992) can help us comprehend the "developmental gap" between representational possibility and "the technical limitations of current videogames and videogame systems" (149). But Milligan takes this notion in a divergent direction, arguing that feelies should be understood as evidence of an essential gap between game and player in which complex forms of embodied reading are generated. In Milligan's view, before we can fully understand the stories we tell with, about, and around videogames, we need to first understand how storytelling works as a haptic, affectively charged, transmedia process.

Where might we find comparable literary imaginings of videogames before videogames existed? Jason Wilson has tracked a common set of visual and performative design principles linking the work of abstract expressionist Barnett Newman's painting *Onement IV* (1949), installation artist Nam June Paik's *Zen for TV* (1963), and Atari's *Pong* (1972). These share not only a common look (a rectilinear space divided down the middle by a bright line) but also a common concern with promoting a new kind of "embodied attention" (87).

I would point to an earlier example, the 1950s US children's television show *Winky Dink and You*. An otherwise anodyne entertainment, it distinguished itself from its competitors by way of a nifty little technological supplement. Fans of the show could mail order a thin electrostatic sheet of plastic called a "magic window," attach it to their television screen, and draw on it with special "magic crayons." Every episode featured moments when the viewer would be asked to complete connect-the-dots puzzles (for example, a bridge over a chasm), reveal hidden messages, or create a character for the actors to converse with. *Winky Dink and You* fulfills the core definition of a videogame: nontrivial interaction between the viewer and an electronic screen. Further, the screen and crayons could be used for more mischievous ends, low-tech "glitch play," like drawing horns on an actor in a commercial pitching breakfast cereal.

Let's go a little farther out on the literary-historical limb. Though I've found no evidence that Crockett Johnson knew about *Winky Dink and You* (or vice versa) when he conceived his *Harold and the Purple Crayon* series (1955–63), his story of a little boy materially altering his world with a magical drawing implement is curiously similar to what the producers of *Winky Dink* designed. The two texts share a vision of a child using a handheld device (a crayon) and a screen (for Harold, the world itself, flattened to two dimensions) to express their imaginations and change their worlds. A more inclusive definition of "videogame literature" that encompasses texts that don't focus on videogames, that focus on antique or conceptually adjacent gaming technologies, or that imagine videogames that don't exist in present reality can alert us to a wider range of videogame adaptation strategies, a more diverse set of gaming literacies, and a more granular understanding of the ideological significance of those literacies.

Ready Reader Two!

Megan and I embarked on this project in part because we wanted to learn more about what videogame literature is. We haven't been disappointed. However, despite our best efforts, we haven't been able to fully cover the field or the questions it raises. Take poetry, for example. The work of Colette Arrand, Ashley Harris, B. J. Best, Sam Martone, Hannah Faith Notess, and August Smith (to name a few) are entirely worthy of attention, even if they're absent from our table of contents. Indeed, poetry provides singular insight into the semantic and affective dimensions of videogames. In "St. Augustine Enters the World's Largest Pac-Man Maze," Notess explores themes of grace and salvation in terms of the iterative travels of Pac-Man through his pellet-punctuated labyrinth. She asks, "What is the soul, my God, / but a point of light / propelled by desire?" Notess's figure intertwines the desire of Pac-Man and player, both "hardwired" by their creators, both intent on finding a kind of temporary freedom from death through iterative, compulsive movement.

Ashley Harris explores a similar contrast between freedom and unfreedom but frames it in terms of the history of race, racism, and the duplicities they obligate. In "For all the masks formed:," Harris avers, "The history of race / Is a history of masks," then turns her attention to Link, the protagonist of *The Legend of Zelda: Majora's Mask* (2000), who "fits into all the masks: / Zora, / Goron, / Deku, / Scrub, / white boy / with blonde hair and blue eyes / fits all sizes." But what cost, she asks, does wearing the mask demand of the player of color? Riffing on Paul Lawrence Dunbar's 1895 poem "We Wear the Mask" ("We smile, but, O great Christ, our cries / To thee from tortured souls arise"), Harris writes, "I tried to be like Link, / wondering / who would have to die / for me to reincarnate into /another shade."

Also missing from these pages is the rich intertextual relationship of rap and videogames. The Notorious B.I.G.'s "Juicy" may be the superlative example ("Super Nintendo, Sega Genesis / When I was dead broke, man, I couldn't picture this"), but is one of countless raps that reference videogames. Games have returned the favor, from *PaRappa the Rappa* (1996), a pioneering rhythm game with a "U Rappin" meter, to *Grand Theft Auto: San Andreas* (2004), which features protagonists based on the rap group NWA, real-world MCs like The Game and Ice-T, and a rapcentric soundtrack. In "The Futurism of Hip Hop: Space, Electro and Science Fiction in Rap," Adam de Paor-Evans argues that videogames not only feature as metaphor and focus in raps like the Dead Residents' "Smash Robot Vs. Packman Ghost" (2008) but also inform its structure and rhythm, too. Dead Resident member Junior Disprol explains, "The song is basically back and forth jousting and tourney style shit kicking" (qtd. in de Paor-Evans 131). This is an example of what I've called "procedural adaptation," in which creators adapt the mechanics of a game as formal structure, including what Paor-Evans identifies as the "transitions between real space and game-space" that are typical of videogame play and videogame culture, rap subgenres like Electro Rap, and intellectual and creative movements like Afrofuturism (131). We agree that the "cultural significance of the videogame within hip hop requires a broader and extensive study" (133).

Though Gallagher discusses Florencia Rumpel Rodriguez's zine *In the beginning we all played Family* and 't Hooft examines the Japanese writer Haruki Murakami's position in an emerging global taste culture, videogame literature outside the United States and Western Europe isn't as well represented in these pages as we would prefer. Obviously, there is much to learn about videogames, videogame players, and videogame cultures beyond the particular stories represented in our essays. Simply take a look at the "five snapshots" with which Phillip Penix-Tadsen starts his book *Video Games and the Global South*. They take us from a family playing videogames with a system powered by a car battery in the Dominican Republic to preteen game designers in India and Australia pitching games to Microsoft and Apple to a girl in Palestine sharing her love for first-person shooters to the crowning of a new international Esports champion in the Philippines to a makeshift entertainment center in a refugee camp in Sudan. These illustrate Adrienne Shaw's point that "to understand video games, we must look at them *in* culture, not just *as* culture" (Penix-Tadsen 6).

But even if the stories told in this anthology don't cover every story ever told about games, our contributors have succeeded at showing us, as Penix-Tadsen puts it, "how much of the 'big picture' of gaming is lost when we neglect experiences outside of the presumed norm, and just how much perspective can be gained by understanding games as complex technological and cultural products whose creation, circulation, consumption, and meaning are shaped by concerns and practices that are fundamentally local and situated in nature" (6).

We've only just begun the work of understanding the stories we tell with, about, and around videogames. We invite you to continue what we started here.

Ready Reader Two!

WORKS CITED

Apperly, Thomas H. *Gaming Rhythms: Play and Counterplay from the Situated to the Global*. Institute of Network Cultures, 2009.

Barr, Jason. *Video Gaming in Science Fiction: A Critical Study*. McFarland & Company, Inc., 2018.

Bowman, Nicholas David, and Megan Condis. "Governmentality, Playbor, and Peak Performance: Critiques and Concerns of Health and Wellness Gamification." *Privacy Concerns Surrounding Personal Information Sharing on Health and Fitness Mobile Apps*, edited by Devjani Sen and Rukhsana Ahmed. IGI Global, 2020, pp. 186–210.

Cebulski, Bryan. "A Model for Referencing Videogames in Literature." *Kill Screen*, 5 January 2016. https://killscreen.com/previously/articles/a-model-for-referencing-video games-in-literature.

Clark, Naomi, and Merritt Kopas [merritt k]. "Queering Human–Game Relations: Exploring Queer Mechanics and Play." *First Person Scholar*, 18 February 2015. http://www.firstpersonscholar.com/queering-human-game-relations.

Cline, Ernest. *Ready Player One*. Random House, 2011.

Condis, Megan. *Gaming Masculinity: Trolls, Fake Geeks, and the Gendered Battle for Online Culture*. University of Iowa Press, 2018.

———. "Playing the Game of Literature: *Ready Player One*, the Ludic Novel, and the Geeky 'Canon' of White Masculinity." *Journal of Modern Literature*, vol. 39, no. 2, Winter 2016, pp. 1–19.

Consalvo, Mia. *Cheating: Gaming Advantage in Videogames*. MIT Press, 2007.

De Paor-Evans, Adam. "The Futurism of Hip Hop: Space, Electro and Science Fiction in Rap." *Open Cultural Studies*, vol. 2 (2018), pp. 122–35.

Eldred, Janet Carey, and Peter Mortensen. "Reading Literacy Narratives." *College English*, vol. 54, no. 5 (September 1992), 512–39.

"FIFA Survey: Approximately 250 Million Footballers Worldwide." FIFA.com, 3 April 2001. https://www.fifa.com/who-we-are/news/fifa-survey-approximately-250-million-foot ballers-worldwide-88048. Accessed 19 May 2021.

Franklin, Seb. *Control: Digitality as Cultural Logic*. MIT Press, 2015.

Gates, Henry Louis Jr. *Figures in Black: Words, Signs, and the 'Racial' Self*. Oxford University Press, 1987.

Gee, James Paul. "Learning and Games." *The Ecology of Games: Connecting Youth, Games, and Learning*, edited by Katie Salen. MIT Press, 2008.

Genette, Gérard. *Paratexts: Thresholds of Interpretation*, translated by Jane E. Lewin. Cambridge University Press, 1997.

"Global Gambling Market 2021." *PR Newswire*, 9 February 2021. https://www.prnews wire.com/news-releases/global-gambling-market-report-2021-market-to-grow-from -465-76-billion-in-2020-to-516-03-billion-in-2021-forecast-to-2030--301224701. html. Accessed 14 June 2021.

Harris, Ashley. "For all the masks formed:." *Cartridge Lit*, 24 June 2017. https://cartrid gelit.com/2017/06/24/if-the-hero-was-black/.

Hoffer, Christian. "Dungeons & Dragons Live Action TV Show in the Works." *Comicbook*, 30 October 2020. https://comicbook.com/gaming/news/dungeons-dragons-television -series-hasbro/.

Huxley, Aldous. *Brave New World*. Harper, 1998.

Jarvis, Matt. "Free Time During Lockdown Helped Board Game Sales to Jump in 2020." *Dicebreaker,* 29 January 2021. https://www.dicebreaker.com/categories/board-game/news/games-and-puzzles-market-2020-2021.

Jenkins, Henry. "Transmedia Storytelling." *MIT Technology Review,* 15 January 2003. https://www.technologyreview.com/2003/01/15/234540/transmedia-storytelling.

Jones, Jeffrey M. "Pro Football Losing Fans; Other Sports Holding Steady." Gallup, 13 October 2017. https://news.gallup.com/poll/220562/pro-football-losing-fans-sports-holding-steady.aspx.

Juris, Carolyn. "This Week's Bestsellers: December 7, 2020." *Publisher's Weekly,* 7 December 2020. https://www.publishersweekly.com/pw/by-topic/industry-news/bookselling/article/85076-this-week-s-bestsellers-december-7-2020.html.

Keane, Steve. "From Hardware to Fleshware: Plugging into David Cronenberg's *eXistenZ.*" *ScreenPlay: Cinema/Videogames/Interfaces,* edited by Geoff King and Tanya Krzywinska. Wallflower Press, 2002.

Leilani, Raven. *Luster.* Picador, 2020.

Lothian, Alexis. *Old Futures: Speculative Fiction and Queer Possibility.* New York University Press, 2018.

MacTavish, Andrew. "Technological Pleasure: The Performance and Narrative of Technology in *Half-Life* and Other High-Tech Computer Games." *ScreenPlay: Cinema/Videogames/Interfaces,* edited by Geoff King and Tanya Krzywinska. Wallflower Press, 2002.

McKenzie, Jon. *Perform or Else: From Discipline to Performance.* Routledge, 2001.

Newman, James. *Playing with Videogames.* Routledge, 2008.

Notess, Hannah Faith. "St. Augustine Enters the World's Largest Pac-Man Maze." *The Multitude.* Southern Indiana Review Press, 2015.

Penix-Tadsen, Phillip, ed. "Introduction: Video Games and the Global South." *Video Games and the Global South.* ETC Press, 2019, pp. 1–32.

Polanski, Lana. "Towards an Art History for Videogames." *Rhizome,* 3 August 2016. https://rhizome.org/editorial/2016/aug/03/an-art-history-for-videogames.

Roig, Antoni, Gemma San Cornelio, Elisendra Ardèvol, Pau Alsina, and Ruth Pàges. "Videogame as Media Practice: An Exploration of the Intersections between Play and Audiovisual Culture." *Convergence: The International Journal of Research into New Media Technologies,* vol. 15 (2009): 89–103.

Sanders, Scott. "Pynchon's Paranoid History," *Twentieth Century Literature,* vol. 21, no. 2 (May 1975): 177–92.

Sell, Mike. "A Defense (Sort of) of *Ready Player One* (Part 2 of 2)," 9 February 2018. http://iblog.iup.edu/thisprofessorplays/2018/02/09/a-defense-sort-of-of-ready-player-one-part-2-of-2.

———. "What Is a Videogame Movie?" *Arts,* vol. 10, no. 2, 2021, pp. 1–32.

"Sports—$614 Billion Global Market Opportunities and Strategies to 2022." *Business Wire,* 14 May 2019. https://www.businesswire.com/news/home/20190514005472/en

/Sports---614-Billion-Global-Market-Opportunities-Strategies-to-2022---Research AndMarkets.com.

Street, Brian. "What's 'New' in New Literacy Studies? Critical Approaches to Literacy in Theory and Practice." *Current Issues in Comparative Education*, vol. 5, no. 2 (2003), 77–91.

Takahashi, Dean. "Game Livestreaming Should Grow 10% to 728.8M Viewers This Year." *VentureBeat*, 9 March 2021. https://venturebeat.com/2021/03/09/newzoo-game-live streaming-will-grow-10-to-728-8m-viewers-this-year.

———. "Global Game Market Will Shrink in 2021 for First Time in Many Years." *Venture-Beat*, 6 May 2021. https://venturebeat.com/2021/05/06/newzoo-global-game-market -will-shrink-in-2021-for-first-time-in-many-years.

Thabet, Tamer, and Tim Lanzendörfer. "The Video Game Novel: StoryWorld Narratives, Novelization, and the Contemporary Novel-Network." *The Novel as Network: Forms, Ideas, Commodities*, edited by Tim Lanzendörfer and Corinna Norrick-Rühl. Palgrave Macmillan, 2020, pp. 181–202.

Walz, Steffen P., and Sebastian Deterding, eds. *The Gameful World: Approaches, Issues, Applications*. MIT Press, 2014.

Whitson, Jennifer R., and Bart Simon. "Game Studies Meets Surveillance Studies at the Edge of Digital Culture." *Surveillance & Society*, vol. 12, no. 3 (2014): 309–14.

Wilson, Jason. "'Participation TV': Videogame Archeology and New Media Art." *The Pleasure of Computer Gaming*, edited by Melanie Swalwell and Jason Wilson. McFarland & Company, 2008, pp. 94–117.

Winchester, Kendra. "Why the Videogame Scenes in Raven Leilani's *Luster* Are So Important." *Literary Hub*, 20 November 2020. https://lithub.com/why-the-video-game-scenes -in-raven-leilanis-luster-are-so-important.

Zimmerman, Eric. "Manifesto for a Ludic Century." *The Gameful World: Approaches, Issues, Applications*, edited by Steffen P. Walz and Sebastian Deterding. MIT Press, 2014, pp. 19–22.

PART I

VIDEOGAME STORIES AS LITERATURE

Gamers of the World, Unite!

Gamification and Governmentality in *Ready Player One* and *For the Win*

MEGAN AMBER CONDIS

"You are a gamer whether you like it or not." That is how McKenzie Wark opens her 2007 book *Gamer Theory*, in which she argues that the logics of gaming have penetrated nearly every aspect of our society. This wide-ranging phenomenon, in which "elements of videogames have seeped into uses and applications beyond merely leisure and play" (Bowman and Condis 187), is called "gamification," and it deploys mechanisms like "points, badges and leaderboards" to "provide players with feedback" and "allow players to understand and compare their performance and progress to that of other players in the system" (189). Proponents of gamified systems believe that they are powerful tools capable of "marshal[ling] the feelings of motivation and empowerment that games provide and to aim those feelings towards productive ends" (188). This is because, according to gamification gurus like Jane McGonigal, "games are providing rewards that reality is not. They are teaching and inspiring and engaging us in ways that reality is not. They are bringing us together in ways that reality is not" (4). Therefore, if "we started to live our real lives like gamers, lead our real businesses and communities like game designers, and think about solving real-world problems like computer and videogame theorists," we "could leverage the power of games to reinvent everything from government, health care, and education to traditional media, marketing, and entrepreneurship—even world peace" (7–8).

At first glance, Ernest Cline's *Ready Player One* (2011) appears to be a novel about the sort of utopian gamified world that McGonigal predicts, a fable about the liberatory potential of gamification. The book follows Wade Watts, a teenager living in a not-so-distant future where a virtual world called the OASIS has become the primary place of business and source of leisure for a world in turmoil. When the creator of the OASIS, an eccentric game designer named James Halliday, passes away and promises to leave ownership of his company to the gamer who can find the location of an Easter egg hidden within his vast virtual world, an evil corporation called IOI makes it their mission to win his final game by any means necessary. Luckily, Wade and his fellow gamers are able to win out over their corporate opponents by using their gaming skills and their in-depth knowledge of gamer culture. "In short," according to critic Doug Stark, "Wade's victory over IOI to maintain Halliday's vision of a free OASIS" appears at first to represent "a triumph of the individual over a faceless corporation, a free internet over a monetized one, teamwork over cheating and, above all, a game well played" (157).

Yet, in spite of the novel's seemingly happy ending, if we read against the grain of the novel (Bartholomae et al.), questioning how Halliday's egg hunt is constructed and what kind of behaviors it encourages, we will discover that it exemplifies the many ways in which gamification can be used as a disciplinary mechanism, a means of control that drives participants to take actions that benefit powerful institutions like corporations. Halliday's game is designed both as an incentive system to encourage participants to engage in activities that are profitable for his company, GSS, and as an onboarding and training exercise for potential future employees. It was created, in other words, as a mechanism for the reproduction and dissemination of GSS's corporate philosophy, a means to ensure its continued existence and profitability in the face of threats from its corporate rivals like IOI. As a result, the novel posits that being a gamer means having the ability to transform oneself into a loyal customer, an individual who is able to achieve success according to the parameters set by the gaming industry, a good consumer who might one day get the opportunity to become a good employee. The measure of their success, therefore, is the extent to which they can help replicate a system built to extract profit from them in one way or another.

Jamie Woodcock and Mark R. Johnson describe this kind of gamification as "gamification-from-above" (543), a system designed to discipline players and to nudge them toward habits of behavior that are productive and profitable for game owners. But in addition to gamification-from-above, we can also imagine "gamification-from-below" that aims at satisfying the needs and desires of players over the desires for efficiency and profitability held by corporations. This version of gamification posits that the essence of what it means to be a gamer is not rooted in conformity or consumption but rather in critical forms of play (Flanagan) that encourage people to question the systems in which they are situated and to "hack" those systems when necessary.

We can find a model of this revolutionary form of gamification in Cory Doctorow's *For the Win* (2010), in which a collection of gold farmers and other digital laborers from all over the world form a union and use their superior gaming skills to negotiate with both their bosses in the real world and the game designers who built the virtual worlds in which they work. In doing so, they recognize the slippages between labor and play in a gamified world, and they demonstrate their elite gamer status by thriving in the blurry space between the two, carving out a space for themselves as players in an economic metagame where they were only ever supposed to be game pieces. As such, the novel defines a gamer not as someone who can achieve success in a game whose rules have been written to benefit powerful institutions but rather as someone who can find unexpected ways to rewrite that game's rules toward radical ends.

By reading these two novels side by side and seeing how they embed the mechanics of gameplay into a narrative context, we are able to see that gamification is not a panacea that automatically leads to increased agency on the part of players. It is a tool, and therefore understanding the ideological context in which that tool is deployed is vital to determining how it is being used and who will benefit. This suggests that in critiquing gamified programs of organization and discipline, one must look at the narratives that have been built to support gameplay in addition to the rules and reward systems that define it.

Hunting for a New CEO: Gamification in *Ready Player One*

Ready Player One is the story of Wade Watts, a typical geeky teenage gamer living in a dystopian future that is riddled with disasters, from an "ongoing energy crisis" to "catastrophic climate change" to "widespread famine, poverty, and disease" and topped off with "half a dozen wars" (Cline 1). Wade has also undergone several devastating personal traumas in his short life: his father "was shot dead while looting a grocery store during a power blackout" when he was just a few months old, and his mother was forced to work as a virtual reality sex worker to make ends meet (15). When Wade was eleven, tragedy struck again when his mother died of a drug overdose and he was sent to live with his aunt and her boyfriend, who view him as an inconvenience at best and a target for their own frustrations and abuse at worst.

Luckily, Wade can escape to a virtual OASIS, the "Ontologically Anthropo-centric Sensory Immersive Simulation" (48). The OASIS is "a massively multi-player online game that had gradually evolved into the globally networked virtual reality most of humanity now used on a daily basis" (Cline 1), and it represents a kind of charitable utopia within the broader dystopia (Nordstrom 240) in that "impoverished children around the globe" are provided with "free OASIS hard-ware and Internet access so that they could attend school inside" (Cline 69) and it enables "even a penniless kid" (like Wade) to gain "access to every book ever written, every song ever recorded, and every movie, television show, vid-eogame, and piece of artwork ever created" (15–16). Furthermore, while most other online games in Wade's world "generate . . . revenue by charging users a monthly subscription fee for access," users can access the OASIS for a nominal "onetime sign-up fee" of just twenty-five cents, "for which you received a life-time OASIS account" (59).

The OASIS is the creation of one James Halliday, who, at the outset of the novel, has just passed away and posthumously announced a contest to deter-mine who will inherit control of his company, GSS, as well as his vast fortune. In a video released to the public following his death, Halliday announces that he has hidden an Easter egg, a secret that can only be uncovered by the most diligent and attentive of gamers, somewhere in the OASIS, and that the first person to find the egg will win the contest, the money, and the power to de-termine the fate of the (virtual) world. Halliday declares that the egg will be hidden behind three hidden gates, which can only be opened by three hidden keys, meaning that, in order to make progress in this game within a game, egg hunters—or "gunters," as they soon come to be called—will have to explore the vast virtual world, solve elaborate puzzles, and overcome challenges that demonstrate their gamer bona fides.

Luckily, Halliday leaves the gunters a "training manual" in the form of *An-orak's Almanac*: "a collection of hundreds of Halliday's undated journal entries" named after his in-game avatar, the wizard Anorak. The almanac is filled with Halliday's "stream-of-consciousness observations on various classic videog-ames, science fiction and fantasy novels, movies, comic books, and '80s pop culture" and is believed by gunters to indicate that "a familiarity with Halliday's various obsessions would be essential to finding the egg." Due to the frenzy surrounding the contest, Wade's world has become immersed in "a global fasci-nation with 1980s pop culture" (Cline 7–8). Meanwhile the specific texts mentioned in the almanac are treated like "hallowed artifacts . . . pillars of the pan-theon" (Cline 14) by gunters looking for an edge over their fellow competitors.

Among these competitors are the employees of a rival corporation, IOI, "a global communications conglomerate and the world's largest Internet ser-vice provider." According to Wade, "A large portion of IOI's business centered around providing access to the OASIS and on selling goods and services inside it. For this reason, IOI had attempted several hostile takeovers of Gregarious Simulation Systems, all of which had failed. Now they were trying to seize control of GSS by exploiting a loophole in Halliday's will." Wade and his fellow gunters fear that, should IOI be allowed to take control of GSS, the OASIS would "become a corporate-run dystopia, an overpriced theme park for wealthy elitists" (33).

IOI is willing to engage in the most brutal, horrific acts to maintain its profit margins. It keeps an army of indentured servant debtors locked up in prison cells deep in the bowels of its corporate headquarters, forcing them to do grunt work like take customer service and tech support calls and to serve as foot soldiers in the in-game search for Halliday's egg. In exchange, they receive food, shelter, and a wage that is insufficient to make a dent in their crushing debt: "Once [IOI] got finished slapping you with pay deductions, late fees, and interest penalties, you wound up owing them more each month, instead of less. Once you made the mistake of getting yourself indentured, you would proba-bly remain indentured for life" (278). The company is even willing to kill if it means getting closer to finding the egg: when it first learns of Wade's real-life identity, it sets off a bomb in his neighborhood, killing his aunt and many of his neighbors. The company later successfully assassinates Daito, a fellow gunter and occasional ally of Wade's.

The main conflict of the novel revolves around Wade and his band of friends trying to stay one step ahead of IOI. Luckily for the fate of the (virtual) world, Wade is the one who ultimately finds the egg, though he does so with a little help from his friends and fellow gunters. Indeed, he is only able to win by en-listing the help of thousands of other players, who mount an enormous attack on IOI's fortified position within the game to prevent it from opening the final gate. He also gets some assistance from Ogden Morrow, Halliday's former cre-ative and business partner and friend, who provides him with a safe place to hide from IOI's goons in the real world. Readers are left with the sense that the plucky underdogs have successfully fought back against "an evil multinational conglomerate intent on ruining" the only thing that makes their ruined world livable (34), proving that, with enough skill, knowledge, and hard work, the little guy can end up as the king of the hill.

However, this interpretation of the novel is missing a key component: an analysis of the conduct of Halliday's company, GSS. Yes, in comparison to the cartoonishly rapacious IOI, GSS is practically an angel of generosity, giving away access to its software for next to nothing and providing equipment to poor children so that they can access an education. But it also is a business, so if we want to read the novel as a repudiation of corporate greed, it is important that we interrogate GSS's business practices. For example, we might ask how GSS can continue to survive as a company (let alone become the most successful company on the face of the planet) if it is willing to give users lifetime access to its virtual world for only a quarter. The answer lies in GSS's free-to-play business model, one "in which the game designers do not charge the user or player in order to join the game. Instead, they hope to bring in revenue from . . . in-game sales, such as payment for upgrades, special abilities, special items, and expansion packs" (Rouse). These "microtransactions" (Crecente) can be for "functional or instrumental props that increase the offensive or defensive power of characters" or for "decorative or expressive props for altering character or pet appearances and for enhancing social or communication tools" (Lin and Sun 271). This business model can create sharp disparities between the experiences of players who can afford to pay for in-game perks and those who cannot.

Indeed, at the outset of the novel, Wade explains that in addition to coming from a poor family in the real world, his in-game avatar is also lacking in resources in comparison to other players. "Aside from my textbooks," he tells us, "my avatar had only a few meager possessions: a flashlight, an iron shortsword, a small bronze shield, and a suit of banded leather armor. These items were all nonmagical and of low quality, but they were the best I could afford. Items in the OASIS had just as much value as things in the real world (sometimes more), and you couldn't pay for them with food vouchers" (Cline 27–28).

He also laments being stuck wearing plain "black T-shirt and blue jeans, one of the free default skins you could select when you created your account," while wealthier gamers are able to choose an "expensive designer skin" to signal their elite status (29–30). Furthermore, Wade's lack of money to spend on in-game microtransactions not only makes him less stylish and less effective in combat but also also prevents him from visiting all but a tiny sliver of the many virtual worlds available within the OASIS. After all, Wade tells us, while "logging into the OASIS was free . . . traveling around inside it wasn't. . . . Charging people for virtual fuel to power their virtual spaceships was one of the ways Gregarious Simulation Systems generated revenue, since accessing the OASIS was free. But GSS's primary source of income was from teleportation fares. Teleportation was the fastest way to travel, but it was also the most expensive" (48–49).

As a result, Wade remarks that he feels "like a kid standing in the world's greatest video arcade without any quarters, unable to do anything but walk around and watch the other kids play" (51). Furthermore, at the conclusion of the novel, although Wade and his friends are ultimately able to achieve great wealth and success and promise to use some of their winnings to alleviate the extreme poverty that many around the world face, they make no indication that they are planning to restructure the OASIS's microtransaction-filled business model, thereby ensuring that a great many players in the next generation of gamers will experience the same second-class citizenship within the game world that Wade has experienced.

We must also assume that some number of them will wind up as indentured servants in the clutches of IOI or some other company like it, for although IOI's repulsive practices are not directly carried out by GSS, Halliday's company most certainly enables them. After all, it would be a simple thing for GSS to refuse to allow companies that are known to use slave labor to operate within its world. It is therefore somewhat disturbing that, even after infiltrating IOI's corporate headquarters and briefly serving as an "indent" in order to hack IOI's servers before escaping, Wade is seemingly unconcerned with the indents' fate once the egg has been secured. It seems as though he was more interested in inheriting the keys to the kingdom than in starting a revolution and that his reign as the new head of GSS will mean that business as usual will continue, both for good and for ill.

When we step back from Wade's individual rags-to-riches story and instead look more closely at the actions of GSS, it becomes clear that Halliday's Easter egg hunt was designed from the start as a philosophically libertarian "meta-game" (Boluk and LeMieux 3) that will incentivize players to increase their participation in activities that are profitable for the company. It works similarly to other gamified customer loyalty programs, such as McDonald's famous *Monopoly* sweepstakes, which uses the player's desire to collect game pieces in exchange for the possibility of winning fabulous prizes to encourage them to buy more fast food (Linehan et al.). If players in Halliday's game are to have any hope of finding the far-flung gates and the keys that open them, they must spend money on in-game expenditures like travel. And if they are to have any hope of defending themselves against their competitors, they must spend money on weapons and equipment. In fact, Wade remarks that although his success in the egg hunt has made him extremely wealthy, he is forced to turn around and dump nearly all of his newfound riches back into the game: "Spacecraft repairs. Teleportation fees. Power cells. Ammunition. I purchased my ammo in bulk, but it still wasn't cheap. And my monthly teleportation expenses were astronomical. My search for the egg required constant travel, and GSS kept raising their teleportation fares" (Cline 206). In other words, the hunt is designed to require players to engage in the kinds of in-game activities that are most profitable to GSS, and player success within the game is measured by determining which players have "most fully internalized its algorithm" (Wark 9).

But unlike the McDonald's *Monopoly* sweepstakes, Halliday's egg hunt has a second purpose, beyond merely incentivizing players to buy more of his virtual goods. It was also built to encourage players in the OASIS to shape themselves into the kind of gamer that Halliday was, to watch what he watched, play what he played, and value what he valued. "Over the course of the contest, he essentially asks his fans to relive his youth via his favorite fiction, movies, television shows, comics, and videogames in the hopes that these experiences will shape their perspectives on gamer culture into something that more or less resembles his own" (Condis 6). Halliday expects players to demonstrate their willingness to internalize the film and TV narratives that provided him with a much-needed escape from his own awful home life by embedding them into his own game and even requiring players to re-create them in every word and gesture. He also expects players to internalize his own narrative, to relive his own life story by visiting a digital re-creation of his childhood home and by reading and studying his journal.

The egg hunt is therefore the perfect mechanism to train up his replacement and ensure that the status quo of life in the OASIS, the good and the bad, will remain intact. Players are encouraged to internalize the idea that the winningest strategy is to make themselves as similar to Halliday as possible and to continue his legacy by preserving the OASIS as it is. In other words, the egg hunt is the ultimate corporate training seminar. It ensures that GSS's next "hire" will have already taken on the goals and thought processes of the institution they are about to join. It also puts legions of fans in the position of acting as a buffer between GSS and IOI. In essence, the hunt serves as a kind of weaponized fandom (Miller) that protects the company from a hostile corporate takeover until a new CEO can arise, one who will be the next best thing to the second coming of Halliday himself. And since this new CEO will have already undergone a great deal of gamified training, they can be relied upon to maintain the profitable systems that GSS has set up for itself within its creation— the very systems that the player mastered in order to rise to their elite position within the company. As such, in Halliday's egg hunt, "elite gamer" is "a code word for customer" (Boluk and LeMieux 3): gamers engage in activities that generate profit for the gaming industry, they seek to protect the corporate interests of the companies that produce their favorite games, and they might someday be converted into devoted employees.

Hack the System: Gamifying Resistance in *For the Win*

Woodcock and Johnson describe the type of program depicted in *Ready Player One* as "gamification-from-above" in that it "entails an elite . . . that decides to impose game elements into the lives of other people" (547) as a way of influencing not only player's behaviors but also their values, their identities, and even their political ideologies. These are games that were deliberately designed and deployed as a form of management or governance (Schrape 26), as a means to convince players to adopt and reproduce the institutional goals of game designers as their own. They therefore function as an "engine for stasis" (Conway 132), a way of ensuring the continuing stability of existing systems.

Gamification-from-above is exceedingly common in the real world; it can be found everywhere from companies that use gamified loyalty programs to retain customers (Fuchs 148) to workplaces that gamify employee productivity (Patella-Rey 285). Such games are in many ways reminiscent of carnival or casino games in that they are designed to provide players with a frisson of fun and excitement as well as the *appearance* of fairness. However, their rules are inevitably rigged to ensure that in the long run the house always wins and the behaviors that the game cultivates are always profitable for its owners.

However, it is possible to imagine another form of gamification, one in which the rules have not been written to benefit the interests of the designer over those of the player. Woodcock and Johnson call this phenomenon "gamification-from-below" (548) and describe it as a means of reimagining the relationship between work and play to benefit workers.

Proponents of gamification-from-below take play seriously even as they seek to resist the manipulative kinds of "playbor" (Kücklich) that has been designed to discipline and organize their behavior. They engage in a reclamation of play that recognizes the productive and motivational power games offer while at the same time demanding their right to have some say in determining the ends toward which that power is directed (and a share of the benefits that accrue from their skillful play). As a result, they occupy the role of the "gamer as theorist" (Wark 10) as they use their knowledge of games to "defamiliarize and recalibrate our sense of things, becoming instruments of representation as well as intervention" (Milburn 8). In so doing, "they pose a provocation to treat the world itself as a game, learning its rules and protocols in order to master them, or tweak them differently." (Milburn 101). In other words, rather than ceding the design of the gamified workplace to managers and productivity experts, they demand to be a part of the game design process, whether that means being allowed into the discussion when the rules of the gamified regime are being written or coming along later to hack and mod the rules to their liking. They see gameplay as a way to enable "the technical subversion of dominant regimes of power from the inside, using the tools and support structures developed by those systems" (Milburn 81).

This is the mode of play described in Cory Doctorow's novel *For the Win*. The novel is set in a not-so-distant future in which massively multiplayer online roleplaying games are a massive source of revenue for the megacorporations that run them. Although these games are played through a traditional keyboard and mouse and not futuristic virtual reality equipment, their economies operate in a fashion similar to that of the OASIS in *Ready Player One*. In addition to paying a subscription fee to access the game worlds in which they play, users also generate value by creating a marketplace for the buying and selling of goods within these worlds, thereby driving the value of the virtual currencies of those worlds. These currencies, in turn, can be exchanged for real-world currency and are subject to stock market trading and speculation just like real-world commodities. In other words, the more that users engage with this economy, the more money the game's creators stand to make.

However, unlike *Ready Player One*, Doctorow's novel does not focus on a single player striving to achieve success within the planned economy outlined by the game's designers, nor is the novel narrated from a single protagonist's perspective. Rather, it focuses on a diverse group of virtual laborers, players from all over the world who have been hired by small, oftentimes shady black market operations to extract resources from the game so that they might be sold for real-world currency outside of the auspices of the game makers. The novel bounces back and forth from one narrator to the next, explaining the various kinds of jobs that each performs within the virtual world, each of which requires a special skillful kind of play. The virtual world does not function for them as an escape from their problems. It is their workplace, and their function within the world is to facilitate the escapist play of others. The novel's narrative style reflects this by largely forgoing descriptions of the storylines of the games that these characters play. The storylines are not for them and are largely irrelevant to the work that they do. Instead, the novel focuses on the intricacies of the mechanics that these player-workers must master to survive.

For example, gold farmers like Matthew Fong search for spots within the game where they can exploit bugs or take advantage of unbalanced economic incentives to generate huge quantities of gold quickly and efficiently and then sell it to other players for real-world currency. Gold farmers "could run a dungeon once and tell you exactly the right way to run it again to get the maximum gold in the minimum time," and "where a normal farmer might make fifty gold in an hour, Matthew could make five hundred" (Doctorow 16–17). They often work in "factories" under the auspices of bosses who pay players a small wage for their work and then keep the lion's share of the profits from the sale of the gold that they gather to themselves.

On the other hand, boosters like Leonard "Wei-Dong" Goldburg and his crew interact more directly with the public, charging newbies for the privilege of experiencing some of the most difficult areas of the game, under their protection. Their typical customer "paid them to run the instance with him, and he could just hang back and let the raiders do all the heavy lifting, but he'd come forward to deal the coup de grâce to any big bosses they beat down, so he'd get the experience points. He got to keep the gold, the weapons, the prestige items, all of it—and all for the low, low price of $75" (20).

Both the gold farmers and the boosters must stay alert for another kind of laborer, the mercenaries, such as Mala and her army of child workers operating out of an internet café in Mumbai (34), who are paid by the operators of gold farming factories to harass and interrupt the work of rival organizations. And they must also constantly remain on the lookout for the employees of the game companies themselves, who think of them as "parasites" (361) or "rats" (238) in need of "de-lousing" (356) because their activities eat into corporate profit margins by undercutting the prices of their own officially sanctioned gold-selling and quick-leveling operations.

Representing the perspective of the game industry in the novel is Connor Prikkel, a former trader of in-game commodities who got so good at predicting the market that he was sought out and hired by Coca-Cola Games to oversee its virtual economies and to sniff out and ban gold farmers and boosters. Even though Prikkel once made his living selling in-game gold and commodities for money, he has been trained by his employer to think of them as "cheaters" who are "ruin[ing] the game for real players" (317). Of course, "real players" in this instance are defined as players whose behaviors are authorized by and profitable to the game designers. As such, Connor admits that he imagines them to be unskilled players. For example, he "had a tendency to think of gold farmers as mindless droids repeating a task set for them by some boss who showed them how to use the mouse and walked away" (319–20).

This assumption makes sense when one considers that Connor is the designer of a game that, much like the OASIS, operates via gamification-from-above. He defines what it means to be "good at games" by measuring players against the incentives that he has designed for them, and so anyone who disregards those incentives must be bad at the game. However, when he plays alongside a group of boosters in order to gather information on their operation, he cannot help recognizing the skillfulness of their play, musing that "the gold farmers played all day, every day, even more than the most hardcore players. They were hardcore players. Hardcore players he'd sworn to eliminate, but he couldn't let himself forget that they were hardcore" (320).

The stories of these various factions of workers, bosses, and game runners come together via Big Sister Nor, a former textile worker in Singapore, who comes up with a plan to fight for better working conditions for virtual laborers all over the world: the formation of a union of the International Workers of the World Wide Web (IWWWW), a play on the famous real-world union, the Industrial Workers of the World (109–10). She and her confederates reach out to laborers within the game world to encourage them to fight for better wages and more humane working conditions, pointing out that virtual workplaces are ideal for unions because, unlike traditional industries such as manufacturing, there is no way for an employer to simply pick up and move their "factory" to another country when the laborers demand too much. No matter where the gold farm is located, whether it is in an internet café in Mumbai or an office building in Shenzen, the farmers all log on to work within the same virtual world. As Nor tells Mala, "We are everywhere, but we are all here. Anyone your boss ever hired to do your job would end up here, and we could find that worker and talk to them" (61–62). While the union starts out small at the beginning of the novel, its growing influence quickly gains the attention of some of the more brutal gold farming factory owners, who hire real-world thugs to violently attack Big Sister Nor and the rest of the union leadership and to serve as strikebreakers when one group of gold farmers revolts against the bosses.

However, despite these vicious attacks, the IWWWW hatches a scheme to use members' gaming talents and knowledge of the financial metagames that are taking place "about, within, around, and without videogames" (Boluk and LeMieux 25) to reconfigure their relationships with both their employers and the game makers who design the worlds in which they work and play. They plan to "seize control of the economies" of four hugely popular virtual worlds at once by gaining control over "the majority of the gold, prestige items, and power" within each and sitting on them (Doctorow 280). This not only allows them to destabilize the in-game economies of each game but also enables them to wreak havoc within the metagames being played by investors and speculators betting on in-game commodities. This ensures that it is not just their fellow players who will be experiencing the consequences of their high-risk maneuver; the game designers and their corporate backers also would now have a stake in the outcome of their gambit. Their goal is not to destroy the games but rather to use their leverage to negotiate for legitimacy. No longer would gold farming take place on the black market, thereby allowing shady mobsters to treat workers with brutality and disdain. Instead, they demand that "union gold that comes out of Coke's games will be legitimate and freely usable. We'll have a cooperative that buys and sells, just like today's exchange markets, but it will be above board, transparently governed by elected managers who will be subject to recall if they behave badly" (447–48).

And while their stunt does end with an agreement on the part of the corporation to enter into negotiations with the union, an important first step toward getting the recognition that they are bargaining for, their victory is marred by outbursts of violence, including the kidnapping and severe beating of Mala, one of the union's most capable in-game generals, and the murder of Big Sister Nor. The game is not over. It has merely entered into a new phase, one that is perhaps even more deadly and dangerous than the one they were playing before. Yet, as a result of their efforts, there is an opportunity to change the rules of this game in a way that might empower the players. The members of the IWWWW take heart in the knowledge that "the bosses were better at firing tear gas at them, but they were better at lobbing fireballs, pulsed energy weapons, photon torpedoes and savage flying fish—and they always would be" (121). They use their skillful play not just to win a single skirmish but also to work toward leveling the playing field upon which future contests will take place.

Conclusion

Ready Player One and *For the Win* are both novels that set out to explore the pleasures and the pitfalls of gamification. *Ready Player One* demonstrates how the powerful motivational pull provided by play can be used to turn "gamers into entities plugged seamlessly into . . . products, according to the will of the corporations who create them" (Phillips 14), imagining what it means to be a gamer as a process of disciplining the self into someone more amenable to the goals of the corporations whose games they play. On the other hand, *For the Win* posits that the most elite, most skilled gamers aren't simply the most prolific consumers or the most compliant laborers. Rather, they are those who, once they have become skilled at navigating the systems that have been placed before them, are willing and able to turn their efforts toward reconfiguring the system itself.

While both novels are nominally about gamers and the gamified worlds they inhabit, they each ask readers to engage with them as narratives in very different ways. *Ready Player One* invites us to ignore the dystopian realities of Wade's world, just as he does, and instead to escape into a libertarian fantasy as we "play along" with him. *For the Win,* on the other hand, refuses to allow readers to ignore the material exploitation that makes the existence of an "apolitical" escapist virtual world possible, instead asking us to work alongside the novel's widespread collection of characters to build an understanding of labor and solidarity that can connect us to one another and enable us to help one another outplay our corporate opponents.

This literature is essential, not just to help readers understand the ins and outs of online gaming subculture but also to help us understand the myriad ways in which everyday life is rapidly requiring us to learn how to navigate digital landscapes, manage our data, and manipulate algorithmic systems in order to succeed. Whether we like it or not, we are living in what Eric Zimmerman terms "a ludic century," a time in which "the ways that we work and communicate, research and learn, socialize and romance, conduct our finances and communicate with our governments, are all intimately intertwined with complex systems of information" (19–20). These systems are essentially gamelike in that they are "machines of inputs and outputs that are inhabited, manipulated, and explored" and can therefore be approached strategically (20).

As such, according to Amanda Phillips, "the way to get ahead is to think in terms of games" in that "games uniquely capture and encourage behaviors that are important for life in the twenty-first century, whether it is learning how to intuit the complicated patterns of interlocking systems," as the proponents of gamification-from-below might teach us to do, or merely figuring out "how to motivate ourselves into maximum productivity," as those who create systems of gamification-from-above goad us to do (Phillips 6). In either case, there is no opting out of this game, so we might as well start thinking about how it is that we want to play and what stories we want our play to tell.

WORKS CITED

Bartholomae, David, Anthony Petrosky, and Stacey Waite, eds. "Introduction: Ways of Reading." *Ways of Reading: An Anthology for Writers.* 12th ed., Macmillan Learning, 2020.

Boluk, Stephanie, and Patrick LeMieux. *Metagaming: Playing, Competing, Spectating, Cheating, Trading, Making, and Breaking Videogames.* University of Minnesota Press, 2017.

Bowman, Nicholas David, and Megan Condis. "Governmentality, Playbor, and Peak Performance: Critiques and Concerns of Health and Wellness Gamification." *Privacy Concerns Surrounding Personal Information Sharing on Health and Fitness Mobile Apps,* edited by Devjani Sen and Rukhsana Ahmed. IGI Global, 2020, pp. 186–210.

Cline, Ernest. *Ready Player One.* Random House, 2011.

Condis, Megan. "Playing the Game of Literature: *Ready Player One,* the Ludic Novel, and the Geeky 'Canon' of White Masculinity." *Journal of Modern Literature,* vol. 39, no. 2, Winter 2016, pp. 1–19.

Conway, Steven. "Zombification? Gamification, Motivation, and the User." *Journal of Gaming & Virtual Worlds,* vol. 6, no. 2, 2014, 129–41.

Crecente, Brian. "What Are DLC, Loot Boxes and Microtransactions? An Explainer." *Variety,* 28 November 2017. https://variety.com/2017/gaming/features/what-is-a-loot-box-1203047991.

Doctorow, Cory. *For the Win.* Tom Doherty, 2010.

Flanagan, Mary. *Critical Play: Radical Game Design.* MIT Press, 2009.

#FreeFortnite Cup." *Happy Gamer,* 22 August 2020. https://happygamer.com/epic-games-continues-to-attempt-to-weaponize-their-fans-with-upcoming-freefortnite-cup-78592.

Fuchs, Mathias. "Gamification as Twenty-First Century Ideology." *Journal of Gaming & Virtual Worlds,* vol. 6, no. 2, 2014, pp. 143–57.

Kücklich, Julian. "Precarious Playbour: Modders and the Digital Games Industry." *Fibreculture Journal*, vol. 5, 2005. http://five.fibreculturejournal.org/fcj-025-precarious -playbour-modders-and-the-digital-games-industry.

Lin, Holin, and Chuen-Tsai Sun. "Cash Trade in Free-to-Play Online Games." *Games and Culture* vol. 6, no. 3, 2011, pp. 270–87.

Linehan, Conor, Sabine Harrer, Ben Kirman, Shaun Lawson, and Marcus Carter. "Games Against Health: A Player-Centered Design Philosophy." *CHI EA '15: Proceedings of the 33rd Annual ACM Conference*, April 2015, pp. 589–600.

McGonigal, Jane. *Reality Is Broken: Why Games Make Us Better and How They Can Change the World*. Penguin, 2011.

Milburn, Colin. *Respawn: Gamers, Hackers, and Technogenic Life*. Duke University Press, 2018.

Miller, Chris. "Epic Games Continues to Attempt to Weaponize Their Fans with Upcoming Nordstrom, Justin. "'A Pleasant Place for the World to Hide': Exploring Themes of Utopian Play in *Ready Player One*." *Interdisciplinary Literary Studies*, vol. 18, no. 2, 2016, pp. 238–56.

Patella-Rey, P. J. "Gamification and Post-Fordist Capitalism." *The Gameful World: Approaches, Issues, Applications*, edited by Steffan P. Walz and Sebastian Deterding. MIT Press, 2015.

Phillips, Amanda. *Gamer Trouble: Feminist Confrontations in Digital Culture*. New York University Press, 2020.

Rey, P. J. "Gamification and Post-Fordist Capitalism." *The Gameful World: Approaches, Issues, Applications*, edited by Steffen P. Walz and Sebastian Deterding. MIT Press, 2014, pp. 277–95.

Rouse, Margaret. "Free to Play (F2P)." *Technopedia*, 18 October 2011. https://www.techo pedia.com/definition/27039/free-to-play-f2p.

Schrape, Niklas. "Gamification and Governmentality." *Rethinking Gamification*, edited by Mathias Fuchs, Sonia Fizek, Paolo Ruffino, und Niklas Schrape. Meson Press, 2014, pp. 22–45.

Stark, Doug. "Ludic Literature: *Ready Player One* as Didactic Fiction for the Neoliberal Subject." *Playing the Field: Videogames and American Studies*, edited by Sascha Pöhlmann. De Gruyter Oldenbourg, 2019, pp. 151–72.

Wark, McKenzie. *Gamer Theory*. Harvard University Press, 2007.

Woodcock, Jamie, and Mark R. Johnson. "Gamification: What It Is, And How to Fight It." *Sociological Review*, vol. 66, no. 3, 2018, pp. 542–58.

Zimmerman, Eric. "Manifesto for a Ludic Century." *The Gameful World: Approaches, Issues, Applications*, edited by Steffen P. Walz and Sebastian Deterding. MIT Press, 2014, pp. 19–22.

Level Up!

Emulating Posthumanity in *Lucky Wander Boy*

JARREL DE MATAS

Videogames, beyond those of the educational kind, can serve as heuristic tools for reflecting attitudes about gender, race, and cultures, among many other things. The potential of videogames to be a source for understanding the world has been intrinsic to the emerging field of game studies, particularly as Tulia Căşvean explains it in her 2016 essay on the mission of game studies. According to Căşvean, "The postmodernism and the 'neo-' trends that dominated the humanist discourses by the end of the previous millennia influenced the emerging field of game studies" (54). This essay emphasizes one such trend, posthumanism, as providing unique theoretical concepts that help explain the reconfiguration of human sensibility through videogames. One of these concepts is posthuman emulation, which I theorize here as a process of encoding human consciousness through game emulation. D. B Weiss's *Lucky Wander Boy* (2003) connects the process of software emulation to changes in human interaction, perceptions of the self, and ways of simulating experience.

I contend that Weiss's engagement with ways of knowing facilitated by gaming emulation challenges the humanist bias in videogame studies. This bias is implicit through a gamercentric privileging of the human actor over the nonhuman game object. Weiss's novel, however, draws attention to videogames as providing an experiential way of knowing that influences the sensibility of the protagonist, Adam Pennyman, as much as he is able to influence the gameplay. Bringing posthuman theory and game studies together in this way bears upon the "ludic aspect of human consciousness" outlined by Simona Livescu (2). This "ludic consciousness" occurs on at least two levels in *Lucky Wander Boy*. The first is through the character Adam, who emulates his life in the way his beloved games have been emulated, and the second is through the author Weiss, who uses videogame tropes as a storytelling device for the effects of videogames on players.

Weiss himself stated in a 2006 interview that he was "always playing games," starting with the Intellivision and Atari 2600 systems when he was nine (Bedigian). His early obsession with videogames, reflected in the character of Adam, informs the content of his novel, which builds toward the eventual emulation of Adam's life. Adam sees himself, the people around him, and his environment as an emulation. Weiss's satirical portrayal of Adam becoming emulated in the same way that his beloved videogame has been emulated draws attention to the dangers involved in videogame addiction. Therefore, as much as Adam sees the potential of videogames to offer unique ways of perceiving the world, his immersion in videogames has pitiful repercussions for his psychological state and interpersonal relationships. However, insofar as Weiss's concept of emulation aligns with theories of posthuman enhancement and sensibility, I explore the kind of posthuman Weiss constructs through videogames and the implications of living life as if it were a videogame.

In the opening chapter of *Lucky Wander Boy*, Adam declares that the videogame *Pac-Man* contains "obvious metaphors, lurking just beneath the surface of the game" (Weiss 20). Over the course of the novel, Adam attempts to unveil the material and sociocultural implications of these metaphors while juggling his relationship with Anya, his Polish girlfriend, who desperately tries to fit in to American society. His attempts to "root out the concealed flux of relationships between the different elements of the game" and "to grow more sensitive to connections" (223) informs my analysis of the posthuman web of being that structures the transactional flow of information from gamer to videogame. This description of the coconstituted ontology arising out of this exchange of information adds to contemporary game studies scholarship and encourages posthuman interventions into game technologies. I explore the ability of videogame technology, particularly emulation, to influence configurations of the self and interpersonal relationships. Although more recent videogame narratives take up questions of game-simulated identity and society,* Weiss's novel predates these texts through its earlier cross-representation of a gamified posthuman condi-

* See, for example, *Omnitopia* (2010) by Dianne Duane, *Ready Player One* (2011) by Ernest Cline, *Insignia* (2012) by S. J. Kincaid, *In Real Life* (2014) by Cory Doctorow, and *The Chalk Artist* (2017) by Allegra Goodman, novels similar to *Lucky Wander Boy* that also explore the intersection of game technologies and identity formation.

tion. By revisiting *Lucky Wander Boy* alongside scholarship in posthumanism, I attest to the impact of game studies in the twenty-first century as described by Jennifer Malkowski and TreaAndrea Russworm, particularly as it relates to "representation, identity, and their intertwined relationship in games and game culture [which] have become (or, rather, have been revealed as) such high-stakes matters" (3). The novel's representation of human (in)ability makes use of videogame anecdotes, analogies, and technologies to reflect changing twenty-first-century (re)configurations of the human, embodiment, and society.

As Adam attempts to document his knowledge of videogames into a book called *The Catalogue of Obsolete Entertainments,* he simultaneously deepens his understanding of himself in relation to games and his lived reality. This re-calls the argument made by Aaron Trammell and Aram Sinnreich: "Whether [games] are read as texts or interpreted as platforms, we imagine them to be evocative of other processes in the world at large" (3). Weiss directs attention to the ability of videogames to enact their own method of world building. In *Lucky Wander Boy,* this world building takes place through classic videogames such as *Pac-Man* and *Microsurgeon* and fictional games that Adam invents, such as *Copy-writer!* and Weiss's fictional, eponymous game *Lucky Wander Boy.* The classic games in particular enact an experience of retrogaming, which adds a nostalgic dimension not just to games but also to the changes in gaming brought on by developments in emulation technology.

Given the novel's starting point of retrogaming, I consider the version of posthumanism depicted in *Lucky Wander Boy* as predating the technological advancements that inform descriptions of the posthuman by the likes of Donna Haraway (1991) and Katherine Hayles (1999). Adam re-creates his perception of the world to suit his gaming sensibility, which is shaped by the nostalgia of retrogaming. As game technologies get more sophisticated, as he moves from the hardware of a physical arcade cabinet to the software of emulation, his life becomes gradually consumed in games, and his posthuman sensibility is nec-essarily nostalgic.

Throughout the novel, Adam attempts to uncover different aspects of the world at large. The first indication of this comes at the end of the first chapter when he says, "There is a world beneath the glass that we can never know" (Weiss 24). With every new game that Adam catalogs, his accumulated archive brings readers closer to his personal quest of unlocking the third stage of *Lucky Wander Boy,* a fictional and "obscure" 1983 game created by the fictional char-acter Araki Itachi (77). *Lucky Wander Boy* is the ultimate challenge not only to

Adam's game expertise but also to his screenplay adaptation of the game. Both acts of engagement with the videogame—the experiential and the archival—parallel the less perceptible, though no less important, philosophical pursuit of the human(e) question. I agree with Richard Grusin that technology is a nonhuman category, and I therefore explore the impact of game technology in decentering and reconfiguring the universality of "the human." As such, videogames as a mode of nonhuman technology present a challenge to liberal humanist conceptions of "the human."

According to Rosi Braidotti, "the human" is a product of pre-Socratic classical ideals, which promoted "the cultural logic of universal Humanism" (15). This cultural logic places human values, experiences, and ways of knowing at the center of human existence. Privileging an essential humanism in this way reduces other, nonhuman forms of knowing. *Lucky Wander Boy* draws attention to one such alternative knowledge base, which the novel's protagonist locates in videogames. Through an attentiveness to features such as game design and emulation, I theorize the posthuman as a material construction that dissolves the boundaries of human epistemologies and consciousness. In the process, my game studies analysis aligns with posthuman interventions into the classical construction of "the human" by providing alternative configurations to what Braidotti calls "our shared understandings of the human subject and of humanity as a whole" (46). However, with a focus on videogames' ability to create alternative forms of knowledge and affect, I add to the field of "critical posthumanities," as Braidotti calls it, by considering the ways in which Weiss utilizes videogames to spotlight the implications of emulation technology on identity formation and social situations.

Economy and Space in *Pac-Man*

The earliest and one of the most direct engagements with posthuman conditions in *Lucky Wander Boy* appears during Adam's cataloging of *Pac-Man*. Because Adam describes *Pac-Man* as "the world's first metaphysical videogame" (Weiss 23), and because Adam-as-player uses the game to understand his world, I begin with an analysis of the ways in which Adam's understanding of *Pac-Man* interfaces with questions of the posthuman economy and existence. Moving from biology to economics to philosophy, Adam explains that *Pac-Man* is an exemplar for reflecting the human condition: "If Pac-Man and the games that followed in its wake mean anything to us," he argues, "if they are central switching stations through which thousands of our most important memories are routed, it is our duty to dig deeper" (21). The videogames that root Adam's memories help route our interpretation of the posthuman condition. As it concerns the interface between posthumanism and the economy, *Lucky Wander Boy* alludes to a form of designer capitalism that is reflected by *Pac-Man's* gameplay. The classic videogame becomes the medium as well as the message through which Weiss criticizes the impact of videogame capitalism and consumerism on the gamer.

Writing on designer capitalism, Jan Jagodzinksi draws attention to the institutionalization of videogame addiction, which "harness[es] young talent into the technology of the software industry—especially designing videogames" (101). This technologized interpellation of youth on a large scale, as Jagodzinski goes on to suggest, creates a capitalist society that depends on, as much as it creates, new forms of videogame design. Interweaving Karl Marx's *Communist Manifesto* with his meditation on the Pac-Man's motive to accumulate wealth, Adam points out that the Pac-Man occupies the role of "corporate antihero in a Utopian fantasy . . . where the agents protesting his unfettered domination of the maze-world actually defeat him in the end" (Weiss 20). *Lucky Wander Boy* illustrates the creation of videogames as a product of capitalism as much as it reproduces what Jagodzinski calls the "larger 'knowledge' economy" of "'interactive' citizen-consumers" (166) who become "prosumers" of game design (113).

Weiss's metanarrative of videogame addiction portrays the protagonist as a victim of designer capitalism by his very cataloging of each videogame. Thus, *Pac-Man* becomes an appropriate starting point for Weiss's story of the far-reaching implications of videogame production. Adam's—and, by extension, Weiss's—nostalgia surrounding videogames reproduces the obsession with playing in order to emphasize the very consequences brought on by this obsession. Although he recognizes the capitalist technologies at play, Adam is nonetheless powerless against the forces of consumerism, which compels him to unlock new levels of gameplay.

The Pac-Man avatar channels the player's addiction, which, like designer capitalism, feeds on player participation. Gameplay consists of an interactive exchange of greed as player and their avatar are co-opted by the game design into accumulating wealth, or gamepoints. Adam reflects the posthuman "citizen-consumer" (Jagodzinski 166) when he observes that Pac-Man was created to be "always hungry, all the time chomping with want just like the player it represents" (Weiss 19). *Pac-Man's* game design creates a posthuman consumer that participates in an endless feedback loop of points accumulation. His participation in *Pac-Man* and other games during the novel realizes Jonathan Boulter's claim of a posthuman fashioning of "the subject as subject," which comes about when "the character within the game in a sense trades himself as a commodity" (121). The singular obsession that Adam finds in the Pac-Man figure comes to resemble his own selfish preoccupation with cataloging other videogames at the expense of social interactions. Adam's life becomes a caricature of *Pac-Man* gameplay by exaggerating the protagonist's immersion in different types of videogames to the point where he becomes a real-life wander boy who appears aimless without videogames. Adam's conscious experience of becoming a composite avatar of different gamed characters is at once a challenge to and a substantiation of Boulter's argument about posthuman play.

In contrast to Boulter's claim that "the human, given its obvious addiction to many forms of play, is deeply involved always in leaving itself behind, becoming something other than a fully self-aware, self-present entity" (11), Adam invites us to characterize the gamer as a more nuanced posthuman who can be more or less self-aware about their position as a consumer. However, where Boulter claims that "in play the game plays us" (11), Weiss deliberately gestures toward the impact of designer capitalism as an ideological game that binds the obsessive gamer to the game. His awareness as a cog that contributes to the capitalist-driven gaming industry enables readers to interrogate the perseverance of designer capitalism in creating posthuman gamers.

Although the book's Los Angeles digital entertainment CEO Kurt Krickstein "emphatically" distances his company from Hollywood, the forces of capitalism are no less apparent in his plan to globalize the convergence of movies, videogames, and the internet. The marketization of this convergence emphasizes lives that are experienced on-screen. In so doing, capitalists like Krickstein continue the production of prosumers like Adam and, eventually, Anya, whose experience of being fashioned into a posthuman "prosumer" is appropriately described through gaming terminology. As Adam explains, "In videogame parlance, she was successfully porting herself to the American platform" (Weiss 81). America thus becomes its own game world, with associative notions of fantasy, designer capitalism, and the creation of type-specific avatars.

But this comes at a cost. Anya's reference to Adam as a "monster of selfishness" (75) emphasizes his becoming something other than human through his game addiction. The monstrosity attributed to him, however, is ironic because she also becomes, like Adam, a monster of selfishness, existing in a different world of designer capitalism. The evocation of monstrosity brought on by immersion into gamified worlds enacts a boundary crossing of the putatively firm categories separating the human, the animal, and technology. For Jay Bolter, this boundary crossing occurs through cybernetics, leading him to speculate that "the computer metaphor may arguably have contributed to the posthumanist perspective." In contrast, *Lucky Wander Boy* trades the computer metaphor for a game console that goes beyond serving as a metaphor and toward being an actual controller of life. Both Adam and Anya share the *Pac-Man* gameplay experience of being converted into posthuman monsters controlled by external forces.

Adam as Pac-Man enacts a posthuman, digital embodiment of designer capitalism. Like Jagodzinski, who argues that game technologies have created a distinct version of "Koreanness" wherein "the 'virtual' and the 'actual' are just the two sides of the same coin" (100), Adam explains that *Pac-Man* gameplay allows us to conceive of the screen as a liminal space that facilitates, not obstructs, our lives as they "play out" on-screen. Describing a "thought-experiment" whereby we "try to occupy Pac-Man's subjectivity," Adam gestures toward the material experience of gameplay. Thus, each dot that Pac-Man must consume for the player to win the game contains a "very specific and distinct joy or sorrow (Weiss 21). From this perspective, the Pac-Man avatar is not about the avatar as such but about what it enables: a process in which the player identifies with the Pac-Man and determines, as much as it depends on, the Pac-Man's ability to evoke an emotional response.

The exchange of joy and sorrow that occurs between *Pac-Man* and player enacts a form of "digitally mediated and distributed subjectivity" identified by Aubrey Anable (xiii). The mediation and distribution of particular emotions through videogames highlighted by Weiss extends the reach of designer capitalism to influencing and even inducing certain emotions that keep players addicted. Adam's dependence on videogames to give meaning and structure to his life resembles the claim made by Anable that videogames "engage and entangle us in a circuit of feeling between their computational systems and the broader systems with which they interface: ideology, narrative, aesthetics, and flesh" (xii). *Lucky Wander Boy* captures in story form the ability of videogames to be a source of cultural commentary on the impacts and implications of technology.

One such impact of game technology that is played out during the novel is the digital connection forged between player and *Pac-Man*. This connection, I argue, suggests a shared posthuman ontology through what Ian Bogost calls the "procedural rhetoric" of computational affordances. In *Lucky Wander Boy*, these affordances take the form of emulated gameplay. Weiss reflects Adam's perception of the world through *Pac-Man* gameplay, thereby inviting us to experience the game's digital world alongside Adam's experience of playing the videogame. The transformation of human experience through gameplay aligns with forms of posthuman boundary transgressions, as argued by Donna Haraway, who rhetorically asks, "Why should our bodies end at the skin, or include at best other beings encapsulated by skin?" (220). Weiss responds with insight into videogame transgression of human boundaries. To continue Haraway's argument of reconstituted embodiment, the *Pac-Man* "interface becomes a tool through which the human acquires a prosthetic, posthuman sensibility (178). This sensibility transforms the understanding of the technologized self as much as its environment, as Adam goes on to explain.

Coinciding with the transgression of bodily boundaries is the transgression of space. Beyond the literal screens, tunnels, and mazes that constitute the game space of *Pac-Man* lies an alternate dimension that calls to mind Haraway's discussion of ideological space. As Haraway explains, "Ideological space [is] opened up by the reconceptions of machine and organism as coded texts through which we engage in the play of writing and reading the world" (152). In *Lucky Wander Boy*, posthuman space is coded through *Pac-Man*'s "narrative architecture" (Jenkins). *Pac-Man* allegorizes the perceived distinction between seen and unseen spaces. As Adam explains, this distinction does not actually exist in Pac-Man's world because its tunnels on the left are connected to those on its right. Therefore, when Pac-Man disappears through the tunnel, it continues to exist, though not physically. Additionally, the game does not end when Pac-Man disappears. Because *Pac-Man* codes seen and unseen space in the experience of gameplay, it requires "truly tapped-in" players (Weiss 23). Only then can players occupy the unseen space inhabited by the Pac-Man.

This augmentation of game space has been taken up by Boulter. Following Haraway's theory of the posthuman as a coded being of machine and organism (152), Boulter draws a direct connection between posthuman and game technologies. According to him, the posthuman (gamer) is a "confluence of human flesh and machine" who "is articulated as a cyborg in her entry in the gameworld" (Boulter 4). In this respect, Adam and Anya become cyborgs through their involvement with gaming, though in two distinct ways. In Adam, the posthuman gamer is more apparent, particularly in terms of the time he spends playing and archiving games. For Anya, it is more a case of her being, as Adam says, "tapped in" to the socioeconomic order of the American Dream, an order shaped by games and play. As Adam becomes increasingly absorbed into cataloging games, Anya retreats into her own virtual world, but both are re-configuring their humanity in the process. To take Boulter's discussion of the posthuman game world further, *Lucky Wander Boy* articulates the human not just as a cyborg interacting with machines but also as a participant in an entire socioeconomic and material environment.

Designing Experience through *Copywriter!*

As I've mentioned, Adam's immersion in videogames is as much a process of cataloging as it is of playing them. Cataloging his addiction is an attempt to "strike through the mask of 'entertainment' and reach the truths hidden behind it" (Weiss 75). This practical approach to reigniting "obsolete" videogames extends into a posthuman theory of what Kurt Squire calls "designed experience," wherein "players' understandings are developed through cycles of performance within the game worlds, which instantiate particular theories of the world (ideological worlds)" (19). Throughout this essay, I've argued that certain games in *Lucky Wander Boy* act as tools for Adam as he conceptualizes his life. Here, I argue that Adam's act of *writing* about games is the proper focus for examination of posthuman interactivity with the outside world.

Adam's growing catalog of obsolete games sees him cross paths with Kurt Krickstein, who, contrary to Adam's wishes, desperately wants to create a film adaptation of the *Lucky Wander Boy* game. He begins working for Krickstein as a copywriting consultant for the film adaptation of *Lucky Wander Boy.* This job coincides with the cataloging of another game, called *Copywriter!*, a game of Adam's own invention. Thus, *Copywriter!* is distinct from the other obsolete games in his catalog because it is the first one that Adam is responsible for designing. In contrast to the closed worlds of *Pac-Man* and *Microsurgeon,* with their preset rules and codes, in *Copywriter!*, we see him setting the rules as he goes along, a task that suits his aim of mastering his job as he would a game. The increasing publicizing of his videogame addiction, however, paradoxically leads him into greater isolation because it requires him to be even more addicted to games that he makes up, such as *Copywriter!*, to emulate his own life.

In this way, Adam constructs a world in which being a successful gamer requires a technosocial practice of performativity as dictated by corporate culture. To take Squire's argument of games as participation in ideological systems further, the ideological (game)world of *Copywriter!* doesn't participate in the ideological system—it creates the system. Insofar as Adam is able to design his own work experience, and in posthuman fashion place himself in that design, *Copywriter!* gives credence to the forecast made by Byron Reeves and J. Leighton Read that "some people will soon do their jobs *inside* a game, and many more will thrive in information environments that have features borrowed from today's best games" (4). Adam fulfills his role as an effective copywriter by pinning his duties to a set of "elegant and nuanced [game] strategies" (Weiss 149).

Although the strategies Adam uses are designed for the games in remarkably nuanced fashion, his application of game design to his job results in the reduction of people to auxiliary game devices. Conceiving—or as he classifies it, formatting—his job as a game allows him to assemble shortcuts, or "cheat codes," for a simplified way of controlling his work environment, including those who work in it, and even cheating to get ahead. For example, Adam quickly learns how to defer tasks to the subordinate interns. Likened to the super zappers and smart bombs of *Tempest* and *Defender*, respectively, the interns are described as precious ammunition; therefore, "you had to save them for when you really needed them" (151). Thinking of his job as comprising game elements allows for a new kind of work environment, one where he excels in his duties, though at the expense of human interaction, because his coworkers become mere data that can be manipulated and controlled.

The "procedural adaption" (Sell) of Adam's conceptual use of cheat codes, super zappers, and smart bombs in his job reveals Weiss's entanglement of non-human videogame tropes with human sensibilities to produce a human subject defined and remediated by particular forms of videogame addiction. In so doing, the juxtaposition of game design and work environment enacts for Adam a form of "posthuman learning," described by Cathrine Hasse as an "understanding that both the novice and the expert become skillful in an evolving process of collective socio-cultural material epistemology" (356). Adam, a novice at his job, relies on his expertise as a gamer to increase his skill level at being a copywriter. His expert ability to sift through mass emails and break down large tasks exemplifies the claim made by Reeve and Read that "game designs will offer new tools to clarify objectives that adapt to external challenges" (8). The company's name, Portal Entertainment and Development, is thus perfectly apt in that Adam formats his duties to fit the innovative demands of his job—games are a portal toward efficiency. However, going through this "portal" causes him to leave something behind—a capacity for emotional responsiveness both to others and his own needs. Thus, the posthuman ability facilitated by *Microsurgeon* and *Copywriter!* are as much disabling as they are enabling.

Adam's copywriting job, along with his experience playing *Lucky Wander Boy*, lands him a scriptwriting position for the film adaptation of *Lucky Wander Boy*, but it also generates critical perspectives. Adam's game design converts his social interactions into a screenplay, which he then uses to criticize Krickstein for his commercializing of *Lucky Wander Boy*. His representation of real-life human communication through screenplay writing is another example of the paradoxical loss and gain of different kinds of experiences that occurs through the processes of remediation and emulation. For example, Adam's game-design sensibility enables him to literally rewrite the power dynamic between him and Krickstein. He confronts Krickstein when he discovers the option agreement that would grant Krickstein exclusive rights to *Lucky Wander Boy*. However, despite his ability to recognize what is happening, the conceptual power of game design does not enable Adam to successfully compete with the practical power of Krickstein's corporate ideology.

In this way, the novel challenges the notion that gaming literacy enables the "loosening up the hierarchy" identified by Reeves and Read (60). The two consecutive and contrasting chapters in the novel in which Adam questions Kricktein's motives reflect Adam's conflicted game and real-world states of existence. At first, Adam's script represents a possible alternative to his challenge of the corporate hierarchy. However, it is inevitably overridden by corporate culture. Krickstein ultimately condemns what Adam seeks to defend in *Lucky Wander Boy*: "*Lucky Wander Boy* epitomizes our struggles, our confusion, our persistence in the face of opponents we cannot even see, much less understand. It *means* something. Think about that—it has *meaning*" (Weiss 250). As I have argued throughout this essay, by showing his character developing high-level forms of game literacy, Weiss reveals strategies of knowing and expression that are enabled by videogames—strategies that successfully decenter a universal humanist claim to knowledge and power. However, that knowledge and power remain limited. Adam learns that designing particular experiences as games can only go so far when it comes to the corporate world.

The second of the chapters ends with Adam's acquiescence to Krickstein's management style. This experience segues into Adam's cataloging of *Frogger*, a game of survival, which Adam extrapolates to *Copywriter!* and his subsequent job as scriptwriter. Although Adam accepts the defeatist overtones of *Frogger*, which "draws its power from our shared memories of powerlessness" (269), he nonetheless perseveres because of his ability to (re)design his experiences—to change his strategy from one game to another. His perception of a shared state of powerlessness between the frog and him is one of the few moments in the novel when he steps out of his privately held opinions of videogames. Notwithstanding his misplaced conception of the power of videogames to transform power relations, it is his nostalgic connection to videogames, in particular to *Lucky Wander Boy*, that encourages Itachi to withdraw Krickstein's involvement in the film adaptation of the game.

Cartridgeration of the Self in *Lucky Wander Boy*

Adam's involvement in the screen adaptation of *Lucky Wander Boy* sees him necessarily immersed in playing the videogame, if only for source material. The intersection of writing about a videogame while playing that videogame is a significant narrative strategy in *Lucky Wander Boy*, which connects to posthuman configurations of existence, specifically to the process of becoming consumed by games that Adam refers to as "cartridgeration." As Weiss explains, the cartridgerated life is a way of being in a game world in such a way that the player can materialize their existence in different ontological formats. In his supplementary essay to the catalog entry of *Lucky Wander Boy*, Adam explains the progression of cartridgeration from arcade games to ROM chips to videogame computer systems to the present-day multiple arcade machine emulator (MAME), which prevents "vintage software from being lost and forgotten . . . by documenting the hardware and how it functions" ("What Is MAME"). Again we see Weiss create a parallel between the transformation of subjectivity and the transformation of software. MAME gaming represents a technological advancement from the obsolete forms of the coin-op arcade machine or Intellivision console—a way to sustain play across technologies. In terms of Adam's attempt to reconfigure his life and shed its pesky "human" dimensions, MAME gaming represents an emulated sensibility in which game experiences become hardwired in the gamer's mind even as they are played out across new computer software and hardware. In sum, emulation is itself being emulated by Adam—he is procedurally adapting technological history into his own being. The overlapping moments of MAME gaming magnify Adam's ongoing descent into videogame addiction.

Further, MAME gaming shows how Weiss's narrative of self-creation illustrates the importance of ontological consideration to game studies, demonstrated by Simon Egenfeldt-Nielsen and others. In mounting a philosophical inquiry into games and gaming, the emphasis on ontology aligns with posthuman interventions into the question of what constitutes the self. While all of the games Weiss examines up to this point offer philosophical inquiries into the nature of existence, the *Lucky Wander Boy* game works differently. First, it is the one game that has eluded Adam's skill—it's not a game he can win. Second, it is the game that keeps him motivated to complete his catalog of obsolete entertainment, which in turn allows for other impactful games to be explored. Finally, the game is significant because it frames one of the central ideas of the novel, cartridgeration, which itself undergoes emulation as a representation of posthuman subjectivity.

Ultimately, Weiss invites us to take seriously the idea that selfhood in the world of videogames is an unequivocally posthumanizing process. He does this to demonstrate their contradictory nature. While this posthumanizing process allows for high-order processing of information, it is also addictive in the sense that the empowerment depends entirely on a specific set of ontological and epistemological parameters. As Hayles (1999) argues, posthumanism is as much indebted to technological advancements as it is determined by capitalist forces. Weiss would seem to agree, as *Lucky Wander Boy* frames cartridgeration as a product of both technology and capitalism and its effects as both empowering and addictive. In light of the cartridgerated self's relation to developments in technology, Adam draws attention to a constantly recalibrating identity that resembles the ease of switching game cartridges as well as the obsession that software emulation supports.

The MAME system, a remediated form of the arcade machine, represents the culmination of videogame technology for Adam because through MAME a gamer "toggles from cartridge to cartridge, game to game, goal to goal, [and] identity to identity" (Weiss 237). Each cartridge contains its own world wherein the gamer gets to play a given or chosen role. However, the possibilities offered by MAME are overstated by Adam, underlined by the fact that MAME gaming remediates more than the machine; it also remediates the haptic origins of the game, or its modes of embodied interactivity. This remediating principle of MAME gaming is explained by Adam similarly to how N. Katherine Hayles (1999) discusses the metaphoric cyborg. Two examples of this cyborg provided by Hayles—"the computer keyboarder joined in a cybernetic circuit with the screen" and "the adolescent game player in the local video-game arcade" (115)—bear striking resemblance to Adam's naive theory of cartridgeration.

Naive though it may be, the co-formation of the self enabled by emulated gaming results in endless identities that can be infinitely reconfigured, as Adam explains: "He [the gamer] can choose to become two, three, four, or more . . . but he cannot choose to stop choosing, because he is the choosing, the changing, the becoming. Like an open-water shark, he must keep moving, or he as he has come to know himself will cease to be" (Weiss 238). However, there are costs to that reconfiguration. Gaming codes selfhood into the MAME software, to the extent that Adam is unable to extricate himself from the program. To use Hayles's words, cartridgeration "signals the end of traditional concepts of identity even as it points towards the cybernetic loop that generates a new kind of subjectivity" (115).

Adam's cartridgerated way of thinking not only emulates a single-player experience of life but also obscures the real-life implications of his actions for other people. Because games have determined Adam's conception of himself, to stop playing would lead to an existential void—an absence of both ontological and epistemological structure. His gamified construction of reality therefore requires him to pursue new experiences in the same way that he would pursue higher levels in a videogame. Searching for new, more "advanced" stimuli—in the case of Clio, sexual stimuli—is once again likened by Adam to a game. He sees Clio as "part of a completely different config than Anya, compares her to "the bouncing bonus treasure in a quest game," and describes her as "far more exciting and worthwhile than the dull, poorly programmed obstacle course I got whenever I plugged in the Home Life cartridge." In sum, Anya and Clio have become "cartridges" that Adam can conveniently replace to ensure fun and challenge, and thus he does not believe he is betraying Anya by having a sexual encounter with Clio, a graphic designer at Portal, because Anya "was in a whole different universe, as different as Stage I of *Lucky Wander Boy* is from Stage II" (Weiss 240).

A whole other universe indeed. Adam's increasing isolation from Anya results in a "Game Over" for their relationship. Unable to process his real world without the use of his game knowledge, he euphemizes that he "paused this round of Dumped!" in an attempt to come to terms with his reality (292). Anya tries to help, but although she wipes his computer of the MAME software, it does not extract him from his cartridgerated self. At this point in the novel, Adam's sense of himself is irrevocably bound to each game he has ever played. Although the physical games no longer exist, each cartridge, with its specific gameplay, has been imprinted on his consciousness, a kind of emulated epistemology and structure of desire. Of all these games, *Lucky Wander Boy*, with its elusive stage 3, remains the ultimate goal for Adam to complete.

To return to Hayles's notion of the posthuman coformed in part through "technological prostheses" (34), the *Lucky Wander Boy* game cartridge functions as a form of prosthesis whereby Adam gradually becomes his Wander Boy avatar. As Adam controls his avatar through a series of jumps onto staggered planes, the novel reveals his own developing consciousness. Explaining his version of *Lucky Wander Boy*'s game design to the original designer, Itachi, Adam says, "It's epistemological—but it jumps, it jumps to the ontological" (Weiss 449). The "level jumping" that he experiences through the completion of stage 2 corresponds to his own expanding awareness of himself and his surroundings. If stage 3, previously unattained, is the game's ontological destiny, then Adam's quest for the nature of his existence is arguably resolved at the end of the novel. Where he previously regarded the gamer–avatar divide as defined essentially by a screen that separates game from real life, he now uses the word "mirror" to emphasize the complete dissolution of that boundary:

> In the mirror I saw my face, broken down into crisp vector polygons, immaculate and sharp, a caricature of myself so economical and perfect that it was not a caricature at all but a pure distillation of the idea of Adam Pennyman.
>
> And then I stepped through the mirror into Stage III—
>
> And time stopped—
> And I was in the picture—(456)

Through the cartridge, Adam's identity is separated, advanced, and reflected. Being "in the picture" is his final design challenge, which, like stage 3, he achieves. This is reflected in the way Weiss structures the story: the final four chapters of the novel are all titled "Replay." These chapters, while suggesting alternate endings, are rather a representation of the feedback loop between human and videogame machine. The repetition of an ending signals an endless cycle of gamified living that embroils Adam in his videogame world. Structurally, the novel's last chapters recall the "infinite regress cliché" identified by Adam earlier in the novel, when he foreshadowed his concept of a cartridgerated self. According to Adam, technological sophistication would ultimately develop a computer "that could perfectly emulate *me* using the computer that could perfectly emulate my dinosaur laptop" (54). As a representation of an ostensibly posthuman configuration of selfhood, Weiss's novel dissolves the human–nonhuman binary through the distillation of Adam's existence, which is spread out in each cartridge, a kind of distributed emulation. Ultimately, the final game to be cataloged is Adam himself:

GAME: ADAM PENNYMAN

Format: Person

Manufacturer: Harold and Joanne Pennyman
Year: 1971. (470)

Like the games before it, Adam as game becomes Adam as catalog. In true cyborg style, his life is extended through technological prosthesis. This expansion of selfhood in the form of a game places the nonhuman technology alongside, not beneath, universal notions of "the human." Thus, the novel achieves a reinvention of the human as coevolving with nonhuman epistemologies but also a troubling gamification of interpersonal relationships.

Conclusion

The potential of videogames to reflect complex modes of being are brought to the fore in *Lucky Wander Boy*. Treated as a single sociocultural artifact, the videogames that Adam catalogs serve a higher purpose, at least for him. It helps him document how he perceives himself and his environment, but without compelling a comprehensive understanding of why he wants to perceive in this fashion. As much as they might be regarded as obsolete entertainment, the emulated games are significant for enabling Adam to tell his personal narrative and for Weiss to build his novel's story of human consciousness merged with technologically advanced game worlds.

Combining a game studies analysis with theories of posthumanism and applying this to *Lucky Wander Boy* reveals converging ways of being that take the form of digital, emulated, distributed identities. With every new game that Adam plays, a feedback loop is created between the human and the machine, to the extent that worlds are created, the self is reconfigured, nostalgic experiences based on now-obsolete entertainments are (re)generated, and Adam can sustain his quest for knowledge and autonomy.

The nonhuman game personas highlighted in the novel destabilize the universality of "the human" by depicting alternate, coconstituting elements of being. What do we make of this? Adam's game sensibility eventually evolves to the stage where his physical reality is indistinguishable from his game world. With all of his experiences mediated by emulated game cartridges, the novel invites us to consider the extent to which our own lives are mediated by technology and the effects of that mediation on our ability to understand ourselves, others, and the increasingly gamified society in which we live. As Adam's screen becomes a mirror, the novel asks, How human are we—and how important is that question, ultimately? While the prosthetic emulator is a stand-in device for Weiss to explore the ability of computers to expand human limitations—a central point of inquiry in posthuman studies—*Lucky Wander Boy* speculates on the ways in which the computer interface becomes less of an exterior attachment and more of an internal probe for questions about the state of the world and our place in it. Understanding the videogame interface and its effects on the body and mind of the gamer brings us closer to understanding the future and our future selves, though potentially at the cost of our ability to understand ourselves, except in nostalgic, gamified terms.

WORKS CITED

Anable, Aubrey. *Playing with Feelings: Videogames and Affect.* University of Minnesota Press, 2018.

Bedigian, Louis. "GZ Interview: Video Game Obsession Is Taken to New Heights in Lucky Wander Boy." *Game Zone,* 4 May 2012. https://www.gamezone.com/news/gz_inter view_video_game_obsession_is_taken_to_new_heights_in_lucky_wander_boy.

Bolter, Jay David. "Posthumanism." *The International Encyclopedia of Communication Theory and Philosophy* (Vol. 1), edited by K. B. Jensen, Robert T. Craig Jefferson D. Pooley, and Eric W. Rothenbuhler. Wiley Blackwell, 2016.

Bostrom, Nick. "Why I Want to be a Posthuman When I Grow Up." *Medical Enhancement and Posthumanity,* edited by B. Gordijn and R. Chadwick. Springer, 2008, pp. 107–36.

Boulter, Jonathan. *Parables of the Posthuman: Digital Realities, Gaming, and the Player Experience.* Wayne State University Press, 2015.

Braidotti, Rosi. *The Posthuman.* Polity, 2013.

Căşvean, Tulia Maria. "What Is Game Studies Anyway? Legitimacy of Game Studies Beyond Ludo-centrism vs. Narrato-centrism Debate." *Romanian Journal of Journalism & Communication,* vol. 11, no. 1, 2016, pp. 48–59.

Egenfeldt-Nielsen, Simon, Jonas Heide Smith, and Susana Pajares Tosca. *Understanding Videogames. The Essential Introduction.* 2nd ed., Routledge, 2016.

Grusin, Richard, ed. "Introduction." *The Nonhuman Turn*. University of Minnesota Press, 2015.

Haraway, Donna J. *Simians, Cyborgs, and Women: The Reinvention of Nature*. Routledge, 1991.

Hasse, Cathrine. "Posthuman Learning: AI from Novice to Expert." *AI & Society*, vol. 34, 2019, pp. 355–64.

Hayles, N. Katherine. "Cybernetics." *Critical Terms for Media Studies*, edited by W. J. T. Mitchell and Mark B. N. Hansen. University of Chicago Press, 2010, pp. 145–56.

———. *How We Became Posthuman: Virtual Bodies in Cybernetics, Literature, and Informatics*. University of Chicago Press, 1999.

Jagodzinski, Jan. *Pedagogical Explorations in a Posthuman Age: Essays on Designer Capitalism, Eco-Aestheticism, and Visual and Popular Culture as West-East Meet*. Springer Nature Switzerland, 2020.

Livescu, Simona. "From Plato to Derrida and Theories of Play." *CLCWeb: Comparative Literature and Culture*, vol. 5, no. 4, 2003, pp. 1–7.

Malkowski, Jennifer, and TreaAndrea M. Russworm, eds. "Introduction: Identity, Representation and Video Game Studies Beyond the Politics of the Image." *Gaming Representation: Race, Gender, and Sexuality in Videogames*. Indiana University Press, 2017, pp. 1–18.

Reeves, Byron, and J. Leighton Read. *Total Engagement: Using Games and Virtual Worlds to Change the Way People Work and Businesses Compete*. Harvard Business Press, 2009.

Sell, Mike. "What Is a Videogame Movie?" *Arts*, vol. 10, no. 2, 2021, pp. 1–32.

Squire, Kurt. "From Content to Context: Videogames as Designed Experience." *Educational Researcher*, vol. 35, no. 8, 2006, pp. 19–29.

Trammell, Aaron, and Aram Sinnreich. "Visualizing Game Studies: Materiality and Sociality from Chessboard to Circuit Board." *Journal of Game Criticism*, vol. 1, no. 1, 2014, pp. 1–11.

Weiss, D. B. *Lucky Wander Boy*. Penguin, 2003.

"What Is MAME." *MAME Documentation*. https://docs.mamedev.org/whatis.html.

"Why Can't a Game Make Us Understand More, See More, and Feel More?"

The Avatar and Temporality-Function in Dennis Cooper's *God Jr.* and Jeanette Winterson's *The Gap of Time*

AARON HEINRICH

For those who love videogames and novels, the imaginative multiplicity of their union—the videogame novel—provides even more to love. Beyond each genre's normative praxis, their dynamic fusion endows writers, passionate about the motivations of the human heart, with unnerving and unveiling superpowers. The primary goal of this essay is to establish a dialogical relationship between the tools of game studies and literary analysis to unpack the ways two authors incline their readers toward deeper definitions of humanness.

Dennis Cooper's *God Jr.* and Jeanette Winterson's *The Gap of Time* push us beyond the current boundaries of mainstream videogame discourse to address the almost absent cultural and human question of how videogames relate to experiences of traumatic loss and grief, a question that brings the field of psychotherapy to the table. Conversations between the fields of game studies, narrative studies, and psychotherapy are already well under way with the work of scholars like Clarissa Gonzalez and Hope Bell (2016), who consider free play an effective means of trauma therapy for children; psychotherapist and neurobiologist Terry Marks-Tarlow (2017), who documents the therapeutic affordances of creative wordplay; and scholar-performance practitioners like Semi Ryu (2017) and Sabine Harrer (2018), who explore avatars and videogame design and play as effective mediums for therapeutic play, just to name a few. But Cooper and Winterson extend the dialogue by offering their own perspectives on the subject in fictional form, presenting us with two characters who have experienced life-altering traumatic events and choose to engage in videogame play as a coping mechanism and, for Winterson's protagonist, as an explorative platform for communal healing.

For both writers, the power of the videogame to tackle the labor of mourning and the work of inner healing lies, first, in the defamiliarization of a character's everyday skin through the aid of their avatar and, second, in experiencing the multivalent nature of videogame temporality, particularly its cyclical, pause-on-command, and reversible features. Together, the experience of playing an avatar and playing in a different temporality provide the protagonists the tools they need to move on, though only one does so successfully. Cooper's and Winterson's stories are informative and instructive representations of the potential harm and healing coded into the games we play and codified in our playful experiences. Cooper, on one hand, shows videogames facilitating isolation and a fantasy life divorced from reality; Winterson, on the other, shows reflective, conscientious, communally oriented, morally and ethically responsible, and therapeutically charged gameplay.

Jim's Quest and Xeno's Game

Cooper's protagonist, Jim, has made a literal and figurative wreck of his life. He works for a small company that designs and creates specialty costumes for children, and per company policy, every one of Jim's coworkers has a disability. Jim is a paraplegic whose legs ceased to function (temporarily, though he's not informed his employer of this) after a car crash into a telephone pole that killed his only son, Tommy. Jim was high when the crash occurred, and by some "miracle" of the legal system, he wasn't held responsible for Tommy's death. Jim regrets that he never really knew his son beyond getting high with him, a regret he attempts to redress after he discovers the sketches in one of Tommy's old notebooks, including multiple drawings of a building. As a way of monumentalizing Tommy's death, Jim hires a construction crew to replicate that building in his yard. When Jim discovers that the building is part of a videogame world Tommy was obsessed with, Jim adopts Tommy's bear avatar and embarks on a symbolic knowledge quest. Though Tommy's notebooks seem to evince only cannabis-induced daydreams of "skateboard ramp[s] . . . shaped like a pot leaf" or the "Vegas strip" and nude girls inside the building, Jim believes there is something more (Cooper 36). Because the door of the in-game building is locked, Jim must level up to acquire a ludonarrative mechanic that will allow him access, symbolic access, to the real world of love and belonging from which also feels locked out.

As Terry Marks-Tarlow notes, Jim's videogame play is a "fantasy not only to escape but also to disappear inside [himself]," a solipsistic adventure that begins in an existential moment of crisis and leads Jim further and further from reality and relationships (171). By changing his avatar from a simple bear into a godlike persona, Jim subverts the intentions of the game designers. Moreover, Jim's abusive relationship with the nonplayer characters (NPCs) in the game mirrors the dysfunctionality of his relationships outside of it and his inability to move past the loss of his son by grieving well with others. His obsession with a fanta-sized endgame artifact—the ability to undo Tommy's death via a literal restart (suicide)—becomes his paramount goal, the end of a mythic and retraumatiz-ing quest for him and his real-world NPCs: his coworkers, neighbors, and wife.

Winterson's protagonist, Xeno, grew up in a boarding school with his best friend, Leo. When the other kids went home on the weekends, they stayed and played together, "invent[ing] worlds where they could live" (33). The two take divergent paths in life: Leo becomes a slick-suited banker and Xeno a van-life hippie, ponytail and all, who designs videogames. But they remain friends un-til Leo loses trust. Leo's wife MiMi and Xeno spend significant time together, and Leo has an incredibly overactive fantasy life, leading Leo to accuse MiMi of carrying Xeno's baby and to endanger Xeno's life as he rams the Fiat Xeno's driving, over and over, in a parking garage. When Perdita is born, Leo sends her to Xeno's house. Xeno thinks that, if he pretends not to be home, Leo's deliv-eryman will take the baby back to MiMi, but Tony is tragically murdered, and the baby is lost. After this second trauma, Xeno's new game, *The Gap of Time*, comes online.

Unlike Jim's play, which is oriented toward escape, Xeno's game utilizes, in Jean Piaget's terms, the "ludic incentives" of play (150) to reflect on his lived experience, including the dysfunctionality of his relationships and, more im-portantly, how present choices can defamiliarize and reframe past events, un-locking future potentialities (Winterson 4). Because his avatar resembles his real-life self, he reforges a new identity for himself and his community from the brokenness of the past: picking up the shattered pieces, reclaiming the wounded wreckage, and reconstructing it all into food for the soul through a symbolic act he calls "litter duty" (197). While in the real world Xeno's trau-matic experiences convince him he is only fit to fall, his game is designed to rewire neurological pathways and provide a virtual stage for a dramatic reinvention and re-presentation of himself and his community. This is accomplished in a fashion that closely resembles what videogame theorist Lluís Anyó calls "participation time" in virtual rituals that can be semiotically and practically translated into real-world rituals (65).

Ultimately, Winterson's representation of videogame play demonstrates the possibility of healing through an imaginative rethinking of how videogames can work as communal performances. This is in sharp contrast with Cooper's Jim, who invests his grief in a game that only reinforces his selfishness, displaced rage, and extreme narcissism. However, though these writers offer very different stories about videogames, tell very different stories *with* videogames, they help us to understand the ways in which the experience of traumatic loss and grief can transform common videogame affordances into extraordinary psychological experiences. I will explore in detail the affective functions of the two most significant videogame affordances for Cooper and Winterson—the avatar and temporality.

The Avatar-Function: Olympian Stoner Bears and Mortal Garbage Men

When Michel Foucault coined the term "author-function" in 1969, he wasn't aiming for a simple recital of the obvious facts—an author scribbles down words with a pen for the fortuitous sake of a bemused, grateful, or sometimes bewildered audience. Instead, he was accounting for a much larger phenomenon beyond the mere and momentary encounter between a reader and a writer in the interval between a front and a back cover. He wanted to "characterize the existence, circulation, and operation of certain discourses within a society" (Woertendyke 8). In the same vein as Foucault, I employ the term "avatar-function" to suggest that the avatar is more than a mere technological innovation for accomplishing game tasks or obliterating one's game world enemies. As the term has circulated among gamers, designers, scholars, bloggers, and, yes, novelists, the avatar has come to mean much more. As Katherine Isbister notes, avatars provide users a range of "visceral, cognitive, social, and fantasy" possibilities for play and expression (28).

Ryu gives one such avatar possibility a name, Han, a Korean word meaning "one," which exposes and expresses a deep sense of loss and mourning (as one might watch a lover disappear slowly into the horizon) while simultaneously capturing the limitless potential afforded by such moments when the full horizon comes into view and the dramatic tension or paradox between letting go and self-discovery can be successfully held (123, 129). Ryu discovered her own moment of Han when she came face-to-face with a virtual avatar of herself on stage, triggering a tearful "farewell" with a "potential self" (122). Beyond the endurance of the momentary pain of that performative encounter was a healing release, a new and stronger, self-actualized Ryu. She now seeks to re-create that same healing affordance for others through a virtual avatar storytelling project for the elderly, VoicingElder. The dynamic intersection of play, embodiment, and affect that Ryu has discovered between virtual and actual bodies (psychologically layered and highly complex) is a great example of how avatar discourse is constantly changing as the "conceptual," "experiential," and "formal affordances" of the avatar serve different needs within a given context (Sharp 5–6).

Cooper and Winterson provide us with a snapshot of the avatar's expanding meaning, particularly the way avatars can express and mediate loss, whether to promote emotional growth or to inhibit it. Cooper and Winterson use the techniques of speculative fiction to render avatars into fluid ludonarrative affordances. Like innovative game designers, they deploy avatars in their fictions to foreground the "kinds of experiences an audience anticipates having through the consumption of its community's artifacts," doing so to open new imaginative and affective ground for "the things for which a community of practice believes the cultural form can be used" (Sharp 5–6). Videogame stories like *God Jr.* and *The Gap of Time* and platforms like Ryu's VoicingElder contribute to a growing avatar-life discourse, a discourse capable of infusing the avatar-function with life well beyond killing bad guys and rescuing princesses.

For Cooper's protagonist, Jim, a bear avatar and drug use have a synonymous function, a function that ultimately inhibits the success of Jim's symbolic knowledge quest and ludic transformation into someone who has dealt successfully with his grief. Jim's gameplay and drug use are completely immersive experiences that relegate both the traumas and his inability to overcome those traumas to "the world's spookiest wallpaper" (102). The way Jim plays the videogame is fundamentally flawed because his bear avatar is a mirror image of the way he disengages from reality, relationships, and responsibility. His avatar is one of the "druggie bears," as an NPC classifies him, knowing all too well the look and behavior of the intoxicated, which he learned from watching Tommy play (99).

To grow from a failure, one must care about that failure—and accept one's weaknesses. Jim does not, and his refusal to care is reflected in the transformation of his avatar from a bear into a druggie bear and then into a godlike figure who exists beyond human emotion. Exploring the level with the locked building, Jim the druggie bear finds a talking-plant NPC that instructs him on how to locate a special ludic mechanic called the mega-jump that will allow him to land safely on the sacred building's balcony. However, since druggie bear is "the weakest bear I've ever seen," the plant instructs him to play a godlike avatar in bearskin instead of playing through the levels as a genuine game bear (93). Jim describes how he manages the transformation, shifting between third- and first-person perspective: "Then the bear went down and stood around the building while I tried to Method act us into an animal Zeus. . . . When the bear's pose struck me as godlike . . . I walked him toward the exit" (107–8).

Ryu (following drama therapist and theorist Robert Landy) might call Jim's relationship to his avatar a relationship of "over distance" or a play state "characterized by too little feeling, causing a wide separation between the [player] and [avatar]" (Ryu 126). The first challenge Jim's avatar meets on his quest to locate the mega-jump will illustrate this point further.

Following an NPC sunflower's directions, Jim acquires the "dribble," a jump that pounds the earth when he lands (Cooper 112). However, when Jim tests out this dribble mechanic, he unintentionally awakens a snake. Instead of attempting to defeat the snake via his brand-new dribble mechanic, Jim uses his god voice and tells the snake that he will code him out of existence or mod him into a "non-golden rock or something even worse" if he doesn't give the bear a honeycomb (an extra life for the player) (113). Jim refuses to play the game—refuses to grow and mature as a bear. Even if it resulted in multiple failures and retries, dealing with the snake as the rules intend would prepare Jim for the challenges ahead: each new task and level rewarding a skills upgrade as he embraces the ludonarrative risk of presented play moments.

While Jim's choice to burden his bear avatar with "god skills" achieves the desired result of the honeycomb and leveling up, higher-level NPCs don't fall for the mind games of a weak player who doesn't even have the skills to be a decent game bear, let alone a god. While Jim disparages the NPCs as "movement-impaired" or "blue-collar" "peons," Jim's overdistanced, drug-induced inertia prevents him from taking the crucial steps to level up authentically in the game and real life (107, 128). The "extra-special, super-duper honeycomb," the "unbelievable gift" Jim imagines inside Tommy's building, is, ironically, "mobility" or the ability to "go anywhere at any time"—a gift, in Jim's real life, that is not locked away in inaccessible towers but readily accessible in ever-increasing measures as Jim authentically activates it (156–57). If trauma temporarily paralyzes Jim's innate mobility mechanic or sets Jim back to a mobility meter score of nil, he can't cheat or bypass the mourning process designed to reactivate and re–power up the mechanic. Mourning well—facing new conditions and roles—with others is the psychological key to his very solvable inertia puzzle.

When the tragic implications of Jim's avatar-impaired play reach critical game-mass, the bear becomes trapped inside of a well. The well, which turns out to be a talking NPC, proceeds to "lecture" Jim on basic "game strategy" (127). The NPC informs Jim that there was a "labyrinthine" greenhouse that the bear was supposed to explore to find the bombs that would keep him from being trapped. Jim's bear avatar was designed to be bearlike rather than godlike. Not incidentally, that same strategic curiosity might have been employed to know his son when he was still alive, and his wife, coworkers, and neighbors now. However, Jim's overdistanced relationship to his body, and his inability to move on, traps him both in-game and in real life. But as Samuel Zakowski notes, moments of inattentive play often lead players to such "point[s] of no return" (75).

The only solution, the well tells Jim, is to acknowledge failure and restart the game. What happens next is a whiplash movement from over- to underdistance, an emotional crash and restart. In an "impulsive, out of control, flooded with feeling" moment of failed play, Jim pours out his "whole sob story" to the well in the hope that "its walls might spring a leak or two in some surreal take-off on sympathy." What the well says to Jim's now underdistanced avatar before finally letting him out is a revelation of what it's like to be an NPC in Jim's real world: "Think about it this way. If I were a nail, and the bear were a hammer, then why the hell would I care about the carpenter?" (Cooper 127–28). Jim's wife, Bette, is one of the many NPCs who keeps getting emotionally hammered by Jim's fantasy-driven, falsely impaired avatar, who is responsible for his son's death but does not take responsibility.

Cooper's representation of the avatar-function suggests that videogame play, reframed by the Han-like potential of narrative, can be more than what Ian Bogost calls "interactive," with an overt or covert design agenda, or what D. Freeman calls design "emotioneering" (emotional engineering) (qtd. in Harrer 16, 30–31). Cooper gradually and purposefully eradicates the designer from the reader's mind as he forcefully flexes Jim's avatar and game world into a Jim-shaped curvature. For Cooper, Jim becomes an uneasy case study in how the avatar-function can reflect the psychological process of grief, a process that can transform the self into its own dysfunctional and immobile avatar. Jim transfers his trauma and emotional wreckage into a bear avatar who refuses to dribble-jump his way to a mega-jump, who fails to take the obvious microactions of the moment into honeycombs that could be far more rewarding than those he coerces from tyrannized NPCs. If the old adage "Winning is never as important as how the game is played" has lost its personal and cultural resonance in our gamified era, Cooper updates and reincarnates it into the disturbing image of a player and his avatar separated only by a barely perceptible layer of glass: the infusion of Jim's real-life, movement-impaired, stoned, escapist style of habitually disconnected misplay into avatar skin. Though the affordance of an in-game mirror avatar should provide a highly reflective and teachable experience for Jim—a window into his misshapen play and a way out—he can't recognize and embrace the Han-like ludonarrative pain and hope embedded in Tommy's game.

While Winterson's Xeno is also struggling to make sense of his life and losses, he takes a very different approach to play than Jim, even though he too exercises a godlike ability to transform the rules of play. While Leo, Xeno's childhood best friend, likes to play *Grand Theft Auto* and watch porn (and thus maintain the most conventional kind of avatar-function in his virtual life), Xeno wants to design videogames that aren't "all cars, fights, theft, risk, girls, and reward." Games that don't even have cars in them at all. Games where players don't "build alliances" as "instrumental" means for accomplishing solipsistic goals. Games that are all about "relationship-building" and "moral challenge." Xeno believes that videogames like *Grand Theft Auto* are "too passive." Games should "make us understand more, see more, and feel more"—more than adrenaline, as much as books (Winterson 38–39).

To accomplish this, Xeno's game affords two choices of avatars and two possibilities for alliances: with Dark Angels and with mortals (44). Dark Angels are creatures "made, not born" with "two, four, or six wings," who reproduce by shedding their feathers. While the Dark Angels do not control where the feathers land, the fallen feathers can be brought into contact with reactive substances: those contacting fire becoming Angels of the Watch, with eyes in their wings, and those contacting water becoming the Sunken Angels of the underground (196). Mortals, in contrast, are born by choice (the player uploads a selfie into the game), form the resistance to these Dark Angels, and must search for the child who is the key to the game—a generational key to their ultimate resistance. While some readers might dismiss Winterson's videogame inclusion as representative of a traditional good/evil binary and a rehash of the messianic Chosen One trope, there is more at play here in the symbolism of the feathers and the therapeutic possibilities of the avatar—the Han of the game.

In her representation of the avatar-function, Winterson's protagonist, Xeno, is utilizing what Doris Rusch calls "experiential metaphor," in which players use their real-life experiences to analogically make sense of their game worlds (Harrer 23–24, 38–39). Jean Piaget would, similarly, phrase Xeno's good game-play (or grief play) as an activation of his "symbolic imagination" or the use of "unrestricted combinations" to reflect on and defamiliarize his lived experience without—and this is the sharpest contrast with Cooper's avatar-function—losing emotional or memorial touch with that experience (4). Significantly, Xeno's game is a massively multiplayer online game (MMOG), and the four characters who are central to Winterson's plotline are all player characters, not NPCs. Leo is an archangel with many followers. Xeno is what we might call a mortal garbage collector. Leo reproduces Dark Angels like himself by searching out fallen feathers and tragically bringing them into contact with water or fire in a semiotic replication of his real-life under-/overdistanced play states and trauma-inflicting behavior.

But Leo's chaotic and destructive relationship to the material world that is beyond Xeno's control in the real world becomes graspable within Xeno's waste management capabilities, via a clever and imaginative retranslation or "unrestricted combination" of Leo's "dark skills" into the unassuming but powerfully combustible symbolism of feathers. And within the therapeutically charged play space opened up by these constantly cascading but attentively collectible feathers, Xeno discovers, perhaps for the first time in his life, what Ryu calls "aesthetic distance" and Mihaly Csikszentmihalyi (1990) calls a flow state, or "a balance of affect and cognition," which allows one's avatar "to be playful, responding spontaneously to new experience and revisiting old experience as if for the first time" (qtd. in Ryu 127). While in the real world Xeno is a dependable reactive substance to Leo's solipsistically engineered fantasies, in his newfound, avatar-enabled, symbolically combative and unhindered flow state, Xeno has a means not only to contain Leo's fantasies but also to transform them into healing nourishment (chickens) for a relationally cold wasteland where the real Xeno, Leo, MiMi, and Perdita reside.

Xeno, in the words of Toby Smethurst, is playing "interreactive[ly]" with his avatar or "mak[ing] [his] agency felt in the game world by employing game mechanics . . . afforded and delimited by rules" until a "cybernetic circuit" (Brendan Keogh's idea) forms between them and "distinctions between the two are difficult to make, since each is so intimately attuned to the other" (qtd. in Harrer 37). By collecting the semiotically laden feathers—and, more importantly, teaching a new generation to do the same—Xeno is unlocking a therapeutic affordance of the avatar not located in an over-/underdistance binary but in a third option outside the binary. This third avatar has the power to break the binary of futility and redundancy and embrace a Han existence in which the "glory, chance, optimism, bravery, sacrifice, struggle, hope, [and] goodness . . . embedded in the game" are perceptible and accessible (Winterson 197). From two drastically different angles on gameplay and avatar employment—Jim's replication of his real-life habits into an Olympian stoner bear and Xeno's in-flow mortal garbage collector symbolically breaking the power of his out-of-game reactionary rituals—Cooper and Winterson explore the avatar-function in its real-world replicating of harm and its Han-like potential for remediating traumatic experiences to open symbolic pathways for inner healing and future wins.

The Temporality-Function: Cycles, Pauses, and Reversals

I have suggested the idea of the avatar-function to situate and expound the exciting potential of these virtual skins as their existence, circulation, and operation continues to exceed our wildest expectations in videogames and the stories we tell with, about, and around videogames. I'd like to suggest we adopt the term "temporality-function" to denote a similar level of expansive ludonarrative opportunity present in the flexible affordance of time. In *God Jr.*, the temporality-function is most evident in Jim's fleeting tangle with a talking well NPC, mentioned earlier. When Jim initially jumps into the well (before he realizes he's trapped), a bunch of bricks come shooting out of the walls and land in a pile. Next, a digital clock appears on the screen, and the pile, with two rectangular eyeballs, informs Jim that he has exactly two minutes to put all the bricks back "or else" (Cooper 125).

As with his encounter with the snake, Jim refuses to play along. He claims that he has never been good at "jigsaw puzzle[s]," he's not going to start trying now, and even if he wanted to, he doesn't know which button to push, nor did he pay attention to where each brick came from, nor does he even really care (126). Jim literally stonewalls the pile of bricks—"furry poker face to stony red facade"—and demands that they put themselves back because he is God. When

Jim's allotted time to solve the puzzle runs out, the mechanic of the digital clock face disappears and the bricks retreat to their original places.

What Cooper brings to the reader's attention in Jim's failed-because-unwilling-to-try-the-timed-brick-quiz is what Samuel Zakowski calls "cyclical temporality" (62). While Zakowski uses the phrase to examine how temporality "function[s] as the narrative engine" in the *Mass Effect* trilogy (76), perhaps the easiest way to think of cyclical temporality is vis-à-vis the classic movie *Groundhog Day*. In that movie, to escape the time loop in which he is stuck and which causes him to awaken every day on the same day, Phil Connors must "fracture the circularity of historical time and return to the linearity which was present before" the loop began (Zakowski 63). For Phil, the fracturing power lies in curating the perfect day of serving others and surrendering his desire to fall in love to the many variables outside his godlike control. In videogames, this same cyclicality happens when we fail a challenge and must try again or restart a section because we don't like how the game is progressing.

In Cooper's videogame, the powerful ludonarrative tension of defeating cyclical temporality is not a repeated day on the calendar but a two-minute digital clock mechanic meant to motivate, to stir the movement-impaired Jim to meaningful action. Symbolically picking up the pieces of his disordered life and taking responsibility for their aching gaps could break his real-life, movement-impaired cycle and return his fractured cyclical storyline to a linear one: a linear temporality of forward momentum in his marriage and other relationships. When Jim's wife is crying her eyes out in the kitchen, Jim admits that he's "just one raspy breath away from joining her, which I think would save our marriage, but it won't come out" (134). The symbolic act of picking up those bricks could have inspired an attempt at that raspy breath.

Jim's brick fiasco and the missed opportunity to comfort his wife are also good examples of what Zakowski calls "progress-sensitive missions" (75). Basically, the failure to accomplish missions in a certain order or allotted time frame dictated by the rules of the game deactivates the possibility of completing that mission unless the player starts the game over. In Jim's case, starting over to replay the game with more authentic bear strategy (i.e., curiosity), attention to where falling bricks come from, and NPC care could have presented some time-reorienting and life-altering symbolic possibilities. The fracture of the circularity of time and its linear restoration requires Jim to embrace the affordance of what Lluís Anyó calls the "narrative loop" and what I, more aptly for our study, call the ludonarrative loop: to replay the game again and again "as if for the first time" acquiring more player acumen, skills, and knowledge in each and every playthrough (Anyó 71; Ryu 127). In this way, even failures are successes if they hold the power to teach Jim to live in time better. The knowledge Jim desires to gain through his quest is not a prize but the ludonarrative tension of the playthrough, the tension of play and storytelling in and out of the game. Cooper utilizes the ludonarrative tension embedded in the broken cyclical temporality of a game world to heighten the ludonarrative tension of his novel and raise the stakes of a curious, raptly attentive, NPC-oriented readership. In Jim's game world, Cooper's readers just might discover a real world in which digital clocks are not meaningless mechanics but meaningful opportunities to pick up bricks again and again and again.

There is another temporality mechanic in *God Jr.*: the pause. When Jim's bear avatar meets a megaboss called the evil snowman, he's so tired of waiting around for Jim to finish the game that he gifts him with "three nice cheats": invisibility, the power to temporarily melt the snowman, and a move in which Jim must press all the buttons simultaneously to reveal a hidden ladder to climb up the snowman to his hat. Inside the hat, if he can get there fast enough (in other words, if he can progress on his progress-sensitive mission), he will find a spring that will launch him to anywhere he wants to go in the game (152). These three options are symbolic and directly parallel the choices Jim has with respect to his real-life trauma: he can remain invisible by continuing to immerse himself in the trancelike state afforded by his drug use and coercive, tyrannical gameplay; he can continue mistreating his wife, coworkers, neighbors, and others so that they temporarily melt; or he can use this opportunity, this videogame, as a symbolic spring to take him anywhere he wants to go—mobility.

Jim can win the game on his own terms by getting inside the monument and finding love, which he says is the "biggest prize in life. It's like that building . . . You want to be inside that love, even if it's empty, and even if the ones who hide it are divorcing you or dead" (160). Thanks to the snowman, Jim has the ultimate cheat code to get inside that love. He knows where the ladder and the spring are hidden, or in the words of Ryu, he stands in a "paradoxical state of consciousness"—"extreme . . . grief" and "great hope"—with a "springboard" for "overcoming a seemingly impossible situation" or "attaining a state of transformation" (123). But instead of using the code, Jim chooses to subvert the desires of the snowman for a satisfying conclusion to a game that's gone on way too long by standing still, freezing, refusing to choose—effectively pausing the game permanently.

God Jr. ends abruptly when Jim, in his "half dead," paused state, decides to treat all the symbolic import of the game as perma-damage, as if nothing in the game is real or really broken and therefore nothing in his life is real or really broken—not even the glass of the windshield his son flew through or the grass he's buried beneath. To imagine the isolation inside the monument as death and his real world to be as much of a fantastical construction as his game world, to refuse to play by the rules of any world, in the end, proves to be an easier mental and psychological task for Jim than just picking up that damn pile of bricks, just getting to the snowman's hat, just locating that symbolic spring.

Jim tries to solve puzzles, including the puzzle of his own life, by staring them into nonexistence. As the snowman rightly concludes, Jim turns "a puzzle any child could solve into the Sphinx" and a "majestic view into [his] blighted neighborhood" in his paused state or perma-existence (161). The wise NPC plant that Jim met in level 3 knew exactly what the monument meant to Jim all along. It was a vision of Jim's paused world of trauma "eroding . . . peeling away . . . [on] borrowed time and that's rust" (98). The monument was never the glitch that Jim supposed it might be. The way Jim translates his real-life, relationally defunct avatar into a paused, rusting, half-dead bear avatar is the glitch that produces a Game Over. However, all along, Cooper dangles the powerful but missed opportunity for a do-over into the raw gap of Jim's stalled "narrative engine"—his ludonarrative ellipsis between life and death.

Winterson has a different take than Cooper on the temporality-function. All time is present time in Xeno's game, and participation time in that attentive space of presentness becomes a dramatic instantiation and substantiation of the healing process facilitated through our play—grieving well by facing the past head-on and reframing hopeful Han potentialities for renewed relationships in and through the affordance of a transformed play state. Gina Bloom's theory of the pause in *Gaming the Stage* (2018) adds deeper insight into how time operates in Winterson's exceptional conversion of the orthodox game world. Bloom explains that one of the unique features of chess is that all the information needed to analyze the state of play is always available to the players and anyone else watching. If cheating occurs, it can only happen in the pause between moves, and it is only in that same pause that one player can accuse another of cheating, essentially rewriting the history of the game. By fighting and defeating the Dark Angels, the mortals in Xeno's game get to take their wings as a temporary mechanic. With these wings, Xeno can hover, paused, outside of MiMi's window and remember how he loved her when they were alone together in Paris (though Leo stood in the way of that love's contractual fulfillment) and how he can still love her even now.

It's important to note that, in this paused state, Xeno is not rusting or in a half-dead state, like Jim, but is interacting with his game world on what James Newman calls the "ergodic continuum," which treats as meaningful everything in the game (including ambient sounds, NPC interactions, cutscenes, and so on), not just what the player does by pressing a button. It considers the "microdynamics of action" on a continuum along with more overt types of action such as running or jumping (qtd. in Harrer 23, 28–29). If flapping his fading wings accounted for the full ergodic import of Xeno's paused moment of play, the pause would be a useless mechanic, a waste of his hard-earned ability to fly and of valuable playtime—or, worse yet, an evasion of his self-appointed vocational signature. But the emotional ground Xeno traverses as he takes in the fullness of MiMi and reactivates the affective mobility of his love for her makes the pause the most significant mechanic yet, far exceeding the upward mobility of wings. When Xeno emerges from the game world and disconnects from his virtual body, his actual body is right back where it started, but—and this is what ultimately separates Xeno's good grief play from Jim's patented brand of escapist play—he will encounter what Ryu (again following Landy's lead) calls "dramatic paradox": the act of playing in to play out, a "here and now" transformed into a "once again here, and once again now," "a dynamic reflexive state, a returning back to reality with a critical shift in perception, awareness and realization." (129). He is still Xeno and yet is no longer Xeno.

The significance of the pause, for Bloom and for our study, doesn't end there. Bloom explains that the past, present, and future are all contained in the pause. Bloom, using Walter Benjamin's definition, claims that redemption—"a future state of happiness to be achieved, paradoxically, by disrupting the fluid temporality of progress"—is made possible by the pause. Of further use are Benjamin's political interpretations of the "revolutionary" as a person fully conscious "that they are about to make the continuum of history explode" and that the "present" is a temporal state "in which time takes a stand and has come to a standstill" (qtd. in Bloom 148).

The videogame Xeno designs, codes, and plays is based on a dream that Gerard de Nerval once had. The dream involves an angel who gets stuck in a narrow courtyard and dies, but before he dies he gives a little girl two feathers that cannot fly away and become Dark Angels, solid diamond feathers. The feathers symbolize the "flight of time" and the "flight of love" (Winterson 195).

Where Nerval's dream ends, Xeno's game begins. By making the final and ultimate objective of the game to find the lost baby, now seventeen, Xeno's entire game world becomes a revolutionary pause capable of healing the past, present, and future by reclaiming two symbolically crucial feathers that vanished from his community's collective grasp with Perdita and the intentionally inflicted trauma surrounding her disappearance. Winterson's protagonist, Xeno, as a revolutionary videogame designer and player, takes a stand against the progressive tyranny of time and brings time to a standstill through a paused game state until he can make the continuum of history—his and his community's traumatically impaired and well-rutted story—explode.

Another and final twist on the temporality-function in Winterson's game world is one Anyó reminds us of when he claims that "actions are irreversible" in an MMOG (71). Xeno's game, however, intentionally defamiliarizes the MMOG by making time reversible, enabling avatars who reach level 4 to "move around in time . . . deep-freeze an action, event, happening, and . . . make it unhappen" (Winterson 196). When Xeno uses his temporary wings to look into MiMi's window, the game essentially becomes his time-traveling DeLorean. He sees MiMi not as she is now, because "she doesn't sing anymore" after the trauma of losing Perdita, but as she once was, on the night before she gave birth: a moment to which it now seems impossible to ever return (200). In the same way, when Leo thinks about that boyhood day that he caused Xeno to fall from a cliff in the game, he remembers how it's his fault for driving the gap between them wider and wider after the accident, a gap he now considers irreversible. But the narrative engine of the storyline, which traumatically stalled midway through Winterson's tale (with Perdita's unbearable loss), is in full throttle again by the grand finale:

> A woman is standing like a statue in the light. . . .
>
> She doesn't move. Then she does.
>
> "This song is for my daughter. It's called 'Perdita.'"
>
>   *
>
> Leo stood up, went into the aisle. From somewhere in the theatre Xeno came and stood beside him. He put his arm around Leo. Leo was crying now, long tears of rain.
>
> That which is lost is found. (267)

While Leo's in-game behavior and actions mirror his self-centered and reckless out-of-game attitude toward life and relationships (a self-condemned "life sentence" from which he cannot escape), Xeno and Perdita form a resistance to reverse the deadly condition of his gameplay: a reversal to a play state where the "invent[ion of] worlds where they could [all] live" becomes possible again (33, 262). And together Xeno and Perdita prove that the gap of time is ludonarratively reversible and mendable through communal participation time in a game that's so much more than "just a game"—a game that can heal the very fractures of time by re-jump-starting the broken-down, rusting, half-dead engines of our storylines.

From Function to Future

We've seen Cooper's striking representation of the avatar as a virtual skin capable of mirroring our actual traumatized bodies, as well as the psychological disorders and impaired relationships that sicken us and that stem from a failure to hold ourselves accountable or to take definitive action in our present and critical moments of play. We've seen Winterson redefine our trapped states of trauma and victimization, doomed to repetition, by performatively transforming the metaphysical substance of that trauma into healing nourishment instead of harm. Through Cooper's portal into one player's traumatized world, we've seen the effects of cyclical time and paused gameplay on a character who refuses to take meaningful ludonarrative action to fracture the circularity of his rutted existence and to solve the greatest relational puzzle, bringing the game (and by symbolic extension his life) to a happy ending for all.

Through Winterson's masterful storytelling techniques, we've seen the triumph of the pause to rewrite a history of cheats, lies, and deceptions and the power of an MMOG to communally reverse the gaps fissured by our emotional baggage, social bondages, and ultimate inability to reclaim the time and relationships we deem irreparably lost. Beyond the avatar and temporality-functions detailed and deciphered here, I hope you will be inspired to apply the practical tools of a ludonarrative literacy to the videogames and works of fiction about, with, and around videogames that you love to play and read, so that we can continue reaching together toward a better understanding—a deeper discourse on our collectively empowered humanness.

WORKS CITED

Anyó, Lluís. "Narrative Time in Video Games and Films: From Loop to Travel in Time." *Game,* vol. 1, no. 4, 2015, pp. 63–74. https://www.gamejournal.it/anyo_narrative_time.

Bloom, Gina. *Gaming the Stage: Playable Media and the Rise of English Commercial Theater.* University of Michigan Press, 2018.

Cooper, Dennis. *God Jr.* Black Cat, 2005.

Gonzalez, Clarissa L., and Hope Bell. "Child-Centered Play Therapy for Hispanic Children with Traumatic Grief: Culture Implications for Treatment Outcomes." *International Journal of Play Therapy,* vol. 25, no. 3, July 2016, pp. 146–53.

Harrer, Sabine. *Games and Bereavement: How Video Games Represent Attachment, Loss, and Grief.* Transcript Verlag, 2018.

Isbister, Katherine. *How Games Move Us: Emotion by Design.* MIT Press, 2016.

Marks-Tarlow, Terry. "I Am an Avatar of Myself: Fantasy, Trauma, and Self-Deception." *American Journal of Play,* vol. 9, no. 2, Winter 2017, pp. 169–201.

Piaget, J. *Play, Dreams, and Imitation in Childhood.* Translated by G. Gattegno and F. M. Hodson. Routledge & Kegan Paul, 1951.

Ryu, Semi. "Avatar Life-Review: Virtual Bodies in Dramatic Paradox." *Virtual Creativity,* vol. 7, no. 2, December 2017, pp. 121–31.

Sharp, John. *Works of Game: On the Aesthetics of Games and Art.* MIT Press, 2015.

Tedx Talks. "Virtual Reality for Han, Semi Ryu, TEDxRVA." *YouTube,* 20 September 2017. https://youtu.be/BLPARGjvwfc.

Winterson, Jeanette. *The Gap of Time.* Hogarth, 2015.

Woertendyke, Gretchen. *Hemispheric Regionalism: Romance and the Geography of Genre.* Oxford University Press, 2016.

Zakowski, Samuel. "Time and Temporality in the Mass Effect Series: A Narratological Approach." *Games & Culture,* vol. 9, no. 1, January 2014, pp. 58–79.

"We Really SLAY Everywhere"

Virtual Reality, Identity, and Black Girl Magic in Brittney Morris's *SLAY*

RIZIKI MILLANZI

Videogame literature provides readers the opportunity to consider how both videogames and our own realities are shaped by issues of identity, representation, and culture. Novels such as *Ready Player One* (2011), *Warcross* (2017), and *88 Names* (2020) engage ideas about race, poverty, and oppression, and Brittney Morris's 2019 novel *SLAY* is no different. *SLAY* contributes to the argument that videogame literature is a promising and exciting way of considering and representing contemporary thought about the issues and ideas that matter most in our everyday lives. Ernest Cline's *Ready Player One* gives us the opportunity to consider the ways in which American popular culture imagines our future, but it also scrutinizes our present and past (Alexander 525; see also the essays by Sell and by Condis in this volume). In Marie Lu's *Warcross*, the eponymous videogame's use of virtual reality (VR) allows "the real and virtual worlds to mesh" (Ingall 33), and as a result, explores the power structures that surround videogames. This is taken further in Matt Ruff's *88 Names*, which explores the idea of "trying on different skins" and considers how both videogames and virtual reality create a "sense of empowerment" for their players (Seidlinger 36), nesting these ideas in larger geopolitical conflict.

Videogame literature provides us with a unique lens through which we can examine the issues in and around videogames, and that are also present within wider popular culture, such as issues of race, identity, and representation. Not coincidentally, all of the novels I've mentioned provide us with depictions of virtual reality and massively multiplayer online roleplaying games (MMORPGs). But they are far from the only ones. Indeed, representations of virtual reality are among the first and most common examples of videogame literature. Instances include Laurence Manning's *The Man Who Awoke* (1933), Stanislaw Lem's Professor Corcoran and his "personoids" in *Memoirs of a Space Traveler* (1961), Daniel Galouye's *Simulacron-3* (1964), *Tron* (1982), and William Gibson's *Neuromancer* (1984), among others. Virtual videogame environments provide writers a unique opportunity to explore the intersections and multiplicity of identity in a way that other speculative tropes and genres are not quite as successfully able to do. This is because they give writers the opportunity to explore how we represent ourselves, the way that we are perceived by others, and how we try to either control or fight back against dominant images and representations. These depictions also provide us with literary representations of contemporary and real-life societal discourses, such as the discussion about the oppression and marginalization of Black women, which is explored in the 2019 young adult novel *SLAY*.

When the protagonist of *SLAY* is first told, "You are a queen, and this is your game," it is one of the most empowering and significant sentences in Morris's novel (164). It is representative of the celebration of Black culture, creativity, and identity that takes place throughout the book. *SLAY* follows Kiera, an African American teenage girl and the creator of *Slay*, a virtual reality MMORPG which she both develops and runs. In *SLAY*, Kiera is forced to navigate the friction between the empowerment and inclusivity that she has designed into her MMORPG utopia and the pressure and monotony of her family's, boyfriend's, and society's expectations. This is a dichotomy that both challenges and inspires her, and we see it play out both within and outside of the world she has created.

Both Kiera's *Slay* and Morris' *SLAY* have been identified by critics and fans as examples of Black Girl Magic (BGM), a movement that celebrates Black women, identity, culture, and excellence. As Rasha Ali explains, the BGM movement aims to highlight the achievements and talents of Black women and girls, something that has been historically neglected by the wider society, including the videogame industry. BGM is enabled in specific ways in the novel. The game *Slay* is specifically aimed toward Black gamers and attracts a diverse player base from across the world. Access to the game is invite-only, with invitations shared between Black gamers through passcodes and social media. It features a turn-based combat system using dueling cards that are themed around various aspects of Black culture and history, such as the Gabby Douglas card, which grants the player great gymnastic ability, and the Anansi card, which is themed after West African folklore (Morris 41, 69).

But the power of Black Girl Magic is constantly endangered, both in Kiera's game and in her real life. In *SLAY*, Kiera attempts to fight against the backlash that takes place in the aftermath of a *Slay* player's murder, a tragedy that is heavily racialized by newscasters and social media. Through this plot, *SLAY* provides readers the opportunity to explore how the racial stereotypes and tropes that we find in and about videogames can be considered, responded to, and subverted within works of videogame literature, though *SLAY* is unusual for its focus on Black characters and Black experience. In *SLAY*, the reader is immersed in the captivating virtual world of Kiera's game but is also made conscious of the racial and discriminatory narratives that take shape beyond the bounds of her VR headset. Videogame scholars have argued that "extreme and blatant racial tropes flourish within videogames" and that these racial stereotypes help to create reductive and pervasive "cybertypes" (Higgin 4; Leonard, "Not a Hater" 83). Lisa Nakumara writes that the term "cybertype" can be used to "describe the distinctive ways that the internet propagates, disseminates, and commodifies images of race and racism" (3). *SLAY* adds to this discussion by examining both real-life racial stereotypes and the damaging cybertypes that we find represented within videogames.

Anna Everett and Craig Watkins suggest that Black people in videogames have long been portrayed as "digitally manipulated Black caricatures," a viewpoint that is both shared and built upon by the primary antagonist of Morris's novel (149). The character of Malcolm, Kiera's boyfriend and the eventual antagonist of the novel, provides an opportunity to consider how a caricature-like representation of Black people within videogames affects the Black community and potentially shapes their own notions of how they are perceived and what society expects from them. Therefore, *SLAY* can be usefully considered as an example of how the representation of Black people within videogame literature is shaped by established depictions of African Americans within videogames, combined with wider literary tropes and stereotypes.

It is significant that Kiera's game includes both VR and avatar customization as key elements, as it has been suggested by Janet Murray that VR is "an optimistic technology for exploring inner life" and sends the user "back to the real world all the stronger" (28), and Laura Tampieri has written that VR avatars create "a very close identification between the real and the virtual person" (3). In *SLAY*, Morris adopts the strong links that exist between VR, avatars, and identity in videogames to explore wider issues of representation, both in real life and in the wider gamer culture. In this way, Morris both examines and usurps stereotypes and tropes while exploring their effect and legacy in videogames and gamer culture.

To these ends, I will consider how *SLAY* portrays the way in which Kiera and the wider Black community of gamers that she forms are able to center and celebrate their Black culture in a way that they often are unable to in conventional videogames and the wider society. Next, I will explore how *Slay* facilitates the empowerment of its players through both its game mechanics and its ethos of inclusivity, and how it exemplifies the Black Girl Magic movement, both for the characters in *SLAY* and for readers of the novel. Following this, I will consider how Malcom, Kiera's Black boyfriend, allows Morris to examine the dialogical relationship between virtual and real life that VR creates and that Malcom tries to control. Finally, I will explore how Morris's use of videogame and VR conventions links to wider questions about identity, videogame culture, and representation.

Videogames and Virtual Reality as a Safe Space

Videogames have traditionally been considered a space that is dominated by white males, which both excludes and alienates minority gamers (Gray 19; Gray and Leonard 7; Nakamura 40; Patterson 40). This perception of a predominately white gamer culture is reinforced by how Black gamers often find themselves portrayed within videogames as supporting characters and as heavily racialized stereotypes, such as impressive athletes or nameless bystanders (Leonard, "Not a Hater" 85). This is not just a representational issue, as this exclusionary space is also established by gaming companies' historical and ongoing unwillingness to implement effective and inclusive moderation within their communities or to properly address the racist and toxic behavior that takes place within them (Lapolla 19; Paul 70). As Adrienne Shaw argues, "Simply adding diversity to games will not automatically make the gamer audience more diverse," since it will still be a space catering mainly to a white-dominated audience (39). In this respect, we can consider *SLAY* a response to a "growing danger and anxiety that some games are functioning as stewards of White masculine hegemony," but it also serves as recognition of the power and influence that is possessed by virtual reality communities (Higgin 3).

Representations of Black people within popular culture are significant because not only do they harbor harmful stereotypes and systems of oppression but also they affect how Black people "see their place in society" and how members of different minority groups see both "themselves and others like themselves" (Dyer 2). In particular, racialized tropes and representations within videogames serve to perpetuate what has been considered the most important function of stereotypes, which is "to maintain sharp boundary definitions" and restrictions (16). Considered in this context, Morris uses the ongoing discussions concerning race, stereotypes, and identity in videogames and gamer culture as a prompt to explore the ramifications of a game that challenges white hegemony and established racial representations. While Morris could have used film or another form of popular culture to explore these ideas, she uses a virtual reality videogame because videogames are uniquely situated to pose questions about our everyday lives, dominant contemporary culture, and the communities and identities that we form, particularly when we want to play and excel.

Through her depiction of the MMORPG *Slay*, Morris examines how videogames can use virtual reality and avatar creation to empower Black people through gaming instead of oppressing and degrading them through reductive cybertypes and tropes. But Morris goes a step further by emphasizing the pressures placed on Kiera as a game developer. She first creates *Slay* as a safe space, a virtual reality that provides respite from the predominately white high school that she attends. In her everyday life, Kiera is forced to constantly code-switch as she continuously "tries to fit in by keeping her head down and her grades up" (Wright-Redford 48). Kiera creates *Slay* as somewhere where she can truly be herself, without having to change her voice or hide her opinions to fit in. Furthermore, Kiera isn't just responding to the everyday pressures of code-switching; she also navigates the roles of a game designer, player, and community leader. Through *Slay*, Kiera creates somewhere she doesn't have to live up to the unrealistic expectations that are placed upon her by different social groups within society, a space where she is not trapped between her ambition to defy societal expectations and the pressure to internalize and reinforce established white narratives and stereotypes (Cokley 477).

However, *Slay* provides more than a source of escapism. Kiera has created an intersectional and international platform where gamers can freely explore and celebrate Black culture. Throughout the novel, Morris provides the reader with chapter-length snapshots of Kiera's diverse and widespread player base, showing the effect the game has on their relationship with their identity and Blackness. For example, *Slay* provides Jaylen with the opportunity to explore not only their Blackness but also the intersections of their race and gender identity. When Jaylen battles Kiera, they state, "I don't think she'll ever understand what she's done for me. To have a place like this where I can be who I am is indescribable. It feels like waking up for the very first time" (124). These snapshots of the player community demonstrates that Kiera's creation is not only a videogame but also a complex virtual community where people can come together, interact, and support each other as individuals and as a community (Chan and Vorderer 89). In other words, *Slay* is a safe haven for Black people across the world and a social structure for gamers and nongamers alike.

And most importantly, it is free to play. Unlike subscription-based MMORPGs like *World of Warcraft* and *Runescape*, *Slay* players only require a basic VR headset and a passcode, eliminating some of the intersecting race, class, and monetary barriers that a paid service might create for Kiera's intended player base. Beth Wright-Redford describes Kiera's game as "the oasis she created for her community," drawing comparisons to the OASIS in Ernest Cline's *Ready Player One*, which was created as an affordable, accessible, and open-source gaming platform even for those who, like Cline's protagonist, are poor or lack disposable income (Wright-Redford 48; Cline 37).

Like Halliday, the developer of the OASIS in *Ready Player One*, Kiera creates a virtual world enriched by gamer culture and tropes, but in contrast to Cline's overwhelmingly white and male-centered virtual world, she uses them to enable a wider community and to recognize and empower Black culture, creativity, and identity. This can be seen in *Slay*'s combat system. On one hand, Morris uses long-standing videogame mechanics such as the three-round death match present in fighting games *Soulcalibur* or *Mortal Kombat*. However, the combat depicted in *SLAY* is made distinctly Black by how the combat presents itself as physical manifestations of Black cultural tropes and icons. This includes the Mom's Mac and Cheese card, which makes the game environment hazardous to the player as it becomes "thick and gooey" like quicksand (Morris 121). I'll return to the way *Slay* gamifies Black culture in the next section.

The other MMORPG in *SLAY*, *Legacy of Planets*, favors a gamer culture centered around a white, male player identity and focalizes Eurocentric, Western gaming conventions and representations. Kiera characterizes *Legacy of Planets* as "symptomatic of the whole online multiplayer universe" and the racism that takes place in online gamer culture (Morris 97). For example, while playing *Legacy of Planets* for the first time, Kiera finds that the only way she can make her character's skin as dark as her own is to select the dwarf class during character creation. Morris's representation of avatar creation is in conversation with wider representational issues within gaming, one of which is game designers' failure to include diverse options for their players. In this respect, *SLAY* affirms real-life efforts to diversify in-game representation, such as the #EAListen social media campaign that pushed back against the lack of diverse hair and skin tone options in EA's *The Sims 4* (Jackson).

Ultimately, *Legacy of Planets* proves an unwelcoming and prejudiced environment that Kiera abandons despite how badly she "wanted" to love it (Morris 96). Morris demonstrates that MMORPGs often "function as hegemonic fantasy by filtering the racial imagery that threatens the safety and political coherence of White dominance" (Higgin 6). These harmful representations of Blackness preserve white hegemony by presenting Black people in a way that doesn't threaten established depictions and social structures. In contrast, *Slay* shows readers how independently developed and Blackcentric games can provide a liberating and welcoming environment for Black people in a way that many mainstream and established games often do not. As in *Legacy of Planets*, players can "have a world at their fingertips" when they play *Slay*, but can do so without the risk of racial prejudice and denigration—indeed, quite the opposite (96). *Slay* is a place where Black people can play and exist with pride.

Slay is an excellent example of how fictional videogames can cast critical light on real-life issues. The depiction of the game provides readers with food for thought about what can be done in the videogame industry to make it more inclusive, while also highlighting why such inclusivity is beneficial, if not absolutely necessary. In other words, Morris uses the videogame novel to both comment on the culture of videogames and provide a model for both meaningful change and a better way to play. *SLAY* advocates for videogames that celebrate different cultures and identities and provide players with opportunities for meaningful representation. But it also shows us how fictional representations of virtual reality are embedded in utopian fantasies and the politics of embodiment. In *SLAY*, those fantasies and politics are the power of Black Girl Magic.

Black Girl Magic and Black Culture in *SLAY*

The Black Girl Magic movement has evolved from a social media trend into an amplification of pride, empowerment, and self-love that is championed by Black women throughout wider societal discourse and popular culture. The phrase was coined in 2013 in a hashtag used by African American educator CaShawn Thompson (@thepbg) on Twitter. Since then, Black Girl Magic has provided the opportunity for Black women to celebrate their accomplishments and heritage and to both highlight and communicate the wider societal struggles and difficulties they continue to face. The BGM movement challenges narratives that portray Black women as a monolith, pushing back against damaging racialized stereotypes and representations. The movement brings together Black women from all over the world, connected by their shared experiences, common values, and empathy for one another. BGM also encourages participation in other social movements that concern Black women, such as the Black Lives Matter movement. BGM's reach is due not only to its online presence and vibrant community but also to its presence across popular culture, such as in young adult literature and videogames.

Kiera's creation and development of *Slay* is an important part of the novel's portrayal of Black Girl Magic. Morris envisions game-based virtual reality as enabling creative freedom, such as providing the opportunity to challenge traditional representations of Black people, culture, and experiences. Although she is only seventeen years old, Kiera codes, designs, and creates a platform that is used and adored by gamers all over the world. One of the key elements of the game's BGM is its uniquely diverse, complex, and inclusive avatar-creation system.

Avatars are the player's representation within the videogame world, giving gamers the opportunity to create a virtual extension of their identity, interests, and imagination. Jaime Banks and Nicholas David Bowman describe avatars as an extension of players' agency into the space of the videogame itself, while Katherine Warren argues that "avatars expose much about how a player understands her place in a game world" (Banks and Bowman 1; Warren 34). In *SLAY*, Morris proposes the world of virtual reality and avatars as important spaces in which Black women's agency, creativity, and thought—their Black Girl Magic—is allowed to manifest and exist. Morris' depiction of videogame-based BGM emphasizes the expression of identity and creativity in a videogame system that is not inherently designed to accommodate Black female players. Kiera's game allows Black women not only to exhibit their agency but also to examine their experiences in relation to what they're playing and seeing in the world around them. In *SLAY*, Kiera envisions a form of avatar that unites Black gamers across the world by way of Black Girl Magic. In short, *Slay* is the cumulative result of Kiera's own BGM, just as the novel itself is the result of Brittney Morris's.

A key part of the BGM movement is the sharing of Black culture, experiences, and achievements. This is evident in *Slay* via its combination of traditional MMORPG and fantasy tropes combined with Kiera's inventive gameplay and innovation. For example, the Fufu card, named after the staple West African maize dish, creates a huge ball of dough that players can use to damage their opponents (Morris 305). The Twist-Out card, based on the protective natural hairstyle used by Black women, deals no damage but entangles and traps the enemy player with magical, enchanted hair (36). Dueling players in *Slay* are forced to learn and memorize the hundred or so cards within the game so that they can use them correctly and strategically in battle. This also contributes to a sharing of culture and ideas among players as they learn about the different cards and their varying significance and origins throughout the African diaspora, and it allows players to push back against mainstream Western portrayals of Black culture that perpetuate the idea of a monolithic experience. After all, in most videogames, "Blackness is only allowed visibility in very specific and calculated moments that enact the desires of the dominant audience" (Higgin 7). However, in *SLAY*, players across the world use Kiera's gamified Black Girl Magic to showcase fashions, traditions, hairstyles, and music from across the African diaspora:

> Everyone's configured their characters to be different shades, from Zendaya to Lupita, and I am living for it. There's forehead jewelry and face paint, flowers, feathers, beads, glitter, Afros the size of small vehicles and braids just as long and thick as pythons. I spot dashikis, Mursi lip plates, otjize clay, Ulwaluko blankets, Marley twists, Michael Jackson's glove, and a man in a purple cape twice as tall as me in the front row who's trying a little too hard to be Prince. (Morris 27)

By way of its gamified BGM, *SLAY* advocates both for the inclusion of Black female players within the wider gaming community and for more well-rounded and complete representations of them within videogames themselves.

Slay also stands apart from traditional gamer culture through its interactions with wider Black culture and social issues, such as the Black Lives Matter movement. Further, Morris shows how movements like BGM and Black Lives Matter are targets of conservative critics, exemplified in the wake of Jamal's murder (Morris 101). In *SLAY*, Kiera uses Black Girl Magic to fight back against the unfounded hostility directed at her game and the Black women and other players who inhabit the space and keep it running. Thus, Kiera's game engages not only with the organizing and activist sides of Black movements but also with their ability to inspire and empower the wider Black community.

Ultimately, Kiera's game is made possible by videogame conventions and culture, but it is enriched by Black fashion, experiences, and creativity. Tanner Higgin suggests that "game companies must understand the importance of tearing fantasy from its Eurocentric and colonial roots" and that they must destroy the long-standing "connotation of humanity with whiteness" (21). After her frustration with character creation in the fictional MMORPG *Legacy of Planets*, Kiera does just this, creating a customization suite that embraces Black culture, Black identities, and Black creativity—in other words, Black Girl Magic. However, *Slay* also provides gamers with the opportunity to consider the uncertainties of being a Black gamer as well as a Black woman in a world where you have to carve out your own spaces of community, pride, and acceptance.

Identity in Videogames, Virtual Reality, and *SLAY*

In *SLAY*, Morris endorses the opportunity to celebrate and engage Black identities and experiences as well as the more problematic and complex issues faced by Black gamers and the Black community more generally. In addition to creating an opportunity for empowerment and discussion, like the Black Girl Magic movement itself, videogame literatures such as *SLAY* also become a space for examining the uncertainties and contradictions of such spaces. Like *Ready Player One*, *SLAY* illuminates what Megan Condis calls the "anxieties and uncertainties of embodiment and identity in the digital age" through its representation of virtual reality, identity, and videogames (1).

As noted, Morris's depiction of avatar creation and customization form a massive part of the gameplay in *Slay*. This is not unique to *Slay*; avatars are an important part of a gamer's identity and are "often based on an exaggerated version of their own self-image" (Mack 108). However, opportunities for avatar creation can be damaging if such systems privilege whiteness and players are not given the opportunity to properly represent themselves, in terms of both their appearance and their identity (Higgin 3).

In *SLAY*, Kiera creates an inclusive character creation suite that provides a visual representation of Blackness that often is not present in many fantasy games and MMORPGs. By allowing Black gamers to create avatars that mirror their own skin color and features, Kiera both acknowledges and empowers "minorities and other traditionally disenfranchised groups in online environments by making them obvious, visible participants" (Nowak and Rauh 174). This kind of representation is important, as it legitimizes the lived experiences and visibility of Black people.

Morris reminds us that avatars empower players in two ways. As Katie Salen and Eric Zimmerman have argued, a player relates to their in-game character or avatar through a "double consciousness of play," in which the avatar acts as the gamer's "immersive persona" but also as their tool and puppet—a representation, in other words, of agency (453). This agency is increased in virtual reality games because of their immersivity and the increased connection between player agency and avatar agency. Kishonna L. Gray theorizes that in response to exclusionary and discriminatory practices within videogames, people of color often create "their own spaces within virtual worlds," in which they are free to explore and represent their own identities without restriction (76).

This is true of those who make and play *Slay*. Like her players, Kiera values the transformation and escape from reality that the VR game allows, the distinctly Black forms of agency it provides players, as well as the virtual and real-life communities that the game creates. Players of *Slay* have created a coded question that they use to find members of their community in real life: "Did you thaw the meat?" (Morris 30). This greeting exemplifies the empowering duplicity of Kiera's game, combining shared elements of the African American experience (the need to carefully manage one's food and budget) with aspects of the gaming community to which they also belong and in which they participate.

Ironically, when discussing why the passcodes to *Slay* are only given to Black people, Kiera's white friends Harper and Wyatt state that it is discriminatory, as "the game excludes people based on race" (108). Both Wyatt and Harper, like many gamers and developers throughout the world, are seemingly unaware of the exclusionary practices that take place within mainstream gamer culture, such as privileging whiteness and marginalizing the other, and the effect that these have on Black people's mental health and experiences in game and out (Gray 12). This is something that many gamers don't seem to accept or acknowledge, as exemplified by Wyatt, who ultimately hisses, "You're going to stir up all this hate because you can't play as a character with dark skin? Is that it?" (Morris 110).

Another character in *SLAY* who disagrees with the exclusivity of Kiera's game is her Black boyfriend, Malcom, who believes that *Slay* does not empower Black people but in fact helps to perpetuate the racial stereotypes and narratives that oppress them. Malcom's behavior is representative of the anxieties that he feels about the portrayal of Black identity in the wider society and popular culture. But he also represents the prejudices and anxieties that many people feel about videogames as cultural artifact and activity. This is why Malcom creates an avatar that masks his identity and race, manipulating Kiera's avatar creation suite to adorn his avatar with swastikas. Malcom is unable to see past the way that videogames have traditionally centered white normativity and featured caricatures of Blackness, nor is he willing to accept anything other than the limited conception of Blackness and Black consciousness that he has developed in response to such dominant controlling images and institutional racism—a conception limited by his inability to think beyond the actual into the virtual. Though Malcom claims to be "decolonizing" and attempting to "level the field," he is really trying to impose a singular kind of Blackness upon his community, one that does not have a place for play, Black womanhood, or self-construction (Morris 18, 20).

Malcom is unable to acknowledge the game's potential as both a safe space and a celebration of Black culture because of his own constructions of race and identity. Malcom tells Kiera that videogames are just "another distraction to keep us from becoming great," yet he spends much of the novel trolling Kiera and, by extension, the rest of her player base (Morris 278). Morris uses the character of Malcom to explore how videogames might perpetuate racial stereotypes or overlook the wider oppression and injustices that are present within our society—and the way that even well-meaning members of the Black community can fail to understand the power of videogames as platforms for and expressions of Black culture and identity. Morris's naming of the character as Malcom is reminiscent of Malcom X, and the character's opinions are also evocative of Malcom X's ideas concerning Black nationalism and Black womanhood (Bosničová 79).

Malcom becomes one of Kiera's first in-game trolls, using a passcode given to him in good faith by another player to infiltrate *Slay* and the inclusive, accepting space that she has designed. Malcom participates in so-called flaming by using emotionally fueled statements and actions to upset and torment others, in addition to participating in other kinds of griefing behavior that, as has been recognized by researchers, uses his and the other players' experiences of intergenerational and personal trauma against them (Cook et al. 3329, 3324). And he does this by exploiting the opportunities for self-construction that Kiera intended to empower her players. Kristine Nowak and Christian Rauh note that unlike face-to-face encounters in real life, games are "mediated environments" in which avatars "can be tailored to elicit any number of impressions and reactions" (155). Malcom's actions are clearly intended not just to shock his fellow players but also to turn the game's virtual reality into a traumatic space.

After Malcolm's behavior is discovered, Claire asks Kiera why her Black boyfriend would do such heinous things. Kiera responds that it is simply "because he doesn't recognize Black excellence when he sees it" (Morris 290). On this point, Kiera fails to recognize the depth of Malcolm's misbehavior. Whitney Phillips argues that it is a "mistake to dismiss trolls' behaviors as politically meaningless" even when they appear bratty or petulant (6). In this case, it is clear that Malcom's objections to *Slay* go beyond his objection to videogames alone. Malcom's objection to *Slay* is also shaped by his narrow view of what Black excellence should be: a Black nuclear family, giving in to respectability politics, and, above all, "relentless drive and undying ambition" (Morris 295). Morris portrays Malcom as a threat to the inclusive and intersectional utopia of Blackness that Kiera has created and to emerging discussions about what Blackness is and can be, both in the real world and in the games we play.

Moreover, Malcolm fears the particular kinds of excellence that Black women can achieve in the videogame space. When he reveals his true identity within the game, Malcom tells Kiera that he wanted to show her "why Black women should stay focused on being Black women," a viewpoint that Malcom intends to be empowering and supportive of Black women but that ultimately just perpetuates already existing stereotypes and expectations (Morris 278). Morris's idea of what a Black woman should be is in direct conflict with those of Malcom, who believes that Black women should be aspiring toward education, motherhood, and gaining society's respect rather than creating and excelling in games. Malcolm does not see gaming as an appropriate part of a Black women's identity, and further, he fails to understand the significance of videogames as an enduring part of Black culture and identity, particularly for Black women. Malcom's actions, as Kiera's sister states late in the novel, are "ironically the most white-boy troll shit" she's ever seen (295).

Morris' depiction of Malcom shows how the perception of Black people in society can be informed by their representation in videogames, but also how these representations shape and reflect the oppression that Black people face within their everyday lives—sometimes from the very people who claim to care about them. In contrast, Morris's representation of Kiera, Claire, Steph, and other *Slay* players emphasizes how videogames, gamer culture, and videogame literatures can be used to build self-confidence, acceptance, and pride in our own identities. But *SLAY* also participates in and contributes to the Black Girl Magic movement by centering the celebration and consideration of minority identities around the particular perspectives, powers, and achievements of Black women.

Videogame Literature as a Reflection of Our Realities

Ultimately, Morris's novel establishes and explores the connections among games, identity, and race that exist both within the novel and in our everyday and virtual lives. Furthermore, *SLAY*, like other virtual reality narratives, shows the ways in which virtual reality can explore ideas of identity and community, both those operative in the real world and those possible in imaginary worlds. Additionally, Morris's writing also contributes to a discourse that seeks to "overcome the one-sided view of digital games as a risk to health and society" by portraying videogames as something that can promote well-being, empowerment, and self-care (Reer and Quandt 2). But she goes a step further by recognizing how this can apply to those who play videogames and to those who make them.

The celebration and inclusion of Black identities and culture in Kiera's game subverts the systemic exclusion and white normativity that is found in many commercialized, popular, and AAA games. This is one of the reasons why the character of Kiera is so remarkable—and such a perfect example of Black Girl Magic for the young adults to whom her book is dedicated. Kiara is the creator of *Slay* and the creator of a community that uses videogames and virtual reality as a tool to create lasting social connections and a supportive network of Black gamers. Felix Reer and Thorsten Quandt have stated that "the idea of the 'lonely gamer' who plays shooter games in a darkened room without any social contact" is an "outdated and unrealistic stereotype" (14), and *SLAY* supports this argument by emphasizing the importance of the virtual community that Kiera has created. The players of *Slay* aren't just not lonely—they are recognized.

SLAY presents us with a narrative that explores how videogames can be a platform to uplift others and offer support and affirmation. Most interestingly, the book does the same, as it is clearly intended to inspire readers to embrace their identities, create similar communities, partake in similar acts of solidarity, and use their powers of creation, no matter what anyone else says. But *SLAY* is not naive about the challenges facing readers. It is one of many examples of authors creating utopian spaces that "provide an optimal environment for a pleasurable escape from the restrictions and difficulties of the real world" (Reer and Quandt 3). However, like Marie Lu's virtual world in *Warcross* or Charlotte Perkins Gilman's *Herland,* these utopian spaces are threatened by ideologies and modes of embodiment that are difficult, if not impossible, to avoid or disable, particularly because they take advantage of the very empowerment that the player community finds in those games.

This is particularly true of the "escapism" affirmed in *SLAY*. Morris's portrayal of the Black community finding a safe space for play challenges established portrayals of escapism surrounding game culture by imbuing it with revolutionary ideas of Black excellence and empowerment. Even more remarkably, Morris usurps one of the core ideas that sustains sexist, racist, queerphobic movements like Gamergate: that escapism means ignoring the existence of racism, sexism, and even women and people of color gamers themselves (Mortensen 792). *SLAY* consequently serves as a critique of how racialized and gendered stereotypes and portrayals continue to inhibit Black people and their participation in gamer culture and other communities. *SLAY* sets a precedent for how other works of videogame literature and novels can be used as a lens to explore real-life reactions to videogames as well as the issues that are created and perpetuated by them. Just as campaigns for racial justice like Black Lives Matter get censured by critics as "promoting violence," the MMORPG *Slay* becomes the target of a public rhetoric that portrays it as promoting racial violence and exclusionary practices (Morris 128).

Videogames, as well as the literature that engages with them, often mirror prominent societal ideas, both those that operate in the real world and those that exist in gaming spaces. However, they also can be used as a facilitator of change or to respond to and challenge these ideas. David J. Leonard believes that "videogames are not just games or sites of stereotypes but a space to engage American discourses, ideologies, and racial dynamics" ("Live in your world" 3). *SLAY*, understood as a work of videogame literature and as a Black Girl Magic text, highlights how videogame literature can respond to such discourses and provide readers ways to imagine other worlds and other ways to play. Because of its inherent Black Girl Magic and its address to young adult readers, *SLAY* has the potential to inspire not just a whole new generation of gamers and developers but also a generation of Black people who can imagine new ways to design their selves and their communities.

WORKS CITED

Alexander, Jonathan. "The Uses and Abuses of Pop Culture in *Ready Player One* and *Grandmother's Gold*." *Journal of Popular Culture*, vol. 53, no. 3, 2020, pp. 525–46.

Ali, Rasha. "What Is Black Girl Magic? A Short Explainer." *TheWrap*, 30 June 2016. https://www.thewrap.com/what-is-black-girl-magic.

Banks, Jamie, and Nicholas Bowman. "Some Assembly Required: Player Mental Models of Videogame Avatars." *Frontiers in Psychology*, 15 July 2021.

Bosničová, Nina. "Malcolm X and the Fair Sex: Representation of Women in Malcolm X's Autobiography." *Brno Studies in English,* vol. 32, 2006, pp. 77–85.

Chan, Elaine, and Peter Vorderer. "Massively Multiplayer Online Games." *Playing Video Games: Motives, Responses, and Consequences,* edited by Peter Vorderer and Jennings Bryant. Taylor & Francis, 2006, pp. 88–101.

Cline, Ernest. *Ready Player One.* Crown, 2011.

Cokley, Kevin O. "Testing Cross's Revised Racial Identity Model: An Examination of the Relationship Between Racial Identity and Internalized Racialism." *Journal of Counseling Psychology,* vol. 49, no. 4, October 2002, pp. 476–83.

Condis, Megan Amber. "Playing the Game of Literature: *Ready Player One,* the Ludic Novel, and the Geeky 'Canon' of White Masculinity." *Journal of Modern Literature,* vol. 39, no. 2, Winter 2016, pp. 1–19.

Cook, Christine, Juliette Schaafsma, and Marjolijn Antheunis. "Under the Bridge: An in-Depth Examination of Online Trolling in the Gaming Context." *New Media & Society,* vol. 20, no. 9, September 2018, pp. 3323–40.

Dyer, Richard. *The Matter of Images: Essays on Representations.* 2nd ed., Routledge, 2002.

Everett, Anna, and S. Craig Watkins. "The Power of Play: The Portrayal and Performance of Race in Video Games." *The Ecology of Games: Connecting Youth, Games, and Learning,* edited by Katie Salen. MIT Press, 2008, pp. 141–66.

Gray, Kishonna L. *Race, Gender, and Deviance in Xbox Live: Theoretical Perspectives from the Virtual Margins.* Taylor & Francis, 2014.

Gray, Kishonna L., and David J. Leonard, eds. "Introduction. Not a Post-racism and Post-misogyny Promised Land: Video Games as Instruments of (In)justice." *Woke Gaming.* University of Washington Press, 2018, pp. 3–23.

Heineman, David S. *Thinking about Video Games: Interviews with the Experts.* Indiana University Press, 2015.

Higgin, T. "Blackless Fantasy: The Disappearance of Race in Massively Multiplayer Online Role-Playing Games." *Games and Culture,* vol. 4, no. 1, December 2008, pp. 3–26.

Ingall, Marjorie. "Y.A. Fantasy." *New York Times,* 12 November 2017, p. 33.

Jackson, Gita. "Black 'The Sims 4' Players Are Changing One of the World's Biggest Games." *Vice,* 12 August 2020. https://www.vice.com/en/article/4ay5a9/black-the-sims-4-play ers-are-changing-one-of-the-worlds-biggest-games.

Lapolla, Matthew. *Tackling Toxicity: Identifying and Addressing Toxic Behavior in Online Video Games,* 15 May 2020. Seton Hall University, PhD dissertation.

Lebowitz, Josiah, and Chris Klug. *Interactive Storytelling for Video Games.* CRC Press, 2011.

Leonard, David J. "High Tech Blackface: Race, Sports Video Games and Becoming the Other." *Intelligent Agent,* vol. 4, no. 4, 2004, p. 5.

———. "'Live in Your World, Play in Ours': Race, Video Games, and Consuming the Other." *SIMILE: Studies in Media & Information Literacy Education,* vol. 3, no. 4, November 2003, pp. 1–9.

———. "Not a Hater, Just Keepin' It Real: The Importance of Race- and Gender-Based Game Studies." *Games and Culture*, vol. 1, no. 1, January 2006, pp. 83–88.

Lu, Marie. *Warcross*. G. P. Putnam's Sons, 2017.

Mack, Jonathan. "Evoking Interactivity: Film and Videogame Intermediality since the 1980s." *Adaptation*, vol. 9, no. 1, March 2016, pp. 98–112.

Morris, Brittney. *SLAY*. Hodder, 2019.

Mortensen, Torill Elvira. "Anger, Fear, and Games: The Long Event of #GamerGate." *Games and Culture*, vol. 13, no. 8, 2018, pp. 787–806.

Mou, Yi, and Wei Peng. "Gender and Racial Stereotypes in Popular Video Games." *Handbook of Research on Effective Electronic Gaming in Education*, edited by Richard E. Ferdig. IGI Global, 2008, pp. 922–37.

Mukherjee, Souvik. *Video Games and Storytelling: Reading Games and Playing Books*. Palgrave, 2015.

Nakamura, Lisa. *Cybertypes: Race, Ethnicity, and Identity on the Internet*. Taylor & Francis, 2002.

Nowak, Kristine L., and Christian Rauh. "The Influence of the Avatar on Online Perceptions of Anthropomorphism, Androgyny, Credibility, Homophily, and Attraction." *Journal of Computer-Mediated Communication*, vol. 11, no. 1, November 2005, pp. 153–78.

Patterson, Christopher B. *Open World Empire: Race, Erotics, and the Global Rise of Video Games*. New York University Press, 2020.

Paul, Christopher A. *The Toxic Meritocracy of Video Games*. University of Minnesota Press, 2018.

Phillips, Whitney. *This Is Why We Can't Have Nice Things: Mapping the Relationship Between Online Trolling and Mainstream Culture*. MIT Press, 2015.

Reer, Felix, and Thorsten Quandt. "Digital Games and Well-Being: An Overview." *Video Games and Well-Being: Press Start*, edited by Rachel Kowert. Springer International, 2019, pp. 1–21.

Ruff, Matt. *88 Names*. Harper, 2020.

Salen, Katie, and Eric Zimmerman. *Rules of Play: Game Design Fundamentals*. MIT Press, 2003.

Seidlinger, Michael J. "The Great Pretenders: PW Talks with Matt Ruff." *Publishers Weekly*, vol. 266, no. 46, November 2019, p. 36.

Shaw, Adrienne. "Do You Identify as a Gamer? Gender, Race, Sexuality, and Gamer Identity." *New Media & Society*, vol. 14, no. 1, February 2012, pp. 28–44.

Smith, Stacy L. "Perps, Pimps, and Provocative Clothing: Examining Negative Content Patterns in Video Games." *Playing Video Games: Motives, Responses, and Consequences*, edited by Peter Vorderer and Jennings Bryant, Taylor & Francis, 2006, pp. 64–87.

Tampieri, Laura. "Second Life as Educational Space for the Simulation of Enterprises' Start Up and for Managerial Culture Development." *Virtual Reality*, edited by Nada Bates-Brkljac. Nova Science Publishers, 2012, pp. 1–49.

Trepte, Sabine, and Leonard Reinecke. "Avatar Creation and Video Game Enjoyment: Effects of Life-Satisfaction, Game Competitiveness, and Identification with the Avatar." *Journal of Media Psychology,* vol. 22, no. 4, January 2010, pp. 171–84.

Warren, Katherine. "Who Are You Here? The Avatar and the Other in Video Game Avatars." *Rhetoric/Composition/Play through Video Games,* edited by Richard Colby and Matthew Johnson. Palgrave Macmillan, 2013, pp. 33–43.

Williams, Dmitri, Nicole Martins, Mia Consalvo, and James D. Ivory. "The Virtual Census: Representations of Gender, Race and Age in Video Games." *New Media & Society,* vol. 11, no. 5, August 2009, pp. 815–34.

Winget, Megan A. "Videogame Preservation and Massively Multiplayer Online Role-Playing Games: A Review of the Literature." *Journal of the American Society for Information Science and Technology,* vol. 62, no. 10, 2011, pp. 1869–83.

Won, Daehyun. *Avatar in Digital Games: Embodied Rhetorical Agency or Disembodied Algorithm?* SWPACA 2021.

Wright-Redford, Beth. "Young Adult Book Reviews." *School Library Journal,* vol. 65, no. 6, July 2019, p. 48.

"It's As If We're Free of Ourselves"

Minecraft and Techno-Utopias in Keith Stuart's
A Boy Made of Blocks

HOLLY PARKER

Keith Stuart's 2016 novel *A Boy Made of Blocks* employs *Minecraft* as a techno-logical utopia where Alex and his son, Sam, who is diagnosed with autism spectrum disorder (ASD), can "be free of [themselves]" (133).* This techno-utopia allows the pair to experience adventure within the safety of the game and to build an emotional connection with each other in a space informed by neoliberal regimes and evolving videogame culture (Marantz). Stuart adopts the novel form as a unique way to engage with techno-utopianism as he focuses on the angle of familial relationships. The novel provides a space for Stuart to unpick the complicated knot of feelings, gameplay, and political ideologies beyond viewing gameplay as an isolated experience. This essay interrogates how Stuart's novel tackles cultural perceptions of ASD and how Sam's representation interlinks with the novel's representation of neoliberalism. Stuart's depiction of Alex's and Sam's performances as avatars both critiques and subscribes to postmillennial

---

* While there is much debate around the terms used surrounding autism, I am using "autistic" and "autism spectrum disorder" throughout the essay to denote Sam's autism. In their survey of the terms used to describe autism, Kenny et al. state, "Examination of the figure clearly shows that people use many terms to describe autism. The most highly endorsed terms were 'autism' and 'on the autism spectrum,' and to a lesser extent, 'autism spectrum disorder (ASD),' for which there was general agreement across groups." Nonetheless, these authors acknowledge that "community members disagreed . . . on the use of several terms." "When participants were asked to choose which one term they would use to communicate about autism, the results revealed little consensus between and within groups" (447). *A Boy Made of Blocks* engages with cultural perceptions of ASD and uses the term "autistic" throughout, so I shall follow the language of the novel.

neoliberal society, engaging with dispossession, self-help culture, and the focus on "family" (Crossley).

Minecraft was launched in 2009 and has shaped a generation's engagement with videogames (Garrelts). The game itself is laborcentric, and players spawn on a randomly generated virtual world that they uncover as they explore. They can play in "creative" or "survival" modes, enabling the players to moderate their level of risk and reward—the more that is at stake, the more loot you can acquire. The game encourages players to mine for materials and offers almost infinite possibilities for world building. This game narrative was vastly different from the first-person shooters that caused authorities so much anxiety throughout early twenty-first-century Western culture (Isbister). Rather, it promotes adventure, exploration, and harvesting.

My interrogation of Stuart's fictional representation of *Minecraft* centers on the game's internal structure and logic, focusing on the players' affective experiences due to their shared gameplay and how that experience is informed by neoliberalism. I will analyze the novel through the lens of performance studies. The term "performance" is broad and contested, and many studies, such as Jon McKenzie's *Perform or Else* (2001) and Marvin Carlson's essay "What Is Performance?" (1996), have acknowledged this in their compiled definitions of the term. For Carlson, the term "performance" can denote that something fulfills its task (such as a working car) or achieves a certain level of skill (such as actors reciting lines). McKenzie's work discusses the emergence of "performance management" to review efficiency in the workplace. Carlson identifies what ties these different understandings of performance together: "According to [Richard] Bauman, all performance involves a consciousness of doubleness, through which the actual execution of an action is placed in mental comparison with a potential, an ideal, or a remembered original model of that action. . . . Performance is always performance *for* someone, some audience that recognizes and validates it as performance even when, as is occasionally the case, that audience is the self" (6).

Whatever we are performing, there is always a previous standard that we assimilate. Performance is always a copy—it is iterative. My analysis of Stuart's novel keeps this definition in mind. Alex and Sam perform in all aspects of their lives. Alex upholds expectations of the neoliberal workplace and of a father; Sam is governed by an insidious model of neurotypical social expectations. As avatars, they negotiate these expectations within the microcosm/techno-utopia of Stuart's literary version of *Minecraft*.

Through the lens of avatarial performance, this essay interrogates *A Boy Made of Blocks* by engaging with affect theory in a digital age, informed by twenty-first-century videogame culture. Applying Sherry Turkle's work on technology and Daniel Muriel and Garry Crawford's research on videogames in the "cyborgian age" to Stuart's novel, my analysis is situated within current debates on videogames and popular culture. My discussion of neoliberalism within the novel is informed by Judith Butler and Athena Athanasiou's conversations on dispossession. This concept is key to Alex's and Sam's ability to embrace the inherent unpredictability of life within *Minecraft* as a "universe where the rules are unambiguous" (133). As Colin Fanning and Rebecca Mir argue, "*Minecraft* does not require an adult facilitator, but the structure of the game world itself provides a framework that places restrictions on the player" (44). These restrictions are vital for Sam and Alex because they allow Sam to tackle the precarious and ever-changing concept of "adventure" within the confines of *Minecraft* and to extend this experience to material reality. Ultimately, *A Boy Made of Blocks* is a novel that engages with and embraces the difficulties of critiquing neoliberalism from within that very culture.

Stuart's novel opens with Alex, a newly jobless and separated father who struggles to connect emotionally with his son, Sam. Sam has ASD and struggles to navigate the uncertainties and complexities of everyday life—from attending school to requiring perfectly cut cheese and piccalilli sandwiches. In real life (IRL), Sam is expected to follow the unspoken rules and etiquette of neurotypical society and to perform his role of son, student, or friend in normative fashion, but Stuart's novel leaves these expectations behind at the log-in screen, when the pair creates "Sam and Daddy's World" (141). In contrast to Sam's IRL "breakdowns," Alex can show Sam how to embrace "adventure" in the game. Sam and Alex adopt *Minecraft* as a digital space where "the logic is unerring" to reconnect with each other (133). The virtual world removes the emotional barrier between the pair, allowing them to discuss adventure, excitement, fulfillment, and loss. Later, Sam and Alex take a trip to London, after having prepared Sam for these experiences.

But Alex too benefits from their gameplay. IRL, he is burdened by the weight of working a nine-to-five job as a mortgage adviser, until he is made redundant and separates from his wife, Jody. The game creates a space where Alex can open up emotionally and appreciate his son in a world separated from the performative roles of father and son. Both characters experience such affects as happiness, anger, and grief from their performances as avatars, respectively and together, but can do so only through the programmed and profitable space of the videogame. As such, *A Boy Made of Blocks* navigates the complexity of building relationships in a neoliberal and digital age.

Performativity and Neoliberalism

Michael Glass defines neoliberalism as a "pervading hegemonic discourse that shapes the economic, social, and political world." It is a regime that positions the individual at the center and focuses on maximizing profits. But neoliberalism cannot do anything by itself, requiring what Glass calls "agents" that help it "develop into such a significant ideological feature on the landscape of late capitalism." Glass turns to performativity to understand how "neoliberalism is made through discourse, signs and authority" and argues that "for neoliberalism, in particular, the consequences of performativity are profound. . . . Performativity holds that there is no preexisting or stable category known as neoliberalism and that it is instead created and recreated as the consequence of active and embodied practices" (352–53). In short, our behaviors and choices are shaped by these neoliberal affects, which mold the political practices we enact to perpetuate the regime. Alex and Sam perform that cycle.

Stuart presents Alex as a product of neoliberalist ideologies, such as through his engagement with self-help culture. On a trip to Blackwell's bookshop, Alex buys self-help books on marriage, ASD, and even *Minecraft,* and these books provide a scaffold for Alex's ability to manage all aspects of his life:

> I get to a small collection of books on autism. I have resolved to read one. Actually read it. We've got a few at home—most of them desperate online purchases made after a long day of exhausting meltdowns. Some are overly officious and instructional, treating the condition like a challenging DIY [do-it-yourself] job; some are more like hippy lifestyle manuals, so you end up feeling like *you're* the problem for ever viewing autism negatively in the first place. (85)

Alex is openly cynical about self-help books in this passage and references the neoliberal focus on individualism as a source of success or failure. This individualism operates on multiple levels, creating an endless cycle. The consumer purchases the books to instill a sense of agency and of seizing the problem with their own hands, but as Alex stresses, "You end up feeling like *you're* the problem," thereby needing to purchase more books to fix yourself.

Although he mocks the political ideologies of the self-help books, he still "desperately" seeks their guidance. He browses the bookshop and selects a couple of books that "sit somewhere between the 'you can fix your broken child' and the 'hey, man, it's *society* that needs to be fixed' schools of thought." On his way to the register, he "spot[s] a huge display of *Minecraft* books . . . On a whim, I pick up something that promises to be a complete guide to the game" (86). Almost despite himself, Alex admits that, "as I walk out of the shop, I am hit by an unfamiliar wave of optimism. . . . I am going to understand Sam; I am going to crack either autism or *Minecraft,* one of the two" (87). Alex chooses to purchase self-help texts in a bid to understand Sam. He even experiences a sense of optimism before he has read the books, as though he has taken control of the situation just through the act of purchasing them.

Stuart frames *A Boy Made of Blocks* around Alex's dissociation from his own emotions, beginning with the first line of the novel, which reflects a wider "numbness" that stems from the sensory overstimulation of contemporary life. Alex confesses, "I am estranged" (1). This statement is isolated and separated from the rest of the narrative on the novel's printed page, and it physically reflects the isolation Alex acknowledges. Moreover, his statement lacks context. While one may infer that Alex is referring to his marriage, his confession has a double meaning in that it represents his emotional state, too. Indeed, Alex suffers from what he calls an "emotional vacuum"; he is dissociated from his emotions, even having to consciously register that "Oh, oh right, I'm crying" (4). The novel narrates Alex's attempt to "connect to everything again" (24).

Stuart explores dimensions of personal and interpersonal experience that are best understood using affect theory. Affect theory, broadly, is a theory of the structure and performance of emotions. Stuart's novel is productively understood as part of the broader conversation on how we negotiate emotions in a digital and precarious age. Hua Hsu posits that affect theorists like Sara Ahmed, Sianne Ngai, and Ann Cvetkovich "began exploring the emotional contours of life during increasingly precarious times." Precarity is an integral part of the neoliberal regime, and these scholars draw a correlation between this instability and mental health. According to Hsu, affect theorists focus on "a kind of overstimulated numbness, considering everything from what it meant to call something 'interesting'—a hedge against actual judgment—to the relationship between economic anxiety and mental health." Stuart's focus on Alex's reconnection to his emotions fits this cultural backdrop, and he presents a narrative focused on negotiating a path back to emotional well-being in the face of, and because of, precarity. I shall return to this in reference to Butler and Athanasiou's work on dispossession. My analysis concerns how Alex's emotional estrangement is reflective of this cultural state.

Alex must open himself to vulnerability and disorder to resist the regimentation that is the cause of the emotional vacuum. After he and Jody make their separation permanent, Alex sinks into depression. During a trip to the corner shop, he observes that the woman behind the counter "gives me a look that manages to combine both sympathy and fear; when I get home I realise I'm wearing tartan pyjama bottoms, a crumpled Marks and Spencer shirt and two trainers that don't match. Add the fact that I haven't shaved in five days and I look like what I am—a pathetic shuffling husk of a man." Ironically, the disruption of Alex's formerly well-managed self demonstrates a shift toward his emotional reconnection. This moment is phrased in his sudden declaration, "Oh God, I'm the mad woman in the attic. Or, more accurately, the sad man in the spare room" (76). This mess and emotional awareness of it create a "stepping stone" for Alex to open up both to Sam and to himself, even before they play *Minecraft*.

Alex's process of self-management is similar in some ways to Sam's need for logic and control; the way they mirror each other is telling of the wider need for regimentation in twenty-first-century life. The notion of work–life balance that's promoted within the neoliberal workplace, for instance, is centered on the ability to divide and manage emotions and external distractions to encourage efficiency at work. Stuart represents different styles of self-management in each of the central characters, and as such, highlights how ingrained and insidious this ideology is. For example, Alex struggles to connect to his emotions and seeks to separate himself from his grief. Similarly, Sam thrives on a world of "unerring logic" (133). I shall return to the representation of ASD later in the essay, but I note now that Sam's characterization as an autistic child character reflects wider anxieties surrounding the nuclear family. Sonya Freeman Loftis argues that autistic child characters tend to "stand in for larger cultural anxieties regarding the instability of the postmodern family and the struggle to establish emotional connections in a postmodern world" (108). In *A Boy Made of Blocks*, Sam stands for precarity: the precarity of Alex and Jody's relationship and their "family unit," of Alex's job loss, and of Sam's struggle to fit into an unstructured and unpredictable world. *Minecraft* plays a vital role in the novel; its 8-bit design offers a logical and self-contained space that counters the chaos of everyday life.

Minecraft as Performance Space

Stuart's fictionalized version of *Minecraft* is successful as a performance space because of its regimentation and associated safety. He uses the videogame as a clearly defined and contained microcosm that focuses on life under neoliberalism, including the key aspect of negotiating risk. First, Alex and Sam must log in to Sam and Daddy's World to access the blocky virtual world. This immediately distinguishes the virtual world from the material one. The game constitutes the performance space. Fanning and Mir assert that the structure of *Minecraft* provides a restrictive framework for the player. Alex's narration supports this argument: "While everything else was chaos in our lives, we had somewhere that we could escape to and explore—a place that had logic and rules and definite borders. . . . We were safe and we could make anything we wanted" (Stuart 360). This is especially important for Sam, as Alex notes, "To Sam, the world is a gigantic engine that needs to work in a certain way," but "in this universe, where the rules are unambiguous, where the logic is clear and unerring, Sam is in control" (133). The game, then, provides a clear and safe techno-utopian space for Sam and Alex to reconnect.

The two modes of gameplay in *Minecraft* are "survival" and "creative." As the term "survival" suggests, there are greater risks involved in that mode. In contrast to creative mode, in survival mode players can be killed and lose their loot, but with this increased risk there also are higher rewards. Stuart utilizes these modes of gameplay to allow Sam to negotiate levels of risk and precarity. Sam first plays in creative mode, then survival mode, and then applies these experiences to material life. Thus, Stuart's representation of Sam's growing confidence reflects the wider neoliberal concerns of control and precarity. Sam processes virtual loss and frustration through the mediated risk of *Minecraft*, and its role in Sam's development can be seen when Alex convinces Sam to play the game in survival mode. Subsequently, when the pair die in-game, Alex responds that "the spoils are lost" and the progress they have made in the virtual world lost, too. Sam becomes "lost in his own disappointment and frustration" and blames Alex for convincing him that no risk would befall them: "That was your fault . . . you said it was safe" (135). Yes, he loses his loot, but he gains the experience and knowledge to avoid a repeat. In this way, the game is a beta-test version of life under neoliberalism. As Fanning and Mir argue, where playing on a playground allows children to learn and grow, "*Minecraft* provides this without the risk of a concussion or broken bones" (50). For Sam, there are no real-world negative effects on his health, but he can learn how to overcome some of his anxieties.

The benefits of the game I have discussed so far lie within the safety of the virtual world, but this safety and mediated risk can be applied materially, too, and *A Boy Made of Blocks* highlights the wider cultural uses of online role play. Sherry Turkle asserts that, from the advent of online roleplaying games, some people already "saw virtual places as essential" to life off the screen "because online experiences were helping them grow" (*Alone Together* 214). She describes "a young woman who lost a leg in a car crash and now wore a prosthetic limb" and felt "awkward and anxious" about resuming real-life sexual relationships. So, Turkle states, she created an avatar with a prosthetic leg so she could "practice" talking about her prosthetic limb in virtual relationships. "She grew more comfortable with her physical body through the experience of her virtual body." (214). *A Boy Made of Blocks* reflects similar rehearsals in its engagement with digital culture, and Sam's behavior reflects a wider cultural trend in which users practice emotions, events, behaviors, and other performances that they may not feel comfortable with IRL.

Affect: Virtual, Material, Other?

A Boy Made of Blocks can be situated within current conversations on the materiality of affect and videogames. Alex and Sam do free themselves through their avatars, but there is still a physical aspect—using the Xbox controller—that must be addressed. Aubrey Anable's research investigates affect within screen-based games. Anable discusses mobile apps such as *Candy Crush*, seeing in them evidence that "bodies are not machines and that affect is not virtual" (xxi). Anable further argues that affect must pass through a material body, and that this body is not technological: "At the screen, we touch the game and the game touches us" (66). While I agree with Anable's acknowledgment that the screen plays a vital role, and I argue that both Sam and Alex experience happiness in their material bodies, Anable's work fails to recognize the symbiotic relationship between the virtual and material worlds that can be achieved through videogame play. *A Boy Made of Blocks* suggests that gameplay can be a porous membrane. While playing *Minecraft*, Alex narrates, "Somehow we lose the sense that this is a screen; we are no longer controlling digital characters in a computerised environment. It is *us* peering into the jagged caverns, then hiking across the grassy plains beneath the bright square sun" (124). Here, the distinction between the material/virtual and the screen/player has dissolved.

The ability to provide what Isbister terms the "'social level' of experience" in videogames is an integral part of the medium and forms the focus of several academic discussions in the field (11). Turkle recognized the empathetic potential of videogames in 1985 when she stated, "The polarization between action and imaginative identification breaks down in the presence of the computer. With the computer behind them the videogames provide imaginative worlds into which people enter as participants" (*Second Self* 75). As Isbister astutely points out, this sense of empathy with the players' avatar is a key factor in the players' ability to evoke emotions: "This capacity to evoke actual feelings of guilt from a fictional experience is unique to games. . . . Because they depend on active player choice, games have an additional palette of social emotions at their disposal" (11). She notes, "Of course we engage this delusion willingly—it allows us to experience alternate situations and ways of being human, which in turn informs our own experience of being human" (8). Sam and Alex are active players in the *Minecraft* world; they are the ones peering into the jagged caverns, and they form a relationship within that space. Stuart, then, engages with the embodied emotions and affective structures that are inherent to the medium of the videogame itself, which encourage empathy and "inform" Alex's and Sam's experiences of being human. The benefit of narrating this through the novel form is that Stuart is able to articulate these emotions and directly track/present the effect their gameplay has through his linear narrative.

Moreover, Alex's and Sam's absorption in Sam and Daddy's World is reflective of wider contemporary politics as the game's frontier narrative reflects the privileging of the individual that is central to neoliberalism (Bull). This sense of individual agency translates into Alex's and Sam's immersive gameplay. According to Muriel and Crawford, representations of players' agency often centers on their role as protagonist (70). Although Muriel and Crawford do not engage novels such as *A Boy Made of Blocks*, it is an apt description of Alex's experiences. He is enveloped within the virtual world as he "hike[s] across the grassy plains beneath the bright square sun" (124). His avatar is not in the adventure; he is.

A (Nuanced) Techno-Utopia

In the novel, Stuart allots some of *Minecraft*'s power as a techno-utopia to Sam's ability to depart from the social expectations of his everyday life. Sam and Alex's ability to step outside their everyday roles and responsibilities, immersing themselves within *Minecraft*, is reflective of the concept of dispossession within wider neoliberalist ideologies and demonstrates how the novel engages with the complexities of the regime. IRL, Sam is held accountable to neurotypical standards. Freeman Loftis astutely identifies that terms associated with autism, such as "mental illness" or "mental disorder," present their own problems: "'Mental disorder' is accurate from the perspective of the psychiatric community but is generally rejected by proponents of neurodiversity. The question becomes 'disordered compared to what standard?' and one could argue that the term 'disorder' prioritizes the neurotypical way of thinking as normal, natural, and neutral" (4). Sam is repeatedly held to the same social expectations as the neurotypical "standard," and such comparisons affect Sam's everyday life.

For instance, during a "play date" with Alex, Sam is approached by a dog. Sam is distressed by the dog. The dog begins "barking and jumping" and Alex sees that Sam "is shaking with terror and sobbing," but the dog owner does not understand Sam's reaction. Rather, Alex says, "She's smiling. It's that dog-owner smile. The smile that seems to say, 'I like dogs, everyone likes dogs.'" Alex asks, "Can you call it away?" but is greeted with disdain, and the woman is confused as to why Sam would be "terrified" of the "friendly dog." The exchange ends as "the woman audibly tuts, grabs the dog's collar and hauls it back. . . . I [Alex] watch her walk off, utterly oblivious to the terror her wretched mutt has caused, oblivious to the possibility this may be about more than a kid who doesn't like dogs" (Stuart 25–26).

Sam's encounter with the dog is significant in relation to neurotypical social expectations and exchanges and when analyzed in contrast to the way Sam deals with encounters in game. Alex's interpretation of the dog owner's response indicates that Sam's terror does not fit the neurotypical social model and highlights that this sort of exchange is part of Sam's everyday life. Inside *Minecraft*, however, there is no judgment for failing to conform. Rather, as Alex says, "It's as if we are free of ourselves," and Sam is no longer bound to conform to social expectations of material reality (133). Stuart presents *Minecraft* as a space where Sam can disrupt and be free from expectations but also can manipulate and navigate the affective structures themselves. He is free not only from the fear of dogs but also from experiencing the guilt he feels because he is afraid when he should not be. Stuart troubles the naturalized social encounters and expectations through Alex's narration of Sam's experience.

The novel's depiction of utopias as separated from social expectations is not all-encompassing, however, and it, too, is informed in part by neoliberalism. This evolution of utopian spaces echoes a wider shift toward complexity rather than idealism, and Stuart's novel engages with those more contemporary conceptualizations of techno-utopianism. IRL, Alex's conversations with Sam are difficult: "It would be great if I could chat to Sam—ask him about school, about home, about his mum—but that's not how he works. He doesn't do chat" (28). In contrast, Sam and Daddy's World opens up a safe and logical space where Alex and Sam can "escape" their roles and responsibilities. Here, within the landscape and labor-centered adventure of *Minecraft*, they can enjoy playing and reconnecting with each other. Rather than stilted conversations, Alex notes that "while we build and reshape, we talk" (143), and his use of "we" here is important; this performance is not simply about Sam's development, but equally about Alex's, and the building of their relationship.

Ultimately, however, these experiences take place only during gameplay. As such, *A Boy Made of Blocks* represents the shift from idealistic, all-encompassing techno-utopias by presenting what Caroline Edwards terms "utopian moments." Edwards argues that we must "disambiguate the utopian impulse and, in particular, liberate it from fixed notions of utopia-as-totality," noting that in contemporary representations of utopias, "there is no journey to the utopian island." While utopian narratives are "traditionally located at the edges of the known world, of capitalist circuits of trade and exchange," a utopian work can also include narratives "set in mimetic and recognisable worlds, but which also contain non-contemporaneous moments . . . that punctuate what is otherwise a relatively realist straight forward sort of narrative" (*Utopia* 50). Edwards clarifies that contemporary utopian narratives are often set within "mimetic and recognizable worlds" and offer moments of escape from material life.

Applying Edwards's argument to *A Boy Made of Blocks*, we see *Minecraft* as a momentary escape. Alex can temporarily "step outside" the neoliberalist ideologies by which he is usually oppressed, and he and Sam can explore a techno-utopian "enclave" filled with adventure. The novel, then, makes steps toward navigating a more rounded techno-utopia that focuses on moments rather than totality. However, Stuart's version of *Minecraft* is ultimately optimistic; there is no critique of the human–nature relationship and the precarity is presented as a positive experience for Sam.

Nonetheless, there remains the question of Stuart's use of neurodivergence. IRL, Sam is labeled with ASD, yet he is still expected to conform to neurotypical social expectations. Children with ASD are often taught to conform with normalized conceptions of the socialized self, to "fit in." Catrina Silva et al.'s study of ASD and "social exclusion and pro-social behavior" concludes that "programmes aiming at developing social skills . . . have proved to have beneficial outcomes assisting autistic individuals in their daily socio-emotional difficulties." They add that autistic individuals "may not be completely shut off from social stimulation" but rather are "distinctly motivated" about whether to act upon it based on the perceived "reward value" of a social context (242).

According to Silva et al., it is a question of motivation rather than comprehension, in terms of ASD and emotion, yet despite the autonomy and agency associated with that argument, the researchers support the continuation of programs that are "beneficial" to the "difficulties" of autistic figures. The term "benefit" in Silva's work appears to denote an autistic person conforming to wider social expectations; stereotypically, this may include rituals such as hugs. My observation here is not concerned with the ethics surrounding these programs (which are contentious) but with the idea that it is beneficial to mold people with ASD into a set of normative social-emotional expectations in order to "fit in." *A Boy Made of Blocks* engages with this notion of neurotypical social expectations. When Sam logs in to *Minecraft*, he opens a space where his role changes and he can escape the socio-emotional difficulties of everyday life.

Alex's and Sam's immersion into their *Minecraft* world creates techno-utopian moments but also embodies a sense of dispossession from everyday life. Alex, separated from his wife, has been made redundant. He moves into his best friend's flat and embraces the transient lifestyle of sleeping on an air mattress. It is at this point, following the dramatic shifts in Alex's life, that Stuart introduces Sam and Daddy's World. At the *Minecraft* competition, appearing at the end of the novel, Alex says, "It seems like a lifetime ago that we first created Sam and Daddy's World together; that space we share while apart. That connection between us. While everything else was chaos in our lives, we had somewhere that we could escape to and explore" (361).

Stuart represents *Minecraft* as the space "we share," the space to which his characters "escape," where they can build a "connection" but are also able to connect because their attitudes to material life shift as they experience what Butler and Athanasiou describe as "dispossession." Butler and Athanasiou argue that neoliberal economic regimes are characterized by "entwinement with multiple forms of doing, undoing, being undone, and becoming, as well as multiple forms of giving and giving up" (193). Sam and Alex's emotional reconnection strengthens as they adapt their systems of self-control to embrace a sense of precarity. On one level, they are separated from their everyday lives, undone and redone in the form of avatars, thereby subscribing to a sense of dispossession. This, in turn, opens a space for vulnerability and other new experiences of affect.

The risk and precarity Alex and Sam experience is mediated by the game, but the sense of dispossession they feel is not solely due to the game. Rather, as Butler and Athanasiou assert, "We can only be dispossessed because we are already dispossessed. Our interdependency establishes our vulnerability to social forms of deprivation" (5). Alex and Sam experience dispossession IRL, too. Their relationship is presented as precarious from the outset.

After Alex and Jody first separate, Alex spends the day with Sam, taking him to the park and coffee shop, but he observes that "the moments between us are fragile—I don't know how to make more of them without breaking everything" (28). Alex fears the disruption or separation and fears the precarity and dispossession so often associated with the twenty-first century. But the novel engages with the fear of precarity by presenting it as more "rewarding." In-game, the rewards are far greater when playing *Minecraft* on survival mode rather than creative mode, but there is also a greater sense of risk. Sam explicitly acknowledges the privileged role of precarity and risk when he embraces Jody's life lesson that "life is an adventure, not a walk. That's why it's difficult" (375). When the pair attends a *Minecraft* convention in London, Sam is faced with large crowds and uncertainty. Alex asks Sam if he's okay, to which he responds, "I'm overcoming my fear" (361). Alex, too, embraces the "adventure" of life when he muses, "That's why it's difficult—because life is extraordinary and it means something, and those things are costly" (375). Athanasiou states that in the age of dispossession, we must embrace a sense of "response-ability toward human vulnerability and precarity"(119), and for Alex, life "means something" *because* it's difficult and risky, and he achieves the sense of "response-ability" toward Sam *because* of that precarity. Again, Stuart explores the idea of dispossession to present a fictional version of *Minecraft* in which the game's focus on labor and commodity production stands as a microcosm.

Perceptions of Autism Spectrum Disorder

Stuart utilizes ASD as a figurative device in his novel, and it is important to recognize and engage that choice. For example, during the *Minecraft* expo at the end of the novel, contestants are asked to re-create "the most important building in London" (364), and Sam chooses to recreate the café Alex visited with his brother, George. Sam is even awarded a "special commendation" (371), and the re-creation of a building of individual "importance" is recognized and celebrated. However, the concept of "most important" here becomes charged and demonstrates the significance of place and objects to Alex, and Sam's emotional intelligence in recognizing this. Sam tells the judges that he built "the café my daddy went to. He was with his brother." After the adjudicator asks if that's why it's important, Sam acknowledges, "Yes, because Daddy always remembers it. It makes him sad and happy. Some buildings are important because they are big, but some are important because they have memories in them" (374). Sam's understanding that "the most important building in London" is one of sentimental value aligns with Sonya Freeman Loftis's argument that "although the idea that people on the spectrum do not feel emotion is a false and damaging one, it is sometimes true that they express emotion in unexpected ways or that their emotions may not be outwardly apparent to others" (85). While Sam's expression of emotion does not necessarily fit neurotypical models, the novel fruitfully represents Sam's "emotional intelligence" and embraces Alex's and Sam's attempts to understand each other through gameplay.

Stuart draws attention to and challenges stereotypes often depicted in fictional representations of the disorder. In *Imagining Autism*, Freeman Loftis argues that, "while they may prove central to the plot, these figures generally appear on the margins of the story. This is a particularly pervasive and significant facet of characterization for figures with intellectual disabilities, reflecting real-life perceptions that deny the subjectivity of those with cognitive differences" (63). Freeman Loftis's argument helps to situate Sam's character and *A Boy Made of Blocks* within the wider canon of autistic characters. Sam is one of the central characters and is a focal point of Alex's narration. However, while Sam is a central character in the novel, it is also true that his behavior is always mediated through Alex's narration, a characteristic of the literature that Freeman cautions against. Yes, Alex is the novel's sole narrator, but *A Boy Made of Blocks* engages with cultural stereotypes through Alex's self-aware neurotypical narration.

For instance, Alex says, "Here is an important lesson I learned fairly early on about autism. The 1988 movie *Rain Man* starring Tom Cruise and Dustin Hoffman is *not* a documentary. Autistic children do not all have special powers" (Stuart 23). In the journal *Autism*, Kenny et al. (2016) discuss "the need to challenge commonly held beliefs about autism, especially the 'Rain Man' stereotype, that are perpetuated in the media and in communities" (450). They call for enhanced awareness of "the gritty truth about autism," and Alex's narration challenges his own preconceived notions of ASD as a disorder that produces stereotypes such as Rain Man figures. While the novel achieves little in terms of an unmediated representation of an autistic character, then, Stuart does make steps in challenging cultural stereotypes about ASD.

Overall, Stuart's novel utilizes *Minecraft* as a nuanced techno-utopia that helps Alex and Sam emotionally reconnect. *A Boy Made of Blocks* appreciates the ever-evolving role of videogames in a digital age and its importance in helping to form relationships. While Sam's experiences and emotional expressions are mediated through Alex's narration, Alex's self-reflection does engage fruitfully with cultural stereotypes of ASD and promotes less reductive understandings of the disorder. Sam is an emotionally intelligent and complicated character, in contrast to often two-dimensional stereotypes of autism, and therefore he contributes to the production of a more complex canon of autistic characters. Both Alex and Sam benefit from their gameplay, as Alex processes his grief and learns to understand Sam's methods of emotional expression.

Initially, Alex and Sam mirror each other's need for self-management and control but embrace a necessary sense of precarity to open a space for vulnerability and change. Alex distances himself from the neoliberal machine's cogs of the nuclear family unit, which allows him to process his grief and bond with Sam. The novel leans into the difficulty of critiquing neoliberalism from within that very culture, and as such, it grapples with the larger difficulties of precarity in twenty-first family, work, and social life. *A Boy Made of Blocks*, then, is a novel that attempts to unpack and critique the aspects of postmillennial society that encourage us to self-manage our relationships and emotions, but does so while navigating the challenges of living in a naturalized world of neoliberalism, embracing the inherently contradictory and complex nature of feelings in that context.

WORKS CITED

Ahmed, Sara. *The Cultural Politics of Emotion.* 2nd ed., Edinburgh University Press, 2014.
———. "Happy Objects." *The Affect Theory Reader,* edited by Melissa Gregg and Gregory J. Seigworth. Duke University Press, 2010, pp. 29–52.
Anable, Aubrey. *Playing with Feelings: Videogames and Affect.* University of Minnesota Press, 2018.
Bull, Iris Rochelle. "Just Steve: Conventions of Gender on the Virtual Frontier." *Understanding Minecraft: Essays on Play, Community and Possibilities,* edited by Nate Garrelts. McFarland, 2014, pp. 88–106.

Butler, Judith, and Athena Athanasiou. *Dispossession: The Performative in the Political.* Polity Press, 2013.

Carlson, Marvin A., ed. "Introduction: What Is Performance?" *Performance: A Critical Introduction.* Routledge, 1996, pp. 1–11.

Couldry, Nick. "Reality TV, or the Secret Rheater of Neoliberalism." *Review of Education, Pedagogy, and Cultural Studies,* vol. 30, no. 1, 2008, pp. 3–13.

Crossley, Stephen. "Realising the (Troubled) Family: Crafting the Neoliberal State." *Families, Relationships and Societies,* vol. 5, no. 2, 2016, pp. 263–79.

Dolan, Jill. "Performance, Utopia and the 'Utopian Performative.'" *Theatre Journal,* vol. 53, no. 3, 2001, pp. 455–79.

Edwards, Caroline. "What Is a Utopian Narrative?" Paper presented at *Crisis in Contemporary Writing,* BACLS Virtual Conference, 26 June 2020.

———. *Utopia and the Contemporary British Novel.* Cambridge University Press, 2019.

Fanning, Colin, and Rebecca Mir. "Teaching Tools: Progressive Pedagogy and the History of Construction Play." *Understanding Minecraft: Essays on Play, Community and Possibilities,* edited by Nate Garrelts. McFarland, 2014, pp. 38–57.

Freeman Loftis, Sonya. *Imagining Autism: Fiction and Stereotypes on the Spectrum.* Indiana University Press, 2015.

Garrelts, Nate, ed. "Introduction: Why Minecraft Matters." *Understanding Minecraft: Essays on Play, Community and Possibilities.* McFarland, 2014, pp. 1–7.

Glass, Michael R. "Performing Neoliberalism: Practice, Power and Subject Formation." *Handbook of Neoliberalism,* edited by Simon Springer, Kean Birch, and Julie MacLeavy, Routledge, 2016, pp. 351–60.

Gu, Jandy. "A Craft to Call Mine: Creative Appropriation of *Minecraft* in YouTube Animations." *Understanding* Minecraft: *Essays on Play, Community and Possibilities,* edited by Nate Garrelts. McFarland, 2014, pp. 132–48.

Hsu, Hua. "Affect Theory and the New Age of Anxiety." *New Yorker,* 18 March 2019.

Isbister, Katherine. *How Games Move Us: Emotion by Design.* MIT Press, 2016.

Kenny, Lorcan, Caroline Hattersley, Bonnie Molins, Carole Buckley, Carol Povey, and Elizabeth Pellicano. "Which Terms Should Be Used to Describe Autism? Perspectives from the UK Autism Community." *Autism,* vol. 20, no. 4, 2016, pp. 442–62.

MacCallum-Stewart, Esther. "Someone Off the Youtubez." *Understanding* Minecraft: *Essays on Play, Community and Possibilities,* edited by Nate Garrelts. McFarland, 2014, pp. 148–60.

Marantz, Andrew. "The Dark Side of Techno-utopianism." *New Yorker,* 30 September 2019.

McKenzie, Jon. *Perform or Else: From Discipline to Performance.* Routledge, 2001.

Muriel, Daniel, and Garry Crawford. *Videogames as Culture: Considering the Role and Importance of Videogames in Contemporary Society.* Routledge, 2018.

Shaw, Adrienne. *Gaming at the Edge: Sexuality and Gender at the Margins of Gamer Culture.* University of Minnesota Press, 2015.

Shinkle, Eugénie. "Video Games and the Technological Sublime." *The Art of the Sublime*, edited by Nigel Llewellyn and Christine Riding. Tate Research Publication, January 2013. http://www.tate.org.uk/art/research-publications/the-sublime/eugenie-shinkle-video-games-and-the-technological-sublime-r1136830.

Silva, Catarina, Chloé Jover, David Da Fonseca, Francisco Esteves, and Christine Deruelle. "Acting on Observed Social Exclusion and Pro-Social Behaviour in Autism Spectrum Disorder." *Autism*, vol. 24, no. 1, 2020, pp. 233–45.

Stuart, Keith. *A Boy Made of Blocks*. Sphere, 2016.

"This Is War." *High Score*, episode 4, Netflix, 2020.

Tremblay, Alexandra Jean, Jeremy Colangelo, and Joseph Alexander Brown. "The Craft of Data Mining: *Minecraft* and the Constraints of Play." *Understanding Minecraft: Essays on Play, Community and Possibilities*, edited by Nate Garrelts. McFarland, 2014, pp. 76–88.

Turkle, Sherry. *Alone Together: Why We Expect More from Technology and Less from Each Other*. Basic Books, 2011.

———. *The Second Self: Computer and the Human Spirit*. Touchstone, 1985.

PART II

VIDEOGAME STORIES AS DISCOURSE

From Players to Storytellers

Machinima, In-Game Photography, and Gamics

JOSÉ BLÁZQUEZ

Videogames are a powerful storytelling medium that has inspired millions of people around the world to create, organize, remediate, and circulate their own content. Forum discussions, dedicated websites, fan fiction and art, mod development, online guides, songwriting, walkthrough video recordings and live streaming, and many more art forms and discursive materials are available in one way or another on the internet. In some of the more interesting cases, audience members employ a different medium to express and represent their playful interests and creativity. These are narratives and experiences around videogames. However, there are other instances in which videogames and their assets are used as vessels to communicate the audience members' own narratives and emotions. These are stories they tell with videogames.

Based on interviews and the analysis of discursive material, this essay examines three practices—machinima, in-game photography (IGP), and gamics—and looks at the opportunities that these can give to audiences. First, I consider the use of machinima, an animation technique that employs videogame engines and assets to produce Web series and movies. Second, I look into in-game photography, which refers to capturing stills within videogame worlds. Finally, I delve into the production of gamics, a practice in which artists use images or resources from videogames to produce comic strips and graphic novels. By considering these three practices, I identify the permeating influence of videogames in society and culture while emphasizing the importance of audiences' creative practices in the understanding of the gaming culture.

In the digital age, being a gamer is not just about playing videogames but also about engaging in a common culture around the medium. This often involves learning, developing, and employing broader media literacy skills that frequently lead to the production and circulation of content (writing texts). Videogames are a powerful storytelling medium for both developers and audiences, the latter finding ways to take a certain amount of creative control, even if the games do not provide them with the required mechanisms to assert that agency. As I will explain, gamers engage with these transformative practices for a variety of reasons and to different degrees. Fan communities foster these practices with their informal mentorship, knowledge exchange, inspirational support, and the creation of mods and other tools. As a consequence, videogame audiences can both explore their interests and create new value.

Participatory Culture and Videogames

The transition to a digital age was underpinned by a series of cultural, social, economic, and technological transformations, ranging from the development and adoption of new technologies and the expansion of access to cultural and media production at an affordable price to the creation and spread of Web 2.0 (O'Reilly). These provided audiences with more opportunities to get involved in the production and circulation of culture, information, and knowledge (Benkler). In this line, Henry Jenkins coined the concept of "participatory culture" to differentiate the creative and social activities performed by fan communities from other sorts of audience behaviors. The meaning of this term eventually extended to more general domains involving participation "in" and "through" media (Jenkins et al.). Participation "in" the media covers audience contributions to the production and decision-making processes of media outputs, whereas participation "through" the media refers to opportunities for mediated self-representation and engagement in public and social spheres (Carpentier).

Jenkins et al. define participatory culture as "a culture with relatively low barriers to artistic expression and civic engagement, strong support for creating and sharing creations, and some type of informal mentorship whereby experienced participants pass along knowledge to novices. In a participatory culture, members also believe their contributions matter and feel some degree of social connection with one another (at least, members care about others' opinions on what they have created)" (7). Therefore, the concept of participatory culture encapsulates the contrast between the traditional perception of audiences as mere consumers of content and a more contemporary view that also recognizes their role as producers and circulators of culture, information, and knowledge. Indeed, some media gurus and scholars have talked about "pro-ams" (Leadbeater and Miller), "produsers" (Bruns), and "prosumers" (Tapscott and Williams). This enables the identification of "productive audiences" and "user-generated content" when describing their outputs, and "co-creation" of value (Zwass) when referring to their contribution to industrial and commercial processes. For Schäfer, participatory culture exists as an extension of the media and entertainment industries, providing additional content and knowledge about an intellectual property, and unfolding in three domains: accumulation (collection, alteration, and remix); archiving (organization, maintenance, and circulation); and construction (production). Lawrence Lessig gives the title "Read/Write culture" to a society that promotes the creation of derivative works, lowering the barriers to participation and increasing economic opportunities for both the "professional" and the "amateur" in the production of culture. For Lessig, everyone "reads" culture by listening, playing, reading, and viewing, but it is through the development of writerly skills that we can intervene in the culture surrounding us.

Fandom and other practices involving audience participation are mostly developed from the bottom up, underpinned by communities around an intellectual property (see Brooker; Hills) or practice (Wenger). Communities play a key role in the performance and evolution of productive, formative, and social practices as they provide their members with inspiration, motivation, and mentorship as well as a space to share a common culture, artworks, knowledge, and innovation. Communities of practice often facilitate the adaptation of techniques and development tools that fill the absence of commercial or official resources. Consequently, audience participation in the creation and circulation of content contributes not only to the expansion of fictional worlds but also to the life span and affordances of media products, and videogames are not an exception.

Manifestations of videogame fandom are numerous and well documented (see Newman; Schott and Burn; Swalwell et al.; as well as Brooks; Carey; Lovins, in this volume). These include fan art and fiction, guides and walkthrough videos, cosplays, and gameplay streaming. For Katie Salen and Eric Zimmerman, audiences indulge in "transformative play" when there is a reappropriation of the game for creative expression in ways that were not originally intended. The performance of these creative practices conducted by videogame users (whether fans or not) sometimes requires the employment, extraction, and alteration of game assets, as often happens on private dedicated game servers, which in many cases involve modifications (or "mods") to the original game files and resources in order to create custom elements such as maps, skins, weapons, and mechanics (Postigo). These mods and their applications, which often infringe upon end-user license agreements and may trigger cease-and-desist legal actions from the game developers and publishers (see Ng and Schreier), provide opportunities for game users to explore and create their own expressions of the game beyond the game.

Boluk and LeMieux call such practices "metagaming," the phenomena occurring around, before, during, and after playing a game. Metagaming "functions as a broad discourse, a way of playing, thinking, and making that transforms autonomous and abstract pieces of software into games and turns players into game designers" (9). For Matteo Bittanti, artworks in which videogames play a significant role in their production and display are considered "game art." Sharp explains that "game art is art made of games. . . . Artists creating game art approach games as tool sets and cultural tropes rather than as a medium or craft unto itself" (14). In the following sections, I will discuss the techniques and motivations behind three creative practices involving the use of videogame assets for the creation of game art: machinima, IGP, and gamics.

Machinima

Machinima is a creative practice that has been widely studied in academic and nonacademic literature, with an upsurge of major works published between the mid-2000s and the early 2010s (see Hancock and Ingram; Johnson and Pettit; Kelland et al.; Lowood, "Found Technology," "High-Performance Play"; Lowood and Nitsche; Marino; Ng). One of the most quoted definitions comes from Paul Marino, machinima filmmaker and cofounder of the Academy of Machinima Arts and Sciences, who defines it as "animated filmmaking within a real-time virtual 3D environment" (1). By "virtual 3D environment," Martino means computer graphics engines that render three-dimensional graphics in real time. The academy conceived machinima as "the convergence of filmmaking, animation and game development" and expanded this definition to highlight that real-world filmmaking techniques are often applied in machinima, albeit within an interactive virtual environment where "characters and events can be either controlled by humans, scripts, or artificial intelligence" (Academy of Machinima Arts and Sciences). For Nitsche, there are two types of machinima: "outside in," which centers on the use of videogame engines for storytelling purposes, and "inside out," or the use of machinima as a recording of gameplay. According to Jenna Ng, both inside out, which "rel[ies] largely on gaming references and inside jokes to underpin their narratives," and outside in are opposite ends of a spectrum, with many machinima occupying spaces in the middle (291).

Machinima originated from the bottom up, and although there are examples in which media and entertainment industries have adopted the practice, it is still performed mostly by audiences. The origins of machinima take us back to the first demo files used by players of *Doom* (1993) and *Quake* (1996) to register their gameplay. Demos were not actually videos but sequences of commands recorded in a log, which could be read by the videogame, which then reproduced the action as it originally occurred (Lowood, "Video Capture"). Generally, demos captured exhibitions of individual prowess and multiplayer matches within first-person shooters, and modifying the demo file required certain programming skills. As a consequence, authorship was limited to a small number of players, most of whom were male, and viewership was concentrated within the game community.

Machinima gradually evolved from gameplay to narrative demos (such as *Diary of a Camper*, 1996) and eventually to screen-recorded films (the first of which was *Quad God*, 2000). However, it was not until a few years later when there was a visible shift in the diversity of machinima creation. The breakthrough came with the release of *The Sims 2* (2004), a life-simulation videogame that was based not on competitiveness but on creativity and attracted mainly female players (Jones). *The Sims 2* allowed players to record their gameplay with a single button, moving away from installing third-party programs and changing the demographics and genres of machinima production (Kelland). *The Movies* (2005), a business simulation game in which players run a movie studio, also boosted production as machinima creation was part of the gameplay.

As genres and demographics expanded, more accessible mods, tools, and dedicated real-time 3D rendering software, such as Moviestorm and iClone, became available. Some tools enabled machinima makers to access game assets, letting them extract and manipulate elements such as characters, objects, and maps to create customized settings. This made massive multiplayer online games such as *World of Warcraft* (2004) a popular choice for practitioners in the second half of the 2000s (Lowood 2011). Certain mods have also enabled control over cinematography (such as camera position and lighting) and direction (character poses and animations), which is still one of the most popular approaches to machinima making. Recognizing its value, media and entertainment industries have adopted the practice to create their own content. Valve released its movie-making tool, Source Filmmaker, including *Team Fortress 2* (2007) assets, in 2012, and other games, such as *Fortnite* (2017) and *Grand Theft Auto V* (2013), offered built-in director's or replay modes, an accessible way to create machinima regardless of the game platform. These lower barriers to the practice attracted a vast number of creators worldwide.

With machinima, gamers are able to turn the medium they love into a creative tool and to engage with filmmaking, something that many of them would probably not be able to do otherwise, gaining useful storytelling and technical skills while having fun. Some, such as Josh Lee (of the YouTube channel JBS Gaming), started to create machinima films without having any interest in, knowledge about, or experience with filmmaking: "I did not even know where and how [to] edit my videos" (interview July 14, 2020). For Janik Jehkul (Crazy Fox on YouTube), the initial motivation to make machinimas was more conscious, to "learn new software, programming, and storytelling" (interview August 14, 2020). For many gamers, videogames are not just a commodity to be consumed but also a source of inspiration and creativity. Machinima makers learn new skills, develop their professional careers, and engage in the creation of media that they may not be able to access in any other way. From altering the code of demo files to using third-party tools to extract and manipulate assets, the journey of machinima has been closely intertwined with gamers' will to explore and create their own stories—to write culture and not just read it.

In-Game Photography

The term "in-game photography" refers to the practice of capturing images from and within videogame environments. These "photos" generally resemble still 2D digital images, although there are other, emerging forms that can be considered part of this practice (Blázquez). Rokošný considers IGP to be both a mixed-media art and a photographic genre. IGP is currently gaining momentum as a practice, particularly among owners of videogame consoles with built-in photo modes. There are websites, digital magazines, and numerous collectives that promote the practice. As such, IGP is associated with other terms, such as "gametography" (a synonym); "virtual photography," which refers to the practice of taking screenshots from virtual environments, including but not limited to videogames; "screenshot art," which Rokošný considers equivalent to IGP, although the concept has a wider scope; and "virtual tourism," in which visitors to virtual worlds take pictures of their experiences as they might do when traveling to holiday destinations in real life (Book). As I will explain later, IGP and its associated terms and practices illustrate both the productive nature of gamers and their ability to create their own texts, as well as the increasingly common practice of videogame producers providing the creative tools for that creation.

For Gerling, "photographic recordings" in computer games began with *Doom* demos, with players taking images to comprehend gameplay and distribute them for training purposes. Poremba observes the general use of screenshots to document gameplay experiences such as glitches, bugs, victories, or mementos. In this sense, gaming becomes more than just playing; it is also creating, documenting, and collecting. However, some would argue for distinctions based on intention. Gerling, for example, defines the difference between screenshot and photography in terms of the latter's effort to "retain a specific theme: a situation or a scene" (157). For Gerling, the intention (or what he calls the "function" and "use") of the image capture is key, identifying this more aesthetically conscious mode of IGP as a form of what Tekinbaş and Zimmerman would designate as transformative play, since it is not an activity within the rules of the game.

However, this distinction is more blurred when the videogame integrates the use of a photo camera as part of gameplay, as is the case with Nintendo's *Pilotwings 64* (1996) and *Pokémon: Snap* (1999). In an early study, Poremba describes two strands of IGP, depending on whether photography is integrated within the gameplay mechanics. She also describes two types of photography as part of the gameplay ("photo as play"): content-centered, which just requires players to use a camera to meet certain objectives, and practice-centered, which employs photographic conventions and techniques as a framework for play.

Rokošný would agree, designating two types of in-game photographers, those who play by the rules and those who do not. The ones who do not follow the rules go beyond the intended playstyle of the game, utilizing bugs, exploits, tools, and mods to customize game elements and physics, camera location and movement, and postprocessing effects in order to accommodate creative expression. A few of these have made IGP a professional practice, the most notable example being Duncan Harris, one of the IGP pioneers, who under the alias Dead End Thrills "often reverse-engineer[s] games to fulfill publisher briefs without burdening studios and their staff" (deadendthrills.com). Other practitioners, such as Petri Levälahti, are on the payroll of big videogame publishers—EA's DICE in this particular case—to capture images in-house.

The cases of Harris and Levälahti are evidence of a genuine and growing appreciation in the industry for the practice of IGP, which is becoming a valuable asset internally (for developer–publisher communications) and externally (for marketing and promotional content). Not surprisingly, the industry is becoming more open to providing players with accessible tools. For Pascal Grüner, a well-known practitioner who goes under the alias of ItsYFP, this is a sign of the popularity of the form: "Players did demand photo modes and the developers listened" (interview August 5, 2020). One of his peers, Frans Bouma, notices a similar trend: "Game developers have realized that the potential of having a massive group of people posting images of your game is huge" (interview November 3, 2020).

According to Wakeford, photo modes have also facilitated new ways for players to become immersed, while also increasing their appreciation of the virtual worlds that are carefully crafted by game developers. Indeed, photo modes have opened the practice to the enormous population of console-based players, diversifying the platforms of expression and boosting the numbers of practitioners around the world. Similar to how smartphones have boosted the practice of photography, photo modes have done the same within virtual worlds, providing players with the possibility to suspend gameplay, move the camera around, and adjust lens and settings for better performance.

Motivations to capture images within videogames are, as one might expect, quite varied. For Rokošný, IGP practitioners "share the same motivations as real-life photographers—capture appealing images, share an idea, preserve memories, or demonstrate . . . technical expertise" (220–21). Poremba explains how IG photos can act as "surrogate possessions," representing memories or "trophies" from personal game experiences. Unsurprisingly, the exploration of immersive and detailed game worlds prompts some players to capture their beauty, mystery, and rawness even when a photo mode is not available. In this way, as Möring and de Mutiis suggest, many IG photographers feel that they do not tell their own story but highlight or emphasize what the game world and story already do. Vikneswaran, aka Vikster, a prominent IG photographer who works on PS4 and PC, subscribes to this feeling: "Over the years, I have used more transformative methods to make more complicated works, [but] what I create is more emphasized to the appreciation of the game and its elements" (interview September 18, 2020).

But for some practitioners, such as Bouma, "the motivation is mostly about being able to show the world a given scene I stumbled upon, which can be a different view of a scene of a game which tells a completely different story than the shot does." In addition to being a computer-based IG photographer, Bouma is a software engineer who develops his own camera tools for games and shares them with the community of practice. His tools give IG photographers more control over the camera and settings, and when possible they offer options to modify the environment (such as fog and weather/time control) and image quality. This has certainly brought opportunities for the performance of the practice to "tell a different story than the game tells you . . . It's way more fun to create something worth looking at from something that's not art-directed for you."

Once again, this highlights the importance of the tools that are available to creators, since they increasingly make purchasing decisions based on their availability. As Grüner states, "Games are my motivation. I can say that virtual photography ruined gaming a little bit for me, because these days I choose my games [based] on what photography tools are available." There is indeed a common feeling among practitioners that IGP has changed the way they approach games, as the photographer inside of them sometimes takes them away from the intended paths of gameplay. IGP, like other transformative practices, has not only changed the way these practitioners choose their games or play them but also altered what it means to be a gamer. As Vikster puts it, "One can use videogames as a source of enjoying creative expressions."

Gamics

The last practice I will discuss, which I call "gamics," employs videogame assets to produce comics, graphic novels, cartoons, and other illustrated stories. Despite the variety of genres related to this practice, it has been largely neglected by scholars. My use of "gamics" here will need some clarification, as the term has been employed elsewhere to refer to comics based on videogames (Champion) and other media (see Jupin; McGregor; Sommerseth). I use it here as Nathan Ciprick defines it, simply as "gaming and comics as one." Ciprick adds that gamics "tell new and unique stories based on the video games you know and love in a cool screenshot comic format." For Ciprick, gamics are limited to in-game screenshot comics, a subpractice of which he is a pioneer. A related concept is "game comics," alluding to videogames that employ the affordances associated with comics (Goodbrey). A rarer term is "machinomics," a portmanteau of "machine" and "comic," which describes a particular section of the practice involving screenshots of 3D games ("Machinomics"). None of these interpretations capture the concept of comics made with videogame assets, which is my emphasis here, whether this involves the use of sprites, in-game screenshots, 3D asset compositing, or animated visual resources.

The origins of the practice are as diverse as the techniques; however, the practice as a whole can be said to be closely related to the development of the webcomic. The origins of webcomics can be traced to the mid-1980s, when Eric "Monster" Millikin distributed *Witches in Stitches* (1985) through CompuServe, followed by Jans Bjordahl's *Where the Buffalo Roam* (1987), which Bjordahl claims was the first regularly updated comic strip on the internet and was published on the Usenet newsgroup Shadowculture starting in 1991, and David Farley's *Doctor Fun* (1993), the first webcomic to have its own website (Dowthwaite). However, it was not until the second half of the 1990s that webcomics started to gain traction, a trend related to the growing popularity of sprite comics.

Sprite comics, as the name suggests, are made with sprites (2D bitmaps typically used to animate characters, objects, and backgrounds) extracted from 2D videogames and/or created/modified by pixel artists, which are then composed in a conventional comics layout. Maragos identifies *Neglected Mario Characters* (1998) as the first sprite comic to appear on the Web, a collection of strips kicked off by Jay Resop's *The EVIL-Luigi Story*, which was published on the fan site *Super Mario Bros Headquarters* from September 1998. This multiauthor collection of sprite comics represents a parody of the game's storyworld and its characters.

These kinds of webcomics increased in popularity at the beginning of the 2000s with the release of *Bob and George* (2000) by Dave Anez, which uses *Mega Man* (1987) sprites, and Brian Clevinger's *8-Bit Theater* (2001), based on *Final Fantasy* (1987). As happened to most gamics, the production of sprite comics started to decline in the second half of the decade. However, as with the other genres I've explored here, sprite comics provided opportunities for their creators to develop certain skills. Carmelo Sampayo and Marcelo Prado, for example, are two active "spriters" who specialize in action-drama. Both confess to not being talented enough to create good quality hand-drawn comics, but thanks to their ability to appropriate and repurpose sprites, they were able to communicate the stories they wanted to tell. Along the way, they learned valuable skills such as pixel art, image manipulation, and comic literacy, which they have had the chance to put into practice in other third-party projects.

The extraction and manipulation of game visual assets does not occur exclusively within the 2D videogame domain. Dedicated software such as Asset-

Studio and Ninja Ripper makes it possible to "rip" 3D meshes, textures, and bone data from videogames for use in a viewer and posing program (such as XNA Posing Studio, also known as XNALara) or with 3D computer graphics software (such as Blender, 3D Studio Max, or Maya) to compose images for comic strips. The ability to alter expressions, poses, clothing, and textures, along with the customization of lighting and backgrounds, gives artists endless possibilities for storytelling, in some cases enabling creators to explore topics and subgenres that are missing in most videogames. This is the case for Lito Perezito, a French artist who uses videogame assets to explore gay romance stories, or Romero1718, who turns fighting games into romantic narratives and scenes. Megan Miller uses Mine-imator to import and combine *Minecraft* and custom-made assets to create graphic novels set in fantasy worlds. As she puts it, "I want to create appealing stories for kids (seven to eleven) that draw them into the amazing world of reading and books, and occasionally bring up 'food for thought' topics in an open and nonpatronizing or authoritative way, and hopefully a laugh or two. I also hope to satisfy or interest kids in the aesthetic experience of graphic novels, if I can" (interview October 21, 2020). Miller, whose work has been commissioned by Hollan Publishing and published by Skyhorse, is one of the few examples of practitioners who have been able to professionally publish their own work. One of the main reasons for this is the relaxed approach that Mojang, the developer of *Minecraft,* has had with regard to derivative works produced by end users.

Similar to sprite comics, in-game screenshot comics also became popular in the mid-2000s, with works such as James "BrashFink" Brandt's *Apostasy* (2005) and Christopher C. Livingston's *Concerned* (2005), based on "Garry's Mod" for *Half-Life 2* (2004), leading the way. Nowadays, the production of these webcomics is quite scarce. Grace Dinis, a practitioner who makes use of the vast variety of custom content available to create webcomics with *The Sims 2,* got into gamics naturally when, as she puts it, "I realized how much I could do without having to rely on my poor drawing skills to bring to life the stories inside of my head." Like so many creators, she values the way that simple creative tools foster the acquisition of new skills: "If I could really master 3D modeling, I could probably make the jump to the next better thing" (interview August 7, 2020).

However, Dinis perceives that the comic format is not really popular within *The Sims* community, as audiences prefer "Simlit," stories illustrated with screenshots, generally in the form of episodic accounts circulated on blogs and websites. When Jessica Brown began creating Simlit, she did not even know how to take a proper screenshot. Now she is a prolific and renowned author within *The Sims* community. She considers the learning journey rewarding and fun, as she gained useful literary, media, and information technology literacy knowledge and skills to tell her stories, while simultaneously engaging in gameplay and being supported by a welcoming gaming community: "As a woman—a Black woman—gaming is not widely accepted as an acceptable hobby. . . . When you are passionate about a thing, it is difficult to keep that passion inside. . . . So, when you find other people just like you, it is such a relief" (interview August 7, 2020). As with IGP and machinima, gamic creators depend on communities of gamers and practitioners. These provide the tools, resources, mentorship, and knowledge to enable authors to tell their stories, learn new skills, find new career pathways, and change their understanding of the medium.

Conclusion

I've examined three creative practices in which audiences (as end users) of videogames use videogame assets to produce game art. Machinima, in-game photography, and gamics are closely related with regard to the techniques and tools employed to produce artworks. These works are certainly influenced by the videogames on which they are based, especially in terms of visual framing and storytelling. However, the degree of influence varies.

Active machinima makers, for example, often produce their works by employing directors'/replay modes or mods to accommodate settings, storytelling, and performance, giving them a certain degree of freedom to tell the stories in which they are interested. This is also the case of screenshot comics, which use a similar approach to arrange and capture images. Gamics based on ripped game visual elements, such as sprite and 3D asset compositing comics, certainly provide creative freedom, but unless these resources are further modified, combined, or expanded, the representations tend to be limited to the existing extracted assets. IGP can also be carried out in mods and related tools (such as Mine-imator), but this is often not the case. Generally, the practice is performed in-game and as part of the gameplay, and although there are instances in which practitioners have more agency, such as in *Fortnite*'s creative mode and *The Sims 4* (2014), the stories they can tell are frequently driven by the game aesthetics, theme, genre, and storyline.

Sometimes, storyworlds and events are a source of inspiration for creative practitioners, who, through the appropriation and remix of game assets, fill gaps in or retell game narratives and lore from different perspectives. Others find their inspiration in a more indirect way, using the games and their assets as the means to create their own worlds and stories. Fortunately, many videogame companies have come to understand that a gamer is not just a consumer, a reader of the text, but also a creator who welcomes the agency to engage with a wider array of game experiences. While creative and fan communities are crucial to supporting the practice (as the creators I've interviewed have made clear), there is no question that developer support has enhanced the visibility and reputation of these practices, empowering players to become authors and to share their creative expressions.

Machinima, in-game comics, and gamics are only three examples of participatory culture deeply embedded in gaming culture. These practices suggest a different model of gaming, a different model of the gaming community, and a different way of telling stories with, about, and around videogames. In this case, becoming a gamer involves not just playing the game but also being exposed to the content the community has created and, to a varying extent, the skills and knowledge required for their performance. The creators I've talked to all agree that their creative practices have changed the way they approach, play, and understand videogames. This has affected videogame design, as content production and writing skills are increasingly widespread in videogames and gaming culture. Practitioners "read" and "write" about the intellectual properties, techniques, and tools that can be used to produce original content, and they regularly participate in discussions with their peers and the gaming community across multiple discursive spaces and platforms. While these creator communities function like most fandoms in terms of inspiring and supporting active participation, they have the additional value of enabling their members to develop powerful technical and critical thinking skills.

Machinima, in-game photography, and gamics are interesting texts in and of themselves. However, as I've argued, these texts are also evidence of empowering community practice. Learning and enhancing media literacy and writerly skills, such as the creation and manipulation of assets, critical assessment of the medium's storytelling principles, and the awareness of how videogames are made (including the limitations and opportunities for self-expression they offer) no doubt have a positive influence in making these gamers better consumers and creators of stories. While we cannot say that the future is bright for all these practices, they surely will be the foundation for new practices, particularly as more technological possibilities arise for the telling of videogame stories.

For further reading on machinima, in-game photography, and gamics, see Blázquez (2021), and visit https://participatoryworlds.org/research/press_start.

This work was supported using public funding by the National Lottery through Arts Council England [ACPG-00296850] as part of the project "Press Start": The Use of Videogame Assets in Audience Creative Practices.

WORKS CITED

Academy of Machinima Arts and Sciences. "The Machinima FAQ." https://web.arch ive.org/web/20121010063429/http://www.machinima.org/machinima-faq.html. Accessed 24 July 2023.

Benkler, Yochai. *The Wealth of Networks: How Social Production Transforms Markets and Freedom.* Yale University Press, 2006.

Bittanti, Matteo. "Game Art: (This Is Not) a Manifesto, (This Is) a Disclaimer." *Gamescenes: Art in the Age of Videogames,* edited by Matteo Bittanti and Domenico Quaranta. Johan & Levi, 2008, pp. 7–14.

Bjordahl, Jans. "Where the Buffalo Roam—First Comic on the Internet." *Shadowculture.* https://www.shadowculture.com/wtbr/site.html.

Blázquez, José. (2021) *Press Start: The Use of Videogame Assets in Audience Creative Practices.* Participatory Worlds, 2021.

Boluk, Stephanie, and Patrick LeMieux. *Metagaming: Playing, Competing, Spectating, Cheating, Trading, Making, and Breaking Videogames.* University of Minnesota Press, 2017.

Book, Betsy. "Traveling through Cyberspace: Tourism and Photography in Virtual Worlds." Paper presented at the conference *Tourism and Photography: Still Visions—Changing Lives,* Sheffield, UK, 20–23 July 2003. http://dx.doi.org/10.2139/ssrn.538182.

Brooker, Will. *Using the Force: Creativity, Community and Star Wars Fans.* Continuum, 2002.

Bruns, Axel. *Blogs, Wikipedia, Second Life, and Beyond: From Production to Produsage.* Peter Lang, 2008.

Carpentier, Nico. "Contextualising Author–Audience Convergences." *Cultural Studies,* vol. 25, no. 4–5, 2011, pp. 517–33.

Champion, Erik. "The Nonessentialist Essentialist Guide to Games." *Travels in Intermedia[lity]: Reblurring the Boundaries,* edited by Bernd Herzogenrath. Dartmouth College Press, 2012, pp. 192–210.

Ciprick, Nathan. "About Gamics." Gamics, 2004. https://web.archive.org/web/20061023 043257/http://www.gamics.com/about. Accessed 24 July 2023.

———. "What Is a Gamic?." Gamics, 2004. https://web.archive.org/web/20061101212147
/http://www.gamics.com. Accessed 24 July 2023.

———. "What the Heck Is Gamics?." Gamics, March 12, 2013. https://web.archive.org
/web/20160320175235/http://gamics.com/?p=8. Accessed 24 July 2023.

Dowthwaite, Liz. *Crowdfunding Webcomics: The role of Incentives and Reciprocity in Monetising Free Content.* 2017. University of Nottingham, PhD dissertation.

Gerling, Winfried. "Photography in the Digital: Screenshot and In-Game Photography."
Photographies, vol. 11, no. 2–3, 2018, pp. 149–67.

Goodbrey, Daniel Merlin. "Game Comics: An Analysis of an Emergent Hybrid Form."
Journal of Graphic Novels and Comics, vol. 6, no. 1, 2015, pp. 3–14.

Hancock, Hugh, and Johnnie Ingram. *Machinima for Dummies.* Wiley, 2007.

Hills, Matt. *Fan Cultures.* Routledge, 2002.

Jenkins, Henry. *Textual Poachers: Television Fans and Participatory Culture.* Routledge,
2022.

Jenkins, Henry, Katie Clinton, Ravi Purushotma, Margaret Weigel, and Alice J. Robison. *Confronting the Challenges of Participatory Culture: Media Education for the 21st
Century.* MIT Press, 2009.

Jenkins, Henry, Sam Ford, and Joshua Green. *Spreadable Media: Creating Value and
Meaning in a Networked Culture.* New York University Press, 2013.

Johnson, Phylis, and Donald Pettit. *Machinima: The Art and Practice of Virtual Filmmaking.* McFarland, 2012.

Jones, Robert. "Pink vs. Blue: The Emergence of Women in Machinima." *The Machinima Reader,* edited by Henry Lowood and Michael Nitsche. MIT Press, 2011, pp.
277–300.

Jupin, Tanner. *Gamic Fiction: The Intermediation of Literature and Games.* 2014. University of California, Davis, PhD dissertation.

Kelland, Matt. "From Game Mod to Low-Budget Film: The Evolution of Machinima."
The Machinima Reader, edited by Henry Lowood and Michael Nitsche. MIT Press,
2011, pp. 23–36.

Kelland, Matt, Dave Morris, and Dave Lloyd. *Machinima: Making Animated Movies in 3D
Virtual Environments.* Thompson Course Technology, 2005.

Leadbeater, Charles W., and Paul Miller. *The Pro-Am Revolution: How Enthusiasts are
Changing our Economy and Society.* Demos, 2004.

Lessing, Lawrence. *Remix: Making Art and Commerce Thrive in the Hybrid Economy.*
Bloomsbury, 2008.

Lowood, Henry. "Found Technology: Players as Innovators in the Making of Machinima." *Digital Youth, Innovation, and the Unexpected,* edited by Tara McPherson. MIT
Press, 2008, pp. 165–96.

———. "High-Performance Play: The Making of Machinima." *Journal of Media Practice,*
vol. 7, no. 1, 2006, pp. 25–42.

———. "Video Capture: Machinima, Documentation, and the History of Virtual Worlds."

The Machinima Reader, edited by Henry Lowood and Michael Nitsche. MIT Press, 2011, pp. 3–22.

Lowood, Henry, and Michael Nitsche, eds. *The Machinima Reader.* MIT Press, 2011.

"Machinomics." *TVTropes.* https://tvtropes.org/pmwiki/pmwiki.php/Main/Machinomics.

Maragos, Nich. "Will Strip for Games." 1up.com, 7 November 2005. https://web.archive.org/web/20151208074942/http://www.1up.com/features/strip-games. Accessed 24 July 2023.

Marino, Paul. *3D Game–Based Filmmaking: The Art of Machinima.* Paraglyph Press, 2004.

McGregor, Georgia Leigh. "Terra Ludus, Terra Paidia, Terra Prefab: Spatialization of Play in Videogames and Virtual Worlds." *Proceedings of the 5th Australasian Conference on Interactive Entertainment,* 2008, pp. 1–8.

Möring, Sebastian, and Marco de Mutiis. "Camera Ludica: Reflections on Photography in Video Games." *Intermedia Games—Games Inter Media: Video Games and Intermediality,* edited by Michael Fuchs and Jeff Thoss. Bloomsbury Academic, 2020, pp. 69–94.

Newman, James. "Playing (with) Videogames." *Convergence: The International Journal of Research into New Media Technologies,* vol. 11, no. 1, 2005, pp. 48–67.

Ng, Jenna, ed. "Machinima." *Debugging Game History: A Critical Lexicon,* edited by Henry Lowood and Raiford Guins. MIT Press, 2016, pp. 287–95.

———. *Understanding Machinima: Essays on Filmmaking in Virtual Worlds.* Bloomsbury, 2013.

Nitsche, Michael. "Claiming Its Space: Machinima." *Dichtung-Digital,* 2007. http://www.dichtung-digital.de/2007/Nitsche/nitsche.htm.

O'Reilly, Tim. "What Is Web 2.0: Design Patterns and Business Models for the Next Generation of Software." *Communications and Strategies,* no. 65, first quarter 2007, pp. 17–37. https://papers.ssrn.com/so13/papers.cfm?abstract_id=1008839.

Poremba, Cindy. "Point and Shoot: Remediating Photography in Gamespace." *Games and Culture,* vol. 2, no. 1, 2007, pp. 49–58.

Postigo, Hector. "Of Mods and Modders: Chasing Down the Value of Fan-Based Digital Game Modifications." *Games and Culture,* vol. 2, no. 4, 2007, pp. 300–313.

Rokošný, Ivan. "Screenshot as an Art: An Aesthetics of In-Game Photography." *Marketing Identity,* vol. 6, no. 1/2, 2018, pp. 220–31.

Salen, Katie, and Eric Zimmerman. *Rules of Play: Game Design Fundamentals.* MIT Press, 2003.

Schäfer, Mirko Tobias. *Bastard Culture! How User Participation Transforms Cultural Production.* Amsterdam University Press, 2011.

———. "Participation Inside? User Activities between Design and Appropriation." *Digital Material: Tracing New Media in Everyday Life and Technology,* edited by Marianne Van den Boomen, Sybille Lammes, Ann-Sophie Lehmann, Joost Raessens, and Mirko Tobias Schäfer. Amsterdam University Press, 2009, pp. 147–58.

Schreier, Jason. "Blizzard Says They Had to Shut Down *World of Warcraft* Fan Server Nostalrius." *Kotaku,* 26 April 2016. http://kotaku.com/blizzard-says-they-had-to-shut-down-world-of-warcraft-f-1773089312.

Schott, Gareth, and Andrew Burn. "Art (Re)production as an Expression of Collective Agency Within Online Fan Culture." *Works and Days,* vol. 22, no. 1, 2004, pp. 251–74.

Schott, Gareth, and Bevin Yeatman. "Participatory Fan Culture and *Half-Life 2* Machinima: A Dialogue Among Ethnography, Culture, and Space." *The Machinima Reader,* edited by Henry Lowood and Michael Nitsche. MIT Press, 2011, pp. 301–14.

Sharp, John. *Works of Game: On the Aesthetics of Games and Art.* MIT Press, 2015.

Sheely, Kent. "DoD [2009–2012]." *Kent Sheely,* 2012. https://kentsheely.com/dod.

Sommerseth, Hannah. "'Gamic Realism': Player, Perception and Action in Video Game Play." *Situated Play, Proceedings of DiGRA 2007 Conference,* vol. 4, 2007, pp. 765–68.

Swalwell, Melanie, Helen Stuckey, and Angela Ndalianis, eds. *Fans and Videogames: Histories, Fandom, Archives.* Routledge, 2017.

Tapscott, Don, and Anthony D. Williams. *Wikinomics: How Mass Collaboration Changes Everything.* Portfolio, 2006.

Wakeford, Alex. "Why Photo Mode is One of the Best Things to Ever Happen to Gaming." *Universally Speaking,* 31 October 2019. https://usspeaking.com/blog. Accessed 24 July 2023.

Wenger, Étienne. *Communities of Practice: Learning, Meaning, and Identity.* Cambridge University Press, 1998.

Zwass, Vladimir. "Co-creation: Toward a Taxonomy and an Integrated Research Perspective." *International Journal of Electronic Commerce,* vol. 15, 2010, pp. 11–48.

VIDEOGAME REFERENCES

Doom. id Software, 1993.

Final Fantasy. Square, 1987.

Fortnite. Epic, 2017.

Grand Theft Auto V. Rockstar, 2013.

Halo 2. Bungie, 2004.

Mega Man. Capcom, 1987.

Minecraft. Mojang, 2011.

Pilotwings 64. Nintendo and Paradigm Entertainment, 1996.

Pokémon: Snap. HAL Laboratory and Pax Softnica, 1999.

Quake. id Software, 1996.

Team Fortress 2. Valve, 2007.

The Movies. Lionhead, 2005.

The Sims 2. Electronic Arts, 2004.

The Sims 4. Electronic Arts, 2014.

Unreal Tournament 2004. Epic Games and Digital Extremes, 2004.
World of Warcraft. Blizzard, 2004.

ARTWORK REFERENCES

8-Bit Theater. Brian Clevinger, 2001.
Alice and Kev. Robin Burkinshaw, 2009.
Apostasy. James "BrashFink" Brandt, 2005.
Bob and George. Dave Anez, 2000.
Concerned. Christopher C. Livingston, 2005.
Diary of a Camper. United Ranger Films, 1996.
Doctor Fun. David Farley, 1993.
The EVIL-Luigi Story. Jay Resop, 1998.
Quad God. Tritin Films, 2000.
Red vs. Blue. Roster Teeth. 2003.
The Silver Shroud. Altervlife, 2018.
Where the Buffalo Roam. Jans Bjordahl, 1987.
Witches in Stitches. Eric Monster Millikin, 1985.

Them's Fighting Words!

Explorations of Boss Battle Language in
The Legend of Zelda: Ocarina of Time Walkthroughs

JESIKA BROOKS

Videogames are an interactive medium in which physical actions are translated into a virtual space. For some kinds of games, these actions might include moving objects to solve puzzles or time-based fighting that requires spatial navigation. While games don't have to be goal-driven—sandbox games, for instance, have rules to constrain play while not necessarily having an end point outside of achievement lists—many games are designed with discrete end goals. What happens, then, if a player doesn't know how to meet these goals? They turn to walkthroughs.

Videogame walkthroughs, a genre of shared, mostly online texts, are an offshoot of the printed, bound materials published in the game manuals and guides popular in the 1990s and 2000s. These works of technical communication provide guidance on how to beat a game, whether by enhancing a player's knowledge of the game world or by providing insight on maps, puzzles, monsters, and bosses, the latter often the narrative goal of a game and typically the most challenging aspect of the game. This last aim, sharing boss strategies, typifies the textual qualities of the walkthrough genre, particularly in its nascent, early internet days before the advent of widespread video sharing, which is now the most common and popular way of spreading such knowledge. As defeating a boss indicates not only a player's mastery of game systems but also their knowledge of the game world itself, these strategies are vital, regardless of medium.

Walkthroughs, as a whole, have their peculiarities as a genre of videogame literature. They have a generalized form, style, function, and audience. Although the genre has shifted over time, there are still specific aspects that typify these texts. This essay not only explores the idea of walkthroughs as a genre of videogame literature but also looks into a specific part of walkthroughs, the boss battle strategy, as a vehicle through which writers invoke genre qualities and instruct readers on actions with a temporal-spatial basis.

Agency and Rhetoric in the Walkthrough Genre

Before considering the walkthrough as genre, it's helpful to understand how genre works. Genre studies explores how genres are built and how both rhetors and audience interact with items within that genre. Two ways to approach genre include the academic fields of English for specific purposes and rhetorical genre studies. In their book *Genre: An Introduction to History, Theory, Research, and Pedagogy*, Anis S. Bawarshi and Mary Jo Reiff explain that scholars of English for specific purposes view genres as "forms of communicative action," whereas rhetorical genre studies scholars see genres as "forms of social action." Thus, genre can explore how transactions, or turns, achieve certain tasks or how media shapes and is shaped by its audience.

Walkthroughs are written for those who play games. This audience is what sets walkthroughs apart from the wider genre of technical communication, though technical communication also focuses on purpose-driven writing, often with a focus on achieving a particular goal. Many walkthroughs provide general instructions for games, such as highlighting a game's collectible items, easy-to-miss locations, opportunities for achievements, narrative beats, and, yes, boss battles. Beyond those kinds of general guides, however, there exists a spectrum of hyperspecific walkthroughs that cover single game aspects—for example, bestiaries of game creatures. In *Cheating: Gaining Advantage in Videogames*, Mia Consalvo notes that "one item that [official] game guide writers consider essential to their job is unusually not included in the final product: cheat codes" (61). If a player sees 100 percent completion as a win, then a guide with speedrunning advice will cause them to lose. Writers of unofficial walkthroughs must take readers' needs—and agency—into account, and they can do so without concern about constraints that limit officially licensed game guides, such as personal playstyle.

Playstyle and its connections to walkthroughs are explored by Daniel Ashton and James Newman in terms of how control is navigated in the written walkthrough. As they point out, "The walkthrough . . . is both a document of the game as designed and record of investigations into the vagaries and imperfections of its implementation and how these may be enacted and exploited." A walkthrough writer isn't documenting *the* way to play. They are documenting *their* way to play. Walkthroughs can provide information as basic as turn-by-turn directions, as complex as glitch lists, and as personal as the writers' own imaginative associations. In an early study of fans and walkthroughs, Consalvo describes walkthrough writers as not just providing technical information to the reader but also engaging in narrative exploration and construction. As she puts it, "Gamers' creation of these walkthroughs . . . can serve as an aid to creating a story line in a game" ("Zelda 64" 331). There is a metatextual element to many walkthroughs through which personal remarks give particular affect to otherwise plain, goal-oriented directions.

An idiosyncratic viewpoint can be both boon and burden, and as with most discourse, it can reflect broader societal concerns. On the one hand, in finding a writer with a playstyle similar to theirs, a reader can more deeply enjoy a game, combining the pleasures of *finally* solving a difficult puzzle with that of sharing the experience with another player. On the other hand, viewpoints can steep into the writer's interpretation of the game and into the way that textual information is delivered in the walkthrough, potentially blurring the line between technical communication and personal writing. This self-expression, which acts as motivation for many walkthrough writers, is a genre quality that fulfills multiple needs for both writer and reader. In an extensive study using the GameFAQs (www.gamefaqs.gamespot.com) platform, Michael J. Hughes found five major themes in walkthroughs and the motivations for writing them, which he characterizes as "a shifting mix of motivations, including altruism, community belonging, self-expression, and recognition—primarily in the form of feedback and appreciation but also from compensation." This creative, community-oriented labor—what researcher Hanna Wirman calls "player productivity"—connects both to audience and reception. Walkthroughs as a genre have an audience of gamers, which includes the writers themselves.

On *The Legend of Zelda: Ocarina of Time*

I'm particularly interested in how these multiple motivations are reflected in the temporal-spatial language used in walkthroughs that explain how to defeat the major nemeses of a game, so-called bosses, as this is an act with both narrative and gameplay-specific weight. I focus on walkthroughs centering on four bosses from *The Legend of Zelda: Ocarina of Time* (*LZ:OT*). This game, released in 1998 for the Nintendo 64 console, is an action-adventure roleplaying game. Unlike previous titles in the *Zelda* series, it uses 3D graphics, blending fighting, puzzle-solving, and exploration elements in ways that could be especially challenging for players at the time of its release. In particular, this title's fully realized three-dimensional world and immersive plot have resulted in a surfeit of user-created walkthroughs, evidencing writers' interrogation of both the game and its story.

Beyond those qualities of *LZ:OT*, it's worth considering the particulars of its historical moment. *LZ:OT* was a big deal upon its release, with its Nintendo affiliation and high budget classifying it as an AAA title. Games need to be popular enough to be worth the fan labor of documentation, and complex enough that players will require assistance in solving puzzles and completing tasks. When you further add in the high costs of file storage through the mid-2000s, it's understandable why there are so many text-based walkthroughs on Game-FAQS written for AAA titles from the late 1980s through the early 2000s. Games released in the late 1990s were documented online mostly through the occasional still image and pages of digital text. What's more, it was during this period when AAA games began shifting to 3D. This meant that writers had an additional level of challenge in explaining tasks that hadn't existed before. They had to provide clear descriptions of tasks that occurred in a time and space very different from that of earlier games, with only words as their medium.

Boss battle strategies exemplify the challenge of vivid temporal-spatial language. To defeat a boss, players must move in specific ways with specific timing. Given how boss battles demarcate progress in plot-driven games like *LZ:OT*, boss battle strategies can be found in even the most general of walkthroughs. The boss battles I selected for analysis do not encompass all the bosses in the game; rather, I chose to look at those that were particularly difficult—thus, more complex in terms of their spatiotemporal challenges—and of particular importance to the story—thus, more significant in terms of the battle's spatial communication. In this respect, these boss battles are interesting examples of technical writing that is both purpose-driven and rhetorically stylish.

Methodology and Ethical Considerations

As mentioned, the body of texts I consider here contains portions of walkthroughs for *LZ:OT*. I approach these texts in terms of the English for specific purposes and rhetorical genre studies frameworks, identifying specific narrative and rhetorical strategies using a combination of close and distant reading methodologies. The first set of texts describe strategies for four bosses from this game: Gohma, Bongo Bongo, Morpha, and Ganon. These bosses were chosen due to their perceived difficulty (or lack thereof) and their narrative weight. The snippets of text that I analyze, totaling seventy-one text files from eighteen general walkthroughs, were explored through a corpus analysis tool called AntConc, created by Laurence Anthony, which looks at how often words appear in a corpus and how those words collocate, or appear beside, other words in the text. I'll describe my use of this tool in more detail later.

The second set of texts I consider takes a closer, more nuanced look at strategies for Ganon, the final boss of the game. These excerpts not only focus on strategy (the primary purpose of the first set of texts) but also situate the boss battle at a specific location and invoke the importance of the battle to the game's narrative. The qualities of this fight make for unique textual markers, and as such, I explore these texts using close, rather than distant, readings. Additionally, while Ganon is the primary focus, there often are references to previous boss battles, as the genre conventions and the narrative backbone of the corpus connect to prior texts.

Many walkthroughs, including some that I consider here, were written before the advent of Google and other search engines. Additionally, given Hughes's findings on how some walkthrough writers write for community clout and the need for acknowledgment within fan spaces, I had to take into account other considerations when selecting texts for this exploration. One of those was the use of GameFAQs. Although these corpora are publicly available online, and although GameFAQs is not a solely fannish space, the fact that the walkthroughs published there are written by gamers for gamers (as is the case for almost any walkthrough) creates concerns around possible expectations that these texts are for fans alone—a rhetorically limited group of writers and readers. For this reason, in the interest of providing pseudonymity while still giving due credit, walkthroughs will be indirectly referenced if possible. Exceptions include a screenshot of AntConc's concordance tool in the distant reading section and unavoidable direct quotes in the close reading section. This indirect referencing utilizes ethical paraphrasing, suggested by Brianna Dym and Casey Fiesler in their work on ethics in fandom research. While this isn't a perfect solution, it is a good-faith effort to maintain ethical standards for this corpus of fan-created texts.

Distant Reading: Information, Identification, and Style

To see broader patterns in the texts, I first created two lists of key terms, both pulled from the corpus of the full set of boss battle strategies. The corpus of text files, excerpted and saved individually, includes only the strategy text snippet beneath each boss's heading in the eighteen general *LZ:OT* walkthroughs available on GameFAQs. If the walkthrough writer included a specific boss battle strategy section (for ease of navigation, many writers opt to create a separate section for boss information), that text snippet was used. A few writers copied and pasted the boss battle strategies from their general walkthrough into this section, but that redundancy didn't affect the analysis.

In the first key term list, "Full List," all words are included, no matter how small. In the second list, "Stopped List," all stop words (words that are common and are generally considered to have minimal narrative or rhetorical significance) have been removed (see tables). For reference, I used the Buckley & Salton Stopword List (Onix Text Retrieval Toolkit). In her guide on using AntConc for research in *Programming Historian,* Heather Froehlich notes that retaining stop words can make for interesting insights: "As readers we tend not to notice [stop words] very much. Computers, especially software like Ant-Conc, can show us where these words do and do not appear and that can be quite interesting, especially in very large collections of text." This is especially true for this walkthrough exploration. For example, spatial language often uses prepositions, considered by many to be stop words, but these are critical terms when considering both the space and timing of battles. In the case of boss battles, "insignificant" words like prepositions, pronouns, and adverbs can provide insight into the technical, narrative, and stylistic aspects of the texts:

eye. This is Queen Gohma. She'll see **you**, <u>then</u> *descend* so you can see her full
out of the tentacle and bring it toward **you**. <u>Then</u> *hit* IT with your sword. Another method
, you're screwed. Sorry, I can't help **you** <u>there,</u> *now* CAN I? 2. Z-Target the face,
they can hover overhead and stomp on **you**. *They can* KNOCK you out of the arena
this level so much. I can end it! **You** <u>think</u> *it's* HARD to play through it?
When **you** <u>think</u> *its* OVER no its not! Ganon rises

However, for all the importance of such words, articles do the heaviest lifting in these texts. The most frequently used word in the full corpus is "the." This might not seem special at first: what value has "the" when it's not even worth capitalizing in title case? But "the," as a definite article, gives specificity. It pro-

Full List

WORD	IN-TEXT REFERENCES	RANK
the	916	1
you	506	2
to	447	3
and	403	4
it	316	5
a	296	6
of	242	7
will	203	8
is	195	9
with	194	10
this	167	11
s	162	12
sword	158	13
your	149	14
in	139	15
her	135	16
he	131	17
his	123	18
she	109	19
when	109	20
him	105	21
boss	103	22
eye	101	23
if	101	24
on	101	25

vides two important rhetorical contexts, that of a single object or group and that of a particular, intentional reference. For walkthrough writers, using "the" indicates to readers that they don't need *a* sword, they need *the* sword. The difference between "a" and "the" can be the difference between success and failure.

"A" appears on Full List at rank six, with 296 references in the text. This is compared to 916 uses of the word "the." Although walkthrough writers can offer choice, the use of "the" versus "a" more often than not suggests that objects are given a deliberate technical and narrative weight. Given that names aren't usually referenced with "the," the articles in question are likely appended to nouns used as objects or locations. In such cases, the walkthrough writers specify a

Stopped List

WORD	IN-TEXT REFERENCES	RANK
sword	158	1
boss	103	2
eye	101	3
attack	92	4
hit	68	5
ganon	66	6
hands	54	7
water	54	8
master	52	9
bongo	50	10
shoot	46	11
red	44	12
target	44	13
arrow	41	14
biggoron	41	15
back	40	16
fight	40	17
morpha	40	18
slash	40	19
gohma	39	20
run	39	21
light	38	22
tail	37	23
time	37	24
deku	36	25

particular weapon, using their presumed authority to be more prescriptive in their advice.

The second most used word is "you," which naturally lends itself to the genre of technical communication, and more specifically, of instructional texts. Most, if not all, instructional text is you-focused, as soft commands and hard imperatives have implied second-person subjects. That said, "you" doesn't seem to be used only in this manner when it comes to boss battle instructions. Looking at the concordance tool, which shows how the word is used in context, "you" also relates to the fan-oriented side of the walkthrough genre. Walkthroughs not only aim for purpose-driven writing but also are imbued with the authorial purpose of meeting audience needs within a community-oriented content—that is, proving and providing a fan connection.

However, this use of "you" is not only a conventional imperative address; it is also a reflection of the ways videogames connect the player to their avatar. In their study on avatar identification, Jasper van Vught and Gareth Schott explore how people embody their on-screen avatars as they play games. They find that identification is shaped by camera angle, the player's sense of in-game embodiment, and their identity as the virtual character—in other words, identification depends on circumstance. While the game in their study was a first-person shooter, not an action-adventure roleplaying game, both it and *LZ:OT* feature the ability to swap between first- and third-person camera views. Regardless of the particular dynamics of identification in *LZ:OT*, it's evident that it is part of these texts: the word "Link"—the hero of the story and the on-screen protagonist—only appears eight times in the corpus. Even "he" and "his" appear a relatively small number of times (131 and 123, respectively), with the masculine bosses muddying the waters with regard to how often those pronouns directly refer to Link, who is gendered male.

With stop words stripped away, the most used word in the full corpus is "sword." At 158 uses, its rank outnumbers "boss" (103) and "eye" (101). It also appears on Full List at rank thirteen. Other top words include "attack," "hit," "ganon," "hands," "water," "master," and "bongo." ("Bongo," referring to the boss named Bongo Bongo, might be a bit overrepresented due to its doubled presentation.) The stopped list's words show the importance of specificity in videogame walkthroughs. Just as "the" provides a pointed precision, so too do the nouns and verbs at the top of the ranked-word list. Reflecting the way in which boss battle instructions communicate both technical information and the personal style of the writer, the words further down in the list tend to showcase writers' creativity and idiosyncratic writing styles. For example, consider the word "whamming," used only once in the full corpus, to describe Gohma's tentacle attack. The top ten words, in contrast, are obvious in their connection to the act of fighting in the fantastical world of Hyrule.

One surprising absence in the stopped list is adverbs. Adverbs can be helpful in indicating time, mentioned as being key to complex, three-dimensional challenges, as well as playstyle. That's not to say there are no adverbs in the corpus, but the strongest focus within this small selection is on nouns and verbs—and, of course, on the proper nouns necessary to know thine enemy, such as boss names like "ganon" and "morpha." Likewise, some words have multiple readings, such as "light." While bosses often leave behind light portals, there are also light arrows as an inventory item, which are particularly potent against Ganon.

It's also worth noting the types of verbs in the stopped list. Walkthrough writers generally use a mix of generic and specific verbs in their writing, both to give concrete information and to make things entertaining to read. This "edutainment" value is common to the walkthrough genre, as viewed through the lens of the full corpus. While "attack" and "hit" are fairly generic, "slash" implies a specific type of attack in *LZ:OT*. Link can either slash or stab, and one of his more powerful attacks includes a jumping slash. "Shoot," too, can only be performed with certain weapons, such as the Longshot found in the Water Temple. In this light, the lone use of verbs like "shimmy" or "hollers" feels like a writer trying to keep their readers engaged.

Close Reading: Spoilers

While reading distantly provides insights that would otherwise go unnoticed without the aid of computational analysis, deconstruction makes holistic meaning a bit harder to grasp. As such, reading excerpts more closely allows for a greater understanding of how writers met genre aims and how they indicated time and space through text. This close reading explores one subset of the full corpus, that of boss battle strategies for Ganon, the final boss of *LZ:OT*. For this particular boss, one walkthrough on GameFAQs did *not* include a strategy for Ganon, instead focusing on Ganondorf, Ganon's earlier incarnation. As such, that walkthrough was not included in the Ganon corpus, bringing the total number of texts to seventeen. Its absence, however, is an example of one aspect of walkthroughs that's somewhat unique: the idea of spoilers.

On GameFAQs, depending on the game, there will be walkthroughs designated as "spoiler-free." In these walkthroughs, instructions become brusquer and more clipped. Rather than writers writing in their own unique voice—as seen in some close reads of Ganon's boss battle strategies—text is flat, without suggestions of impeding events. For walkthroughs without the spoiler-free designation, writers may reveal plot twists or otherwise spoil game events. In the case of the missing walkthrough text, there is *technically* a boss battle strategy, but it's obfuscated due to the connection between Ganondorf and Ganon. That is, the writer didn't want to reveal the then-surprising twist that Ganondorf had a final form, that of the piglike Ganon. Here is how the writer dances around the issue, providing information while respecting fans' desire to remain unspoiled: "Eventually you'll defeat [Ganondorf]. I'm not going to give away the rest of the game after this, but if you get stuck, here are some hints" (Zauron).

Given that Ganon is the game's final boss, spoilers are a big concern for writers. Do they ruin the impact of the game's final cutscene, or do they lead up to the final blow? Of the seventeen texts in the Ganon corpus, only two discuss content after Ganon's defeat, with one being vague on the details. The rest mention cutscenes, the ending, or just "a nice relaxing movie" (N64Gamerz). One writer specifically decries spoilers. Another tells readers that they can discover what happens for themselves.

This refusal to elaborate seems fairly unique to walkthroughs, compared to other forms of technical communication. Imagine a set of instructions that leaves the final step open-ended, particularly when the rest of the text uses extreme specificity (naming tools, actions, and objects with proper nouns). If walkthrough as genre can be viewed through a lens of social action, then some walkthrough writers' adherence to keeping readers spoiler free can be seen as an extension of norms within fan spaces. They are writing how they'd prefer to read, and perhaps how they'd prefer to play. A game's reliance on narrative thus can shape how instructions are delivered.

Close Reading: Fan Labor, Embodiment, and the Space-Time of Boss Battles

I now turn to a different reading method and a more specific subset of boss battles in *LZ:OT*. In looking at texts in the Ganon corpus, we see another aspect of walkthroughs that sets them apart from similar genres such as software documentation or instruction manuals. Walkthroughs can be highly subjective, in both the flavor of the text and the instructions themselves. Understood in terms of rhetorical genre studies, walkthroughs as a genre cater not just to those who need help with a task but also to a community of self-identified gamers or fans of games in general. This is a matter not just of rhetoric but of labor. Walkthrough writers provide fan labor, putting in innumerable hours to document the games they write about and to support the community around those games both practically (enabling successful play) and discursively (sustaining a particular style of communication). In an editorial for *Transformative Works and Cultures*, Mel Stanfill and Megan Condis connect fan labor to audience explicitly, stating, "Fan work creates fan community—fandom itself—through the production and maintenance of affective ties." Hughes affirms this notion, adding that some walkthrough writers feel a need to give back to the fan community, while others desire to show expertise. In both the intros and outros of walkthroughs, writers often remark on the number of hours they spent grinding through games. In this way, they both serve the community as experts and exemplify the gamer identity as fans.

But labor isn't only about time. Walkthrough writers may also state whether a boss is challenging or not. Difficulty seems to be aligned on two axes for these writers: perceived difficulty and expected difficulty. When difficulty is mentioned within the context of boss battle strategies, its sentiment is colored by the writers' perceptions of where it falls on those axes. These views are then turned into either practical advice (writer as expert) or fan discourse (writer as fan).

Within the Ganon corpus, difficulty becomes a talking point for several reasons. As Ganon is the final boss of the game, many of the writers remark on the boss battle's difficulty, in how it either met or fell short of endgame expectations. One writer expresses disappointment directly, saying the final boss was uncreative. Another writer suggests that the spectacle of the battle makes up for the lack of challenge, stating, "If you were hoping for a big and challenging boss battle you likely won't find it here, but still you're in for an impressive fight against an enormous enemy, which still works out quite well" (A_l_e_x).

Unlike other forms of technical communication, which often sacrifices clever or entertaining turns of phrase for the sake of clarity, walkthrough writers have no such obligations. It's unlikely you'll find instructions for putting together a bookshelf that state, "Too bad this shelf is so easy to put together!" The same can't be said for walkthroughs. For walkthrough writers, the ability to complete a task is tempered by the way that task aligns with expectations, both of the narrative and the quality of gameplay. Likewise, the reasons behind writers' remarks on difficulty—to brag, to reassure, to complain, or to geek out—are as idiosyncratic as the writers themselves.

Just as a writer's idiosyncratic writing and playstyle are evident in a close reading, so too is the authorial attempt to rhetorically duplicate the dynamics of reader-avatar identification. As seen in the distant reading, "you" is an important word in the full corpus, and indeed in walkthroughs more generally. With imperatives—that is, instructions or commands—the subject is implied. The command "Halt!" can be diagrammed with an implied subject of "you." Likewise, in an instructional manual, this same sort of technique is employed: "[You] insert tab A into slot B." You, the reader, are expected to be the one putting the shelf together, even if you are merely the reader and a second party will be doing the assembly. However, in walkthroughs, the second-person address is more complex and shifting. Many games scholars have looked into the ways that players embody their characters, or how game worlds use embodiment to explore themes, build empathy, or create emotional experiences (Johnson). It is this complex, shifting form of embodiment that's indicated in walkthroughs, with the combination of direct address and the need for writers to communicate with their readers as fellow fans being two other reasons for the prominence of the second-person address.

Instructions can be written in three ways: with an implied-you instruction, with an explicit address to "you," or with reference to the in-game character. This third option, of having the in-game character serve as a proxy for the player in the instructions, also bleeds into the implied-you text. All of the boss battle strategies reference actions that you, the player, must do as Link, the actor. These actions are ones that would be impossible (or at least inadvisable) to do in public. The player must "strike Ganon" through Link, even though their physical body is on the couch. What makes this embodied, second-person instruction so interesting is how the forms of address shift. In a single paragraph, one walkthrough writer goes from telling players to "Z-target" Ganon (a physical action on a controller) to suggesting they do a backflip (embodied action). This becomes a common motif, particularly when mentioning specific button presses, like the aforementioned Z-targeting, or in one walkthrough that explains how to lunge with the Z and A buttons. As there are multiple on-screen characters—Link, Ganon, and Zelda—the embodied address is constantly shifting.

In order to clarify the particular "you" being addressed at a given moment, walkthrough writers must provide a way for readers to locate themselves in the game world, a challenge that is particularly daunting in games that are narratively dense and that take place in three-dimensional spaces, as is the case with *LZ:OT*. Doing so requires writers not only to describe game locations but also to conceptualize them as landmarks to guide action and to mark narrative beats. For boss battles, there's an additional challenge: the battles are action-driven rather than static, and the battles' spatial organization is influenced by the mechanics of the fight itself. It's not enough for players to find the boss; they have to take an active role in defeating them, and that activity requires careful attention to position and movement. All of these goals require the use of temporal-spatial language.

When discussing spatial language, many scholars use Levinson's frame of reference (FoR) taxonomy as a lens through which a speaker or writer interprets location. The FoR is a reference point that provides the home base, so to speak, for any directions, and in Levinson's taxonomy it is categorized into absolute, intrinsic, and relative frames (Bender and Beller 348). For example, an absolute FoR supposes that directions are given using fixed points such as cardinal directions, while intrinsic and relative frames focus on relationships among objects or on the self in that space. Elena Andonova articulates the differences between the last two frames, noting that an "intrinsic frame of reference is object-centered while a relative frame of reference is viewer/speaker dependent, also construed as egocentric" (36).

In the Ganon corpus, texts tend to utilize the egocentric FoR for spatial navigation on the stage, with Ganon becoming a frame when discussing targets for players to hit. This is unsurprising, given that the narrative focuses on a single protagonist, Link, the camera angles and user interface are oriented around Link's point of view, and the mechanics of navigation and combat depend on an accurate perception of both Link and his targets. There also may be a cultural bias in the inclusion of FoR rhetoric, as there appears to be a preference for intrinsic and relative FoRs with English-speaking groups (Majid et al. 108), but perhaps the fact that these walkthroughs are written in English presupposes its use by English speakers. Regardless, an egotistical, object-centered frame of reference is common in these boss battle instructions.

The Ganon boss battle is staged on a circular platform, with rubble scattered around to block paths and complicate navigation and attacks. Many of the boss battles in *LZ:OT* use this sort of setup, with an environmental area that may have a few blind spots but is otherwise fully visible to the player so long as they have the right in-game objects. However, unlike other parts of the game, the boss battles don't require a map—the navigation of the space is less about exploration than about strategy and tactics. As games have grown in mechanical and spatial complexity, spatial language centered egotistically on the player-avatar's position in space is not only more common but also necessary for instructions to make sense.

In the case of *LZ:OT*, this is also a matter of game mechanics. Z-targeting, often mentioned by writers as a useful strategy, is the ability to lock on to an enemy or object and have the camera follow its path regardless of Link's movement. This ability makes the egocentric FoR an especially helpful rhetorical framework for writers. If Z-targeting is used, then the player's viewpoint becomes less of an unknown, giving walkthrough writers the ability to more accurately describe the relative positions of Link and his opponent. For a boss that doesn't move around much, when Z-targeting is used, Link might be described as positioned to its right or left, but ultimately the boss becomes a background object. Many of the Ganon strategies use multiple FoRs, but most of them appear to be informed by the particular spatial dynamics introduced by Z-targeting. With Ganon Z-targeted, he is always in front, and so directions imply side-to-side movement or frontward-facing hits (such as with swords or light arrows). In sum, Ganon isn't just the culmination of the narrative action; he serves as the primary directional marker.

Which leads us to the question of time and the way boss battle instructions construct temporality. Technical communication tends to use the present tense, with instructions being written as though they're being followed in real time. This expectation is shared by walkthroughs, which also use present and future tense, unless discussing game lore, which is generally set in the past. In an essay on the peculiar temporality of videogame narratives, Lluís Anyó notes that videogame narratives tend to function in terms of "the control of time by the player," resulting in a tension between narrative time (the unfolding of the plot) and participation time (the carrying through of action)—a tension that often takes the form of a temporal loop, as players will often have to attempt an action over and over to succeed, or will replay for fun. This generally is not the case with individuals attempting to install a faucet or prepare a dish for a meal. Given the temporal "loopiness" of games, the use of past tense verbs in walkthroughs is understandably rare, as the player—as addressed by the walkthrough writer—will be in an ongoing or anticipatory state.

This can result in complex rhetorical constructions of time. In this excerpt, note how the player is addressed through present tense commands and how Ganon is described in future tense as a result of player action: "If you're using arrows, just Z-target him and close to him [sic]. Lure him into attacking, and before he completes the attack, do a back flip to avoid the attack! He will just stand there, a bit dazed" (winnie the poop 2). We see the writer using "before" to indicate the timing of the attack, but the simple future tense to indicate the anticipated consequence of a correctly timed attack—and all of this oriented around the particular spatial perspective provided by Z-targeting. In the Ganon texts, this is the norm, and it's typical in most boss battle instructions. By structuring instructions in a specific way, there is a sequence of events implied, with the particular consequences of an action marking intent as well as the possibility of repetition. Again, we see how the dynamics of space constructed by the particular mechanic of Z-targeting shapes the construction of time, the anticipated future shaping the specific beats of timing—the lure, the backflip, the attack—which have an implied order.

But this is also the consequence of the fact that the boss battles in *LT:OZ* are more a challenge of positioning rather than of timing. In the Ganon walkthroughs, there's little emphasis on the tempo of attacks. There are four mentions of doing something "quickly." At least one writer stresses the need for split-second timing, and another suggests that timing is key at a specific spot in the boss fight, but in general, the concern of writers is primarily spatial. For walkthroughs beyond this corpus—such as those for games with bosses whose mechanics feature narrow windows for action, like in the *Dark Souls* series—language regarding timing will likely be more prevalent.

Beyond the GameFAQ: Storytelling, Gamer Expression, and Future Directions

The narrow focus of this exploration has encompassed only text-based walkthroughs, which were the norm when *LZ:OT* was released. As a burgeoning genre, text-based walkthroughs established several organizational, rhetorical, and stylistic norms. That said, it's certain that the introduction of audiovisual media into videogame walkthroughs and the emergence of other, walkthrough-like genres, such as Let's Play videos, have changed how writers express instructions with regard to the conventions I've described here, including specific words, the rhetorical use of the second-person address, and the foregrounding of spatiotemporal narrative strategies. For example, rather than trying to express tempo changes verbally, a video clip can demonstrate speed in real time. GameFAQs itself now shares HTML-format walkthroughs rather than pure text files. With the move beyond plaintext, walkthrough formatting has changed, with less need for referencing previous sections or including typographical navigational cues such as dingbats. Further, video walkthroughs are sometimes silent, with the gameplay itself providing information through visual cues.

What directions might we follow to track the storytelling strategies? Looking at the shift of language to accommodate other media would be an interesting follow-up study, particularly through the lens of "you"-focused language. Researchers might look into walkthroughs selected by genre, year, or series. Given the differences between control schema, particularly between console and personal computer iterations of a game, how would instructions vary? Expanding boss battle strategy texts to include games in other genres could further understanding of how point of view, action, and style are expressed by writers. Research also could analyze language change from text-based to media-rich walkthroughs, and examine whether a trending complexity in game design affects what writers share through text alone. Narrowing the focus to games with specific playstyles could also provide more insight into the temporal-spatial nature of walkthrough language. For example, how do walkthroughs work in the genre of rhythm-action games? Do walkthrough writers in these genres more resemble writers covering the fields of music and dance? Perhaps writers skip over play-by-play details of gameplay in lieu of using walkthroughs to explain more about the game itself. Finally, there's the question of rhetorical cultures—how do the rhetorical and narrative conventions of the genre differ across regions and languages?

Ultimately, walkthroughs are their own genre of videogame literature, and as such, they have their own stylistic conventions. Walkthrough writers may write for many reasons: to convey expertise, to help out their fellow fans, or to express interest in a game that's captured their attention. However, even given the narrow scope of this study, it is evident that walkthroughs enable a unique combination of technical writing and storytelling. Just as each game has peculiarities that enrage and endear its players, writers too have their peculiarities, and that's one of the attractions of these texts. Walkthroughs are their own genre, but they are not a monolith. There's no doubt that walkthrough writers have carefully crafted their works, with the huge number of guides available online standing as testament to their efforts, to their continuing readership, and to the vital presence of the genre in the wider body of videogame literature.

WORKS CITED

A_1_e_x. "*The Legend of Zelda: Ocarina of Time*—Guide and Walkthrough." *GameFAQs*, 15 July 2007. https://gamefaqs.gamespot.com/n64/197771-the-legend-of-zelda-ocarina -of-time/faqs/39038.

Andonova, Elena. "How Frames of Reference Prime Spatial Memory," http://ceur-ws.org /Vol-1419/paper0001.pdf.

Anyó, Lluís. "Narrative Time in Video Games and Films: From Loop to Travel in Time." *Game*, vol. 1, no. 4, 2015, pp. 3–74. https://www.gamejournal.it/anyo_narrative _time.

Ashton, Daniel, and James Newman. "Relations of Control: Walkthroughs and the Structuring of Player Agency." *Fibreculture Journal*, vol. 16, 2010. https://sixteen.fibrecul

turejournal.org/relations-of-control-walkthroughs-and-the-structuring-of-player-agency/.

Bawarshi, Anis S., and Mary Jo Reiff. *Genre: An Introduction to History, Theory, Research, and Pedagogy.* WAC Clearinghouse, 2010.

Bender, Andrea, and Sieghard Beller. "Mapping Spatial Frames of Reference onto Time: A Review of Theoretical Accounts and Empirical Findings." *Cognition,* vol. 132, 2014, pp. 342–32.

Consalvo, Mia. *Cheating: Gaining Advantage in Videogames.* MIT Press, 2007.

———. "Zelda 64 and Video Game Fans: A Walkthrough of Games, Intertextuality, and Narrative." *Television & New Media,* vol. 4, no. 3, 2003, pp. 321–34.

Dym, Brianna, and Casey Fiesler. "Ethical and Privacy Considerations for Research Using Online Fandom Data. *Transformative Works and Cultures,* vol. 33, 2020.

Froehlich, Heather. "Corpus Analysis with AntConc." *Programming Historian,* 15 November 2020.

Hughes, Michael J. "What Motivates the Authors of Video Game Walkthroughs and FAQs? A Study of Six GameFAQs Contributors." *First Monday,* vol. 23, no. 1, 2018.

Johnson, Matthew S. "Authoring Avatars: Gaming, Reading, and Writing Identities." *Composing Media Composing Embodiment,* edited by Kristen L. Arola and Anne Francis Wysocki. University Press of Colorado, 2012, pp. 60–71.

Levinson, Stephen C. "Frames of Reference and Molyneux's Question: Cross-Linguistic Evidence." *Language and Space,* edited by Paul Bloom, Merrill F. Garrett, Lynn Nadel, and Mary A. Peterson. MIT Press, 1996, pp. 109–69

Majid, Asifa, Melissa Bowerman, Sotaro Kita, Daniel B. M. Haun, and Stephen C. Levinson. "Can Language Restructure Cognition? The Case for Space." *Trends in Cognitive Sciences,* vol. 8, no. 3, 2004, pp. 108–14.

N64Gamerz. *"The Legend of Zelda: Ocarina of Time—Guide and Walkthrough."* *GameFAQs,* 23 September 2005. https://gamefaqs.gamespot.com/n64/197771-the-legend-of-zelda-ocarina-of-time/faqs/39092.

Newman, James. "Walkthrough." *Debugging Game History: A Critical Lexicon,* edited by Henry Lowood and Raiford Guins. MIT Press, 2016, pp. 409–17.

Onix Text Retrieval Toolkit. https://eecs.csuohio.edu/~sschung/CIS593/StopwordList1.pdf.

Stanfill, Mel, and Megan Condis. "Editorial: Fandom and/as Labor." *Transformative Works and Cultures,* vol. 15, 2014.

van Vught, Jasper, and Gareth Schott. "Identifying with In-Game Characters: Exploring Player Articulations of Identification and Presence." *Narrative Absorption,* edited by Frank Hakemulder, Moniek M. Kuijpers, Ed S. Tan, Katalin Bálint, and Miruna M. Doicaru. John Benjamins, 2017, pp. 157–75.

winnie the poop 2. *"The Legend of Zelda: Ocarina of Time—Guide and Walkthrough."* *GameFAQs,* 13 April 2003. https://gamefaqs.gamespot.com/n64/197771-the-legend-of-zelda-ocarina-of-time/faqs/22800.

Wirman, Hanna. "On Productivity and Game Fandom." *Transformative Works and Cultures*, vol. 3, 2009.

Zauron. *"The Legend of Zelda: Ocarina of Time*—Guide and Walkthrough." *GameFAQs*, 24 February 2004. https://gamefaqs.gamespot.com/n64/197771-the-legend-of-zelda -ocarina-of-time/faqs/13397.

Zwicky, Arnold M. "On the Subject of Bare Imperatives in English." *On Language: Rhetorica, Phonologica, Syntactica,* edited by Caroline Duncan-Rose and Theo Vennemann. Routledge, 1988. https://web.stanford.edu/~zwicky/bare-imperatives.pdf.

Who's Fooling WHO?

Addiction and Autobiography in *Gamelife: A Memoir*

FRANCIS BUTTERWORTH-PARR

The World Health Organization (WHO) classifies "gaming disorder" under "disorders due to substance use or addictive behaviours." Preventative and treatment measures became mandatory for WHO member nations in 2022, but the classifying gesture itself is a totalizing response to a subject that is more complex than the WHO admits. With the Chinese government's videogame "curfew" controlling adolescent gameplay (see Kuo; Zialcita), the WHO's classification may have already justified interventions; however, there remains a frustrating lack of consensus regarding videogame addiction, and this conversation occurs without the voices of those for whom videogames are a formative medium.

When debates like these become polarized, literary representations can offer a different lens through which to interpret concepts central to discussions. Escapism, leisure, and reality—concepts that define how we generally treat videogames and gamers today—are all represented in Michael W. Clune's *Gamelife: A Memoir*. Books like Clune's are valuable discursive touchstones for interrogating videogame controversies, highlighting how formulations like "critical immersion" can be new descriptors for gaming and part of writerly reflection. Here, I deploy Clune's oscillatory account of videogaming against the clinical debate to balance the language of compulsion and dependency with the language of education and passion, thus generating a vocabulary capable of expressing the space between the two.

Gamelife offers a descriptive counterpart to the clinical community's prescriptivism. An account of Clune's childhood through his most formative medium, it places his gaming between destructive addiction and therapeutic obsession. Both depictions evince different perspectives on videogame addiction, which become more insightful and less dogmatic through their collusion. Alongside other memoirs, like Tom Bissell's *Extra Lives* and Zoë Quinn's *Crash Override*, *Gamelife* exemplifies the emerging autobiographic urge to tell stories with videogames, presenting videogaming as an important relational object in twenty-first-century life-writing.

I will juxtapose the major controversies within the academic discourse on videogame addiction, then argue *Gamelife*'s case as a lens through which to examine the questions arising from the debate. Drawing on aesthetic and educational arguments, I trouble videogaming's position among the family of substances and pastimes the WHO designates as addictive. Finally, I wrestle with the idea of escapism and the inadequacy of that idea to describe gaming, proposing "critical immersion" instead. In particular, I contextualize critical immersion within *Gamelife*'s passages in which Clune describes attempts to process trauma through play.

Debates, Definitions, Disagreements

This essay does not seek to prove or disprove the existence of videogame addiction—that is the clinician's task. Rather, this essay hypothesizes that videogame addiction, if it exists, exists differently from the WHO's classification. The *International Classification of Diseases*, 11th revision, defines "gaming disorder" as follows:

> Gaming disorder is characterized by a pattern of persistent or recurrent gaming behaviour ("digital gaming" or "video-gaming"), which may be online (i.e., over the internet) or offline, manifested by: impaired control over gaming (e.g., onset, frequency, intensity, duration, termination, context); increasing priority given to gaming to the extent that gaming takes precedence over other life interests and daily activities; and continuation or escalation of gaming despite the occurrence of negative consequences. The behaviour pattern is of sufficient severity to result in significant impairment in personal, family, social, educational, occupational or other important areas of functioning. The pattern of gaming behaviour may be continuous or episodic and recurrent. (6C51)

And "hazardous gaming" is described as follows:

Hazardous gaming refers to a pattern of gaming, either online or offline that appreciably increases the risk of harmful physical or mental health consequences to the individual or to others around this individual. The increased risk may be from the frequency of gaming, from the amount of time spent on these activities, from the neglect of other activities and priorities, from risky behaviours associated with gaming or its context, from the adverse consequences of gaming, or from the combination of these. The pattern of gaming often persists in spite of awareness of increased risk of harm to the individual or to others. (QE22)

The WHO's decision to classify disordered/hazardous gaming is the culmination of a decade of fractious debate on videogame addiction's existence and treatment. News outlets clambered to sensationalize this momentous medical occasion; their interest in videogaming moral panics being nothing new (van Rooij et al. 5). Large-scale institutional interventions followed. In 2013, the American Psychiatric Association added "internet gaming disorder" to its *Diagnostic and Statistical Manual of Mental Disorders*, 5th edition. However, the *DSM-5*'s suggestion that an "international consensus" (Petry et al. 1399) for assessing videogame addiction was reached in 2014 was contested one year later by Griffiths et al. (173), and Petry et al.'s attempt to deploy the DSM's criteria for practical purposes catalyzed a series of debate papers.

Given the millions of dollars in industry sanctions and regulations, clinical infrastructure, and research funding that could be the consequence of pathologizing the most profitable entertainment media, this debate was a high-stakes affair for any videogame professional. Two camps have emerged. Mark Griffiths, Halley Pontes, and Daria Kuss are among the defenders of formalizing the definition, while the opposing view counts Christopher Ferguson, Antonius van Rooij, and Espen Aarseth among its luminaries. While the former seem to be winning, those on the losing side are not going quietly, nor have their misgivings been assuaged.

One of those misgiving is that gaming is different in kind from other compulsive behaviors like gambling—different because one tells stories. Both are addictions to games, but gambling games like roulette are not concerned with form or representation as videogames are, and collapsing the two together in metaphor, where videogames become gateways to gambling (a common trope in popular media), constitutes a misrepresentation. Although gambling mechanics in videogames demonstrably encourage gambling (see Molde et al.;

Zendle), game design, not videogames themselves, should be held responsible for this relationship. This category error is what the "social science and medical communities[,] . . . locked in the substance use or gambling disorders metaphor" (Bean et al. 379), are also threatening to commit, having lost, in their focus on videogames as ludic object, too much of their form as art. Regardless, throughout the discourse, there is no recourse to aesthetic arguments. Whether compulsively consuming an entertainment medium can be considered an addiction is certainly one question, but when that medium constitutes an aesthetic object like literature, then the language of its consumption transposes the clinical and medical to taste and culture.

Memoirs like *Gamelife* provide the gamer's voice in this debate, troubling concepts clinicians often take for granted. Although researchers have produced a small study on videogamer ethnographies of addiction (Snodgrass et al.), "there is much left unturned in understanding the videogame from an ethnographic approach: the culture of videogaming itself is another important piece of the puzzle currently left unconsidered" (Bean et al. 379). Videogame addiction stories can and should complement cultural (Penix-Tadsen), feminist (see Gray et al.; Jenson and de Castell), and queer (Harper et al.) ethnographic research, providing clinicians with that "piece of the puzzle" that Bean et al. note is lacking in the discourse. Without that perspective, diagnostic practices validating stereotypes may pollute the "culture of videogaming" when description would better suit.

For example, the WHO relies on clichés that videogames are mere instruments of escapism, but escapism both fails to describe quotidian gameplay (Calleja) and the etiology of problematic gaming. The assumption is that time spent in virtual worlds can be put to better employment in the material world. A Deleuzeian formulation of the virtual would contest this, seeing it not in opposition to the real, but as a process with the elastic potential to actualize (Deleuze 272). Take, for example, the social mechanisms of online videogames. These are not hard-coded into a game's infrastructure, yet the game may incentivize relations. Stories like Mats Steen's, whose life in *World of Warcraft* gave him access to social spaces unencumbered by disability (Schaubert), show the value of emotional connections that are not diminished when produced in virtual settings. Further, the WHO dropped this cliché during the COVID-19 initial outbreak. Raymond Chambers, the WHO's global strategy ambassador, tweeted, "We encourage all to #PlayApartTogether" (March 28, 2020), merely a year after the WHO had declared videogames addictive precisely because they happen in the absence of real-life sociality. Tergiversation like this highlights the classification's socially constructed nature. Apparently, whether videogames are dangerous depends not on what they are but whom the argument suits, and when larger, unexpected issues arise, gaming becomes not so dangerous after all.

The metaphorical collapsing of videogame addiction with other addictions, the underrepresented aesthetic argument for videogames, and the lack of addiction-focused videogaming ethnographic data all overdetermine *Gamelife* as part of a broader movement of players telling their stories—stories confirming, rejecting, or blurring how we think about videogame addiction. As *Gamelife* describes how gaming affected Clune privately and socially, it reaches questions surrounding the gamer's social construction and internal struggles. Ivor Goodson, writing on the need for "theories of context" when exploring life-writing, stresses that life-writing analysis places a text's narratological aspects—what "the story particularizes, details and historicizes"—into the "terrain of the social, into insights into the socially constructed nature of our experiences" (30).

As a memoir, *Gamelife* presents a putatively individualized account of Clune's life in games, but only insofar as any life-writing is divorceable from social and cultural conditions. Life-writing scholarship often deals with stories that produce a decontextualizing effect. It explores elements where the personal gives way—perhaps unintentionally—to social pressures. To underscore this is to identify "the social scripts people employ in telling their life stories" and then to examine how commensurate they are with the text's individuation or "the personal characterizations the life storyteller invokes" (Goodson 31). The videogame addiction debate, itself concerned with societal and linguistic interference in medical discussions, offers an appropriate "theory of context" in which to test *Gamelife*'s divergence from or convergence with stereotyped experiences of playing videogames.

Another benefit of considering *Gamelife* is that it strives to examine the celebrations and contradictions of objects alongside lives. Historically, life-writing has moved from being concerned with how texts construct autonomous subjects within narratives deployed for factual representations to, in contrast, the relationships described in those texts, a turn brought about by feminist critic Marlene Kadar and autobiography luminary Paul Eakin. In this latter approach, the autobiographical "I" is understood as inseparable from others; good life-writing scholarship examines those relationships to access intersubjective identities.

Recently, this significant "other" has been theorized as an object. Anne Rüggemeier suggests this as a helpful blow to the Cartesian model of autonomous selfhood, understanding that objects in autobiographical writing are a "form of resistance against the processes of mind-based epistemology" (36). Similarly, Vera Alexander objectifies relationality, embedding the floaty autobiographical "I" in its transformation "by objects and environments" that expose "the narrated self as a confection which is always partly mediated, invented and imagined." Just as Alexander proposes "factoring two significant non-human others into relationality: books and places" (221–22), I argue for introducing videogames into life-writing's relational inner circle.

Addiction and Passion: Videogames between the Two

Gamelife oscillates. Clune oscillates gameplay between addictive and passionate sensibilities, the videogames he describes oscillate between contemplative and mundane objects, and the reader oscillates between accepting the promise of Clune's authentic childhood experience and acknowledging that autobiographical writing cannot keep this promise. In presenting Clune's specific life in games and what a life in games looks like, *Gamelife* deploys the metaphorical categories of "life" and "game" flexibly. Sometimes videogames bend to events, conversations, and practices; sometimes Clune's life is in the metaphorical employ of videogames. Whether the subject is the videogame or Clune's life, *Gamelife* expresses the compound "gamelife" as totality.

Can this totality be a happy one? Fortunately, the addiction debate comes furnished with definitions for passion and addiction. Using addiction and passion to describe gaming behavior, Jory Deleuze et al. differentiate between addictive and passionate engagements. The distinguishing features are the "autonomous internalization and free will" present in passionately engaged players. By "autonomous internalization," they refer to gaming that builds an integral but healthy part of a subject's sense of self. When gaming is maladaptive, it interferes with day-to-day living, leading to "impulsivity and depressive symptoms . . . [, the use of] gaming to fulfill basic needs, lower game enjoyment, and more negative consequences" (115). These distinctions are a conceptual vantage point from which to analyze *Gamelife*'s representations of highly engaged gaming.

Gamelife begins in a knot of wires, tape, clouds, language:

I wasn't surprised when the computer appeared. I'd seen it coming on TV. Television was pictures on a screen. After television came the words. In the den of our old Victorian house in Evanston, after the VCR tape of *The Parent Trap* was over and my sister Jenny dozed beside me, and my parents were upstairs and hadn't yet noticed the television babble had stopped, I watched the static. I waited for something to emerge. I was seven. . . . After a half hour the static was like a pulverized alphabet. Ten minutes later I saw the first letter. W. . . .

I was ready for the words and the end of television. . . .

The Commodore 64 was a swollen beige keyboard. (3)

Videogames take fourth place in *Gamelife*'s opening media referential race. The "computer" is followed by the "television," and Clune reads the flicker of language in both the W "assembled in a flash from tiny gray and black slats" of the static and in the Commodore 64's programming, in the "ERROR" Clune's fiddling produces below "the pre-words of high clouds" in the skyline (3–4).

Language permeates the metaphorical makeup of all these technologies. Language comes before them as form captured in the primordial static of television and the sun, preparing Clune for "the words at the end of television" that progresses in the computer as an afterlife for language first, not games. It is unsurprising that Clune's first formative videogame, *Suspended* (Infocom), would be an example of the "now-forgotten genre known as 'text-based adventures,'" a genre as heavily indebted to a constellation of language, gameplay, and screen time as Clune's juxtapositions are here. What Mark Hansen wrote of media's vital components—that they do not estrange the medium from users but offer "an environment for life" (Hansen 297)—documents *Gamelife*'s ecology well. *Suspended* completes the metaphor of media as a vector for media DNA, hypostatizing the environs of television, the computer, and language as an afterlife in miniature—a gamelife. *Gamelife*'s initial configuring places the videogame between the archive and the graveyard, between formal menagerie and a mourning for form.

Twice removed from cultural authority as mere entertainment and via formal interactivity that entails a more vocal user, *Suspended*'s primary aesthetic mode is an enabling one. It cultivates a user's autobiographical "I" as an actor in a play. It is a temporary custodian of active self-presence in a way that most literature is not. In this sense, videogames are a less arrogant form than the novel, whose long historical lineage and grand cultural cachet eventually saw its author have to die (Barthes 1967) to broaden readerly appreciation of its polysemy. This quality makes videogames a fascinating avenue for life-writing. *The Sims 3*, for example, is hypothesized by Julie Rak as "a lab . . . to theorize living as a series of scenes with the potential to be connected, rather than a life which must be connected to narrative to be intelligible" (172). Synthesizing this with Alexander's and Rüggemeier's idea of life-writing as a place "to theorize living," the videogame questions a mind-based epistemology by being a place/object for safe experimentation and a relational object, a significant "other" assisting individualization. Rak expresses life-affirming consequences for relationships between players and videogames, a far cry from the pathologizing rhetoric of the WHO and others. Voicing the videogame's especial role in players' lives, however, falls here to life-writing and not to games themselves. *Gamelife* exists, unlike videogames, in a genre most comfortable with its voice.

This comes through in Clune's methodical approach to *Suspended*'s context-dependent language. Clune recounts having to "look in the book," the book being the game's instruction manual, as an event, recognizing it as "the first methodical thing I had done in my life," establishing *Suspended*'s reliance on supplementary materials for its processes (21). To "look in the book" is not to *read* the book. The "look" is barely a moment's rest from solving the game problem presented and Clune's wish to progress in *Suspended*. It is reading borrowed by gaming. Yet Clune's beginning in videogames is also a literary event—if a subordinated one.

Suspended is a text-based adventure game, a genre in which the boundaries between videogames and literature are permeable. The ease with which Clune conjures his videogame's visual sense in *Gamelife* dissipates after the *Suspended* vignette. The input/output process between young Clune and Whiz (20–21), an in-game character, is true to *Suspended*'s form because *Suspended* is essentially textual, not visual. It is gaming borrowed by reading. Thus, Clune's first memorable moment with videogames arrives in a paratactically hierarchized sequence of actions: "look at card, look at keyboard, type word on card on keyboard" (20). Theorizing *Suspended* as media panoply evokes Rak's laboratory, a safe place to puzzle and wonder with words as much as games. Importantly, it uncovers a formative textual quality to Clune's relationality that appears more compatible with educational than with addictive contexts.

If the textual represents what *Suspended* brought to Clune, it falls to visual art, to Goya's *Drowning Dog*, to voice what Clune brings to *Suspended*. As the "vast thickening shapeless yellowy mass" hangs above the imperiled dog, so do *Suspended*'s problems hang over Clune's imaginative faculties. For Clune, the dog depicts "the basic animal experience of wonder" that could go beyond wonder and toward understanding, perk out of its isolation and comprehend the black mass not as a submerging wave but as a verge (Clune 21). Clune thus encourages an understanding of playing games as a reciprocal percolation of subject and object. Just as much as Clune remembers *Suspended*, Clune remembers himself *playing Suspended*, appreciating not just the aesthetic object but also the individualized relational aspect of that aesthetic event.

By modeling his engagement as educational and intermedial, Clune suggests that the idea of videogame addiction reductively resolves the videogame's fundamental contingency. Reviewers knew this about *Suspended*, which received praise as "another milestone in the continuing evolution of the interactive computer novel" (Bang 42), thus exposing how its reception as videogame was predicated on its novelistic qualities. Textuality is sine qua non to *Suspended*, and not merely in textuality's mundane ubiquity—the textuality of *Suspended*'s gameplay, like hands under cloth, is a specifically *literary* textuality granted by its novelistic qualities, not by a theory. Thus, to say that Clune's first experience with an "interactive computer novel" would cause an addiction to videogames is to lose the "novel" in the "interactive computer."

Paradoxically, the first images of Clune's gaming experience suggests that the experience could have been otherwise. This contingency of form discloses the object of inquiry's slipperiness: Clune's account hesitates to impose formal necessity upon *Suspended* even in retrospect. As it is reasonable to define *Suspended* as an "interactive computer novel," then Clune's obsession could instead have sparked an addiction to reading, not gaming—but the cultural bias toward videogames resolves it as a videogame: addictive where novels are not. Clune brings into relief the addiction classification's hypocrisy by tracing the contingent nature of videogaming's addictive attributes. If Clune were addicted to *Suspended*, then the novel that *Suspended* is not, but could have been, must share the blame for drawing Clune in.

Clune describes playing *Suspended* with the language of discovery and growth, preferring to draw upon humanistic metaphors associated with literary education. In contrast to the discourse of addiction, *Gamelife* imagines whether an art form resembling the novel can truthfully be described as addictive but also suggests that form can provide what Kenneth Burke called "equipment for living, as a ritualistic way of arming us to confront perplexities and risks"

(60). By placing videogames within this educational "equipment for living" set, Clune destabilizes its demarcation as an addictive object. Addiction strips life of its armor in the guise of producing it. In contrast, the complex media negotiations *Gamelife* performs as it moves from television's static to prewords to books to Goya represents videogaming as a multiliteracy.

Yet there is something inevitable, almost procedural, about Clune's play. His inputs, "a wheel made out of simple repetitive movements," are mechanical yet primordial, and its repetitive force "wears through the rock of the world like a river" (22). Obsessive passion expresses itself in this inevitability via a paratactic style of description, a heavily extended object–subject dialogue, and metaphors of self-dehumanization, all of which combine into a fragmented autobiographical self. But it is not an incoherent one. Clune's account is clearly revisionist. The job of putting Goya's dog into the mouth of his childhood symbolizes one of life-writing's essential aporias—the silent, introspective work done between acts and the writing about them.

I pause here to place this analysis in the pathological context constructed so far. Perhaps the most obvious debate points touched by *Gamelife* have been the educational and aesthetic potential for videogames. Clune's interactions with *Suspended* developed appreciable attributes; his determination to explore and his obsessive attention to details presents the "off-the-shelf" educational contexts that videogames can create. Clune's imagining of *Suspended* rails against the pathological definition of videogames as an object that (recalling the language of the *International Classification of Diseases*) "appreciably increase[s] the risk of harmful physical or mental health consequences." The addiction construct, in failing to differentiate between videogames and their varied risk-and-reward loops, implicates an entire medium in this disorder, which strains credulity.

The point is this: if a standard of taste applies to videogames as it does across the arts, then the highly engaged consumption of videogames does not mean it is an addictive consumption. Therefore, Clune's "addiction," if accepted as that for argument's sake, is as much an aesthetic problem as it is a behavioral problem, and it concerns the specific videogames comprising his gameplay, not videogames writ large. What Clune insists upon is a differentiation between videogames producing highly engaged harmonious passions and ones that produce obsessive passions. Clune's account of playing *Suspended*, inhabiting as it does a space between addiction and passion, exposes that a deterministic approach to videogame addiction leaves the effect of playing specific videogames unduly resolved, missing the point that some games are more capable of fostering addiction than others—and that others may foster something else.

Escapism and Critical Immersion in *Gamelife: A Memoir*

I now turn to a more positive approach to highly engaged videogaming. During the first two years of the COVID-19 outbreak, videogaming became an important aspect of self-care for many people. This provided more opportunities for extended and highly engaged gameplay, as social isolation freed up more time for at-home leisure while also necessitating strategies to maintain mental health and social connections—and, of course, creating more opportunities for maladaptive gaming. A moment like this suggests that gaming's effect on life has yet to be understood.

This section explores the role of videogaming in the context of social isolation and how Clune deploys videogaming to safely negotiate trauma through productive escapism. Further, in contrast to the assumption of pathologists, Clune suggests that videogames may well be the least fruitful medium of all to sate an escapist urge. If escapism attempts to deploy a medium to escape real-world problems, then using the medium that organizes the systems producing those real-world problems—a process Daniel Muriel and Garry Crawford and term "videoludification" (16)—would logically be a jump from the frying pan into the fire. When all worldly processes are aflame with videogaming's logic, when gamification, for example, becomes a new means for reinventing old-fashioned modes of surveillance and social reward/punishment (see Bowman and Condis), then the inverse can be argued. Videogaming, rather than facilitating escape from reality, allows players to investigate those processes that construct their real-life problems.

This form of obsessive investigation might be called "critical immersion." "Critical" is used here in the sense described in Gilbert Weiss's and Ruth Wodak chapter "Theory, Interdisciplinarity and Critical Discourse Analysis": "making visible the interconnectedness of things" (14). Something is "critical" if that activity creates knowledge about relations or creates these relations outright in a demystified process. "Immersion" is a more familiar term to game and media research, so much so that Alison McMahan decries it as "an excessively vague, all-inclusive concept" (67). Janet Murray's definition, however, is cogent for my purposes. Murray defines immersion as "the sensation of being surrounded by a completely other reality, as different as water is from air, that takes over all of our attention, our whole perceptual apparatus . . . in a participatory medium. . . . Immersion implies learning to swim, to do the things that the new environment makes possible" (98–99). Similarities exist between this kind of immersion and escapism; however, the "sensation of being surrounded by a completely other reality" defines immersion's full phenomenal range, whereas it is merely a tendency of escapism, a difference between the act of immersion and the wish to escape through immersion.

When Murray's immersed subject swims, they "do the things that the new environment makes possible," but because they are surrounded by another reality, they leave the swimming pool dry (to extend the metaphor), not necessarily retaining the experience or the new skills they had acquired. To further extend the swimming metaphor, when you swim, you become a better swimmer, but you also become fitter, you become better at moving on dry land, you have gained that "equipment for living" that Burke saw in literature, but in this case through a different kind of immersive experience. Therefore, I shall take Weiss and Wodak's definition and append it to Murray's immersion, defining critical immersion as the sensation of being surrounded by a completely other reality that highlights or creates a new sense of the interconnectedness of things.

Critical immersion challenges escapism's bifurcation of the real and the virtual by suggesting a "completely other reality" that encourages users to see the interconnectedness of these states of being. Unlike escapism, critical immersion retains the new knowledge about the interconnectedness of the virtual and the real, of simulated and nonsimulated space, of workplace structures and games, and sees it as valuable, at its most optimal as part of the cultural experience of twenty-first-century citizens. It also makes more sense when it is deployed alongside existing concepts. Where escapism and videoludification conceptually fork each other, with escapism deploying the very form it wishes to escape, critical immersion is more obliging. The critically immersive work does not express the real but exposes reality's contradictions—deprivileging the claim to primacy that escapism ascribes to reality.

Gamelife highlights critical immersion and its absence. Chapter 4, "World War II Has Never Ended," chronicles Clune's doctoral studies and his time playing *Beyond Castle Wolfenstein* (Muse Software 1984) and, later, *Call of Duty* (Infinity Ward 2003). By this point, Clune has been exposed to enough fear surrounding videogames to deter him from playing. The belief, instilled in him by "professors and so-called friends," that playing games withholds from him his dissertation, nice clothes, and vacations, planted "an irrational fear of computer games in [Clune's] head" (107–8). Clune's irrational fear of videogames signposts how the malignancy of social demonization—the fear that it can mystify the offending object and its potential benefits to the user—can muddle a writer's efforts to make sense of their life.

Affected by this mystification, Clune's former critical insights give way to prose frozen by insecurity and roundaboutness:

> The computer games know about history because they know about fun. And the only reason to have history anymore is for fun. The world doesn't need it. The world has capitalism now, it doesn't need history. . . . Now we have the global market. There's no one for us all to be against, there's no reason for us to think of ourselves as part of an invincible whole moving irresistibly forward against our enemies. History doesn't make sense. The objective necessity of history is over. History has stopped. And we can find out exactly when it stopped. Because when the fun experts want to make a game that is totally fun, they discover that the closest time period they can set it in is World War II. (115)

Clune describes his desire to play these wargames so he can be a part of history's "invincible whole moving irresistibly forward against our enemies"—but it's a fantasy plagued by Westerncentric nostalgia that mystifies World War II's material consequences. His desire to learn and grow falls prey to escapism. Clune longs to immerse himself in history to efface—not confront—his troubled present. His nostalgic recounting of his longing for games to return him to a simpler, heroic past reveals nostalgia's truth: that it is as much a forgetting as a remembering. He cannot rethink history or games convincingly because his play is escapist instead of critically immersive—and perhaps evidences addiction.

Just as the worst satire tends to affirm the ideologies it aims to mock, Clune's rant about history and capitalism, as lighthearted and irreverent as it may have been intended, is undercut by his antisocial isolationism. Moreover, this is learned behavior. His uncritical escapist play can be linked to social conditioning as much as to videogames. An examination of Clune's prose when he is recounting his critical immersion in *Suspended* shows a youth brimming with direct access to videogaming's insights, but his description of his obsessive play of *Call of Duty* is mired in the stigma-focused discourse of addiction. It weighs too heavily for him to swim in the experience, and so he drowns. It is as though the equipment for living games can provide has been somewhere destabilized and Clune, striving yet failing to demystify his experience, layers fog upon it instead.

Clune appears to be aware of his failure. The hedging apology following this passage—"Okay, okay, but still" (115)—smacks of the deterministic nihilism that falls at a certain kind of postmodern fiction's feet, where ironic self-awareness functions as a proleptic prophylactic to criticism, another deflective tactic in which the object of inquiry is better served by directness. Clune's prose manifests the reality-avoidant tendencies that concern the WHO. Julie Rak's notion that videogames can be a laboratory for telling and retelling stories becomes, in this moment of Clune's memoir, a kind of alchemist's lab that produces only fool's gold—and the most tendentious kinds of stories about gaming.

I insist, then, on warning against dogmatic understandings of videogame play. The understanding of videogame addiction found in the WHO's clinical materials is alive in some of Clune's passages. However, Clune's metaphorical misstep is clearly the result of social pressures, pressures the WHO occludes. Disentangling the two is essential. Yes, Clune's writing suggests that one can be a healthy, passionate gamer, but that kind of gaming can become maladaptive in times of social difficulty, and social stigmas can warp the perception of self and of the self at play.

Marking the Difference

How can we reliably mark the difference between escapism and critical immersion? That's precisely where stories about videogames reveal their value. When correctly deployed, the idea of critical immersion reveals the internal workings of perspectives and difficult-to-articulate affective experiences. When Clune revisits his youth and his youthful gaming, his game life lattice becomes more densely intertwined as he recognizes and negotiates anew the trauma of his parents' divorce. For instance, Clune invites us to "imagine a cup fashioned to resemble the brick-squashed head of Super Mario, with his ears for handles. Now imagine the cup filled with the black milk of my parents' silence" (125). The grotesque countenance staring out of the cup is the metaphorical collusion of two spaces the young Clune cannot formulate.

Representing his mother as a horrifying, abject barrier to his play, Clune reveals the source of his anxieties about escapism: his mother views *Super*

Mario Bros. (Nintendo 1985) as "enough *escapism* for you. All this *escapism* . . . Sometimes I think you kids are living in a fantasy world" (126). The emphasis placed on escapism suggests that it is empathically felt or, in autobiographical retrospect, deduced. Either way, it betrays its heteroglossic appetite, registering as a socially determined implant into private spheres but also borrowing from an intergenerational misunderstanding about play. Escapism here demarcates the traumatic miscommunication between Clune and his mother; as a child, he could scarcely understand, but certainly felt, what causes adults to label his fun as "escapism."

This traumatic miscommunication makes Clune's account of playing *Elite*, written and developed by David Braben and Ian Bell, theoretically valuable. It highlights how a critically immersive experience can undermine traumatic social isolations by making visible the interconnectedness of things—the very opposite of isolation. Enabled by a critical distance from his fractious homelife—the opposite of critical immersion—Clune's language shifts toward the exploratory and scientific, where "*Elite* brings the fundamental truth of science down on life." To explore this "truth," Clune imagines distance between him and home: "*Elite* turned our giant sun into a distant star," and his local concerns miniaturize against his expanding cosmological point of view. This shift in perspective, what Clune calls "a trick of the eyes," is trained into him by his space-explorative play within *Elite*'s celestial sandbox, but also by a childlike act of metaphor, imposing the elements of his private life upon them. The sun—understood by the older Clune as one star among many—is the sun that "lit [Clune's] mother's fantasy-reality, the sun of July 1988" (132). Thus, what may appear like escapism (imagining one's mother as the sun) becomes critical—*Elite* offers Clune access to an objectified present in which he can explore at arm's length "the sun of July 1988" that gave up the secret of his mother's "fantasy-reality," and the power that he discovered through play.

Rak's concept of videogames as a place to experiment in a nonnarrative but autobiographical tense speaks to Clune's critically immersed recollection—and the specifically literary techniques that enable this recollection. That videogames confront players with their mortality is almost a truism, yet Clune explores more mundane finality. Driven by a notorious learning curve, Clune "spent 90 percent of [his] time in *Elite* seeing through [his] own death," highlighting that his play, largely, was observing the secession of play (139). The syntax Clune deploys when describing these moments when the game is ended—

"To live and die like that . . . Listen!," and "To live and die in a world without surfaces . . ." (134–35)—evokes the impressionistic awe of a young mind grappling with systematic thought, as with *Suspended.* Here, the multiple ellipses function as both dreamy drift and signal the collapsing of introspective time.

The final shift blends *Elite*'s lessons with his familial relationships. The familiarity of "the feeling of being about to die on a fundamentally absent surface" is interwoven with an image of reconciliation with his mother, when reflective thinking manifests in the mirrorlike "absent surface" provided by *Elite.* Just as the "wetness" of Clune's immersion left him better equipped to cope with the trauma under the July 1988 sun, in conflating that essential lack at play within *Elite* with "recogniz[ing] [his] mother's face in a crowd" (Clune 139) as the interconnectedness of things (insomuch as his mother and his gameplay here become meaningful to Clune through his ability to find value in their fundamental absence), he is able to extend the lessons learned from *Elite*'s gameplay and by doing so recover his relationship to his mother by making tentative progress with the trauma his mother represents.

In this essay, I've reframed videogame addiction through two arguments. First, I've argued that the WHO's classifying gesture is reductive, particularly its failure to understand the contexts of play. *Gamelife* highlights the contingencies of videogames and gameplay in a way that reveals the complexity of obsessive or impassioned play. Second, one of the key symptoms identified by those who would pathologize videogame play—escapism—is an overencumbered descriptor of videogaming's immersive experience. In contrast, I have offered the notion of critical immersion, sidestepping escapism's negative connotations and generating an understanding of passionate videogaming immersion that is free of escapism's social demerits without excluding its possibility or its negative effects. *Gamelife,* as an act of sustained, indeed immersive life-writing, takes videogaming as its object of inquiry, offering prose that oscillates between critical and uncritical immersion, with critical immersion producing more useful insights than the uncritical. Where Clune's efforts are most successful are in his representation of videogames as a potent relational object emulating the "equipment for living" Burke ascribes to literature. Finally, I would argue that *Gamelife* is an exemplary text in the ongoing literary experiment with videogames, highlighting the potential of storytelling, particularly storytelling that focuses on the lived experience of play, to frame videogames as relational objects.

WORKS CITED

Alexander, Vera. "The Relational Imaginary of M. G. Vassanji's *A Place Within.*" *Life Writing,* vol. 13, no. 2, 2016, pp. 221–36.

Bang, Derrick. Review of *Suspended,* by Michael Berlyn. *Softline,* vol. 2, May/June 1983. https://www.cgwmuseum.org/galleries/issues/softline_2.5.pdf.

Barthes, Roland. "The Death of the Author." *Image, Music, Text,* translated by Stephen Heath. Fontana Press, 1977.

Bean, Anthony M., Antonius J. van Rooij, Rune K. L. Nielsen, and Christopher J. Ferguson. "Videogame Addiction: The Push to Pathologize Videogames." *Professional Psychology,* vol. 48, 2017, pp. 378–89.

Beyond Castle Wolfenstein. Muse Software, 1984.

Bissell, Tom. *Extra Lives: Why Video Games Matter.* Pantheon Books, 2010.

Bowman, Nicholas David, and Megan Condis. "Governmentality, Playbor, and Peak Performance: Critiques and Concerns of Health and Wellness Gamification." *Privacy Concerns Surrounding Personal Information Sharing on Health and Fitness Mobile Apps,* edited by Devjani Sen and Rukhsana Ahmed. IGI Global, 2020, pp. 186–210.

Braben, David, and Ian Bell. *Elite.* Acornsoft, 1984.

Burke, Kenneth. *Philosophy of Literary Form: Studies in Symbolic Action.* University of California Press, 1974.

Call of Duty. Activision, 2003.

Calleja, Gordon. "Digital Games and Escapism." *Games and Culture,* vol, 5, 2010, pp. 335–53.

Carras, Michelle, Antonius Van Rooij, Donna Spruijt-Metz, Joseph Kvedar, Mark Griffiths, Yorghos Carabas, and Alain Labrique. "Commercial Videogames as Therapy: A New Research Agenda to Unlock the Potential of a Global Pastime." *Frontiers in Psychiatry,* vol. 8, 2018, pp. 1–7.

Clune, Michael W. *Gamelife: A Memoir.* Farrar, Straus and Giroux, 2015.

Deleuze, Gilles. *Difference and Repetition,* translated by Paul Patton. Bloomsbury, 2014.

Deleuze, Jory, Jiang Long, Tie-Qiao Liu, Pierre Maurage, and Joël Billiux. "Passion or Addiction? Correlates of Healthy Versus Problematic Use of Videogames in a Sample of French-Speaking Regular Players." *Addictive Behaviors,* vol. 82, 2018, pp. 114–21.

Eakin, Paul John. *How Our Lives Become Stories: Making Selves.* Cornell University Press, 1999.

Goodson, Ivor F. *Developing Narrative Theory.* Routledge, 2013.

Gray, Kishonna, Gerald Voorhees, and Emma Vossen. *Feminism in Play.* Palgrave, 2018.

Griffiths, Mark, et al. "Working Towards an International Consensus on Criteria for Assessing Internet Gaming Disorder: A Critical Commentary on Petry et al." *Addiction,* vol. 111, 2015, pp. 167–75.

Hansen, Mark B. N. "Media Theory." *Theory, Culture & Society*, vol. 23, 2006, pp. 297–306.

Harper, Todd, Meghan Blythe Adams, and Nicholas Taylor. *Queerness in Play*. 1st ed., Palgrave Macmillan, 2018.

International Classification of Diseases for Mortality and Morbidity Statistics. 11th revision, World Health Organization, 2018.

Jenson, Jennifer, and Suzanne de Castell. "Girls@Play: An Ethnographic Study of Gender and Digital Gameplay." *Feminist Media Studies*, vol. 2, 2011, pp. 167–79.

Kadar, Marlene. *Essays on Life Writing: From Genre to Critical Practice*. University of Toronto Press, 1992.

Kuo, Lily. "China Bans Children from Late-Night Gaming to Combat Addiction." *Guardian*, 7 November 2019. https://www.theguardian.com/world/2019/nov/07/china-bans -children-from-late-night-gaming-to-combat-addiction.

McMahan, Alison. "Immersion, Engagement, and Presence: A Method for Analyzing 3-D Video Games." *The Video Game Theory Reader*, edited by Mark Wolf and Bernard Perron. Routledge, 2003, pp. 67–86.

Molde, Helge, Bjørn Holmøy, Aleksander Garvik Merkesdal, Torbjørn Torsheim, Rune Aune Mentzoni, Daniel Hanns, Dominic Sagoe, and Ståle Pallesen. "Are Video Games a Gateway to Gambling? A Longitudinal Study Based on a Representative Norwegian Sample." *Journal of Gambling Studies*, vol. 35, 2019, pp. 545–57.

Muriel, Daniel, and Garry Crawford. *Video Games as Culture: Considering the Role and Importance of Video Games in Contemporary Society*. Routledge, 2018.

Murray, Janet H. *Hamlet on the Holodeck: The Future of Narrative in Cyberspace*. MIT Press, 1997.

Penix-Tadsen, Phillip. *Cultural Code: Video Games and Latin America*. MIT Press, 2016.

Petry, Nancy M., et al. "An International Consensus for Assessing Internet Gaming Disorder Using the New DSM-5 Approach." *Addiction*, vol. 109, 2014, pp. 1399–1406.

Quinn, Zoë. *Crash Override: How Gamergate (Nearly) Destroyed My Life, and How We Can Win the Fight Against Online Hate*. PublicAffairs, 2017.

Rak, Julie. "Life Writing Versus Automedia: The Sims 3 Game as a Life Lab." *Biography*, vol. 38, no. 2, 2015, pp. 155–80.

Rüggemeier, Anne. "Beyond the Subject—Towards the Object? Nancy K. Miller's *What They Saved: Pieces of a Jewish Past* (2011) and the Materiality of Life Writing." *European Journal of Life Writing*, vol. 5, 2016, pp. 36–54.

Schaubert, Vicky. "My Disabled Son's Amazing Gaming Life in the World of Warcraft." *BBC News*, 7 February 2019. https://www.bbc.co.uk/news/disability-47064773.

Snodgrass, Jeffrey G., H. J. Francois Dengah II, Michael G. Lacy, Andrew Bagwell, Max Van Oostenburg, and Daniel Lende. "Online Gaming Involvement and its Positive and Negative Consequences." *Computers in Human Behavior*, vol. 66, 2017, pp. 291–302.

Super Mario Bros. Nintendo, 1985.

Suspended. Infocom, 1983.

Van Rooij, Antonius, et al. "A Weak Scientific Basis for Gaming Disorder: Let Us Err on the Side of Caution." *Journal of Behavioural Addictions,* vol. 7, 2018, pp. 1–9.

Weiss, Gilbert, and Ruth Wodak, eds. "Introduction: Theory, Interdisciplinarity and Critical Discourse Analysis." *Critical Discourse Analysis: Theory and Interdisciplinarity.* Palgrave Macmillan, 2003, pp. 1–35.

Zendle, David. "Beyond Loot Boxes: A Variety of Gambling-Like Practices in Video Games Are Linked to Both Problem Gambling and Disordered Gaming." *PeerJ,* vol. 8, 2020, pp. 1–26.

Zialcita, Paolo. "China Introduces Restrictions on Videogames for Minors." NPR, 6 November 2019. https://www.npr.org/2019/11/06/776840260/china-introduces-restrictions-on-video-games-for-minors.

Reading Fans Reading

The Beginner's Guide to Fan Theories and Videogame Interpretations

CRAIG CAREY

If videogames are played, theories and interpretations of videogames are read and written, which makes them a fruitful site for exploring the stories we create about, with, and around videogames. Writing across blogs, wikis, discussion forums, video essays, and other media platforms, players and fans participate in a metagame in which they puzzle out enigmas, plot hidden connections, build elaborate stories, and participate in the literary movements of videogame criticism. This essay offers a beginner's guide to understanding fan criticism as a multimedia genre of videogame literature that unsettles conventional ideas about reading, writing, authorship, interpretation, and the dialectical relationship between creators and fans. Videogame theories not only transform the literary into the ludic, and vice versa, but surround videogames with an open and neobaroque aesthetic that blurs the line between interpretative performance and popular entertainment.

Take Playdead's critically acclaimed *Inside* (2016). Artfully designed around an enigmatic story, minimalist aesthetics, and a complete lack of dialogue or narration, upon release the game was swarmed by a huddle of online theories. Like its 2010 predecessor, *Limbo,* the game seems to anticipate fan theories through its narrative design. In the final set piece, for example, the player watches as the unnamed boy, whom they have controlled the entire game, is sucked inside a giant blob of flesh plugged into computers. Inside the fleshy meatball—the Huddle, as fans call it—the player then assumes control of the blob as it breaks free from the lab, smashes through concrete walls, and rolls to a stop on a grassy coastline bathed in sunlight. As the credits roll, players are left wondering what it all means.

Fans searching for meaning found themselves confronted—both inside the game's fiction and outside, in the metagame of fandom—by a phenomenon that eludes easy classification. Indeed, the grotesque image of the Huddle offers a good metaphor for the swarm of players that surrounded *Inside* with theories, speculations, and interpretations. One popular theory framed it as a metagame about Playdead's control of the player, the boy an allegory of players plugged into their machines, blindly executing the Huddle's programming. Readings of this sort accumulated into a messy meatball of speculation in which parts tangled into composites, theories accumulated into plots, and threads multiplied into a chorus of intertextual commentary. How do we begin to read something so tangled in form, so messy and variegated in its content?

We might begin by reading fan theories as a form of "collective intelligence," a term coined by Pierre Lévy and utilized by Henry Jenkins to describe the collective agency and knowledge of fans: "Each of us knows something; and we can put the pieces together if we pool our resources and combine our skills" (*Convergence Culture* 4). However, as James Newman writes, not "all online or offline communication generates the kinds of collective meanings and collaborative authorship celebrated by Jenkins, Lévy or [James Paul] Gee"; it can also lead to conformity, contradiction, competition, and chaos (42).

Multiple methods have been used to study how fans create meaning, share stories, and navigate popular culture through poaching, play, and adaptation. But what about *videogame* fandom? Scholars are just starting to attend to how videogames transform acts of interpretation through metagaming practices. With videogame fandom, and especially videogame fan criticism, we have to climb inside the huddle and investigate the phenomenon as it changes and develops. We can then begin to document and understand how, as Lévy writes, "distinctions between authors and readers, producers and spectators, creators and interpretations will blend to form a reading–writing continuum" with its own aesthetic (qtd. in Jenkins, *Fans* 144). Indeed, videogame fan theories offer a unique literary and ludic reflection of the open, labyrinthine, and serial poetics that Angela Ndalianis finds in other neobaroque media and entertainment.

This essay examines fan criticism as a popular genre of videogame literature and argues that the rise of the independent game market marks a significant moment in the history and development of that genre. Self-reflexive games like *Inside* and Davey Wreden's *The Beginner's Guide* (2015) exemplify a growing trend in which videogame narratives are self-consciously designed to generate ambiguity and the production of bespoke videogame criticism, which I define here as a tangled corpus of theories, interpretations, and think pieces. Drawing on Umberto Eco's theory of the open work, I argue that such games are not just open to interpretation but also self-reflexively integrate interpretive play into "a positive aspect of [their] production," recasting their narrative design to engage players as co-participants in "the open work" of interpretation, configuration, and performance (Eco 5). By articulating "a fresh dialectics between the work of art and its performer," Eco's theory provides a useful lens to analyze these games and the performative role of fan writing in the production of meaning (3). Fan theories and interpretations about indie games register a turn in the direction, purpose, and practice of videogame criticism, providing a means to analyze the changing role of reading, writing, and interpretation in the historical evolution of videogames, videogame fandom, and videogame literature.

Reading Fan Theories

While traffic between game studies and fan studies has increased in the past decade, work on videogame fan theories is basically nonexistent. Henry Jenkins's "Fan Critics," in *Textual Poachers* (1992), was written decades before the rise of videogame fandom, though it does establish the idea that "organized fandom is, perhaps first and foremost, an institution of theory and criticism," and that practices of reading and interpretation underlie genres of fan writing, broadly speaking (88). Matt Hills's notion of "scholar-fans" and "fan-scholars" is also useful to describe fans who engage in intellectual practices outside university walls (xvii). For Hills and Jenkins, fans engage in knowledge production, acquire cultural capital, and comprise interpretive communities—activities that carry over to videogame fandom, but only in the most general terms.

Fan criticism is also scarce in the field of game studies, despite the growing body of work on games as cocreated experiences in which players produce fan-authored genres and assets such as walkthroughs (Consalvo, "Zelda 64"; see also Blázquez; Brooks; Lovins in this volume), fan fiction (Dym et al.; see also Shea in this volume), live streaming (Taylor), and speedrunning (Newman). If mentioned at all, fan theories are typically folded into broader concerns about paratext (Consalvo, *Cheating*), the sociality of gaming (Jones), participatory culture (Newman), or metagaming (Boluk and LeMieux). While these expand the locus of videogames to include what Newman describes as "the myriad ways in which [players] make use of [videogames] besides just playing them—playing *with* them" (vii), none of them focus their attention on fan theories or fan criticism.

The one exception is the recent anthology *Fans and Videogames: Histories, Fandom, Archives*, described as the first book to offer "a historical and critical study of the nature of, and activities around, fandom in game culture." In their introduction, Melanie Swalwell, Helen Stuckey, and Angela Ndalianis argue that game studies and fan studies have failed to address what they call "the videogame fandom phenomenon." They make a strong case for "recogniz[ing] the impact and centrality of videogame fan communities—as a collective intelligence, as a pool of individual creators of games and as interested and engaged parties in the collecting and remembering of game history." With a focus on "particular games, systems, and companies of the 1980s and 1990s," their book draws overdue attention to "fans' documentation of games and game history itself," including "the extent to which videogame fans might differ from other fan communities" (1, 3).

However, compared with archives, systems, and platforms, fan theories are less conspicuous about how they document alternative histories and practices of fandom. With their focus on reading, writing, and interpretation, fan theories nevertheless play an equally critical role in "preserving portraits of the game as a designed experience" (Navarro-Remesal 130), often by drawing attention to how a game's meaning is played out beyond games in "meta" acts of reading, writing, plotting, discovery, and sense making. As a composite of literary skills such as close reading, narrative analysis, fictional world building, and paratextual research, fan theories provide players with a literary *method* for finding meaning in games, a literary *platform* for shaping how games are read and received, and a literary *genre* for participating in the open work of game criticism.

To be clear, I am talking mostly about theories of individual games—meaning interpretation or explanation—rather than theories that posit hidden connections across games, franchises, or fictional universes. The fan theories that interest me include sophisticated forms of textual analysis, description, explanation, storytelling, and other critical-theoretical techniques. Literary forms of "theorycraft" (Paul) have grown with the rise of indie games that cultivate interpretation through ambiguity, symbolism, allegory, metaphor, irony, narrative gaps, and other techniques "designed to serve as the basis for interpretive play," or what Brian Upton calls "interpretive play space" (267, 178). Popular indie titles like *Braid* (2008), *Limbo* (2010), *Journey* (2012), *The Stanley Parable* (2013), *The Beginner's Guide* (2015), *Inside* (2016), *RiME* (2017), *Gorogoa* (2017), and *Gris* (2018), to name a few, have consciously signaled their indie "authenticity," as Jesper Juul argues, by creating "room for interpretation and for think pieces" about their meaning (26).

These games have played a significant role in the development of a more sophisticated and literary-minded form of game criticism. Juul argues that "independent games are an attempt to create a new kind of videogame, not only through design, but also through criticism: to find a new language for talking about games, to create institutions that will honor independent games, and to thereby decide what independent games are in the first place" (25). This critical discourse circulates in awards and festivals, interviews and artists' blogs, and game reviews and game developer conference talks, all of which Juul incorporates into his archival history of indie games. However, Juul does not consider fan writings and critical testimonies, which is surprising, given how many games highlighted by Juul (*Braid*, for example) inspired fans to participate in the metagame of criticism. Fan intimacy with a game often finds expression through detailed close readings as players interpret, research, and honor a game by participating in the critical discourse around it.

So where are these other archives? With Playdead's *Inside*, we might begin with the comments and threads posted on sites like Reddit, Steam, and IGN boards, where theories were initially hashed out in what Newman calls the "participative communication" of fans fueled by "dialogue, discussion, and argument" (42). Here we find the serial work of players puzzling out events, decoding ciphers, and digging up raw material for speculation. Details are cited and circulated, drawn into composite stories about mermaids, pigs, worms, catastrophic floods, secret military bases, nuclear fallout, animal experimentation, and more. Comments subsequently merge into threads, threads into theories, and cooked raw material congeals into a huddle of reference points, allusions, and occasionally wild if entertaining speculations. Within weeks, the critical mass is transformed into more carefully crafted theories appearing on blogs, journals, and video essays on YouTube. Words like "theory," "meaning," and "explanation" appear as a trope to lure fans searching for answers and closure: "*Inside*: The Story & Meaning Explained," "*Inside*: Story Explanation & Analysis," "The *Inside* Theory to End all Theories," "The Meanings and Endings of *Inside*," and so on. From here, the huddle keeps growing, moving to sites like *Kotaku, IGN, Eurogamer, Polygon,* and *Fandom,* where speculation is compiled and curated.

In Patrick Klepek's "The Wild Theories Behind *Inside*'s Secret Ending," for example, or the IGN wiki guide on *Inside*, editors and contributors reframed the game as a reflection on different themes. While poaching and promoting fan theories, mainstream game journalists sealed the metagame with authority, legitimacy, and market promotion. The meaning of *Inside* was thus diffused into a labyrinth of stories, theories, commentary, and speculation. Those searching online for meaning instead found the baroque reflection of themselves and other fans.

Any honest look at fan criticism must contend with Ndalianis's argument about the neobaroque aesthetic of popular entertainment, where open forms of spectacle, seriality, and reflexivity transgress "the limits of the frame" and veer toward the dialectical movement of Eco's open work (25). In her chapter on intertextuality, Ndalianis describes how "meaning" is produced by the seduction of allusions, citations, references, and other paradigmatic relations. Fan theories are no different. "The Sleeping Realm Theory," for example, outlines an elaborate theory about *Kingdom Hearts III* in a 487-page Google document. Coauthored by three fans, the hyperlinked document includes multiple references, allusions, Easter eggs, and intertextual connections, sacrificing linear structure for an open and encyclopedic form. Theory and document are inseparable, wrapped into a form that consists of stories within stories, broken-down timelines, and discrete section breaks, all following the serial logic of contemporary entertainment, "weaving the audience seductively into a series of neo-baroque, labyrinthine passageways that demand that audience members, through interpretation, make order out of chaos" (Ndalianis 27).

In this way, fan theories provide evidence of how players configure videogames into what Eco describes as "open works" that consist of "physically incomplete structural units" designed to be played, interpreted, and reconfigured by a performer (12). While all games are open to interpretation as texts (Fernández-Vara 5), not all games incorporate openness as a formal design strategy, what Eco calls a "a positive aspect of [their] production" (5). Eco distinguishes the "open work" with phrases such as "unfinished" and "work in movement" (12), citing as an example the modular musical pieces by German composer Karlheinz Stockhausen, in which a series of notes is presented to the performer to play in any order they choose. He also turns to modernist literary works like James Joyce's *Finnegans Wake*, whose interpretative play also stems from an aesthetic of serial configuration and composition.

Ultimately, what distinguishes the open work is "the considerable autonomy left to the individual performer in the way he chooses to play the work," distinguishing the "open work" from classical compositions where the assemblage of units is arranged in "a closed, well-defined manner." Open works are "quite literally 'unfinished,'" Eco writes; they exist "more or less like the components of a construction kit" (1–2, 4). It is precisely this structural openness that distinguishes fan theories as open works. Fan theories create new interpretations and performances that set into motion "a new cycle of relations between the artist and [their] audience" and "a new mechanics of aesthetic perception" (22–23). Interfacing games and literature, fan theories document how players and readers transform videogames into literary works whose fictional elements can be played, read, and performed in different ways.

This open movement is frequently contradicted by fans' desire for mastery: a hunt for the ultimate Easter egg or a master plot that unlocks meaning and satisfies the desire for narrative closure. Herein lies the allure of theory and of less academic forms of speculation: conspiracy theories, secret plots, hidden meanings. Theories both fuel and foreclose openness. While generative and intertextual, they can transform the open work into a master plot. Fan theories play the game of interpretation but within circumscribed rules. They poach, combine, and remix material, but they also reconfigure narratives into puzzles and games to be solved.

Fan critics thus are not just agents who actively read, write, traverse, and poach culture; they also seek to master texts through paratextual plotting. "The Sleeping Realm Theory" is not just a neobaroque omelet of intertextual poaching (if I may mix my metaphors); it is also a master theory in which poached eggs are translated into Easter eggs that seduce with the promise of answers, solutions, and meaning. In this respect, fan theories exemplify the duality at the heart of Peter Brooks's *Reading for the Plot: Design and Intention in Narrative* (1992), in which he describes the dynamic process of "plot and plotting" around two competing desires: a metonymic desire for play and movement, and a metaphoric desire for meaning and closure (61). With fan theories, these desires diverge and converge across two axes of reading: one that multiplies the free play of intertextuality, another bound to the formal rules of games and narratives. Both of these movements charge the literature of fan theories with their ambiguity. They provide fan theories with their unique literary and ludic character, marking them as a hybrid metagame in which games and literature converge in the neobaroque folds of reading, writing, and interpretation.

Reading *The Beginner's Guide*

Few indie games invite and deconstruct interpretation more than Davey Wreden's *The Beginner's Guide.* More of a "ludographic essay" than a conventional videogame (Fassone 2018), *The Beginner's Guide* seduces the player into an interpretative trap that invites them to reflect on the relationship of creators, fans, and critics; the challenges and fallacies of videogame interpretation; and the thin line between finding meaning in games and using games as a mechanism for personal validation and ontological security. The game has inspired multiple theories and interpretations, all of which testify to its success as an open work. In this capacity, the game is perhaps best understood not just as "an introduction to the thought of Umberto Eco," as Esteban Grine suggests, but as a historically conscious experiment that anticipates and deconstructs the production of its own videogame literature. Reading the game almost a decade later thus involves close reading of the game and the metagame it produced, a hermeneutic circle that contains not just the game's creator and implied player but all of the historical readers and writers who participated in the game's open work with their own codas and compositions.

Developed after the success of *The Stanley Parable* (2013), *The Beginner's Guide* was released independently in October 2015 under the paradoxically "meta" label Everything Unlimited Ltd. It was sold and described in promotional material by Wreden in characteristic meta fashion: "*The Beginner's Guide* is a narrative videogame from Davey Wreden, the creator of *The Stanley Parable.* It lasts about an hour and a half and has no traditional mechanics, no goals or objectives. Instead, it tells the story of a person struggling to deal with something they do not understand." Its diegesis features Davey Wreden playing a voice-over version of himself—an unreliable "fictionalized author-narrator, or autofictional narrator" named Davey Wreden (Backe and Thon 14)—as he guides the player through sixteen experimental levels (many of them unfinished) created by an equally fictional character named Coda. Throughout the game, the player finds themself caught in a metafictional labyrinth in which they become a reader who participates in the curated production, modification, and criticism of Coda's work—with or against Davey's performance.

The base metafictional layer of the game consists of the short experiments developed by Coda on the Source Engine between October 2008 and June 2011. As it happens, this was the period that saw the development of Source Engine "art mods" such as the original *Stanley Parable* (2011), Dan Pinchbeck's *Dear*

Esther (2011), and experimental mods such as Robert Yang's *Radiator* (2009). All of these were developed as "indie [became] mainstream" (Juul 91), critical writing about games expanded (*Braid* was released in 2008), and changes in the online and social media ecosystem led to more open lines of communication between indie developers and players.

In this context, Coda's "games" can be read as short works that feature experimental mechanics and aesthetics, all of which can be analyzed in detail. Most fall into what Brian Schrank describes as the "radical formal" avant-garde (27), sharing features of Eco's "open work," such as discontinuity, serial poetics, neobaroque aesthetics, and "a constant questioning of any established grammar" (Eco 218). Taken together, the serial configuration of Coda's work thus "assumes the task of giving us an image of discontinuity. It does not narrate it; it *is* it" (90). And it is precisely this "image of discontinuity" that unsettles Davey, fueling his desire to interpret and narrativize the games into a fictional image of continuity, coherence, and closure (Eco 90). Whatever else they are, Coda's works are a discontinuous series that ultimately eludes Davey's interpretation, functions as the inscrutable core of the player's experience, and serves as the base case for all other recursions and metagames that follow.

Davey's unreliable curation and interpretation of Coda's work constitutes the next meta level of the game. Here, Davey's fictional performance documents and satirizes the rise of videogame criticism in the form of curated walkthroughs, Let's Plays, and video essays, which exploded between 2008 and 2011. The website *Critical Distance,* for example, was launched in 2009 in direct response to the increased volume of game criticism, describing itself as "a compendium of the most incisive, thought-provoking, and remarkable discussion in and around games" ("Mission Statement"). This was also a period that saw Reddit's continued growth, the launch and expansion of Steam Community, and the emergence of collective fan writing sites such as Wikia (later to become Fandom). Thus, Davey's "perverse curatorship" of Coda's games, as Stuart Moulthrop writes, materializes as "a supplement to that body of work: Davey's coda to Coda's games," adding another meta layer to the game's transgressive "weirdness" (100). "Woebegone fan that he is" (94), Davey theorizes that Coda uses his games to work out personal issues, ironically oblivious to his own use and abuse of Coda's games as a therapeutic mechanism. Davey interprets Coda's work "more or less like the components of a construction kit"—"quite literally 'unfinished,'" to recall Eco again—which he interprets as a license to stage his own codas to Coda's games, even adding literal lampposts into the game to provide more closure and continuity (Eco 4). *The Beginner's Guide* ultimately exposes the fallacies of Davey's interpretive performance, which is founded "by an urge to define a coherent, stable identity of both Coda's work and person" (Backe and Thon 16). In this way, the game offers an ironic and critical perspective on interpretive walkthroughs, Let's Plays, and other fan writings, particularly those searching for authorial intention.

At the same time, the game offers a fictionalized condensation of Wreden's publicly documented turmoil after the success of *The Stanley Parable*—the period between 2013 and 2015, when Wreden began to work through his feelings about videogame authorship, his relationship to fans and videogame criticism, and his maturing insights into "how this creator/audience thing works." In a 2014 blog post and comic, as well as a 2015 lecture, Wreden recounted how the experience of overnight success produced a situation in which his feelings about the creator/audience relationship were radically unsettled "in a very, very short period of time" ("Playing"). He describes himself as "floating between two emotional states": "a sense of ownership" over *The Stanley Parable* ("this thing I've worked on for years") and "the loss of having turned that ownership over to hundreds of thousands of people" ("Game"). With "an open line of communication to anyone who wanted to get in touch with me when the game launched," he found himself overwhelmed by the growing accumulation of emails and online responses to the game, describing the "weight" as "real" and "heavy" and publicly confessing to his desire for external validation and to his subsequent depression, therapy, and self-reflection. Feeling "adrift in this gap," he documents how he came to terms with "that loss-of-self" that is "at the heart of any kind of performance" and how it reframed his perspective on "how this creator/audience thing works" ("Playing"; "Game").

A few critics have discussed these struggles in the context of *The Beginner's Guide*. Alisha Karabinus, for example, wonders "whether or not *The Beginner's Guide* is a game at all, or just a visualization of that blog post." But nobody has really analyzed how Wreden incorporates his revelations into the game's open and dialectical structure. The conflict between Coda and Davey—their works and compositions, that is—restages the questions and struggles of a creator working through the challenges of releasing his work to fans and critics, challenges that could be ironically performed as "the story of a person struggling to deal with something they do not understand" precisely because the historical Davey Wreden had lived and experienced it.

Which brings us to the final metalayer of *The Beginner's Guide*: the relationship between the game and the theoretical metagame it produced. Here, reading the game involves reading the literature around and about the game, thus reconfiguring the game as an unfinished work intentionally designed to be interpreted by players even as it calls those interpretive performances into question. This metagame plays out in the online chorus of responses to the game, which document a growing divide in online criticism between theories composed by fans and critical interpretations composed by artists, developers, journalists, and academics. These discourses can be read through the logic of the coda as an aesthetic form.

In musical theory, a coda is a concluding passage of a piece or movement, usually as a supplement to a work's basic structure; technically, a coda is "a melodic or harmonic configuration that creates a sense of repose or resolution" (Randel 105). As a sequence that closes a work, a coda can vary in length and complexity, from a few measures in music to a longer section. With *The Beginner's Guide,* codas are found both inside and outside the game, reflected in Stuart Moulthrop's formal analysis of the game around its "adoption of a logic of coda" (91), the use of a coda symbol as the Steam icon for the game, and all of the writings the game inspired.

We might go further and characterize reading and writing as metagaming practices that produce their own historical codas, creating literary passages in which players participate in the interpretative play of videogame criticism. In this case, we can divide these codas into roughly two forms: short texts in the form of threads and comments, and longer texts such as blogs, articles, and video essays. Both participate in the game's open work in different fashion, documenting the growing divergence between popular fan theories and more critically oriented readings.

On Reddit and Steam, the logic of the coda played out in myriad threads and comments: threads announcing movements within a serial discussion, comments playing off each other like a series of notes. With threads about Coda, for example, we get titles like "Coda = Davey?"; "Coda = The Coder"; "Coda Theory"; "THEORY: coda is a woman (spoilers)"; "Coda isn't real"; and "Stop talking about coda. please." Inside, we find countless comments on what or whom Coda represents, including theories that Coda is male, female, gender-neutral, or a trans woman misgendered by Davey; a stand-in for John Ree (a developer for CodaGamer) or Wreden's roommate Robin Arnott; a reference to "R," to whom Wreden dedicates the game; an acronym that stands for "compliments of dumb assholes"; and an abbreviation for Codependents Anonymous (CoDA, for short). Most of these theories are creative and backed by evidence; many are reductive. But all offer surprising connections and archival discoveries.

In other threads, fans share comments about authorship, the intentional fallacy, toxic masculinity, overinterpretation, and other critical topics. (Not coincidentally, development of *The Beginner's Guide* coincided with the period when online harassment and toxic masculinity culminated in Gamergate, leading to theories and interpretations about the game informed by feminism and queer theory.) In comments devoted to the infamous "lampposts" (in-game elements that we discover were inserted by Davey himself), fans accuse each other of imposing meaning on the game, even coining the term "lampposting" as a playful verb to indicate that a person is adding their own meaning to a work (*Beginner's Guide* Wikia).

We also find moments of self-reflection and metacognition: "We're all co-das," writes Niamou, a fan, on Steam (October 2, 2015); another, Rominvictus, speculates that "the whispers [in Coda's games] are the voices of the Steam Community, the collective whispers of gamers and reviewers, like this thread. . . . We are the whisperers. And here we are whispering" (October 8, 2015). In thread after thread, theories and metatheories play off of each other, each completing the work with its own coda and cadence, woven together through the literary play of composition and community.

At this scale, the huddle of fandom registers less as collective intelligence than as improvised play and performance, with fans composing notes and passages like movements in an orchestra. However, what stands out is the logic of the series, in which discrete units play out what Eco and Ndalianis describe as the "poetics of serial thought"—each comment adding to a specific movement, each thread participating in the neobaroque structure of entertainment (Eco 218; Ndalianis 71). Sometimes the codas look like lampposts (an element of intrusion); other times they sound like whispers. But they always play out in serial fashion, performing the open work in the marginal metagame of their individual cadences. Many of these were eventually poached and synthesized by sites like *Fandom*, where *The Beginner's Guide* Wikia distilled them into an organized index and encyclopedia, replacing the idiosyncratic style and personality of fans with the corporate anonymity of collective intelligence.

Authorship was more permanent in blogs, articles, podcasts, and video essays. In these longer texts, criticism veered toward more meta levels of abstraction and analysis, often supplemented by critical theory. For example, less than two weeks after the game's release, Kris Ligman, senior curator of *Critical Distance* at the time, called the game "*catnip* for game critics" in his introduction to a slate of articles about the game—"half of a Critical Compilation already"—that engaged with its interpretative enigmas (Lorischild). Here the work multiplied into meta readings about its interpretative paradoxes: "a game that doesn't want to be written about" (Laura Hudson); "a game about how slippery criticism really is" (Bruno Dias); a game that "resists interpretation" (Liz England); a game that "leaves players confused about the status of the game in relation to their reality" (Aaron Suduiko); a game about the messiness of interpretation (Harper Jay); a game that makes you feel "complicit in the violence enacted by the viewer on the creator of a work of art" (Amsel von Spreckelsen); a game about the misunderstandings that result when we "treat artwork as a window into its creator" (Emily Short); a game "*about the act of reading* . . . about who gets to interpret, under what conditions, and for what audience" (Cameron Kunzelman); a game about "fandom curdling into a sort of illusion of proximity" (Bruno Dias); a game about the death of the author (Hayden Dingman), the death of the critic (Big Joel), and the death of the player (Jed Pressgrove).

Within two weeks of the game's release, the critical response had accumulated into a neobaroque corpus of criticism, a critical mass in which we find at least three critical and self-reflexive turns in the movement of videogame criticism. First, almost all of the interpretations acknowledge the game's resistance to interpretation, along with the author's participation or complicity in trying to discern its meaning. In this respect, Brendan Keogh correctly describes the game not simply as "a self-reflexive exercise for Wreden" but also as "a self-reflexive exercise for the player," "a videogame about videogames" that intentionally "wants the player to be aware at all times they are exploring, unpacking, and ultimately ruining a videogame work as they trod all over it."

In response, most of the interpretations began to perform their own meta levels of analysis, transforming criticism into a metagame with its own literary, critical, and self-reflexive practice. This is the second critical turn. And just dropping the word "meta" often does the trick: "Before we can talk about it, we need a framework for talking about it. And to build that framework, we're going to have to go meta. Way meta" (Innuendo Studios). Interpretation is now used to deconstruct its own metafictional and metagaming status, often by drawing on critical theory to analyze its structure, ideology, and politics, or to simply play along with the game's critical practice. In essay after essay, the open work of the game becomes "a self-reflexive exercise" not just for the player but also for the reader and writer who thinks and theorizes around it (Keogh).

This is the third turn of criticism, which is perhaps most visible in early negative reactions to the game that criticize its metafictional premise. Ligman, for example, after curating the essays for *Critical Distance*, moved to Tumblr and in a post dated October 11, 2015, called the game "bullshit," "a critic-targeted neurotoxin. . . . finely tuned to lure in and trap critics" with an argument about the perversity of interpretation that "is *utter rhetorical garbage*." Liz Ryerson also reacted with skepticism, later wondering whether "the game criticism sphere blow-up with thinkpieces on the game" represented "the discourse around videogames' first awkward baby steps into the realm of taking on complexities in art" or was nothing more than "mainstream videogame culture's first foray in trying to actually make sense of their position of privilege." Here, criticism turns back on itself. Compositions still play out the logic of coda and complete the game through acts of reading, writing, and interpretation, but they also question the game's privileged and political status as a platform for raising questions about videogames, videogame criticism, and the cultural and ontological status of videogame literature.

In the end, all of these critical movements combine to illustrate how the open work of *The Beginner's Guide* produces its own neobaroque metagame layered with new levels of intelligence, new forms of self-reflexivity, and new critical insights into the literary and historical practice of videogame criticism. On all levels and scales, the game marks an increasing divergence in culture between videogame fan theories (a popular method of reading and writing *within and across* games) and videogame criticism (a collection of disciplinary methods for reading and writing *about, around, and with* games). While *Inside* produced a metagame about theories and enigmas, *The Beginner's Guide* produced a metagame about the metagame of interpretation, restaging videogame criticism as a reflexive process with no end or closure—just a series of codas that play, perform, and participate in the critical turns and movements of videogame history.

Coda

In his reading of *The Beginner's Guide*, Stuart Moulthrop examines the "logic of coda" adopted by the game but then stops short of extending the logic to the cultural metagames produced about and around the game by fans, critics, and scholars (91). He only briefly reflects on this broader dimension when he moves outside the game in his brief conclusion, reflecting that "just as *The Beginner's Guide* is revealed from a certain high angle to consist entirely of codas, we can similarly unmask culture as nothing but cultural series" or "a chain of resonances stretched across a landscape of chaotic fracture" (101). Concealed in this bit of theorizing is a practical reminder that the logic of coda plays out in particular acts of reading, writing, and interpreting culture. When we adopt the logic of coda and turn back "to add something more," we mark and interpret culture in serial fashion, playing and replaying codas of our own (100). "Inhabiting culture, we become Coda," as Moulthrop writes (101), but interpreting culture, we also become Davey. As readers, writers, and critics, we are all caught in the logic of coda that serially inscribes culture with desire, discontinuity, and fragments of meaning. In replaying culture, we become Coda *and* Davey, the creator and performer of interpretative works that level up the kinds of stories we tell about, with, and around videogames. With a medium still new and evolving, the work of interpretation remains a recursive beginner's guide. In the words of Louis L'Amour, the inspiration behind Wreden's enigmatic title, "There will come a time when you believe everything is finished. That will be the beginning."

WORKS CITED

Backe, Hans-Joachim, and Jan-Noël Thon. "Playing with Identity Authors, Narrators, Avatars, and Players in *The Stanley Parable* and *The Beginner's Guide*." *DIEGESIS*, vol. 8, no. 2, 2019.

The Beginner's Guide. Windows/PC version, Everything Unlimited Ltd., 2015.

"*The Beginner's Guide* Wiki." *Fandom*. https://the-beginners-guide.fandom.com/wiki/Main _Page. Accessed 2 May 2021.

Big Joel. "The Beginner's Guide: The Death of the Critic." *YouTube*, 15 December 2017. https://youtu.be/mN4vAD-jqO0.

Boluk, Stephanie, and Patrick LeMieux. *Metagaming: Playing, Competing, Spectating, Cheating, Trading, Making, and Breaking Videogames*. University of Minnesota Press, 2017.

Brooks, Peter. *Reading for the Plot: Design and Intention in Narrative*. Rev. ed., Harvard University Press, 1992.

Consalvo, Mia. *Cheating: Gaining Advantage in Videogames*. MIT Press, 2009.

———. "Zelda 64 and Video Game Fans: A Walkthrough of Games, Intertextuality, and Narrative." *Television & New Media*, vol. 4, no. 3, 2003, pp. 321–34.

Derrat, Max. "Inside—Story Explanation and Analysis." *YouTube*, 4 July 2016. https://youtu.be/P2NXvDuz520.

Dias, Bruno. "Interactive Fiction: The Beginner's Guide." *Storycade,* 8 October 2015. http://storycade.com/interactive-fiction-beginners-guide. Accessed 2 May 2021.

Dingman, Hayden. *"The Beginner's Guide* Review: A Weird, Fiercely Personal Game." *PC World,* 3 October 2015. https://www.pcworld.com/article/2989032/the-beginners -guide-review-a-weird-fiercely-personal-game.html.

Dym, Brianna, Jed Brubaker, and Casey Fiesler. "'theyre all trans sharon': Authoring Gender in Video Game Fan Fiction." *Game Studies,* vol. 18, no. 3, December 2018. https://gamestudies.org/1803/articles/brubaker_dym_fiesler.

Eco, Umberto. *The Open Work,* translated by Anna Cancogni. Harvard University Press, 1989.

England, Liz, and Samantha Kalman. "The Game Dev Letters: A Series on *The Beginner's Guide." Game Developer,* 4 November 2015. https://www.gamasutra.com/view /news/258342/The_game_dev_letters_A_series_on_The_Beginners_Guide.php.

Fassone, Riccardo. "Ludo Essay and Ludophilia: *The Beginner's Guide* as a Ludographic Essay." *Cinergie—Il Cinema E Le Altre Arti,* vol. 7, no. 13, 12 July 2018, pp. 67–76.

Fernández-Vara, Clara. *Introduction to Game Analysis.* 2nd ed., Routledge, 2019.

Graeber, Brendan, Lostnotislaz, and Jason Burton. "Ending Theories." *IGN,* 6 July 2016. https://www.ign.com/wikis/inside/Ending_Theories.

Grine, Esteban. *"The Beginner's Guide,* une introduction à la pensée d'Umberto Eco." *Chroniques vidéoludiques,* 7 August 2016. https://www.chroniquesvideoludiques.com /the-beginners-guide-une-introduction-a-la-pensee-dumberto-eco. [In Spanish.]

Hills, Matt. *Fan Cultures.* Routledge, 2002.

Hudson, Laura. *"The Beginner's Guide* Is a Game That Doesn't Want to Be Written About." *Boing Boing,* 2 October 2015. https://boingboing.net/2015/10/02/the-beginners-guide -is-a-gam.html.

Innuendo Studios. "The Artist is Absent: Davey Wreden and the Beginner's Guide." *YouTube,* 26 July 2016. https://youtu.be/4N6y6LEwsKc.

Inside. PlayStation 4, Playdead, 2016.

Jay, Harper. "The Beginner's Guide—Minicrit." *YouTube,* 4 October 2015. https://youtu.be /mZGa0DMHLtw.

Jenkins, Henry. *Convergence Culture: Where Old and New Media Collide.* New York University Press, 2006.

———. *Fans, Bloggers, and Gamers: Exploring Participatory Culture.* New York University Press, 2006.

———. *Textual Poachers: Television Fans and Participatory Culture.* Routledge, 1992.

Jones, Steven E. *The Meaning of Video Games: Gaming and Textual Strategies.* Routledge, 2008.

Juul, Jesper. *Handmade Pixels: Independent Video Games and the Quest for Authenticity.* MIT Press, 2019.

Karabinus, Alisha. *"The Beginner's Guide* and Definitions of Play." *NYMG,* 24 October 2015. https://www.nymgamer.com/?p=11881.

Keogh, Brendan. "On the Beginner's Guide." *Brendan Keogh*, 3 October 2015. https://br keogh.com/2015/10/03/on-the-beginners-gude.

Klepek, Patrick. "The Wild Theories Behind *Inside*'s Secret Ending." *Kotaku*, 13 July 2016. https://kotaku.com/the-wild-theories-behind-insides-secret-ending-1783552341.

Kunzelman, Cameron. "*The Beginner's Guide*: Good Evening." *Paste*, 1 October 2015. https://www.pastemagazine.com/games/the-beginners-guide-review-good-evening.

Lorischild, Kris. "This Week in Videogame Blogging." *Critical Distance*, 11 October 2015. https://www.critical-distance.com/2015/10/11/october-11th-2.

"Mission Statement." *Critical Distance*. https://www.critical-distance.com/about.

Moulthrop, Stuart. "'Turn Back from This Cave': The Weirdness of *Beginner's Guide*." *Journal of Gaming & Virtual Worlds*, vol. 12, no. 1, 2020, pp. 91–103.

Navarro-Remesal, Víctor. "Museums of Failure: Fans as Curators of 'Bad,' Unreleased, and 'Flopped' Videogames." *Fans and Videogames: Histories, Fandom, Archives*, edited by Melanie Swalwell, Helen Stuckey, and Angela Ndalianis. Routledge, 2017, pp. 128–45.

Ndalianis, Angela. *Neo-Baroque Aesthetics and Contemporary Entertainment*. MIT Press, 2004.

Newman, James. *Playing with Videogames*. Routledge, 2008.

Paul, Christopher A. "Optimizing Play: How Theorycraft Changes Gameplay and Design." *Game Studies*, vol. 11, no. 2, May 2011. http://gamestudies.org/1102/articles/paul.

Pressgrove, Jed. "Review: *The Beginner's Guide*." *Slant*, 4 October 2015. https://www.slantmagazine.com/games/the-beginners-guide.

Randel, Don Michael, ed. *The Harvard Concise Dictionary of Music and Musicians*. Belknap Press of Harvard University Press, 1999.

Ryerson, Liz. "The Beginner's Guide and Videogame Criticism's Awkward Baby Steps." *Ellaguro*, 19 January 2016. http://ellaguro.blogspot.com/2016/01/the-beginners-guide-and-videogame.html.

Schrank, Brian. *Avant-Garde Videogames: Playing with Technoculture*. MIT Press, 2014.

Short, Emily. "The Beginner's Guide (Davey Wreden) and Intimacy Inside Games." *Emily Short's Interactive Storytelling*, 5 October 2015. https://emshort.blog/2015/10/05/the-beginners-guide-davey-wreden-and-intimacy-inside-games.

"The Sleeping Realm Theory." 2 February 2019. https://docs.google.com/document/d/11d1TKd4ZKZd41pJKQ77bKz4YxJx8_Mojz2KMpNvTrvU/edit#.

Suduiko, Aaron. "Video Game Structural Aesthetics: Why 'The Beginner's Guide' Is Masterfully Confusing." *With A Terrible Fate*, 13 November 2015. https://withaterriblefate.com/2015/11/13/video-game-structural-aesthetics-why-the-beginners-guide-is-masterfully-confusing/.

Swalwell, Melanie, Helen Stuckey, and Angela Ndalianis, eds. "Introduction." *Fans and Videogames: Histories, Fandom, Archives*. Routledge, 2017, pp. 1–18.

Taylor, T. L. *Watch Me Play: Twitch and the Rise of Game Live Streaming*. Princeton University Press, 2018.

Upton, Brian. *The Aesthetic of Play*. MIT Press, 2015.

von Spreckelsen, Amsel. "The Trip to Sacramento." https://medium.com/optional-asides/the-trip-to-sacramento-50c6dd7d31e5. Accessed 2 May 2021.

Wreden, Davey. "Game of the Year." *Galactic Cafe*, 21 February 2014. Archived at http://archive.is/chRUO. Accessed 25 July 2023.

———. "Playing Stories." Games Now! lecture series, Aalto University, 13 April 2015. Video. https://livestream.com/accounts/6845410/gamesnow/videos/83818176.

The Uses of Ludobiography

How to Read Life-Writing About Videogaming

ROB GALLAGHER

In the age of Twitch, watching other people play videogames has become commonplace. However, *reading* about other people playing videogames remains a niche pursuit. And yet, as I would insist, firsthand accounts of digital gameplay can be entertaining, illuminating, and profoundly thought-provoking. In what follows, I analyze a generically diverse selection of texts, all of which recount specific individuals' experiences of digital play, and propose some ways to read them. One way is to read these as historical sources, but unlike documentary sources, these have the capacity to unsettle received wisdom. Histories of gaming often assume the function of "comforting us with ever more specific facts about techno-geniuses and providing us with an exciting narrative of nemesis rivalry, truth-deciphering and industrial grandeur" (Therrien and Picard). By providing evidence of how particular players in particular circumstances have engaged with particular games, firsthand accounts of gameplay can supplement, complicate, and contest such reductive and overfamiliar framings of the medium's development while also asking us to reconsider who counts as a "gamer" (a term that continues to be used for and against particular players and play communities). In so doing, such accounts often demonstrate the capacity of life-writing to challenge dominant narratives by foregrounding the experiences of the marginalized and excluded.

As this suggests, memoirs, auto/biographies, diaries, letters, and other narratives of the emerging self also spur us to reckon with the nature and function of life-writing and, by extension, with changing forms and understandings of identity, selfhood, and subjectivity in digital culture. Autobiographical literature has historically functioned to propagate "the master narrative of 'the sovereign self'" (Smith and Watson 3). But works of life-writing have also called that master narrative into question, interrogating "the 'givens' of autobiography (literally 'self,' 'life,' and 'writing')" (Poletti and Rak 6).

Gamer life-writing offers a particularly rich object of analysis for those interested in pursuing these lines of inquiry, in part because it is such a contradictory enterprise. Where autobiography involves giving an account of oneself, videogames typically invite us to *lose* ourselves, to assume new identities, immerse ourselves in other worlds, succumb to states of flow, and become entangled in the networks and feedback loops that subtend and sustain play. Consequently, gamer life-writing is characterized by an interplay between the *auto*biographical mode and what I am calling the *ludo*biographical mode. The texts I consider here are autobiographical to the extent that they involve individuals recounting and reflecting upon their own memories and experiences, but they are also ludobiographical, attesting to the way that gameplay can "undercut our sense of ourselves as conscious individuals in possession of our own bodies, identities and stories," putting selfhood into play (Gallagher 360). Across these texts, experiences of losing one's self in videogames are variously represented as exhilarating, angst-inducing, or revelatory.

In the attempt to render such experiences, authors often experiment with form, the handling of time, and the framing of the autobiographical "I," showing that gamer life-writing can enrich both our understanding of gaming cultures and our sense of what life-writing can do and be. To clarify this, I will begin with a discussion of academic sociologist and musician David Sudnow's 1983 book *Pilgrim in the Microworld*, which documents his obsession with Atari's *Breakout*. Sudnow is often amazingly perspicacious, especially for someone writing at the dawn of the commercial videogame industry. He is also minutely attentive to his own sensations and impressions. But his is very much the perspective of a well-educated, well-to-do white American male—a viewpoint that would hardly go underrepresented in later writing about videogames—and the delight he takes in play reflects this.

Next, I will discuss journalist, author, and, latterly, videogame scriptwriter Tom Bissell's *Extra Lives*, a 2010 collection of essays that incorporates profiles of prominent game designers alongside anecdotes detailing Bissell's complicated relationship with gaming. Bissell occupies a demographic similar to Sudnow's, but where Sudnow is curious about what videogames could become and is beguiled by their brash simplicity, Bissell, having grown up a gamer and made a name for himself as a "serious" writer, is desperate for videogames to evolve into the kind of sophisticated artform that people like himself—literate, cultured, self-reflexive adults—can enjoy without embarrassment. Ultimately, however, Bissell cannot banish his nagging sense that gameplay appeals to him primarily as a way of escaping his own self-loathing. The result is a conflicted and often anguished text in which the autobiographical and the ludobiographical are at loggerheads.

From this point, I turn to texts that center other sites and subjectivities. If commercial videogame publishers still tend to understand "the gamer" as a cisgendered, heterosexual, middle-class male living in North America, Japan, or Europe, these texts explore how individuals who fall outside this category have used videogames to lose and find themselves. As its title suggests, Zoë Quinn's *Crash Override: How Gamergate (Nearly) Destroyed My Life, and How We Can Win the Fight Against Online Hate* describes Quinn's experiences as the target of a networked hate movement committed to upholding narrow and regressive conceptions of games, gamers, and gaming culture. But Quinn's text has other things to offer. Here I consider how *Crash Override* portrays the formation of Quinn's gaming tastes, foregrounding its attention to the role of gender and class in shaping the terms on which individuals encounter and engage with videogames.

I then move to Florencia Rumpel Rodriguez's 2019 digital zine *In the beginning we all played Family*. Supplementing US- and Japancentric accounts of gaming's history, Rodriguez looks back on her childhood in Argentina, where the "console wars" waged by rival hardware manufacturers played out rather differently, and where gamers evolved their own unorthodox methods of accessing and engaging with products designed with other audiences in mind. The final section of the essay considers trans speedrunner Narcissa Wright's poem "all the categories are arbitrary." Finding in the practice of speedrunning a model for the reformulation of subjectivity, Wright's text shows how ludobiographical writing can open fresh perspectives on gaming, life-writing and subjectification alike.

No "I" in *Breakout: Pilgrim in the Microworld*

David Sudnow's *Pilgrim in the Microworld* extrapolates a dizzying array of perspectives from the Atari game *Breakout*, which for Sudnow is at once a "a game, puzzle, electronic pencil and paper, learning device, 'brown study' kit, new form of worry beads, childish toy, the perceptual psychologist's most perfect incongruity tool, [and] a first immature token for what could one day be a significant means of rationalized artistic expression" (162). In recounting his experiences with this strange artifact, Sudnow adopts a style in which the autobiographical mode and the ludobiographical mode coexist in dynamic tension.

As I have already observed, autobiography has traditionally been about agency and reflexivity, centering subjects who show themselves capable not just of taking action but also of reflecting upon and accounting for their actions. *Pilgrim* suggests that gameplay can be difficult to integrate into such a template but may be compelling for precisely this reason. Much of the book consists of minutely attentive descriptions of in-game events and Sudnow's physiological responses to them. For example, "an instant or maybe two later, my pulse rising a few points per shot, I glanced somewhere to the side at just the wrong time and missed a fast slam." Within the space of a paragraph, he will go from the high of "a super-speedy rush" to feeling "thoughtless, numbed, deceived" (59).

While there is still an autobiographical "I" in these passages, it is often under considerable strain. As Darshana Jayemanne notes, gamers' accounts of playing story-driven games often "involve very complex terminologies that negotiate tense, voice and other grammatical categories . . . mov[ing] between the first, second, and third person" (146). Sudnow's narration is subject to frequent shifts and repositionings that describe how he is playing but also how he feels about how he is playing and how his feelings affect his capacity to play: "You get within near range of the finish and mess up. The temptation of completion increases, a diffuse subcutaneous malaise gnaws and festers to mobilize a new degree of caring for the first shot of the next attempt, and you play a bit better because each move is charged with an attentiveness" (59). Sudnow is aware that he is annoyed, but also hopeful that this will nudge him toward a win state; he wants himself to "care more" (178), but not so much that he becomes counterintuitively self-conscious.

For Brendan Keogh, Sudnow's writing offers a way past the "mechanical, ludic and narrative essentialisms" that have dominated the field of game studies (971–72). "Intoxicated by the ways the videogame reflect[s] the movement of his hands back at him from the other side of the screen," Sudnow anticipates modes of writing about gameplay that foreground aesthetics, affect, hapticity, and embodiment (1). *Pilgrim* is not a Cartesian description of a mind let down by the body's inability to execute its edicts; rather, we get a sense of how gameplay sensitizes Sudnow to the multiple levels and registers of apprehension and cognition that coexist within him. At times, his prose anticipates that of avant-garde life-writers like Kenneth Goldsmith, whose text *Fidget* logs his body's every action—conscious and otherwise—across a thirteen-hour period, "extend[ing] the project of a posthuman embodied subject" (Emerson 95).

We will return to the idea that gamer life-writing resonates with posthuman perspectives on agency, identity, and subjectivity (see also de Matas in this volume). For now, it is enough to note that Sudnow's text sets a precedent for writers interested in the questions gameplay poses about autonomy, identity, and subjectivity. The games industry has long framed gaming's appeal in active terms, promising to indulge players' fantasies of individual mastery. As Sudnow shows, however, games simultaneously undercut claims to sovereignty, offering experiences that can be pleasurably mindless, acutely frustrating, and all but addictively compelling.

But while Sudnow offers a forensically precise account of what is happening within his field of perception, *Pilgrim* sometimes feels unwilling to look beyond those immediate surroundings and to address how Sudnow's circumstances inform his experiences of play. By writing a book about losing months of his life to *Breakout*, there is a sense that Sudnow the academic and classical musician is slumming it. Digital play figures in *Pilgrim* as a pleasurable, because temporary, abdication of autonomy on the part of a well-to-do white professional who can be confident that he can recover the privileges he is momentarily forgoing.

Gaming of Age: *Extra Lives*

While Tom Bissell writes from a position similar to Sudnow's, his stance is crucially different. Worried that his gaming habit is incompatible with his sense of who he is, he desperately wants games to develop into a medium capable of offering something more than viscerally engaging escapism. To this end, *Extra Lives* is best understood as a series of journalistic bulletins from the cutting edge of videogame development—both an account of how games are changing and what Bissell, as both an avid gamer and a feted author, hopes they will become. There is a biographical dimension to the book, which sees Bissell meeting designers he believes are pushing the medium forward. There is also an autobiographical dimension, as Bissell grapples with his fear that an unbridgeable gulf separates the part of him that loves videogames from "the part that values art" (44). And there is a ludobiographical dimension. Where Sudnow presents gaming as a fascinating holiday from subjectivity, for Bissell it facilitates an anguished flight from it, providing a means of losing himself in what he acknowledges are often crude and regressive masculinist fantasies. These dimensions are connected: it is because Bissell is troubled by his own tendency to retreat into games to escape himself that he wants to believe in the ability of heroic auteur developers to transform the lowly videogame into a vehicle for personal expression, psychological insight, and social commentary—the sort of medium a person like him could love without shame.

These desires were shared by many adult gamers during a period when videogames were still widely seen as a children's medium. It is easy to imagine why such desires would have been keenly felt by an author who had already developed a reputation as a writer of substance by the time *Extra Lives* was published, a writer versed in topics ranging from geopolitics to literary history. As we might expect from such a writer, references to artists and novelists are scattered throughout *Extra Lives*, providing a sense of the kinds of cultural figures Bissell esteems and hopes to emulate. For example, he invokes Martin Amis and Henrik Ibsen, portrays *Braid*'s designer Jonathan Blow as gaming's answer to "Seurat or Monet," and bonds with designer Clint Hocking over their mutual regard for Thomas Pynchon and David Foster Wallace. Through these references to canonical white male writers and emerging innovators, and through Bissell's own willingness to lavish his writerly attention on them, *Extra Lives* attempts to confer a certain kind of cultural legitimacy on videogames and on those who make and play them.

While Wallace is only mentioned once by name, *Extra Lives* often reads as a companion piece to *Infinite Jest* (1996), an acutely self-conscious novel about play, addiction, and what Wallace portrays as a fundamentally infantile desire for vicarious gratification through media (indeed, Bissell would write the foreword for a twentieth-anniversary edition of the novel). *Extra Lives* begins with Bissell worrying that, if his hypothetical children ever "ask me where I was and what I was doing when the United States elected its first black president," he will have to confess that he was playing *Fallout 3* (Bethesda Game Studios). "When I slipped the game into the tray of my Xbox 360," he confides, "the first polls were due to close in America in two hours. One hour of *Fallout 3*, I told myself . . . Seven hours later, blinking and dazed, I turned off my Xbox 360, checked in with CNN, and discovered that the acceptance speech had already been given" (4–5).

If autobiographies tend to address experiences of momentous significance, whether historic, personal, or both, gaming features here as that which Bissell was doing when he should have been doing something worthier of inclusion in his memoirs. The final chapter of *Extra Lives* recounts Bissell's intertwined addictions to cocaine and *Grand Theft Auto IV* (Rockstar North). Its confessional framing situates it within a long tradition of life-writing running from Augustine through Thomas De Quincey to the myriad contemporary memoirs that "publicly tell stories of some form of addiction or dependency" (Smith and Watson 202). For all his shame, Bissell holds that his lone, coke-suffused forays into Rockstar's Liberty City have vouchsafed him "moment[s] of transcendence" as well as "moment[s] in the gutter." He also insists that videogames deal "not [in] surrogate experiences, but [in] actual experiences, many of which are as important to me as any real memories" (87). The very phrasing of this claim, however, with its opposition of in-game experience to the "real," suggests a lingering uncertainty.

Bissell is not always alone while playing *Grand Theft Auto*. Relating an encounter with one of the game's virtual citizens that ends with her "vanishing under my tires in a puff of bloody mist," Bissell writes, "With a nervous laugh I looked over at my girlfriend, who was watching me play. She was not laughing and, suddenly, neither was I" (82). This scene is not unique. Women may be noticeably underrepresented in the canon against which Bissell measures gaming's cultural ambition and achievement (and his own), but a particular feminine figure recurs throughout his text: that of the sexually desirable woman who watches Bissell play and whose bafflement, disapproval, or exasperation underscores his fear that gaming is fundamentally childish and trivial, an activity incompatible with heteromasculine virility and desirability. At one point, Bissell is playing a roleplaying game with dialogue so embarrassing that "the woman I lived with announced she was revoking all vagina privileges" (7). Later, he tells us that, if he is playing a game "and my response to a woman of any foreseeable nudity walking into the room is to turn the game off, I know what I am playing does not have much adult nourishment" (50). We seldom get a sense, however, that women themselves might play videogames—or indeed make them. Visiting Ubisoft's Montreal headquarters, Bissell is surprised to see a "number of attractive young women wandering about the premises" and "wonder[s] if the company had expanded to include an escort service or modeling agency or both" (65).

So, what kind of games *does* Bissell feel capable of playing unashamedly? When *LittleBigPlanet* (Media Molecule) wins console game of the year at the 2008 DICE awards, Bissell receives the judges' decision as "a rebuke of everything games had spent the last decade trying to do and be[,] . . . everything I wanted them to become." It is bad enough that the prize has gone to a "game aimed largely at children . . . which has no real narrative to speak of"; worse is the fact that the judges have snubbed such "warheads of thematic grandiosity" as "*Fallout 3*, *Metal Gear Solid 4*, *Gears of War 2*, and *Grand Theft Auto IV*" (44). As this list suggests, Bissell values story-led single-player games about violence and its consequences—as befits a writer who was once "embedded with the Marine Corps in Iraq" (31). All the better if these games are explicitly informed by literature. Bissell approvingly cites Hocking's account of *Far Cry 2* (Ubisoft Montreal) as an attempt to make "*Heart of Darkness* the video game," describing it as a game about "the behavioral and emotional consequences of being exposed to relentless violence" (69–70).

Bissell also likes games that can be seen as reflecting the subjectivity of a creator. His account of *Gears of War* (Epic Games) (the first entry in a series for which Bissell has since written) argues that the game is elevated by its "autobiographical" dimension and its "melancholy" undertones. Bissell observes that the childhood home of *Gears*'s protagonist resembles the house where lead designer Cliff Bleszinski grew up and that the game's aesthetics were inspired by a formative "trip to London, taken when [Bleszinski] was in his late twenties" (29). He also notes that some players have detected similarities between an enemy tank featured in *Gears of War 2* (Epic Games) and the tank in *Blaster Master* (Sunsoft)—the game Bleszinski was playing "when he learned of his father's death" (29). Noting that Bleszinski was unaware of the similarity "until someone else pointed it out to him" (29), Bissell deploys the venerable biographical trope of the artist unconsciously working through traumatic childhood memories.

While Bissell's attempts to read *Gears* biographically feel rather strained (it is, after all, a blockbuster science fiction shooter made by a team of hundreds), *Braid* proves more amenable to this framing. Graphics and music aside, the game is essentially the work of one person, Jonathan Blow. While *Gears* and *Braid* are very different games—one a grisly 3D shooter, the other a lysergic 2D puzzle-platformer—Bissell praises the latter in similar terms: Blow has taken the quintessentially "childlike" genre of the platformer and, by adding "scaffolds of sneaky biography," has lent it an "unusual melancholy" and "emotional significance" (50). With its allusions to the Manhattan Project and the life of J. Robert Oppenheimer, moreover, *Braid* too can be seen as a game about living with the consequences of military violence.

Today, Bissell's essays are legible as artifacts of a particular phase in gaming's history. In the late 2000s, players like Bissell often were looking for alibis to continue engaging with a medium still widely perceived as juvenile and culturally inconsequential. "Prestige games" like *BioShock Infinite* (Irrational Games) offered one answer, aiming to invest genres like the first-person shooter with cultural gravitas and philosophical heft (Parker). Indie games offered another. Undercutting the assumption that artistic breakthroughs would result from technological advances, these smaller-scale projects traded on their artisanal authenticity.

However, for Mike Sell, *BioShock Infinite* and *Braid* should also be seen as expressions of what he terms "patriarchy lite." Like Bissell's writing, they perform a masculinity that is "vulnerable, self-conscious, talkative, pitiful" ("Bittersweet"). All these writers evince a nostalgic regard for games past, even as they acknowledge that aspects of their inspirations now appear embarrassing, outmoded, or irrevocably problematic. Rather than offering something truly different, they attempt to redeem what has come before through referentiality and reflexivity: "run and gun, jump and smash, kill the boss, get the girl. But do it 'critically,' do it 'historically.' Do it in air quotes" ("Bittersweet").

Far from offering an escape from the dead end of hegemonic gamer masculinity, however, the addition of these "air quotes" only seems to make things more claustrophobic for Bissell. By the end of *Extra Lives*, he has apparently abandoned his former hopes for videogames, arriving at the realization that "all a game can do is point at the person playing it" (87). This formulation, however, feels like a poor fit for Bissell's ludobiographical accounts of gameplay, which often represent games as a means of *getting away* from the person he is, from feelings of "depression" and "piranhic self-hatred" that only roll back with renewed force once he has put down the controller (5). That some game designers had begun to share Bissell's ambivalence ultimately appears to intensify his self-consciousness.

For Sell, one way out of gaming's creative cul-de-sac would come not from prestige shooters or knowing indie pastiches but from the emergence, in the early 2010s, of a culture of independent, avant-garde, queer, and do-it-yourself developers using new tools to create and share experimental games ("Modernist Afterlives"). In many cases, these games were both rooted in and concerned with the lives of women, queer and trans subjects, and people of color. Where Bissell writes about games created by and for people like him, people who revere the same literary and ludic canon, these games would draw on different experiences and express different orientations toward the culture and history of games—experiences and orientations like those *Crash Override* documents.

Trash or Treasure? *Crash Override*

As a game designer, Zoë Quinn is best known as cocreator of the interactive fiction *Depression Quest* (Quinn and Lindsey). To many, however, they will be familiar as one of the primary targets of the so-called GamerGate movement, which began waging war on Quinn after their ex-boyfriend Eron Gjoni falsely accused them of trading sexual favors for positive press coverage of *Depression Quest*. While *Crash Override* tells Quinn's side of this harrowing story, it also performs many other functions. Quinn offers cybersecurity tips, sets out policy recommendations for creating a safer and more equitable Web, and discusses the dynamics of online subcultures, defending the value of anonymous and pseudonymous spaces where subjects can experiment with their identities and make embarrassing mistakes. For my purposes, I am most interested in *Crash Override*'s account of Quinn's early encounters with videogames and the formation of their gaming tastes. This account highlights the degree to which both conventional framings of gaming's history and critical perspectives like Bissell's reflect often unacknowledged norms and assumptions.

If gender is important here, class is crucial, too. As the child of "blue-collar small business owners," Quinn spent their early childhood at a socioeconomic remove from mainstream gaming culture, playing videogames at friends' houses and borrowing gaming magazines from the local library. Quinn portrays their father, a motorbike mechanic, as too kindly for his own good, noting that "he'd accept weird trades and pay-you-laters from less-than-honorable sources" and "bring home a ton of junk because it was 'a good deal'" (23–24). It is thanks to one of these ill-advised transactions that Quinn becomes the owner of a 3DO console, acquired along with fifty games for a knockdown price.

Released in 1993, the 3DO was, in Quinn's words, part of an "exploratory push to put the 'video' back in 'video games'" that ended in "spectacular failure" (24). This push had serious momentum behind it: 3DO founder Trip Hawkins had worked for Apple before starting the enormously successful publisher Electronic Arts, and the hype behind "interactive cinema" was considerable at the time. The 3DO would, however, be quickly vanquished by Sony's PlayStation, while full-motion videogames would become a punch line, notwithstanding their recent rise to popularity and big-studio funding. Derided at the time for their histrionic acting and choppy, pixelated footage, such games were also guilty, in the eyes of many gamers, of a bigger sin: at a time when gaming magazines were developing a notion of "gameplay" as the quality that set videogames apart (Kirkpatrick 14), these games prioritized storytelling over responsive controls, complex systems, and ludic challenge.

For Quinn, however, the 3DO's library possessed a strange allure. Quinn frames their fascination with this ludic "buffet of . . . trash" as evidence of a budding "love of all things camp" (25). But their account also suggests the importance of questioning the criteria that see some games dismissed as "trash" while others are lauded—and some (like *Depression Quest*) accused of not being "real" videogames at all. Recent scholarship has argued that we should "think of interactive movies not as valueless . . . but as experiments worth examining on their own terms" (Perron et al. 233), and developers like Kazutaka Kodaka and Sam Barlow are revisiting and reinventing the genre. Historians, meanwhile, have shown how the valorization of "gameplay" is bound up with forms of gendered gatekeeping (Kirkpatrick 103).

Such developments suggest that there was nothing inherently bad about full-motion videogames, and their supposedly inferior qualities as gameplay experiences enable us to see titles like *Depression Quest* as part of histories that encompass different and diverse games and play cultures. In describing how they came to love games generally disdained by their peers, Quinn's text shows how tastes, preferences, and formative encounters that have a deep personal significance are also the result of circumstances that the individuals concerned may have no control over or knowledge of, whether that is a family's socioeconomic circumstances or corporate strategists' wrongheaded projections.

Quinn's narrative also highlights the fact that understandings of what counts as "next gen" often depends on assumptions about gender, class, geography, language, and personal circumstances. While Quinn was exploring the 3DO's library (25), some of their classmates were gaming on Sega's Dreamcast, a console that launched in the United States in 1999, nine months after its Japanese debut. Where official histories are often content to follow the neat cadences of corporate release schedules, Quinn's experiences are tellingly out of sync with this rhythm. But while Quinn offers an alternative to the male, middle-class orientation of many gaming histories, theirs is still a distinctively North American perspective. In contrast, Florencia Rumpel Rodriguez's zine *In the beginning we all played Family* shows us the value of looking beyond the "conventional centers for the production and consumption of game technologies" to address other contexts and histories (Penix-Tadsen 10).

House Rules: *In the Beginning We All Played Family*

Produced for curator Emilie Reed's 2019 *Lost Histories Jam*, which solicited accounts of "personal experience[s] with videogames you haven't seen in many discussions of videogame history," *In the beginning we all played Family* relates Rodriguez's experiences of growing up as a console gamer in Argentina, where only the wealthiest gamers could afford "current gen" systems. In Argentina, *la Family*—a pirated version of Nintendo's Famicom, a system originally launched in Japan in 1983—maintained its popularity for years, thanks largely to a steady flow of bootlegs and pirated software and, of course, the continued economic precarity of the country's gaming community. Games were sold in *ferias*, where vendors "would set up shop by laying their wares on display mats, dingy tables, or metal booths" and shoppers were invited to browse catalogs of "books, comic books, trading cards, and pirated movies, games, and miscellaneous software . . . filled with pages full of lists printed in A4 pages, using a combination of the Arial 32 font and non-existent design skills" (Rodriguez 4).

Such details might seem inconsequential to historians who focus only on new technology and those who can afford to work and play with it. As Boluk and LeMieux argue, however, all manner of factors—from the design of game controllers to the way games are described in advertisements and instruction manuals to region-specific systems for determining age-appropriate content—play a part in "structur[ing] the lusory attitude players unconsciously assume when picking up a controller" (36). Such paratexts, objects and protocols are typically configured to ensure that the actual player coincides as closely as possible with the ideal player—the player the game expects, solicits, and addresses. But this fit is inevitably imperfect, especially when games circulate beyond their intended contexts of reception.

In this vein, Rodriguez evocatively describes how house rules and national norms shaped her experiences of gaming. In her household, Rodriguez's father "would buy this [sic] magazines that were printed in Spain and play the games while I read the magazines and told him what he should be doing next" (7). The single-player games he favored would become multiplayer experiences, played in a kind of intergenerational co-op mode. And thanks to her father's laissez-faire stance on "mature content"—a stance Rodriguez sees as typically Argentinian—the young Rodriguez would encounter all sorts of scenarios deemed adults-only by other countries' ratings boards.

The interplay between the autobiographical and ludiobiographical modes in Rodriguez's text reminds us that the intended player a game hails may bear little resemblance to the actual player who encounters it, and that this lack of fit can generate pleasurable and productive forms of disorientation, affording novel perspectives on game design and identity alike. As Rodriguez's account of games like *Metal Gear Solid* (Konami Computer Entertainment Japan) shows, Japanese games can make a different kind of sense to Argentinians, just as games that objectify female characters for the delectation of "mature" straight men might read differently for young queer women. Similarly, there are the forms of play videogames expect and those that they afford.

Expanding our sense of how and by whom games are actually played, Rodriguez's firsthand accounts of situated play ask us to rethink what videogames can be and who they can be for. In a context where most gaming histories "trace a series of commercially successful home consoles," reducing the past to "a linear progression where videogames simply became more technologically advanced," such texts are potentially of great historical and cultural significance (Reed). At the same time, the quotidian experiences of gameplay memorialized by writers like Rodriguez and Quinn—gamers who grew up with what mainstream gamer culture would consider failed or obsolete systems—pose a subtle and salutary challenge to hegemonic understandings of gaming. As Reed stresses, the terms on which gaming's past is narrated inform its future. When "dead ends [are] trimmed" in order to foreground "popular characters and franchises that will most likely be re-sold to us" and "people who make and talk about games are presumed to be working from the same set of references," the possibility space shrinks. However, even those videogames best represented in histories of gaming can afford novel forms of play and subject-formation—as Narcissa Wright's spoken-word poem "all the categories are arbitrary" attests.

Gaming Beyond the Human: "all the categories are arbitrary"

Reflecting on her exploits as a speedrunner alongside her experiences of gender transition, Wright's text presents her experiences as proof that "all the categories are arbitrary"—a refrain that recurs across the poem's fourteen stanzas. In this final section, I wish to tease out the resonances of this refrain, drawing on Boluk and LeMieux's reading of Wright's poem as a text that "deftly weaves descriptions of videogame hardware, speedrunning techniques, community history, personal biography, and gender identity together . . . challeng[ing] the default categories of the normative ways we play" (50).

Wright attained fame running *The Legend of Zelda: Ocarina of Time* (Nintendo EAD). Unlike the 3DO titles Quinn came to love, *Ocarina* is eminently canonical, a fixture in the lists and retrospectives through which gaming culture shores up its narratives of excellence and progress. For speedrunners, however, it is often games' flaws that render them rich play experiences, creating possibilities for "collision detection failure, out-of-bounds exploration, and sequence breaking due to discrepancies between physics systems and animation states, especially at extreme velocities or angles of approach" (Boluk and LeMieux 44). For Boluk and LeMieux, such feats show that, from a certain angle, all gameplay is a matter of "manipulating memory": what the player experiences in terms of collecting items or traversing the game world is, from a computational perspective, a matter of writing "hexidecimal values to memory addresses." In *Ocarina*'s case, discoveries about how the game stores and loads data have enabled runners to radically reconfigure gamic space-time (44–45). For Wright, speedrunning is in part a matter of assuming such nonhuman perspectives, of sensitizing oneself to "the dropped frames . . . the bitrate . . . the interlacing . . . the deadzone."

Wright's poem requires a similar shift on the part of its listeners and readers (the full text is reproduced in the description field of the YouTube video). The poem is studded with terms that are meaningless or misleading to lay audiences. Wright's pronunciation of certain terms is idiosyncratic, as is her text's use of lowercase letters throughout, including for acronyms and proper nouns. These idiosyncracies attest to Wright's deep knowledge of the ordinarily irrelevant or imperceptible details that make all the difference to runners—and to poets.

Rather than representing the speedrunner as a virtuoso imposing her will on the game, Wright's poem shows her painstakingly accommodating herself to the quirks and foibles of particular configurations of hardware and software. Writing ludobiographically, she frames herself as one of many players in an ensemble that encompasses everything from the intangible stuff of computer code to the base matter of "rubber band[s], tape, and grease." In search of loopholes and shortcuts, Wright cultivates an intimate knowledge of each component of the ludic assemblage, finding meaning in the minutest differences between the original game, "the sloppy port, [and] the hd remaster."

It is significant that Wright did not run the original Nintendo 64 version of *Ocarina* but the port produced for the iQue player, a system produced in collaboration with a Taiwanese American technologist to circumvent Chinese legislation banning the sale of games consoles for the sake of "the mental and physical development of the nation's youth" (Boluk and LeMieux 41–42). The iQue version of *Ocarina* features "a decreased number of polygons loaded at a time . . . result[ing] in less lag." Further, it is translated into Simplified Chinese (a standardized character set endorsed by the postwar Chinese government as a means of promoting literacy), displaying text at a "rate . . . slightly faster than Japanese text and significantly faster than English" (42). As this suggests, runners' performances are enabled and constrained not only by code and hardware design but also by culture, language, history, and politics.

Biology and anatomy also matter, and speedrunning figures in Wright's text as a form of metagaming that pushes not only the limits of the game but also of the embodied player. This player must endlessly repeat intricate sequences of inputs in the hope that random number generators will produce an optimal set of circumstances, playing a "statistical waiting game / grinding endless attempts, waiting for the outlier" (Wright). For Wright, the "human cost" of speedrunning manifested primarily as carpal tunnel syndrome (Boluk and Le-Mieux 50), as gameplay gradually "destroy[ed] my wrists" (Wright). Her biography, then, shows how susceptible bodies are to debilitating changes—changes that may be a matter of incremental attrition rather than sudden incapacitation. But along with the changes caused by persistent play, Wright recounts her experiences of hormone therapy and experiments with gender presentation, illustrating how subjects can chemically and culturally reconfigure the codes of gender in ways that are affirming and enabling: "painting my nails, doing my makeup . . . / buy a new dress / feel the pain from the laser . . . / leaving the clinic, bottles in my hand / spironolactone, estradiol."

Maxi Wallenhorst argues that in readings of trans life-writing, "the complexity of lived experience" is too often "reduced and romanticized to a site of exemplary and inherent transgressiveness, or even transcendence." For some, the parallels Wright draws between her subversion of *Ocarina*'s explicit rules and her rejection of gender norms may smack of the kind of reductive romanticism Wallenhorst cautions against. But while Wright presents her biography as proof that bodies and selves are mutable and malleable, she also acknowledges that we cannot fully control or foresee the forms they will take. As her evocation of "the pain from the laser" hints, the pursuit of self-realization is seldom without sacrifice or discomfort.

The laser and its pain hark back to earlier stanzas, wherein Wright's "mind wanders . . . / to the ique player, the fast memory card, the old gamecube laser / to the ps2 disc speed." This transition from the vagaries of human reminiscence to the vicissitudes of digital data retrieval is characteristic of the poem as a whole, as is the technique of listing. Wright's lists evoke Ian Bogost's discussion of "ontographical cataloging" as an "inscriptive strategy . . . that uncovers the repleteness of units and their interobjectivity" (38). By reminding us that the components of a system may be intimately entangled while "remain[ing] utterly isolated, mutual aliens," such cataloging "hones a virtue: the abandonment of anthropocentric narrative coherence in favor of worldly detail" (40, 42).

So it proves in Wright's poem. Asserting that her experiences have granted her a sense of "the grand decentralization of it all," her poem resonates with calls to develop forms of posthumanist life-writing in which, as Cynthia Huff puts it, "the individual would be displaced from the center and the center displaced in favor of the surround." For Huff, such writing would "emphasi[ze] . . . interrelationship and interconnection," limning "a space where many beings—some of them readily visible, some not—continually affect each other in contradistinction to the story of an individual human moving through and dominating space" (280). Undercutting the conventional narratives of lone speedrunners asserting their excellence and their identities by imperiously dominating game space, Wright's poem represents her success as the result of a confluence of factors beyond any single being's control. Animated by the tension between the autobiographical and ludobiographical, her poem complicates familiar framing of gaming's history and bring into focus the kinds of posthuman encounters that gaming has rendered commonplace.

Conclusion

This essay has presented firsthand accounts of digital gameplay as historical sources, examples of life-writing, insights into the dynamics of subjectification, and articulations of a kind of vernacular posthumanism. While its purview has been confined to written texts (rather than, say, podcasts, documentaries, or virtual reality installations), the examples I've considered have been formally and generically diverse. By discussing examples ranging from relatively conventional memoirs to zines and spoken-word poetry, and by talking in terms of modes rather than genres, I've sought to better understand the way writers align (or fail to align) the autobiographical and ludobiographical dimensions that exist in all manner of writing about games, from walkthroughs, reviews, and other kinds of popular and journalistic texts to scholarly articles and monographs. There is already a wealth of writing out there shedding light on how individuals within and beyond the industry's traditional demographic parameters have lost and found themselves through play. We just need to know how to read it.

WORKS CITED

Bissell, Tom. *Extra Lives: Why Video Games Matter.* Vintage, 2010.

Bogost, Ian. *Alien Phenomenology.* University of Minnesota Press, 2012.

Boluk, Stephanie, and Patrick LeMieux. *Metagaming: Playing, Competing, Spectating, Cheating, Trading, Making, and Breaking Videogames.* University of Minnesota Press, 2017.

Emerson, Lori. "Digital Poetry as Reflexive Embodiment." *Cybertext Yearbook 2002–2003,* edited by Markku Eskelinen and Raine Koskimaa. University of Jyväskylä, 2003, pp. 88–106.

Gallagher, Rob. "Humanising Gaming? The Politics of Posthuman Agency in Autobiographical Videogames." *Convergence,* vol. 28, no. 2, 2022, pp. 359–73.

Goldsmith, Kenneth. *Fidget.* Toronto: Coach House, 2000.

Huff, Cynthia. "After Auto, After Bio: Posthumanism and Life Writing." *A/b: Auto/Biography Studies,* vol. 32, no. 2, 2017, pp. 279–82.

Jayemanne, Darshana. *Performativity in Art, Literature, and Videogames.* Springer, 2017.

Keogh, Brendan. "Instantaneously Punctuated Picture-Music: Re-evaluating Videogame Expression Through *Pilgrim in the Microworld.*" *Convergence,* vol. 25, no. 5–6, 2019, pp. 970–84.

Kirkpatrick, Graeme. *The Formation of Gaming Culture: UK Gaming Magazines, 1981–1995.* Springer, 2015.

Parker, Felan. "Canonizing *BioShock*: Cultural Value and the Prestige Game." *Games and Culture,* vol. 12, no.7–8, 2017, pp. 739–63.

Penix-Tadsen, Phillip, ed. "Introduction: Video Games and the Global South." *Video Games and the Global South.* ETC Press, 2019, pp. 1–32.

Perron, Bernard, Dominic Arsenault, Martin Picard, and Carl Therrien. "Methodological Questions in 'Interactive Film Studies.'" *New Review of Film and Television Studies,* vol. 6, no. 3, 2008, pp. 233–52.

Poletti, Anna, and Julie Rak. "Digital Dialogues." *Identity Technologies: Constructing the Self Online,* edited by Anna Poletti and Julie Rak. University of Wisconsin Press, 2014, pp. 3–22.

Quinn, Zoë. *Crash Override: How Gamergate (Nearly) Destroyed My Life, and How We Can Win the Fight Against Online Hate.* PublicAffairs, 2017.

Rak, Julie. "Life Writing Versus Automedia: The Sims 3 Game as a Life Lab." *Biography,* vol. 38, no. 2, 2015, pp. 155–80.

Reed, Emilie [Coleo Kin]. "Lost Histories Jam." *Itch.Io,* 2019. https://itch.io/jam/lost-histories-jam.

Rodriguez, Florencia Rumpel. "In the Beginning We All Played Family." *Itch.Io*, 2019. https://rumpel.itch.io/in-the-beginning-we-all-played-family.

Sell, Mike. "The Bittersweet Pleasures of Patriarchy Lite: A Reconsideration." *This Professor Plays*, 25 July, 2018. http://iblog.iup.edu/thisprofessorplays/2018/07/25/the-bittersweet-pleasures-of-patriarchy-lite-a-reconsideration.

———. "Modernist Afterlives in Performance—Playing the Avant-Garde: The Aesthetics, Narratives, and Communities of Video Game Vanguards." *Modernism/Modernity*, vol. 4, no. 3, 2019.

Smith, Sidonie, and Julia Watson. *Reading Autobiography: A Guide for Interpreting Life Narratives*. University of Minnesota Press, 2001.

Sudnow, David. *Pilgrim in the Microworld*. Boss Fight Books, 2019.

Therrien, Carl, and Martin Picard. "Techno-Industrial Celebration, Misinformation, Echo Chambers, and the Distortion Cycle." *Kinephanos*, 2014. https://www.kinephanos.ca/2014/history-of-games.

Wallace, David Foster. *Infinite Jest*. Back Bay Books, 2016.

Wallenhorst, Maxi. "Scaling Hotness to Life." *Texte zur Kunst*, 3 July 2020. https://www.textezurkunst.de/articles/scaling-hotness-life.

Wright, Narcissa. "All the Categories Are Arbitrary." *YouTube*, 18 December 2015. https://youtu.be/EHA1qxsLH-0.

VIDEOGAME REFERENCES

Bioshock Infinite. Irrational Games, 2013.

Blaster Master. Sunsoft, 1988.

Braid. Number None, 2008.

Breakout. Atari Inc., 1976.

Depression Quest. Zoë Quinn and Patrick Lindsey, 2013.

Fallout 3. Bethesda Game Studios, 2008.

Far Cry 2. Ubisoft Montreal, 2008.

Gears of War. Epic Games, 2006.

Gears of War 2. Epic Games, 2008.

Grand Theft Auto IV. Rockstar North, 2008.

The Legend of Zelda: Ocarina of Time. Nintendo EAD, 1998.

LittleBigPlanet. Media Molecule, 2008.

Metal Gear Solid. Konami Computer Entertainment Japan, 1998.

Resident Evil. Capcom, 1996.

Super Mario Bros. Nintendo EAD, 1985.

The Wrath of Disgruntled Fandom

Canon, Representation, and *Mass Effect: Deception*

CHRISTOPHER LOVINS

BioWare's *Mass Effect* franchise spans four videogames with more than forty supplementary releases between them (eleven of which are significant expansions), an upcoming fifth mainline game, four spin-off games, various comic book series, and even an amusement park ride. The original trilogy received both critical acclaim—the second game being cited by numerous publications as one of the greatest videogames of all time—and strong sales of 14 million units. Its continued popularity and influence spurred a 2021 re-release in the form of remastered versions carrying the price tag of a contemporary AAA release.

In addition, the original trilogy generated four novels. Rather than novelizations of the games' plots, these were interstitial stories expanding the story and game world. The first three were generally regarded as solid if unspectacular, but the fourth, *Deception,* was widely denounced by the franchise's fan community as inconsistent with series canon, with one fan expressing displeasure by uploading to YouTube a video of themselves burning a copy. The backlash spurred BioWare to promise a "revised" version correcting the errors. This hostile reaction to *Deception* served as a kind of dress rehearsal for the infamous campaign against *Mass Effect 3* when it was released two months later, though only in the case of the videogame did BioWare issue a revised version intended to address fan complaints.

Fan dissatisfaction with violations of canon is often considered elitist gatekeeping, as fans police the boundaries of acceptable content through demonstration of obscure and arcane knowledge (Carruthers). However, I contend that not all canon violations are equal and that disputes over canon can be a force for inclusion rather than exclusion. I will demonstrate this through analysis of online forum threads discussing *Deception*'s alleged violations, including a fan-produced Google document that marks these violations according to purported severity. Strikingly, the most glaring violations were largely those inconsistent with BioWare's history of including less-represented groups, in this case LGBTQ+ characters and characters with disabilities (see Jerreat-Poole; Pelurson). Though BioWare never released the promised revised edition of the novel, fans nevertheless demonstrated their willingness to hold the company to its statements about inclusion (Collins 17). Couched in the discussion of canon, *Mass Effect* fans debated the "symbolic annihilation" that Adrienne Shaw has identified as a common strategy for gay characters in videogames (231).

Fan studies pioneer Henry Jenkins has explored the potential of fan spaces as areas of greater inclusion. He argues for fandom as the counterbalance to media corporations, noting that feedback between videogame fans and creators is greater than that between fans and creators of other media such as film or television (*Textual Poachers* 154, 169). This empowered participation of the fan community can be an enormous boost to the success of a videogame franchise, to the point where fans are often willing to perform volunteer labor that enhances the value of brands (142, 171). Jenkins describes "the ideal consumer" as "active, emotionally engaged, and socially networked . . . [and] inside the brand community," where they can "become protectors of brand integrity and thus critics of the companies that seek to court their allegiance" (*Convergence Culture* 20). Similarly, Kevin Roberts describes "inspirational consumers" who "act as moral guardians for the brands they love. They make sure the wrongs are righted and hold the brand fast to its stated principles" (192).[*] This essay presents an example of inspirational consumers who criticized a major videogame developer for violating its stated commitment to inclusion.

Novelization, Transmedia Stories, and *Mass Effect*

Novelization is the adaptation of a visual media work, typically a film or videogame, into a novel (see Shea in this volume). By its strictest definition, it is the direct adaptation of a film's plot, essentially its script expanded and revised

---

[*] This is not to say that this notion of fandom as a force against the dominant culture has gone unchallenged. For just a few examples, see Condis; Leonard; Stanfil.

into novel form. But any novel that is said to be "based on" a film or franchise is often treated the same as strict novelization (Benson). Because the author of a novelization is rarely involved in the creative process of the original work, the literary world does not regard novelizations highly. This is reflected in the poor pay these authors receive, buttressed by Writers Guild of America rules that stipulate that a film's original screenwriter is to receive significantly more money for a novelization of their film than the actual writer of that novelization does, with the latter usually denied royalties as well (Kent and Gotler 93–94).

Small wonder, then, that few screenwriters write novelizations of their films when they stand to make more money doing almost anything else with the required time and effort. Thus, novelizations do not enjoy anything approaching the prestige of the reverse form of adaptation, turning books into films. Johannes Mahlknecht has written about the enormous difficulties facing novelization authors "via tight deadlines and limited creative freedom, to deliver a product whose actual quality is of secondary importance" (Mahlknecht 141; see also Van Parys 305).

Videogame tie-in novels typically pay better than novelizations and are not held in quite as low esteem, but they do still tend to be work-for-hire projects done for money rather than creative expression, at least according to *Deception* author William C. Dietz. Dietz's article "How to Novelize a Game" illustrates that original stories based on games are not clearly distinguished from strict novelizations when it comes to industry respectability, as the article appears to use the terms "tie-in" and "novelization" interchangeably. So even if it is a completely original story, a videogame tie-in novel garners little respect in the literary world on account of its connection to the existing property.

Novelizations and tie-ins remain relevant in the second decade of the twenty-first century, since twenty-first-century media creators pitch a world where multiple stories can be told in multiple forms rather than a single story (Jenkins, *Convergence Culture* 116). The *Mass Effect* universe exemplifies this, being conceived from the beginning as a transmedia franchise (see "Mass Effect: Interview"; VGS). Jenkins defines a transmedia story as one that "unfolds across multiple media platforms, with each new text making a distinctive and valuable contribution to the whole" (*Convergence Culture* 97–98). In this case, the original trilogy was accompanied by four interstitial tie-in novels. The first three were written by Drew Karpyshyn, at the time a staff writer at BioWare, who had cowritten a number of the company's flagship titles, including the first two *Mass Effect* games, rather than a freelance author commissioned to write tie-in novels, as is the industry standard (see "Mass Effect: Interview"; Takahashi; VGS). *Deception* was written by Dietz, a freelance author hired in the standard manner, who otherwise had no involvement in the *Mass Effect* series.

The original three games were created by Canadian game developer BioWare and released in 2007, 2010, and 2012, respectively. A space opera set at the end of the twenty-second century, *Mass Effect* sees humanity discover that Pluto's moon Charon is a massive gateway permitting instantaneous travel among a galaxy-wide network of such gateways. Humans are not alone in the Milky Way and are latecomers to a thriving galactic civilization made up of more than a dozen alien races. The eponymous "mass effect" is the manipulation of mass to propel ships faster than light, create artificial gravity, or move distant objects through gravity effects. Certain individuals in the game world can be trained to create and manipulate these mass-effect fields, to the extent that they can be described as having "biotic powers" to move, throw, or damage people or objects.

Deception was published on January 31, 2012, five weeks before the release of the concluding game of the trilogy. This essay will focus on the characters of Gillian Grayson, a girl with potentially great biotic powers, and the chief of security at Gillian's school for biotics, Hendel Mitra, a biotic himself who eventually becomes her protector. At the end of the second novel, Hendel and Gillian are forced to abandon the school and seek refuge with the alien Quarians. They board a Quarian ship bound for an unexplored part of the galaxy so remote and unknown that they will be safe from those seeking to harm Gillian. *Deception* picks up some years later, the exact number being one of the canon inconsistencies that so outraged fans. It is to these inconsistencies that we now turn.

The List

The reaction to *Deception*'s representation of Gillian and Hendel that I express here is that expressed on the dedicated *Mass Effect* forums on BioWare's Social Network website. These forums were shut down in 2016 but were archived by Fextralife. Forums are a useful source for understanding players' reactions to games, as these reactions are "organic and unprompted" rather than induced by a researcher for the purposes of a study (Burgess and Jones). The first major thread on *Deception* was deleted for copyright reasons arising from fans' posting of long excerpts from the manuscript. However, during its four days of existence, the thread accumulated around four hundred pages (and so, at ten comments per page, nearly four thousand comments). Because it was deleted entirely rather than locked, it was not archived and therefore was unavailable for this project. Instead, I focus primarily on the successor thread, which was locked after ten days and 1,140 pages (a staggering 11,393 comments), and on the thread discussing BioWare's announcement that it would republish *Deception* in response to fan feedback, at 184 pages (approximately 1,800 comments). Many of the posters in the original, deleted thread were active posters in these two later threads. For comparison, about half of the contemporary threads on the same forum had ten comments or less, and the other half generally had between two and ten pages (twenty to one hundred comments). Only about one in twenty-five threads had more than twenty pages.

The first post of the 1,140-page thread is a brief introduction to the controversy that raged in the deleted thread and contains a link to a Google document listing ninety-nine issues. Titled *Errors In: Mass Effect Deception*, the document is introduced as follows: "While this list may seem nit-picky considering some of the errors, there are a handful worth mentioning that have very legitimate reasons for being upset over. This includes a character 'growing up' from being autistic, turning Mass Effect's only gay male character straight and then killing him, and being literally impossible to reconcile with the timeline made by the games, comics and other books."* It is telling that Chris Priestly, the compiler of the list, felt compelled to immediately defend it as not "nitpicky," at least not entirely.

Game developer Tom Dowd discusses the list in his guidebook for developing transmedia franchises. For Dowd, *Deception*'s great sin is its "significant continuity errors in the areas of . . . pretty much everything" which "implies a lack of respect for the property" on BioWare's part (70). But Dowd overlooks the list's severity grading. Its compilers flagged grievous errors in red and major errors in blue to demarcate them from the mere "continuity errors." This, combined with its introductory paragraph that highlights three issues (two of them being discussed here), makes it clear that contributors were concerned about more than just continuity. A brief exchange among users JamesFaith, izmirtheastarach (one of the most involved contributors to the list), and Heraxion illustrates this point:

---

* All forum posts and titles are presented as written, including spelling, grammar, punctuation, and use of capitalization. This includes the title of this forum thread, which gives the misspelling "Del Ray" for Del Rey Books. Since all posts are made under pseudonyms, I will use gender-neutral third-person pronouns (they/their/themself/themselves) for all posters.

JamesFaith: Yes, the big ones were Dietz's doom. If he made only those little, we would only smirk "star-shaped Citadel . . . suuure" and it will be all. But there were so many great mistakes, that people started looking for others and when they started, they found all those little ones too.

izmirtheastarach: Exactly. It's what is so frustrating about so many of these errors. A bunch of them would be seriously softended [softened] if Dietz had taken two seconds to explain them. Instead he just presents a bunch of illogical things as facts, and expects us to buy them.

Heraxion: Very good point. [Drew] Karpyshyn makes alot of small mistakes in his books aswell. . . . But Dietz crossed a line. ("Del Ray" post 472, 478, 485)

These Aren't the Characters We're Looking For

The first item on the *Errors In* list, under the heading "Characters," reads, "1. Gillian's autism is never mentioned—The closest the book gets is noting that she was an 'unstable twelve-year-old' and a passing reference to her having a 'temper.' This is not presented as a disability, but rather an adolescent phase she has largely 'gotten over.'" This symbolic annihilation of disability is a far cry from the other entries in the *Mass Effect* franchise. Rather than erasing disability from the future through technological cures, as much science fiction (and particularly military science fiction) does, *Mass Effect* includes the prominent character of Joker, a staple throughout the trilogy, who directly confronts the ableism of his society. The *Mass Effect* trilogy does not cut disability out of the future but instead offers what Adan Jerreat-Poole terms "crip futurity," in which the lived experience of disability is represented rather than technologically cured out of existence.

Thus, *Deception*'s erasure of autism is particularly problematic for this franchise. Unlike the question of Hendel's sexuality, which will be discussed later, the text leaves no ambiguity about Gillian's autism, as she is explicitly identified on page 41 of *Ascension*: "At age three she [Gillian] had been diagnosed with a mild form of high-functioning autism." Later Gillian herself outright states to another character that she is autistic (Karphyshyn 244), and some of her behavior is meant to indicate autism. For example, she eats meals by taking one bite out of each item on her food tray at a time (for which she is mocked by another student), frequently sits in silence with her father without acknowledging him, and prefers solitude to the company of other children, whose social interactions, we are told, she struggles to understand (91–92, 105–110). As noted in the list, *Deception* mentions neither autism nor any behaviors suggestive of autism from *Ascension*. Many fans took exception to this and posted their displeasure on the forums, with crimzontearz referring to it as "the whole autism debacle" to which "people took real offense" ("Del Ray" post 962).

User Ryo Bondiko writes that they noticed only "the most obvious" inconsistencies with series canon, as they were "not that deep in the lore," but pointedly writes, "We have a very powerful and autistic (Mr. Dietz, you might want to wiki that word or read the prequels to your story at least . . .) girl" (post 732, ellipsis in original). SweetJeeba writes, "What's really appalling is this company really went out of its way to take a stand for it's [*sic*] decisions with gay characters, yet has no issues with dismissing a psychological disorders and reducing autism to anger issues. Completely hypocritical" (post 1282). Heimdall writes, "The issue with Gillian is more that her autism is never referenced in any way. The closest she comes to it is mentioning that she had anger issues when she was younger. Which makes it sound like a phase she grew out of" (post 1275). In sum, these posters criticized the characterization of autism as "anger issues" and as a temporary state that disappears upon reaching adulthood. Jerreat-Poole notes how vital it is for the representation of disability in science fiction that "Joker does not overcome his illness," while *Deception* turns crip futurity on its head, with Gillian's autism turned into "anger issues" that simply vanish with maturity.

Some fans countered that six years had ostensibly passed (Gillian is eighteen years old in *Deception*), and so her condition might have changed. dreman9999 argues that "it is possible that she can deal with it and be a normal person" (post 881). This post and further defenses of it by dreman9999 brought a number of responses. One poster calling themself BentOrgy writes, "Dreman, honestly; what the hell are you trying to achieve here? Gillian's no longer autistic, that's a massive problem. What is there to debate? Its not that it 'Wasn't handled well,' its that it wasn't handled AT ALL" (post 887). For BentOrgy, this defense of *Deception* amounts to "overcoming" autism, exactly the curing-out-of-existence trope for which Jerreat-Poole criticizes military science fiction in general. (It may be worth mentioning here that Dietz is a prolific author of, yes, military science fiction.)

MissOuJ offered this rebuttal to dreman9999:

Seriously, this is my main problem with how Gillian's autism is handled. Coping with autism can be incredibly challenging, and people with autism have many different coping mechanisms/ways to deal with their disability. To hand-wave this by claiming autism is just a childhood phase she got over is incredibly insulting. You don't really get over the fact your brain and nervous system function differently from the rest of the population (and the problem for most high-functioning autistics is to learn to live in a world that has been built by neurotypical people for neurotypical people so they have to learn to live in it by trial and error). Having autistic characters is awesome. Displaying them as individuals who have learned to live among neurotypical population and discussing the different way they see the world isn't a problem. It's handwaving the disability in the first place that makes my blood boil. (post 886)

This poster appreciated the Gillian character and made it clear they were not displeased by her ability to function in the world but rather by the elision of how she would achieve this and how her experience of the world would be different from that of neurotypical characters. Just as Joker's ability to walk in a way that rejects being "fixed" is a "resistance to the hypermasculinist super-able-bodiedness celebrated by the [military science fiction] genre" (Jerreat-Poole), Gillian's navigation of "a world that has been built" by and for neurotypicals could have furthered the franchise's inclusivity. Instead, she thinks and acts no differently from neurotypicals in *Deception*, and it is this annihilation of disability that makes MissOuJ's "blood boil."

After further dispute between dreman9999 and BentOrgy, the latter ended their side of the discussion by concluding that the idea that "Gillian could have coped with her condition to the level Dietz potrayed (Again, highly unlikely.) is not the issue, its fact that he made it possible because she's now just another teen with a troubled past. That's. Not. Okay. No matter how you look at it" (post 899). Jerreat-Poole discusses how *Mass Effect 3* "complicates the cyborg super-crip archetype" by depicting a character's "slow process of healing and recovery that is rarely present" in the genre. For BentOrgy, *Deception* could have done something similar if it had depicted the process by which Gillian adjusted to the neurotypical world, why she made such a decision, and how she felt about doing so. Not depicting this process, and portraying her as having "dealt with" these issues, is the symbolic annihilation that so inflamed MissOuJ and Bent-Orgy. Perhaps izmirtheastarach best sums up the thread's consensus: "Literally any explanation would have served better then Dietz's decision to simply pretend that he[r] Autism had never existed" (post 341).

The *Errors In* list's second major point of contention, again under "Characters," is the rewriting of an established gay character as straight, a note highlighted in red as an error of canonical magnitude: "7. Hendel Mitra is described as ogling Asari strippers, a very heterosexual reaction—Hendel was established as homosexual in *Ascension*." A few forum posters disputed this claim along two lines. First, was Hendel's sexuality established as gay rather than bisexual, or was it not firmly established at all? Second, even if Hendel was gay in *Ascension*, was the list correct to characterize his "ogling Asari strippers" as altering this?

Turning to the text, *Ascension* does not directly state that Hendel is a gay man, as it does that Gillian is autistic, but it is implied. For instance, Hendel's close friend (and the novel's main character), Kahlee Sanders, laughs at her (male) lover's insinuation that she is romantically involved with Hendel, telling him, "I'm not Hendel's type. You might be, though." The lover is momentarily confused, but then "grasp[s] what she meant" (Karpyshyn 78). Two pages later, he jokes with her that "maybe Hendel's got a crush on" another male character. A few pages after this, the narration describes a young woman lightly flirting with Hendel while Kahlee thinks to herself, *"You're wasting your time, sister"* (85). Ultimately, Gillian suggests that Kahlee and Hendel marry, causing Kahlee to think, *"This wasn't the time to explain why that would never happen"* (117). Given all this, it is reasonable to conclude that Hendel's attraction is primarily if not exclusively toward people expressing a male gender identity, particularly in light of Kahlee's thought that the unnamed woman cannot interest him romantically; her anonymity in the narrative implies his lack of interest in women generally rather than in Kahlee specifically, as a number of forum commenters suggested.

The user I can Hackett offers this response to contributors to the list, writing, "In my opinion Hendel Mitra was never confirmed to be homosexual it was suggestive at best" ("Del Ray" post 508), and Bluko concurs: "Yes this . . . I missed the part where Hendel was explicitly labeled as being strictly homosexual. Yes it was implied, but never outright said" (post 535). Blacklash93 counters that Kahlee knew Hendel well and indicated "he was gay at least 4 times," finishing with, "It was not suggested. It was outright stated" (post 589). AVPen and Yuoaman—two contributors to the list—also challenge Bluko and I can Hackett. AVPen asserts that it was canon that the Asari were an all-female species and Hendel was queer (being so established in *Ascension*), and "the idea of a homosexual human male becoming sexually attracted to an alien that resembles a human female is utterly ludicrous. <_< Never mind the fact that Dietz had either no f***ing clue that Hendel was gay (because he didn't read the previous novel/s) or he did and just didn't care cause he was gonna write Hendel as being straight for whatever reason" (post 463). InvincibleHero jumps into the fray on the side of Bluko and I can Hackett. They argue that "people change," seemingly citing the problematic practice of gay conversion: "Gay men have publicly proclaimed to be cured and consider themselves monogamous heterosexuals" (post 503). Yuoaman counters with "sexual preference is not a disease to be cured, I don't even know if you're serious right now" (post 505).

We must briefly address the alien species known as the Asari, as this was a major point of contention among forum writers. *Mass Effect*'s lore is not entirely consistent when it comes to the Asari and gender. However, most sources identify the Asari as having only one gender, female. This comes from dialogue by the series' most prominent Asari character, Liara T'Soni, and from the Codex, the in-game repository of game world information, which describes the Asari as "an all-female race." There are numerous indirect indicators, as well. Asari have feminine secondary sex characteristics such as breasts and wider hips, are voiced and modeled exclusively by female actors, and use language such as she/her pronouns, the title "matriarch," and the word "daughters" for their offspring.

The forum includes extensive discussion of these points. BluSoldier argues that "just because a gay character was 'ogling Asari strippers' does not make him straight or bisexual. Remember that Asari have the ability to look appealing to all forms of sentient life, no matter what gender race or sexual orientation he or she may be" ("Del Ray" post 835). BentOrgy replies that this supposed ability was unproven (post 838)—and indeed, BluSoldier provides no evidence for this ability—while Yuoaman concedes the possibility but notes that "such an event would probably still warrant some sort of comment, there was none" (post 836). Forum user Direwolf0294 argues that the Asari are sexually appealing to all species and all genders, as evidenced in a scene from the first *Mass Effect* game that can only be accessed if the player, playing as a female character, pursues a romantic relationship with both Liara and Kaidan Alenko (a human male). In the scene, Kaidan, accompanied by Liara, confronts the player and demands that she choose one of them to continue a relationship. Kaidan says, "I didn't know you were—that you prefer other women," to which Liara replies, "I am not exactly a woman, Lieutenant. My species only has one gender." For

Direwolf0294, Liara's "I am not exactly a woman" means that Hendel's interest in the Asari does not indicate he was sexually attracted to women ("Del Ray" post 449). Direwolf0294 does not mention the very next line, though, which has Kaidan responding, "Yeah, but you look—" He cuts himself off before saying, presumably, "like a woman," "feminine," or words to that effect. TMA Live responded, in a somewhat crude post, that gay men would not be attracted to bodies that appear feminine, as Asari bodies do, while not addressing the suggestion that the Asari are able to appear attractive outside their physical appearance (post 462).

Wulfram, on the other hand, agrees with Direwolf0294, claiming, "The ability of Asari to be attractive outside of people who'd normally find a more or less human female form attractive is established elsewhere too"—though they, like BluSoldier, neglect to list any such occasion (post 455). Yuoaman responds by citing the behavior of the character Kai Leng, established in *Retribution* as loathing the Asari and their sexuality, repeatedly calling them "whores" and finding aliens "disgusting." Kai Leng, then, was a person who clearly did not find Asari attractive . . . except in *Deception*, which was another red-highlighted mistake (number 14 under "Character") on the *Errors In* list: "Kai Leng is physically repulsed by aliens. In *Retribution*, he is completely uninterested in [Asari] Liselle's nudity, thinks of Asari as 'whorish,' and finds the sights of Afterlife [a club filled with Asari dancers] disgusting." Yuoaman notes, "Nowhere in the text does Dietz mention Hendel's sexuality, and there was no need to have him ogle Asari—they're fetishized enough in other media" (post 458). Wulfram concedes that Dietz was likely unaware of any of this, since there was no "acknowledgement of the oddity of the situation" (post 470). WizenSlinky0 opines that, while they regarded a gay man finding Asari desirable as "a conceivable notion based on what we know of the Asari . . . I would have also expected a writer to do it in a way that made that aspect clear" (post 477).

Strikingly, there is no trace of the "don't bring politics into this" position found by Megan Condis in fan responses to the addition of a gay male romance to another BioWare game, *Star Wars: The Old Republic*, released just a few years earlier, in 2009, and so common in contemporary popular media discourse. In the discussion of Hendel's sexuality, disagreements centered solely on whether previous novels established him as a gay man and whether sexual attraction to the alien Asari challenged this, not on the appropriateness of discussing sexuality at all, as on the Old Republic forum. Even forum users who offer defenses of *Deception* nevertheless criticize it for not even mentioning Hendel's established sexual attraction to males. Unlike fans on the Old Republic's forums in 2009, or so many today, fans on *Mass Effect*'s forum in 2012 largely agree that Hendel's sexuality *should* be considered, and they condemned Dietz and BioWare for eliding it.

The closest response to "Don't discuss it" comes from The PLC, with regard to Gillian's autism. They think it "just downright bizarre" that other fans were "OFFENDED because a character in a sci-fi book 'grows out' of" autism, because "Dietz doesn't write anything about growing out of your autism being the normal thing to happen, and it's clearly one of the many mistakes in the book" ("Del Ray" post 965). The PLC was alone among posters, however, with others responding, "I find the idea of telling people not to be offended by things kind of ridiculous" (post 973), and "You will never fully understand until you were in situation od [of] these offended people" (post 972). These users in effect suggested that The PLC decenter their own experience and take account of those of others when it comes to including a character with autism in the *Mass Effect* universe.

Ultimately, the forum posts took on questions of neurodivergence, gender, and sexuality in remarkably responsible if impassioned ways, their ire more often directed toward questions of narrative, character, and storyworld coherence. However, this would turn out to be just as "political" a concern as a larger issue was looming: Who had the ultimate say when it came to the question of videogame storytelling, the intellectual property owners or the fans?

The Desired Outcome

Four days after *Deception* was published, a BioWare employee created a new thread on the *Mass Effect* LiveJournal forum:

> *Mass Effect* fans have been asking for a comment on recent concerns over *Mass Effect: Deception*. We have been listening and have the below response on the issue.
>
> The teams at Del Rey and BioWare would like to extend our sincerest apologies to the *Mass Effect* fans for any errors and oversights made in the recent novel *Mass Effect: Deception*. We are currently working on a number of changes that will appear in future editions of the novel.

We would like to thank all *Mass Effect* fans for their passion and dedication to this ever-growing world, and assure them that we are listening and taking this matter very seriously.

What did the fans dissatisfied with *Deception* want? The same day that *Deception* was published, SpartHawg948 posted an open letter addressed to "[project director] Casey Hudson, [lead writer] Mac Walters, William C. Dietz and the teams at BioWare and Electronic Arts": "We only wish to express our deep disappointment in the quality of this product in the hopes that in the future more thought will be put into the quality of ancillary products, and more respect given to the Mass Effect Community."

While many eagerly looked forward to BioWare's promise to reissue the novel with corrections, others were more cynical: "It's nice to see that something has come of this," writes JeffZero ("Del Ray" post 27). However, most considered it not just a victory but a recognition of their power as a community of creators and fans: "We did it guys," adds LGTX. "Go ME fanbase! And Bioware/Del Rey, you guys rock for listening to us" (post 36). Many fans posted comments similar to this one by felipejiraya: "This is the main reason why I love BioWare, they really care about the fans . . . BioWare has the balls to come to the public and say 'we ****ed up and we're working to satisfy our fanbase'" (post 270). Others compared the response favorably with hypothetical responses (and nonresponses) from other game developers, such as Bungie, Blizzard, and Bethesda.

But the company's promise did not end the discussion or settle the question of the relationship between the company and its consumers. Kusy posts that the apology was "deserved" and so fans need not thank BioWare for it (post 68). Similarly, mulder1199 calls the apology "nice" but refuses to be "impressed" until the rewrite is actually published (post 236). roflchoppaz thinks BioWare should have proved it valued fans by "not publishing this poop in the first place" (post 62), a sentiment echoed by Reptilian Rob: "You show your fan base you care by maintaining a high standard from the START, not a half assed one later on down the road" (post 312). alex90c criticizes what they see as fans' about-face after getting noticed by the company: "Funny how everyone is hating on Bioware, and then the moment they send some vague apology, a whole session of arse-kissing begins" (post 704). One lucidfox is even less enthusiastic: "People, it's a vague promise from a mainstream corporation known for regularly breaking and twisting its vague promises. Wake up" (post 651). SolidusSnake1 likewise does not believe a corrected edition would be published, but they were not troubled by this: "[BioWare will] bury it in a grave where they will never talk about it again. And that is all I ask for" (post 195).

In the end, though, the most common sentiment was that, however un-likely it might be that a corrected version would actually be realized, it was the thought that counted. BioWare had listened to its fans' concerns and, many of them hoped, would not repeat the mistakes it had made with *Deception*. Finding middle ground, izmirtheastarach responds to the "vague promises" post with, "Thanks for the contribution, equally vague voice of doom and gloom. No one is expecting anything. For me, the actual acknowledgement of a problem was enough" (post 652). They also approve of BioWare's lack of censorship as fans conducted "a campaign torpedoing one of their own products from their own official forum" (post 135). Tridenter agrees: "If this was any other developer . . . there wouldn't have ever even been an apology. Nothing. No acknowledgement . . . Be grateful you at least got a reply. But then again, that's probably asking too much of most of the self-serving, delusionally-entitled masses" (post 309). roflchoppaz adds, "I wouldn't say I'm 'happy.' I'm just glad that they finally ac-knowledged it sucks, that they listened. Most companies just ignore ****ty re-ception and move along" (post 722). JamesFaith opines that the fans had shown BioWare they would not tolerate a "half-made" product and the company "will be now more careful with choosing freelancers and editing their work" (post 597), and ZLurps concurs: when it "comes to victories, I'm with James Faith who wrote earlier that this incident will probably lead to better Q&A process regarding tie-in products. I don't believe anyone in the industry wants to be an international joke" (post 726). So, at least for many of the fans, the goal was not a correction of *Deception* or an airing of political grievances but improved future products and, perhaps most importantly, the establishment of a line of communication between fans and producers.

The Actual Outcome

Not everyone was so optimistic. Marta Rio captures the mood in her post: "So the optimist in me says: 'Great, Bioware cares about us and listens to our opin-ions. Yay!' But the pessimist in me says: 'Bioware made this announcement so that we will all shut up about it. In a few weeks when ME3 launches we'll forget it ever happened" (post 690). And so it was. The fans got their apology, but the promised revised edition never materialized and was, as Rio predicted, buried under the controversy over the disastrously received ending of *Mass Effect 3*. Saberchic saw it happening in real time, writing, "The backlash the ending caused in ME3 pretty much sealed this book's fate. They'll let it quietly fade out of people's memories" (post 1747).

However, if the desires of fans were forgotten when it came to the novel, they were instrumental to the development and release of *Mass Effect 3: Extended Cut*, a free-of-charge downloadable file that altered the original ending of the game to address fan complaints. After the release of the downloadable content, Eski.Moe contrasted BioWare's response to fan displeasure with *ME3* to its response to *Deception*: "I was afraid that the movement against the ME3 endings would go the way of this. I mean, we were so passionate and the thread continued to grow and grow. We ended up getting a small placating message from Bioware that they're taking care of things and the spark just died" (post 1580). Poster Genshie expressed their feeling that BioWare's response implied future work would be better vetted, adding that "this has improved the relations between Bioware and its fanbase showing that both sides care" (post 599).

It is impossible to know, but one is tempted to conclude that BioWare's rapid response to fan displeasure with *Mass Effect 3*, promising and delivering an improved ending that dealt directly with fan complaints—and doing so free of charge, despite the enormous costs of development—would not have happened as it did without fan outrage over *Deception*, a spin-off product in a different genre. Perhaps Genshie is correct that this controversy prepared BioWare for how the ending of *Mass Effect 3* would be received, how passionate fans would be about it, how vocal they would be in displaying that passion.

BioWare seemingly did learn from the experience when it came to future tie-in products; all three novels connected to the fourth game, *Mass Effect: Andromeda* (2017), were well received, due in part to BioWare's contracting of respected science fiction authors and avowed fans of the *Mass Effect* franchise, like Catherynne M. Valente and Hugo Award winner N. K. Jemisin. And true to the desires of fans who wanted clear and consistent representation of gender and sexuality, the first of these novels includes not one but two gay male characters, explicitly described as married so as to remove any doubt about their sexuality, and the second makes reference to gender nonbinary beings (humans, not Asari). It seems XXIceColdXX, among others, was correct when they wrote, "Its great that they acknowledged it. And hopefully [it] shakes them up enough that it wont happen again" (post 653).

Second-wave fandom studies generally refuted first-wave descriptions of fandom as an engine of progressive change. Scholars in this wave took a sober look and found fandom was generally not a site for emancipation from the larger culture industry but a continuation of it, not a challenge to existing hierarchies but agents of them (Gray et al. 6). The emerging third wave is, perhaps not surprisingly, finding a messier reality, one that mixes challenge and co-optation, acceptance and rejection, calls for progressive change and defenses of status quo prejudice. If fans at times consciously or unconsciously enact and embody the mores of mainstream culture rather than a liberating counterculture—as some *Star Wars* fans did in the *Star Wars: Knights of the Old Republic* (2003) forums—they can also speak out against symbolic annihilation when a major media company fails to uphold its commitment to inclusion and diversity. Many fans of the *Mass Effect* franchise valued it as another feather in BioWare's cap of increasing representation in videogames, and they regarded *Deception* as a disappointing step back. Their response forced BioWare to make up for lost ground in the following *Mass Effect* game and its tie-in products, to ensure its promise of diverse representation would be realized.

We've examined here an early case of fan-led intervention into a broader vision of how stories are told by media corporations. Such intervention remains an ongoing process in which cases like the misogynist backlash against the 2016 remake of *Ghostbusters* and the internet harassment of *Star Wars* actor Kelly Marie Tran sit uneasily alongside powerful fan-led movements like #OscarsSoWhite and #MeToo. While the struggle is far from over, fan influence of the latter sort—the kind exemplified by *Mass Effect* fans as discussed here—seems to be in ascendance, such that media corporations are intensely cognizant of representation in their properties and how that representation is received. The recent success of *The Witcher*, which occupies both the number 6 (season 1) and number 10 (season 2) spots on Netflix's all-time most watched series, is a case in point. Its success is perhaps the ultimate statement of a fan's influence on a media product, as avowed fan of *The Witcher* videogames Henry Cavill lobbied hard for the title role as an expression of his fandom. Contrasting strongly with the overwhelming whiteness of both the videogames and the previous Polish TV adaptation (titled *The Hexer*), Netflix's *Witcher* includes a significant presence of actors of color, including two of the three central female roles (all of whom were previously portrayed as white). That the final *Witcher* game and the series' first episode were released a mere four years apart is testament to the momentous changes that are now occurring.

WORKS CITED

Benson, Raymond. "The Tie-In Life." *Suduvu*, February 2011. web.archive.org/web/201506 14082245/suvudu.com/2011/02/the-tie-in-life-by-raymond-benson.html. Accessed 25 July 2023.

BioWare. *Mass Effect.* Version 1.02 for Windows PC, Electronic Arts, 2008.

Burgess, Jacqueline, and Christian Jones. "'I Harbour Strong Feelings for Tali Despite Her Being a Fictional Character': Investigating Videogame Players' Emotional Attachments to Non-Player Characters." *Game Studies*, vol. 20, no. 1, 2020. gamestudies .org/2001/articles/burgessjones.

Carruthers, Fiona. "Fanfic Is Good for Two Things: Greasing Engines and Killing Brain Cells." *Participations*, vol. 1, no. 2, 2004, www.participations.org/volume%201/issue %202/1_02_carruthers_article.htm.

Collins, Jennifer. "And Nothing He Has Wrought Shall Be Lost: Examining Race and Sexuality in the Mods of *Dragon Age: Inquisition.*" *Women and Video Game Modding: Essays on Gender and the Digital Community,* edited by Bridget Whelan. McFarland, 2020, pp. 9–35.

Condis, Megan. "No Homosexuals in *Star Wars*? BioWare, 'Gamer' Identity, and the Politics of Privilege in Convergence Culture." *Convergence: The International Journal of Research into New Media Technologies,* vol. 21, no. 2, 2015, pp. 198–212.

"Del Ray [sic] and BioWare Comment on Mass Effect: Deception." *FextraLife*, 3 February 2012. fextralife.com/forums/t511897/del-ray-and-bioware-comment-on-mass-ef fect-deception.

Dietz, William C. "How to Novelize a Game." *International Association of Media Tie-In Writers,* 2005. iamtw.org/articles/how-to-novelize-a-game.

———. *Mass Effect: Deception.* Del Rey, 2012.

Dowd, Tom. *Storytelling Across Worlds: Transmedia for Creatives and Producers.* Routledge, 2013.

Errors In: Mass Effect Deception. Google Docs. https://docs.google.com/document/d/1XBp MF3ONlI308D9IGG8KICBHfWKUosXhontukv-_cmo/preview. Accessed 2 August 2023.

Gray, Jonathan, Cornel Sandvoss, and C. Lee Harington, eds. "Introduction: Why Study Fans?" *Fandom: Identities and Communities in a Mediated World.* New York University Press, 2007, pp. 1–16.

JeffZero. "Mass Effect Deception Discussion Thread." *FextraLife*, 25 January 2012. fextra life.com/forums/t509271/mass-effect-deception-discussion-thread-updated-2220 12-now-with-30-more-links.

Jenkins, Henry. *Convergence Culture: Where Old and New Media Collide.* New York University Press, 2006.

———. *Textual Poachers: Television Fans and Participatory Culture.* Routledge, 1992.

Jerreat-Poole, Adan. "Sick, Slow, Cyborg: Crip Futurity in *Mass Effect.*" *Game Studies*, vol. 20, no. 1, 2020. gamestudies.org/2001/articles/jerreatpoole.

Karpyshyn, Drew. *Mass Effect: Ascension*. Del Rey, 2008.

———. *Mass Effect: Retribution*. Del Rey, 2010.

———. *Mass Effect: Revelation*. Del Rey, 2007.

Kent, Roberta, and Joel Gotler. "Exploiting Book-Publishing Rights." *The Movie Business Book*, edited by Jason E. Squire. McGraw Hill, 2006, pp. 91–97.

Leonard, David J. "Not a Hater, Just Keepin' It Real: The Importance of Race- and Gender-Based Game Studies." *Games and Culture*, vol. 1, no. 1, 2006, pp. 83–88.

Mahlknecht, Johannes. "The Hollywood Novelization: Film as Literature or Literature as Film Promotion?" *Poetics Today*, vol. 33, no. 2, 2012, pp. 137–68.

"Mass Effect: Interview with Casey Hudson—Project Director at Bioware." *Xbox Gazette*, August 2007. www.xboxgazette.com/interview_mass_effect_en.php.

Pelurson, Gaspard. "Mustaches, Blood Magic and Interspecies Sex: Navigating the Non-Heterosexuality of Dorian Pavus." *Game Studies*, vol. 18, no. 1, 2018.

Roberts, Kevin. *Lovemarks: The Future Beyond Brands*. PowerHouse, 2004.

Shaw, Adrienne. "Putting the Gay in Games: Cultural Production and GLBT Content in Video Games." *Games and Culture*, vol. 4, no. 3, 2009, pp. 228–53.

SpartHawg948. "An Open Letter Regarding Mass Effect: Deception." *Mass Effect Wiki*, 31 January 2012. masseffect.fandom.com/wiki/User_blog:SpartHawg948/An_Open _Letter_ Regarding_Mass_Effect:_Deception.

Stanfill, Mel. "'They're Losers, but I Know Better': Intra-Fandom Stereotyping and the Normalization of the Fan Subject." *Critical Studies in Media Communication*, vol. 30, no. 2, 2013, pp. 117–34.

Takahashi, Dean. "BioWare's Casey Hudson: From Mass Effect Burnout to HoloLens and Back for Anthem." *VentureBeat*, 13 June 2018. venturebeat.com/2018/06/13/ea -casey-hudson-bioware-mass-effect-hololens-anthem-e3-interview.

Van Parys, Thomas. "The Commercial Novelization: Research, History, Differentiation." *Literature/Film Quarterly*, vol. 37, no. 4, 2009, pp. 305–17.

VGS—Video Game Sophistry. "VGS Radio Interview: Bioware Writer Drew Karpyshyn on KOTOR, Revan and Mass Effect." *YouTube*, 15 June 2013. https://youtu.be /B9LeXz298K8.

Murakami and Me

My Quest to Understand Why Haruki Murakami's Novels Give Me Videogame Vibes and What to Take Away from That

NIELS 'T HOOFT

A Writer Who Plays Games

Imagine living on an island with an enormous egg on top of the mountain at its center. Wherever you travel, that huge oval shape is always looming over you. Where'd it come from? Why is it there? No clue. It just is.

The image of that egg has stuck with me since playing *Link's Awakening* (1993) on my Game Boy as a teenager. For that game, Nintendo's Japanese development team took the core of their *Zelda* series, threw out the standard fantasy fare, and added a ton of quirkier ideas, including the egg. But not just the egg. As I played, I discovered the island's nature: it was merely a dream—not Link's, which would have been expected, as he's the protagonist—but the Wind Fish's. The Wind Fish was a kind of airborne whale, slumbering within the egg; waking the Wind Fish would complete my quest but also destroy the island and all its inhabitants!

The vulnerability of the Wind Fish's imagination made so much sense to my teenage self. Digital experiences were far more scarce back then, but with *Link's Awakening*, wherever I was, I could switch on my Game Boy and be gobbled up by its fantasy world. Yet if my batteries ran out, all of that would be gone instantly. My current digital life is much less fickle. It's everywhere and it's impossible to turn off, more like a parallel track than a fragile dream. And pretty much everybody I know is in it. In the 1990s, although a lot of kids in the Netherlands were already into videogames, it was still easy to feel like an outsider, not just for playing and liking videogames but also for thinking there was something special there. Especially as I happened to be into literature as well.

I remember, in the early 2000s, bringing my brand-new Nintendo DS to a drinks reception for the publishing company that had just put out my second novel. A small crowd gathered as I demonstrated the console, looking on with equal amounts of awe and detachment. I think many of them just had no way to relate to this device, even though similar tiny touch screens would soon change how they'd all communicate and consume media, and in so doing, put their industry into increasing amounts of trouble. But maybe they weren't really responding to the device but to me, this reader of tea leaves, harbinger of the future, all-around weird guy so unlike them.

As I've grown older, I've gotten used to this kind of response, using it to my advantage, even taking comfort in it. It's just who I am: someone who's often not really in a group but standing at the edges, looking in. Honestly, I think I *need* that feeling of uniqueness, of having an original perspective, because I get bored when I lose it, and when I find it again, it helps me persevere. Like when I wrote about videogames for conventional newspapers, always fighting to get some space on their pages. Or when I founded a startup creating a new way of reading books, trying to meld tech with literature. Or when I fell into a rabbit hole trying to discover and then verbalize why a Japanese author's novels made me feel so much like videogames. Which is what I intend to do here.

When I first became a novelist, I still felt out of place. I'd written a book because I enjoyed reviewing games and thought it would be a nice challenge to create something longer and less utilitarian. In high school, I'd begun reading more adventurously, and I was impressed by all the things books could do. And, of course, the barrier of entry was low. If I could've made a movie or a videogame all by myself, I would have, but alas I could only write a novel. When it was picked up by an agent, published, praised by the press, nominated for a prize, and even translated into German, it didn't do much for my confidence. I got to know a lot of other authors and became friends with some of them, but I mostly felt intimidated. They were so much more serious about writing! Their biggest dream had been to get published, and now that they were, all they wanted to do was read, write, and publish more. I liked being a published author too, but to me, writing books was just one of many things a person could do. Reading books was just one way to immerse oneself in a world—and writing them was just one way to enable others to do the same.

It didn't help that I wanted to write books in which giant eggs lie on mountainous islands, or whatever else my own Wind Fish could dream up. This didn't match well with the Dutch literary tradition, rooted as it is in grim Calvinist realism. Frankly, some of my friends' books bored me, and while I managed to mix some games inspiration into my first novel, it wasn't that much better. Could I ever be a real writer? And was this all there was to being a real writer?

An Inspiration from Japan

I was working on my second novel when I heard about a Japanese writer named Haruki Murakami. It must've been 2004, and I think it was online that I read about his weird, addictive books. I was still worried about displaying "proper writer behavior," walking through bookstores a few days a week, sifting through new releases, spending most of my disposable income on stacks of bound paper. I remember weighing the few Dutch Murakami translations in my hands, settling for *South of the Border, West of the Sun* (originally published in 1992, translated to English in 2000) because it was so thin. Surely that would be a quick and affordable way to discover whether I'd like this author.

It didn't knock me off my feet, but it was a nice enough read, and I started buying and reading more: *Norwegian Wood* (1987, trans. 1989, 2000), a tragic romance with a mysterious sparkle, and Murakami's Japanese breakthrough; *Sputnik Sweetheart* (1999, trans. 2001), with its eerie image of a doppelgänger in an apartment, observed through binoculars from a Ferris wheel; *Hard-Boiled Wonderland and the End of the World* (1985, trans. 1991), which goes deep into weird fiction territory with its parallel fantasy and science fiction storylines; *The Elephant Vanishes* (1993), a short story collection; and, finally, *The Wind-Up Bird Chronicle* (1994–1995, trans. 1997), the quintessential Murakami novel, if you ask me, long and sprawling, including many of the elements the author is now known for.

Often, it's the first book you read by an author that makes the biggest impression, but for me it was that first batch: an eclectic collection of stories of varying length and blends of the real and the fantastic. I was hooked, and I started devouring Murakami's work as soon as it was released. I imagined I was ahead of the curve again, but in reality the translation machine was already firing on all cylinders. At one point, I was alternately reading Dutch and English editions as Murakami's publishers leapfrogged each other.

If I was an early adopter, however, I wasn't alone. One Saturday afternoon I was blocked from the "M" section in my local bookstore by a crowd of people picking up their first Murakami. I barely managed to pluck out the one book I still hadn't read, annoyed that this author was no longer "mine." Even though my writer friends expressed disdain for this latest literary hype, which they thought was overblown and not all that "literary," I was comfortable enough in my role as outsider that I could firmly stand by Murakami's side.

So what was it about these books? Yes, I liked their dreamy quality and flights of fancy; no giant eggs, but how about talking cats and wells that connect to other dimensions? Most of all, I liked the clarity with which they made the unconscious and the symbolic tangible. One example of this can be found in "The Second Bakery Attack" (1985), a brilliant short story in which a husband and wife are kept awake by an inexplicable hunger, driving them to rob a bakery. As his desire to eat grows, the husband imagines himself in a little boat above a volcano. It's a vivid, almost cinematic image of the deep existential emptiness that underlies the man's appetite. For me, it was the best of both worlds: the deep meaning of "difficult" literature presented in a way that appealed to what I thought was my idiosyncratic sensibility. Sometimes I'd read a passage and wonder how a man more than twice my age, living on the other side of the globe in a culture that had always seemed exotic to me, could be so close to me in terms of aesthetics and interests. How was this even possible?

A Playful Fascination

My novels made me very little money, but I was able to pay the rent as a games journalist. Then, as games became more complex in terms of story and graphics and easier to develop and distribute, I became involved in their creation. Sometimes I wrote storylines and dialogue for local studios, or assisted in designing their story delivery systems, but I was also able to help imagine whole new worlds. It felt powerful, being able to create impressive story experiences with just a small team and to have a lot of influence over the final outcome.

Kafka on the Shore (2002)—the English translation appeared the same year (2005) that the Nintendo DS and my second novel came out—was the first of Murakami's novels that disappointed me. This was another sprawling book oscillating between the real and the uncanny, including a living, breathing version of Johnny Walker from the whisky bottle labels. Comfortable to read, sure, but not as refreshing as his earlier works.

But my fascination with the man Haruki Murakami only grew. I read interviews, articles, blog posts, even whole books analyzing his works, and I never stopped wondering how he could speak to me so directly. Then I stumbled upon an interview in the *Paris Review*, published in 2004. In the interview, Murakami mentioned videogames and used them as a metaphor. A bell went off in my head. Yes, that must've been it! So obvious. I had played games from my early Nintendo days, right up to discovering Murakami. And these games were mostly made in Japan—not just *Mario* and *Zelda* but also *Castlevania, Dragon Quest,* and *Final Fantasy.* That explained why I lined up with Murakami so easily and gladly, while my writer friends were nonplussed. And why his books, to me, were exotic and strange yet so very familiar. I wasn't sure how, yet, but games were part of both of our frames of reference, and somehow part of how both us told stories. But how exactly did we do it?

For a while, I kept a "Murakami and games" scrapbook in my Notes app. In the meantime, I wrote a third novel, a decidedly un-Dutch apocalyptic thriller. Then, around the release of *Killing Commendatore* (2017, trans. 2018), I got more serious. Murakami's Dutch publisher announced a special event. I volunteered to give a talk about the parallels between Murakami and videogames, and the organizers readily agreed. I dug into my scrapbook, reached out to others who'd written about Murakami and games, read an advance copy of his book, did a ton of desk research, and organized my thoughts: parallel worlds, character agency, routines, and the interplay between high and low culture. It would turn out to be only the first step in a quest to get to the core of that mysterious egg: understanding Murakami's role in a broader community of creators, which included myself.

Parallel Worlds and Mini-Game Dimensions

Guan van Zoggel, a friend and Japan scholar whom I interviewed, told me that parallel words are so frequent in Japanese fiction that they constitute a genre called *isekai.* Though Murakami's novels aren't typically considered isekai, parallel worlds are everywhere in them, taking many shapes. We find them in *Hard-Boiled Wonderland,* where they are completely different from each other and highly surreal. One is a grimy sci-fi city full of dark passages, the other a bright fantasy realm with spirit stuff going on, the latter revealed to happen inside the mind of the "calculator" in the first, whose sci-fi job is to calculate integers. And we find them in *1Q84* (2009–2010, trans. 2011), in which the worlds are so similar that its characters have to look at the number of moons to tell them apart.

More often, Murakami's parallel worlds take the form of pocket dimensions, spatial bubbles with curious properties tucked into corners of a more regular reality. In *Killing Commendatore*, for example, there's much ado about an ancient burial site from which a mysterious bell keeps ringing. And there's mention of a "wind cave," no relation of the fish, into which the unnamed protagonist's sister disappeared decades ago, talking about *Alice's Adventures in Wonderland* and then remaining hidden for far too long. When she finally returns, the protagonist plainly narrates, "We went back to the real world" (379). But the classic Murakami pocket dimension is found in *The Wind-Up Bird Chronicle*, in the shape of a deep, dry well.

The book is about an unemployed man called Toru who meets a succession of oddball characters as his wife drifts away from him, all while hearing the titular animal calling from a path behind his house. Initially, the well is just a metaphor. In chapter 2, Toru's wife asks him if he has "a deep well inside [him]" (29) that he can just put all his frustrations into. Toru then tries to recall something, but then it recedes into "that dark region of [his] mind where it had been living until that moment" (33). A few chapters later, Mr. Honda tells Toru he is not suited for his job in the legal sector, nor for the normal world of shadows and light: "The world you belong to is above that or below that" (51). When Toru finally discovers a dry well in a neighboring garden, he smugly notes that he now has one in case he needs it.

It's about one-third of the way into *The Wind-Up Bird Chronicle* that Toru decides he does, in fact, need a well. But the incremental materialization doesn't stop there. The well is first used as a flashback device, allowing Toru to think clearly as he descends into the well and meditates in its depths for days. We finally learn how Toru and his wife hooked up and got married. Then, as the memories become more focused, another character starts physically reaching out to Toru in his dreams. Ultimately (spoiler alert), Toru uses the well to transfer himself to other places. In a few hundred pages, the well has grown from an idea into a metaphysical transportation system!

In an e-mail interview with Arjan Peters, reported in the Dutch newspaper *de Volkskrant* in 2018, Murakami said:

> If you look at it from a certain angle, our daily life may look ordinary, boring and extremely continuous. But from a different angle, it's full of amazing contradictions, cracks and irrationality. And regularly we are overwhelmed at night by incomprehensible dreams. Inside us, things are constantly bubbling up that

are immeasurable with existing standards, that we cannot serve out with existing mugs or bowls. We simultaneously live in those two worlds; that's what I feel it comes down to. The role of fiction is—in my opinion—to focus the spotlight on that "other angle" and magnify it. If possible with a positive attitude.

Fantastic portals into weird spaces aren't unheard of in fiction, but there's something distinctly videogame-ish about what Murakami does with them. By putting his "incomprehensible dreams" inside of "magic circles" within the real world and contrasting them with the ever-present mundane, he hands his characters (and his readers) a more accessible way to zoom out and ponder reality without having to fully escape it. Much like when the Wind Fish summoned me, but I could always turn off my Game Boy and return home.

Agency in a Labyrinth of Dotted Lines

The first quote I jotted down when reading *Killing Commendatore* was "I was simply being dragged along by all kinds of circumstances" (27). A typical Murakami sentence, spoken by someone whose career—commissioning portraits—isn't something he chose so much as stumbled into. A typical Murakami character and a typical representation of agency. Murakami's protagonists often want something but don't decide their ultimate destiny, how to unify what they want with what they do.

In *Dance Dance Dance* (1988, trans. 1994), Murakami lets one of his characters discuss his lack of agency: "I felt like I was in a videogame. A surrogate Pac-man, crunching blindly through a labyrinth of dotted lines. The only certainty was my death" (210). While many would argue that games allow players more agency than most story media, Murakami is more interested in games as limiting structures. In a 2008 interview at the University of California, Berkeley, he said, "Writing a story for me is just like playing a videogame. I start with a word or idea, then I stick out my hand to catch what's coming next. I'm a player and, at the same time, I'm a programmer. It's kind of like playing chess by yourself. When you're the white player, you don't think about the black player. It's possible, but it's hard. It's kind of schizophrenic" (Dooley).

While Murakami might seem a cold, analytical writer here, his comments actually suggest a powerful capacity for empathy: the willingness to treat characters and readers as fellow players. It's tempting to see Murakami as a level designer, creating mazes in which readers gobble like Pac-Men. Then, imagine him splitting in two. Player Murakami sticks with his protagonist, gobbling along with us, while level designer Murakami makes us feel like he's still figuring out what will happen next.

Blogger Nate Davis, who wrote about the relationship between Murakami and videogames as early as 2004, had this nice observation: "While Murakami's characters may explore and learn about their environment by themselves, ultimately they wait for a clue for the action that will take them to the next level. They're looking for the hand of a creator who wants them to advance. And you get the sense that the novel just isn't going to progress until they work it out" (emails to author December 2017–February 2018). This is particularly true of his female characters. Like many videogame writers of the 1980s, Murakami often makes women a "clue for the action." In the *Paris Review*, he comments, "In my books and stories, women are mediums, in a sense; the function of the medium is to make something happen through herself. It's a kind of system to be experienced." Recall how a small remark by Toru's wife in *The Wind-Up Bird Chronicle* sets the story in motion—and how she disappears shortly after. Similarly, in *Commendatore*, the main character's wife divorces him, setting the story in motion. But Murakami's male characters have agency. They actively investigate the world around them, even if they're stuck, until at last the author decides to do something about it. The "system to be experienced" is always tied to what the character desires and, in turn, what Murakami assumes his readers desire, too. Sometimes Pac-Man chases power pellets, sometimes women, and they don't just lead him to his goal but transform who he is.

There's another way to think about the repetitive, sometimes aimless wandering of Murakami's characters: as routines. They go through a loop until something changes, at which point they usually go into another loop. These figures are world-class grinders! *The Wind-Up Bird Chronicle* starts with a phone call from a mysterious woman, who from then on keeps on calling. In "Barn Burning" (1983), the protagonist decides to systematically burn all the barns in his vicinity. In "Sleep" (1989), the heroine stops sleeping as she adopts an energetic new lifestyle that includes swimming, eating chocolate, and rereading *Anna Karenina*. In *Commendatore*, the portrait painting procedure is described in beautiful detail, its repetition revealing unexpected qualities. And there's Wataru Menshiki in that same story, observing the girl who might be his daughter with the patience of a videogame player camping until a victim comes close.

Videogames are made up of routines too: you grow crops and harvest them, drop blocks to form disappearing lines, beat enemies to score money to buy increasingly powerful weapons to beat bigger enemies to earn more money. At their deepest level, any videogame is also a cybernetic routine, running from player input to audiovisual output. The program checks whether you're pressing a button, processes that, changes values in its memory, and shows you the results. Ian Bogost has argued that these routines are rhetorical in nature, constructing the reality of the game world and persuading the player to buy in to that reality, no matter how odd or arbitrary it might be.

Murakami is famous for his routine-heavy life, rising early to write for hours and then doing serious exercise, routines he writes about at length in *What I Talk About When I Talk About Running* (2007, trans. 2008) and *Novelist as a Vocation* (2015, trans. 2022). In a 2011 *New York Times* profile, he told Sam Anderson, "I don't get bored. I'm kind of a big kettle. It takes time to get boiled, but then I'm always hot." Just as I ground away at the Nintendo games of my youth, Murakami grinds away at the patient, looping descriptions of his slightly odd, slightly arbitrary worlds. But Murakami seems to have had a more direct hand in videogame culture, too.

A Very Murakami-like Nintendo Game

Murakami was (or is, I can't tell) friendly with Shigesato Itoi. Itoi is probably Japan's most famous adman, having come up with many catchy slogans as well as brand names like Game Boy. He's a tastemaker, often appearing on talk shows and publishing a haiku-like daily blog for decades now. He's also an actor, voicing the dad in *My Neighbor Totoro* and playing the role of the professor in the film adaptation of Murakami's *Norwegian Wood* (2010). However, to Western gamers, Itoi is probably best known for creating the *Mother* series of roleplaying games, including *Mother 2* (1994, translated as *Earthbound*, 1995). It is a strange game by any standard, even coming with scratch and sniff cards. I recently played it in preparation for this essay, as it had not been released in Europe in my youth. It turns out to have huge Murakami vibes. Quirky characters witness strange events in a "kids with bikes" type of small-town America full of cults, psychic girls, pocket dimensions, and a bunch of Beatles references. And what are we to think of the Mu training in which the player chooses to have their legs, arms, ears, and eyes removed, after which they can only communicate with their mind? Like reaching an enlightened state at the bottom of a well!

The corresponding vibes between Itoi and Murakami aren't just me imposing my experience. Long before his Murakami movie role, Itoi commissioned the author to write short stories for the brands he managed (what we would today call "content marketing"), and in 1981 they wrote and published a story bundle together called *Yume de Aimashou* [Let's Meet In a Dream]. While it was never officially published in the West, fans have put their translations of *Yume de Aimashou* online. They are super short, dense, and cryptic, reminding me of Itoi's blog and the diary entries in *Earthbound*, and *maybe* some of Murakami's earliest novels, the so-called Trilogy of the Rat. They don't have the lucid clarity of Murakami's present-day work at all. But they do represent an early manifestation of a shared set of tastes evident in the future works of both men—and of people like me, far away in age and location.

Unfortunately, I haven't been able to find any historical evidence of a deeper connection among Murakami, Itoi, and videogames. But I *feel* it! I feel that Murakami and Itoi must have had a kind of metaphysical mind meld, with Murakami granting Itoi poetic license and Itoi teaching Murakami the effective copywriting of an advertising wizard. After all, Murakami went on to become a best-selling author, with novels full of crystal-clear copy that are looked down upon by more literary minds, both my own writerly friends and the Japanese literary establishment. And Itoi has done an excellent job finding an audience for an idiosyncratic oeuvre.

I know I'm grasping at straws, but I feel a connection between all of this and videogames, those other "systems to be experienced." With games, it's taken for granted that they must be "usable." They need to *work*. Any regular person must be able to put them to their intended use. Sure, the artistic expression of the creator is important too, especially after the so-called indie game revolution of a decade ago, but expression almost always takes a backseat to general usability. Similarly, I feel like Murakami wants his stories to be readable first. After all, if a deep thought is had in a novel that no one can read, is it a thought at all?

As Rebecca Suter discusses in her book *The Japanization of Modernity: Murakami Haruki Between Japan and the United States* (2008), Murakami isn't just writing for a wide audience; he's writing for a Western audience. His literary influences include American authors like F. Scott Fitzgerald, whose work he has translated into Japanese; he lived in the United States for a while; and he actively solicited US publishers to get his translations picked up. Though his stories mostly take place in Japan, his protagonists eat Western food, listen to Western music, and refer to Western literature. There's a curious parallel with Japanese videogames on this point, which were inspired by the American examples of Atari and its contemporaries—and meant for a global market, too—yet were distinctly Japanese. Suter argues that Murakami is part of a broader movement of Japanese modernization; indeed, he is a mediator of that process.

Lights, Camera, Action

It was January 2018. I'd completed the research for my presentation on Murakami and videogames and so I traveled to the harbor town of Rotterdam, where Uitgeverij Atlas Contact, the publisher, had rented the luxury cruise ship S.S. *Rotterdam* for two days. In its heyday, the *Rotterdam* sailed between New York and the Netherlands, but today its rooms are the backdrop for lectures and other social and intellectual activities. Bands played Murakami-inspired music. Screens showed Murakami-inspired movies. There was origami, calligraphy, sushi. But Murakami was not there—cultivating his image as a recluse, or perhaps just too busy writing. And so it was all about a bunch of white people celebrating the man and his works.

I'm pretty sure there was some orientalism at play that weekend, which I was and am guilty of. There's a comfort in fawning over something you don't fully understand, sticking to the mystery instead of solving it, reading between the lines without ever reaching certainty. The affair brought to mind the documentary film *Dinner with Murakami* (2011), in which director Yan Ting Yuen pieces together what attracts her to her idol. In the same spirit as our gathering, Murakami isn't there, just a chair that remains empty to the end of the movie.

The S.S. *Rotterdam*'s central ballroom included a projector and screen, to which I connected my laptop. I'd painstakingly created a gamelike pixel portrait of Murakami, trying to go full circle from videogames to Murakami and back. It appeared above me and all the other people who loved Murakami's novels, videogames, and pondering both. He was larger than life, scribbling his pen on a piece of pixel paper, looking around, then writing again. As the small crowd gathered, I read a quote from the *Paris Review* interview, presenting it almost as a riddle to solve:

> *Haruki Murakami:* I think videogames are closer to fiction than anything else these days.
>
> *Interviewer:* Videogames?
>
> *Murakami:* Yes. I don't like playing videogames myself, but I feel the similarity.

What did he mean by that? Why are they closer to fiction than anything else? I'd saved the context of the quote for the end of my talk, after all my analysis and artifacts were presented. I revealed that he actually said, "So, fiction itself has changed drastically—we have to grab people by the neck and pull them in. Contemporary fiction writers are using the techniques of other fields—jazz, videogames, everything. I think videogames are closer to fiction than anything else these days." I told the audience that I think the similarity between literature and games is that they allow the end user to consume them at their own pace. But Murakami's observation is much more basic: literature must be attractive, accessible, and engaging if it wants to remain relevant.

People responded kindly enough to my talk, but I was not satisfied. I'd done plenty of digging and worked hard to present my findings in a compelling manner, but in the end it was just as Murakami said. Literature has to be more like games if it wants to appeal to a broader audience. Murakami tries to do that, which may be why I liked his work all those years ago, but there's also something mysterious about his work, like that egg on top of the mountain. The last two of his works that I got my hands on hammered this point home: nonfiction tomes about classical music and his T-shirt collection, of all things! It seemed to me that, no, he really didn't really care about videogames, and I was looking for something that wasn't there.

Still, when I got home, I wrote down my talk, translating it to English and expanding on it where I could. I posted it on my website, linked to it on social media, even created a Reddit account just to put my article on the Murakami subreddit, which turned out to be not too active. But as things tend to find their way in life, a few years later, my article was discovered by the curators of the bundle you're reading right now, weird people like me who may not be into Murakami as much as I am but are definitely into the connections between videogames and literature and pondering those connections. When they got in touch, I'd published my fourth novel as a smartphone app, using color, sound, and animation to help convey the story of two Japanese game makers who excavate the mind of a young programmer. This experimental publication had led to the founding of a startup that's building out these ideas into a new and better way of reading all books—and of engaging the audience in a way I think Murakami would appreciate. Megan and Mike asked me to return to my Murakami project, giving me notes on what to work on, as well as a nice reading list. Like I said, the role of misunderstood outsider can do wonders for your perseverance, and so I started digging again.

An Exegetic Exploration of the Self

One of the more interesting homework assignments Megan and Mike gave me was a talk about detective stories and games. In "The Duality of Playful Plots in Detective Fiction and Games," researcher and game designer Clara Fernández-Vara explores the two different narratives contained in whodunits and other mystery stories: first, that of the detective/player, and second, that of the crime, which is puzzled out by the detective/player. Fernández-Vara calls that puzzling process "exegetic gameplay." Apart from Ushikawa, Murakami's protagonists are not literally detectives, but they certainly behave like them, especially when they are stuck in their routines, meticulously considering everything within their reach: objects, other people, their own thoughts.

In the Q&A after her talk, Fernández-Vara was asked about Japanese role-playing games, which often feature characters who are like detectives of their own lives. For example, in *Final Fantasy VII*, Cloud suffers from amnesia and has to figure out who he is and what happened to him and his world. I was reminded of the *Castlevania* series, filled to the brim with bonuses that could be hidden under any tile, forcing the player to hit them all with their whip, patiently, carefully, always believing they'll get lucky soon. That realization, in turn, brought me back to Toru in his well, feeling the ground, touching the stones, getting used to the dark, finally reaching into the parallel universe of his subconscious, an exegetic exploration of the self through the careful exploration of the world. Which reminds me of me, writing this essay, trying to understand who I am, why I like what I like, why I make what I make, and the world that contains people like me.

Which takes me to games that seem to be directly made by people like me for people like me, like the game *Memoranda* (2017). In their advertising, the creators make a big thing of their Murakami inspiration. The game's Steam page reads, "Memoranda is a 2D point-and-click adventure game inspired by author Haruki Murakami's surreal short stories." Lead designer Sahand Saedi of studio Bit Byterz told games website *DualShockers* that they had the atmosphere of Murakami's stories in mind from the day they came up with the game, and the stories guided them through development: "When I faced blocks in designing the puzzles, often times I opened a Murakami book and searched for ideas . . . The surreal aspect of the stories is fully reflected in the game's puzzles and sometimes they are even more surreal." But there's a more widespread, indirect influence that people like me can detect in contemporary videogames.

While fans clamor for a new *Mother* game, Itoi hasn't developed one for fifteen years now, and the last installment was never even released outside of Japan. Games seem to have been a side quest for Itoi, but other developers have taken his sensibilities and run with them, most significantly Toby Fox, the creator of the hit indie game *Undertale* (2015). Others have since taken Fox's lead, like the makers of *YIIK* (2019), who even got some bad press because of their Murakami love. A character in *YIIK* quotes a character from Murakami's novel *After Dark*, though without attribution, and when they were accused of plagiarism, Ackk Studios told the videogame website *Kotaku*: "That book was an influence on the game and we wanted to pay tribute to it." It's a Murakami Easter egg!

I have to say, though, that these Murakami games don't feel like Murakami stories all that much to me. It's not enough to borrow a quotation or a few story elements or recurring themes. To me, these are surface elements that don't touch Murakami's essence, and the hand-drawn caricatures that populate *Memoranda* even distract from his slightly twisted realities. But what if a Murakami game existed that was all about routines, pocket dimensions, and watching patiently like Menshiki in *Commendatore*? As it happens, I've started working on a little Murakami game of my own, inspired by his writings. I'm not really a game developer, just like I'm not really a writer or a founder of a company, but I've tinkered with hobby game making for years now, enjoying the process of putting together something interesting, step by step, feeling my way through.

It's a smartphone game, a pocket dimension resembling *Earthbound* somewhat, in which Haruki Murakami himself is the protagonist, evolved from the animated guy I'd created for my talk. He first gets inspiration in the "real" world, reading books, talking to people, doing chores, and then he sits down to write, turning his subconscious into a whole new game world, where the routine starts anew. The environments are quite bland and empty, but they're generated according to Murakami's actions, and I haven't gotten around to tiling those talking cats, pots of spaghetti, and oracle-like women. But I'm getting there.

But back to the essay I was writing. Megan and Mike kindly replied that my second draft showed promise but ultimately lacked direction. They were right, of course. And they wrote something that made me think: maybe this essay isn't about Murakami. Or not *just* Murakami. Maybe it is about a new generation of creators and audiences and their way of thinking about their works. Not just Murakami and Itoi, but videogame makers and players too. Like me!

A Kind of Global Mind Meld

So I went to work one last time (well, one next-to-last time, since Megan and Mike are extremely picky editors). I scrapped the draft and began anew, writing about *Zelda* before heading into Murakami territory. This time I wrote the ending first, then layered it with condensed bits of my original analysis. I really tried to crack it this time, but judging from my editors' response, I didn't really get there. The thing is, I never will, and the version you're reading is as good as it's going to get. But if I'm kind to myself, I would say that those who reach this point will surely have stumbled onto interesting ideas and further paths to explore.

And that's the essence right there. With his literary works, Murakami stands in a tradition of Japanese modernity: remixing American pop culture in a distinctly Japanese way, just as his generational peers were remixing early American games culture. Both had a huge impact on the global pop consciousness, and they had a huge impact on me. They gave me ideas, paths to explore, and now I'm using them in my own works. And I'm not alone.

The things I noticed in Murakami and games are in fact all around us: the real and the fantastic, the high and the low, the digital and the analog, the exotic and the native, the impenetrable and the accessible, the interactive and the linear, the mundane and the weird. They're all converging, while at the same time diverging into a multitude of forms, like a worldwide, many-dimensional version of Itoi and Murakami's mind meld. Videogames can't be made without channeling all of that. Books perhaps can, but they would be less boring and difficult if they didn't.

Writing this, tweaking this very sentence one final time (assuming Megan and Mike don't change it again [Editors' note: we did.]), I feel enlightened, but also intimidated. So I can do anything now, in any way I see fit? Well, I still have to do it. Put in the work. Spend the time. Take it seriously. Power through somehow. Finish that essay. Do the routine until the routine changes. Develop that Murakami game. Push through with that startup, grab readers by the neck with attractive and engaging new ways of reading on that phone. Write that egg island maximalist novel. I am a writer, a journalist, a founder, a game developer, and a Murakami essayist all at the same time, building on the things I love to experience, always trying to get to the bottom of that well, meditating on myself and my surroundings, on the path to put together something completely new.

Murakami is in his seventies; I'm reaching middle age (forty-two, and I still don't have any answers). What's exciting is that there's a new generation of makers who should be much more relaxed with all of the above. I can't wait to play their games, read their books, or whatever else they'll end up willing into existence. I'm not sure if there will be giant eggs in them, or parallel worlds, or whatever, but I'm happy they didn't let their Calvinist roots, their artist friends, or for that matter their editors hold them back.

WORKS CITED

Anderson, Sam. "The Fierce Imagination of Haruki Murakami." *New York Times,* 21 October 2011. https://www.nytimes.com/2011/10/23/magazine/the-fierce-imagination-of-haruki-murakami.html.

Bogost, Ian. *Persuasive Games: The Expressive Power of Videogames.* MIT Press, 2010.

Davis, Nate. "Haruki Murakami, Video Gamer?" *Sailing: An Odd Essay,* 13 September 2004. https://snakeandme.typepad.com/snakeandme/2004/09/haruki_murakami.html.

Dinner with Murakami. Directed by Yan Ting Yuen, seriousFilm, 2007.

Dooley, Ben. "Haruki Murakami in Berkeley." *The Millions,* 14 October 2008. https://themillions.com/2008/10/haruki-murakami-in-berkeley_14.html.

EarthBound. Designer Shegesato Itoi, HAL Laboratory, Ape Inc., 1994.

Fernández-Vara, Clara. "The Duality of Playful Plots in Detective Fiction and Games." NYU Game Center Lecture Series, New York University, 7 March 2014. *Vagrant Cursor. https://clarafv.com/speaking.*

Final Fantasy VII. Square Enix, 1997.

Hulst, Auke. "Als ik schrijf, komt er iets kwaadaardigs mee." *NRC Handelsblad,* 11 January 2014. https://www.nrc.nl/nieuws/2014/01/11/als-ik-schrijf-komt-er-iets-kwaadaardigs-mee-1334466-a246263. [In Dutch.]

Kawakami, Mieko. "A Feminist Critique of Murakami Novels, with Murakami Himself." *Literary Hub,* 7 April 2020. https://lithub.com/a-feminist-critique-of-murakami-novels-with-murakami-himself.

The Legend of Zelda: Link's Awakening. Nintendo, 2019.

Meitzler, Ryan. "Memoranda Interview—Lead Designer Sahand Saedi on Adventure Gaming Inspired by Literature. *DualShockers,* 23 January 2017. https://www.dualshockers.com/memoranda-interview. Accessed 20 September 2022.

Memoranda. Bit Byterz, 2017.

Murakami, Haruki. *1Q84,* translated by Philip Gabriel and Jay Rubin. Vintage, 2011.

———. *Dance Dance Dance,* translated by Alfred Birnbaum. Vintage, 2010.

———. *The Elephant Vanishes: Stories,* translated by Alfred Birnbaum and Jay Rubin. Vintage, 2010.

———. *Hard-Boiled Wonderland and the End of the World,* translated by Alfred Birnbaum. Vintage, 2010.

———. *Kafka on the Shore,* translated by Philip Gabriel. Vintage, 2005.

———. *Killing Commendatore,* translated by Philip Gabriel and Ted Goossen. Vintage, 2018.

———. *Norwegian Wood,* translated by Jay Rubin, Vintage. 2010.

———. *Novelist as a Vocation,* translated by Philip Gabriel and Jay Rubin. Vintage, 2022.

———. *South of the Border, West of the Sun,* translated by Philip Gabriel. Vintage, 2010.

———. *Sputnik Sweetheart,* translated by Philip Gabriel. Vintage, 2001.

———. *What I Talk About When I Talk About Running,* translated by Philip Gabriel. Vintage, 2008.

———. *The Wind-Up Bird Chronicle,* translated by Jay Rubin. Vintage, 2010.

Peters, Arjan. "Haruki Murakami: 'Voor mij moet een roman me het gevoel kunnen geven dat er iets verandert in mij.'" *de Volksrant,* 16 February 2018. https://www .volkskrant.nl/cultuur-media/haruki-murakami-voor-mij-moet-een-roman-me-het -gevoel-kunnen-geven-dat-er-iets-verandert-in-mij~b07ba48a.

Rivera, Joshua. "Indie Developer Accused of Plagiarism Says It Was An 'Intentional' Reference [Update]." *Kotaku,* 20 May 2019. https://kotaku.com/indie-developer -accused-of-plagiarism-says-it-was-an-in-1834902499.

Suter, Rebecca. *The Japanization of Modernity: Murakami Haruki Between Japan and the United States.* Harvard University Press, 2008.

Wray, John. "Haruki Murakami, the Art of Fiction no. 182." *Paris Review* 170 (Summer 2004). https://www.theparisreview.org/interviews/2/the-art-of-fiction-no-182 -haruki-murakami.

YIIK. Ysbryd Games, 2019.

PART III

VIDEOGAME STORIES AS ARTIFACTS

Half-Light Histories

Uncovering Videogames' Disorienting Origins in *Kentucky Route Zero* and *Disco Elysium*

ANDREW BAILEY

When a videogame's "realism" is discussed, it is often in reference to how well it visually represents reality, especially if it has photorealistic visuals or its in-game objects behave in an expected manner. Doc Burford comments on these applications of realism in reference to *Microsoft Flight Simulator* (1982–present): "On one hand, you have an abstract representation of reality following a clear set of rules . . . and on the other, you have . . . a thing where you're sitting in the seat of an airplane . . . almost as if it were real life." Looking at realism's nondigital history, however, we see the concept has a wider array of meanings that exceeds the popular conception of videogame realism.

Building on recent interdisciplinary videogame scholarship, this essay explores how metatextual references to real-world histories can be used in videogames to craft productively disorienting stories that entangle material and virtual realities in a fashion reminiscent of older, nonludic modes of realism. This application of realism allows for more complex formations of videogame history, ones in which games function as visual art, literary text, and archival document all at once. What's more, this form of multimodal realism provides unique insight into the stories we tell with, about, and around videogames. To this end, I will analyze *Kentucky Route Zero*, or *KR0*, from Cardboard Computer (2013–2020), and ZA/UM's 2019 *Disco Elysium*, or *DE*, two point-and-click adventure games that have been categorized as deliberately participating in the vaguely fantastical subgenre of magical realism, a genre more often associated with film and print fiction (see Felkai et al.; Hildebrandt).

Lisa Denthridge argues that magical realism is qualified by "the 'irreducible' element of magic, detailed descriptions of the phenomenal world, the creation of unsettling doubts around the contradictions between events described, the emergence of different fictional and real realms, and distortion of time, space, and identity" (263). Although it is beyond the scope of this essay to fully describe these games' sprawling narratives, *KR0* and *DE* both fulfill Denthridge's criteria. Both feature an ensemble of downtrodden characters navigating equally ground-down worlds that correspond with the real-world regions where they were developed (the United States for *KR0*, post-Soviet Europe for *DE*). Additionally, each game's world contains inexplicable, often surreal phenomena with which the player must contend—a mysterious underground highway called the Zero in *KR0* and a strange form of spreading cosmic entropy called the Pale in *DE*.

As a contrast to these fantastical aspects, each game also alludes to real-world political and technocultural histories. In this way, both games use magical realism as a world-building tool, and the player is confronted with intertwining narratives that blur the real and the virtual, the fictional and the documentary, the novel and the referential. Through this complex formation of reality and fantasy, *DE* and *KR0* suggest a particular way in which the "realistic" language of videogames can tell stories about the history of videogames themselves and the way they construct "reality."

Realism: Ludic and Otherwise

Realism first emerged during the nineteenth century as a movement intended to reject the romanticized and idealized portrayals of reality that were dominant in arts and literature. Boris Groys argues that "realism usually involves the reproduction of an average, ordinary, profane view of the world." These completely ordinary representations of the world are typically intended to reveal it as a "sum of necessities and constraints that do not allow us to do what we would like to do or to live as we would like to live." Thus, realist art does not need to be an exact replica of material reality but instead works to communicate how people are always working to interrogate what they consider to be factual, authentic, or real.

In videogame studies, realism has become an increasingly useful tool for scholars aiming to break down the binaries of virtual and real that inform popular conceptions of the videogame experience. Looking at military first-person shooter games, Alexander Galloway argues that the challenge for realist art is to "capture the social realities, in some capacity, of the disenfranchised" (84). To achieve what he calls "social realism," videogames must contain "some kind of congruence, some kind of *fidelity of context* that translates itself from the social reality of the gamer, through one's thumbs, into the game environment and back again" (78). For Galloway, this fidelity must connect experientially with the player's current social milieu rather than impress them with technological spectacle. Photorealistic graphics or physics simulations are not antithetical to social realism, they just need to be used as tools to connect "the material substrate of the medium" with the "specific activities existent within the social reality of the gamer" (84).

Also looking to blend the technological capacity of videogames with the sociomaterial realities they inhabit, Timothy Welsh argues that videogames are emblematic of what he calls "mixed realism." Analyzing how digital experiences cannot be productively separated from everyday life, mixed realism "describes the ways media-generated virtualities reframe or recontextualize the real-world activity of interacting with them. Rather than a particular aesthetic style or technical paradigm, it refers to the capacity for virtual environments and virtual objects to situate their users within social, material, and ethical contexts" (6). To support this theory, Welsh compares metatextual literature with videogames that work to self-reflexively acknowledge their dual status as fictional constructs and media objects. Within Welsh's framework, what is *perceived* and what is *represented* as real coalesce into a singular experience through the player's interaction.

This essay applies this framework to explore how mixed realism functions when applied to historically themed, magical realist videogames such as *KR0* and *DE*. I argue that, through the mixed realist aesthetic, history becomes a narrative to be ambiguously experienced in the present, an "uncertain, temporary, and elusive" inversion of traditional models of linear historical knowledge. Through mixed realism, the boundaries between the real and unreal can be enmeshed, as can "the boundary between historiography and poetics" (Wojnowski 96). Through the double lens of magical and mixed realism, *DE* and *KR0* work not only to narrativize videogame history but also to construct it anew within the present.

Roleplaying Reality in *KR0*'s Historical Caverns

During *KR0*'s opening, the player must descend into the dark basement of a dusty old Equus Oils gas station to flip a circuit breaker and restore the building's power, and it is here that the experience of mixed reality is subtly introduced. The player's current avatar, Conway, needs to access the station's computer to get directions for a delivery he is supposed to make, but when he tries to access the breaker, he is impeded by three ghostly figures playing a tabletop roleplaying game (TTRPG). The spectral players show no awareness of Conway and are seemingly projections from a slightly different time and space. Although they do not directly respond to Conway, the figures describe a game curiously similar to the one the player is playing, and they mention that they have lost their twenty-sided die, lamenting how they need it to continue their game. The player must now search the station's basement to find the missing game piece.

This seemingly innocuous fetch-quest serves three functions. First, the lost die impeding the ghostly trio's gameplay is the same object that is preventing the player from getting to the breaker and thus making progress in *KRO*. This creates a parallel between what is happening in the fiction of the game and what is happening in the reality of the player. For both games to continue, the die must be found. Second, the specificity of the twenty-sided die is an explicit reference to *Dungeons & Dragons*, the popular TTRPG that served as inspiration for many of the first computer games. Finally, the game played by the so-called Basement People involves moving pieces on a map similar to the map of *KRO* itself. In sum, the moment establishes connections between the player's experience and the origins of both TTRPGs and computer games, origins that do not go uninterrogated throughout the rest of *KRO*.

This is particularly evident in the game's third act, when the player characters must once again go underground to make progress. Rather than a gas station basement, they descend into a cavernous, subterranean chamber dubbed the Hall of the Mountain King. The craggy, firelit space features a rickety wooden structure on which several people can be seen working on a disorganized array of computer equipment, desks, and bookshelves. One of these is a man named Donald, an eccentric, aging computer scientist whom careful players will have heard of in earlier parts of the narrative. As the player further explores the cavern, they learn more about Donald's academic history and that the other cave dwellers are graduate students he has hired to help him work on an ever-growing piece of experimental software called Xanadu. After speaking with Donald, the player characters are tasked with investigating the cave's giant, mold-ridden computers and finding the one on which Xanadu has been installed. Once the player finds the correct machine, they are once again confronted with an experience of mixed reality in which the material interface of *KR0* is reflected in what their player character is doing.

Xanadu is revealed to be an archaic text adventure game with a relatively simplistic action-and-noun natural-language parser. Although the platform that runs Xanadu—an ancient machine that resembles 1960s-era PDP-1 computers—differs from the console, personal computer, or tablet the player is using to play *KR0*, there is, as with the twenty-sided die, deliberate reference being made here to the lineage of the adventure game genre and to the origins of computers and videogames. In addition to its connections to Samuel Taylor Coleridge's "Kubla Khan," Xanadu is an explicit reference to *Colossal Cave Adventure*, or *CCA*, developed by William Crowther and expanded by Don Woods, which was one of the first text-based adventures and one of the first popular videogames.

These kinds of references (as well as the setting, which references Henrik Ibsen's *Peer Gynt*) enable *KR0* to poetically and haptically reconnect contemporary modes of videogame storytelling with a digital and predigital past. *CCA* was originally crafted by one person, William Crowther, in an attempt to share his hobbies of cave spelunking and *Dungeons & Dragons* with his young daughters, who were increasingly separated from him due to divorce. Crowther had to ensure the game could be interfaced with using natural rather than machine language, as neither of his daughters could code at the time. *KR0*'s designers deliberately reference Crowther's language parser in their portrayal of Xanadu, as well as with their choice to set it within a dimly lit, cavernous hall. Both choices capture Crowther's efforts to textually represent the twists and turns of subterranean space. Further deepening this mixed realist referentiality is the fact that, instead of building *CCA*'s environments from scratch, the game's titular cave is an accurate map of sections of the Mammoth Cave system in Kentucky, which Crowther regularly spelunked. Indeed, in the years since Crowther released his game, fans have traveled to Mammoth Cave National Park and have been able to use their virtual experiences to successfully navigate sections of its dark contours.

Responding to Dennis G. Jerz's survey of personal accounts and travel logs from these players-turned-spelunkers, ecocritic Alenda Y. Chang argues that Crowther's decision to base *CCA* on Mammoth Cave has allowed for an experiential blending of digital and geologic space. By navigating through *CCA*'s interweaving and permeable forms—ludic, textual, and environmental—Crowther's "ecomimetic" (Morton) creation acts as a prime example of how "game environments cannot consider themselves impervious to correspondence with real-world environments, whether they are based on known places or not" (Chang, "Games" 69). Chang's portrayal of game environments as being reflective of real-world ecologies corresponds with Welsh's description of mixed realism: "Players engage the virtualities of game fictions, not as vicarious visitors to alternate virtual realities but as media users, for whom many everyday practices involve 'artificial' environments. From this perspective, the interactive fictional worlds of videogames extend or update the paradoxes raised by literary metafiction" (61).

Viewed from the perspective of Chang's ecomimesis and Welsh's mixed realism, the Hall of the Mountain King reveals itself as a twice-disguised representation of Mammoth Cave. The aging computer scientist Donald corresponds to Crowther as a pioneering game developer, the relationships among Donald and other characters echo the dysfunctional relationship of Crowther with his family, and Xanadu is a thinly veiled cipher for *CCA*. These details function as "cracks in the narrative façade [that] cannot be ignored." These deliberately authored fissures, created with multilayered historical references, force "the material circumstances" of *KR0*'s "implementation to show through the gaps" (Welsh 61–62). Indeed, the subterranean setting, Xanadu's archaic interface, the intertextual references to Coleridge and Ibsen (both of which pose their own challenges to traditional realism), and Donald's backstory all work together to break the game's immersive framework and encourage the player to consider how *KR0*'s story relates to the world beyond the boundaries of the screen.

By engaging in metaleptic breaks like this and foregrounding narrative fault lines, *KR0* engages and addresses the player explicitly as a real-world media user, prompting them to critically reflect on and ludically engage with the early history of videogames as well as the antiquated materiality of the computers that have been used to construct them, represented through the deliberately low-resolution, glitchy interface of *Xanadu*. Through these allusions to real-world histories, these "points of interface and intersection between virtual and material contexts" function as "self-reflexive, meta-media moments that reflect on the role of media-generated virtualities in the 'real' media ecology" (Welsh 62). Through this self-reflective construction of its own creative and material histories, *KR0* embraces mixed realism as central to its conceit and demonstrates some of the many ways that "game fictions fold together real and virtual contexts" (66). In embracing this particular mode of storytelling, the developers at Cardboard Computer also work to "fold" together much more than many would typically associate with the history of videogames and to tell a broader story of how they relate to the history of interactive art.

Welsh's description of mixed realism as "folding" together material and virtual space draws directly from the field of cybernetics. Similarly, Aubrey Anable builds on Eve Kosofsky Sedgwick and Adam Franks's concept of the "cybernetic fold" to argue that *KR0* works to enfold multiple mid-twentieth-century histories—both "actual and imaginary" (Anable 17)—into itself. One example from *KR0* that illustrates the game's enfolding of fictional and nonfictional histories is "Limits and Demonstrations," a brief interlude that occurs between acts 1 and 2. Here, the player controls the three spectral figures who lost their game piece in the first act and are now touring an exhibition of contemporary art. The exhibit is set within a brick-walled industrial space and features an assortment of new media art installations by Lula Chamberlain—a character the player will encounter throughout *KR0*, notably at the start of the second act. Some of these works are completely fantastical, existing only in *KR0*'s fictional world, but there is one piece that explicitly refers to real-world art and literary histories. Given the lengthy title *Overdubbed Nam June Paik installation, in the style of Edward Packard, 1965, 1973, 1980*, this installation consists of a scattered array of strips of magnetic tape arranged on a white wall, a tape player placed on a pedestal a few feet in front of the wall, and two large speakers positioned on either side.

In 1963, Paik created *Random Access Music*, a work that Chamberlain's piece closely resembles. Paik encouraged audience members to take strips of magnetic tape and run them through the nearby tape player, producing a random combination of noise and transforming how interactivity was perceived within the histories of postmodern art and technoculture. In an essay focused on the parallels between the Fluxus movement, an art movement with which Paik had strong associations, and the commercial origins of the videogame industry, Jason Wilson argues that Paik's art worked against the "various kinds of separation between spectator and object that had pertained in the experience of visual art" (98). Wilson also posits that Paik's playful focus on interactive technology functioned similarly to the goals of early videogame developers in that both wanted to find new ways for consumer technologies to become more interactive. In this way, Paik's work reflects both an urge for greater interactivity and, by way of his association with Fluxus, a blending of high and low aesthetic forms and attitudes.

In these ways, *Kentucky Route Zero* works to enmesh its fiction in the real-world histories of experimental new media art and videogame development. As Anable argues, in *KR0*, "the corporeal and discursive, the analog and digital, are meaningfully entangled and, like magnetic tape, are sites onto which different histories and different affective scripts might be recorded" (33). The image she evokes here is a productive one to apply to the experience of playing through *KRO* and for reflecting on how the game plays with the multiple traditions of realism—including the other artist referenced in Chamberlain's installation, Edward Packard, creator of the Choose Your Own Adventure series. As Noah Caldwell-Gervais states, *KRO* "is so self-consciously dense that it's easy to feel lost in all the different layers of meaning, easy to have difficulty in sorting out which connections are frivolous and which are meaningful" (40:14).

However, Anable provides her own route through the game's dense historical references and disorienting metalepsis, arguing that, rather than attempting to clearly sort through these entangled connections, players should instead celebrate their disorienting effect and use them as a theoretical springboard. She writes, "I am making a case for feeling disoriented—getting a bit lost and being unsure about one's position and what it permits—as a strategy for bringing into relief what we can see and say from a particular location and also for reorienting game studies in ways that might permit other meanings, other games, and other histories to emerge" (11). What Anable describes here is a particularly playful approach not only to realism but also to the many histories that have produced realism as a contested but still vital aesthetic position, reflected in Chamberlain's entanglement of interactive technology (Paik) and interactive narrative (Packard).

Exploring its labyrinthine, cavernous depths, the player becomes aware of the multitude of material, textual, and cultural connections between *KRO*, the console or computer they are using to play it, and the expansive variety of artists, designers, texts, places, and creations that precede both. This mode of densely self-referential realism reorients the player toward videogames' literary and textual origins and, in the process, reframes the medium's potential for documentary storytelling and historiography—particularly the stories of those damaged and left behind by new technologies and their industrial applications. Via its subterranean pseudofiction, *KRO* makes a case for how videogames have already, and might continue to, function as artistic texts and produce meaning through the disruption of linear history and the incorporation of multiple modes of representational realism—a kind of choose-your-own historiography.

In the next section, I will use Anable's description of *KR0* as a tangled ball of magnetic tape to examine *Disco Elysium* and how it addresses videogame history in a similarly mixed realist manner. Not unlike Chamberlain's installation, *DE* features its own representation of how modern tape-recording technology relates to the obscured origins of videogame development, new media art, and interactive narrative. However, as will become clear, *DE*'s particular brand of mixed realism is more strongly filtered through a fictionalizing lens, thus playfully but intentionally obfuscating many of its most exciting historical references.

Disco Elysium's Ruinous Realism

Just as *KR0* references TTRPG history, the opening section of *DE* alludes to cardboard game pieces and multisided dice. In these references to both early and ongoing analog and digital forms of roleplaying and interactive narrative, both *KR0* and *DE* reveal a fascination with the materiality of games and how they are able to construct fictional story spaces distinct from but linked to reality through references and the situation of game development and play. One of the first buildings the player encounters is a bookstore with some of its windows boarded up and a grimy green roof. If the player enters the building and explores the retail space inside, they encounter a table display featuring a number of loosely disguised versions of popular real-world board games. For example, there is *Archipelagos of Insulinde*, which Plaisance, the store owner, tells you is "a very educational game for those interested in geography" and is clearly inspired by the board game *Settlers of Catan* (1995). *Catan* might also be the inspiration for *Suzerainty*, described as "a civilization-building game where you build a civilization, then set off to brutally colonize and repress other civilizations." Although these board games have a distant relevance to videogame history by way of the simulation and strategy genres, the most relevant items here in terms of understanding *DE*'s mixed realist approach to videogame history are the TTRPG sourcebooks and codices that also litter the table. Titles such as *Welkin Compendium, Second Edition* and *The Hunters of Katuak: Boreal Creature Compendium* are a reference to the numerous editions of TTRPG books that have been published throughout the past few decades.

Just as *KR0*'s early-game references to TTRPGs help contextualize later references to the history of computer games, these board games and books act as a loose introduction for later, more complex narratives focusing on how videogames function in *DE*'s fictional world. When the player character speaks with Plaisance, she will eventually tell them about the locked doorway leading to the upper floors above her store. Plaisance explains that she thinks this area is haunted and she will only allow the character entrance as long as they agree to investigate and exorcise whatever supernatural force dwells there. As the player explores the dark recesses of the supposedly haunted space, they encounter an artisanal die crafter and the long-dormant office of a game studio called Fortress Accident SCA (FASCA).

Some broader context is in order. The world of *DE* is presented through a combination of steampunk and Cold War–era Soviet aesthetics. While there are computers, they are closer to the hulking machines of the 1960s than they are to anything most players will have ever used themselves. The fictional technology of *DE*'s setting is important because, as the aspiring inventors of their world's first videogame, FASCA's absent designers had to be quite experimental in their designs. We find another connection to *KR0* here. Just as William Crowther's *Colossal Cave Adventure* was partly inspired by a passion for *Dungeons & Dragons*, the designers at FASCA were working to convert the kinds of TTRPGs featured in the bookstore into something that could be experienced through interactive electronic technology—a motivation shared by the developers of many real-world early computer roleplaying games (Peel). To achieve this within the technical limits of their rudimentary "radiocomputers," FASCA set out to create what it refers to as "revolutionary interactive call-in radio games." By poking around their studio, the player learns that FASCA ultimately failed to deliver the game but was working to create an open-world, choose your own adventure roleplaying game that would be experienced by calling into radio stations that would then give the player new information and choices on how to proceed.

This blending of radio technology, playful interaction, and artistic creation resonates with Lula Chamberlain's remix of Nam June Paik's magnetic tape installation, but FASCA's remix of the pen-and-paper roleplay experience using wired and wireless communication technologies has other real-world historical precedents. A similar approach to transmitting videogames over the airwaves can be observed in a short-lived European trend during the early 1980s called radio wireless data transfer. Attempting to circumvent the then-high price of hard drive technology, a Dutch broadcasting company called Nederlandse Omroep Stichting (NOS) began exploring how audio cassette tape could be used to store computer games and other software. Building on this idea, the NOS started a radio program called *Hobbyscoop* that would play computer game files that had been converted into audio form for listeners to record at home using their own cassette tape recorders (see Skågeby; Veraart, "Basicode," "Transnational (Dis)Connection"). These transmissions of game data sounded similar to the static from a dial-up modem and was, as Trevor English describes it, quite perplexing for "anyone outside of the knowledge of what was going on."

The way in which *Hobbyscoop* worked to disseminate its games using the airwaves functions as a circuitous connection to the second historical precedent for FASCA's failed project. Closer in nature to Chamberlain's and Paik's installations than the more industrialized efforts of NOS and *Hobbyscoop* is an aesthetic genre called "radio art." With origins ranging almost as far back as the medium itself, radio art can be loosely defined as any effort to produce and transmit artwork through novel, experimental, or nontraditional applications of radio technologies. Helen Thorington explains that radio artists during the 1980s "were predominantly engaged with subverting media conventions by presenting something other than familiar radio forms." Similarly, Anna Friz argues that "if radio to date has largely acted as an accomplice in the industrialization of communications, art radio and radio art continue to destabilize this process with renewed explorations of radio and electromagnetic phenomena" (4).

Although FASCA was ultimately a small business aiming to capitalize on its efforts and produce a profitable product, the project not only attempted to revolutionize how its world used radio but also was severely impacted by the kind of electromagnetic phenomena mentioned in Friz's definition. However, rather than a deliberately artistic manipulation of radio waves, the phenomena that FASCA encountered through its subversion of the radio form had an unexpectedly destructive effect on its game development—and casts a decidedly magical realist tone over the entire affair.

Just as *KR0* reconstructs the history of the roleplaying and adventure game genres through the magical realist context of a moldy cave and a fictional but historically referential art installation, the transmedial entropy of the destructive radio phenomena in *DE* provides the player with opportunities to reconsider videogame history's relationship with obsolescence, ruin, and erasure. Later in the game, the player character encounters a stern woman named Soona who is holed up in an abandoned church along with several radiocomputers arranged in front of a decaying yet still impressive stained glass wall. Although Soona's intentions are revealed to be scientific, the dramatic qualities of the dark, aging building and the geometric arrangement of her large, eccentric computer equipment have many visual parallels to the avant-garde new-media art installations of Chamberlain and Paik. And as with Chamberlain, we discover other wordly entanglements.

Through conversation, the player can learn that Soona was a programmer at FASCA before it was shuttered and that she is investigating the boarded-up church because she believes it is somehow linked to the unexplainable technical difficulties her studio encountered. If the player chooses to help Soona, they discover that the upper rafters of the church hide a strange anomaly that consumes sound and radio signals. Due to the studio's heavy reliance on radio technology to both produce and distribute its prototypical game, this seems like it was indeed a major contribution to FASCA's decline. Over the course of this subplot, we learn that the anomaly is a kind of growing hole in reality that swallows everything it touches, enabling the Pale—a cosmic entropic force—to spread out from it.

The Pale is a perfect example of the use of mixed realism to enfold video-game history in metaphorical processes of digital decay and obsolescence. Although *Hobbyscoop* and radio wireless data transfer did not fade away because of some eldritch hole in our world, their original aim to sidestep the high costs of hard drives was made obsolete as data storage technology progressed and became correspondingly cheaper. The result of such evolutions, both *DE* and *KR0* suggest, is not just technological progress but also the loss of specific ways of making and sharing stories. In other words, the overwriting of historical memory is both a loss of stories and a loss of how and where those stories were told. Through these cycles of technological innovation and obsolescence, the very real though oftentimes overlooked materiality of videogames and the computer equipment used to produce and run them are brought to light—as are the people who made, used, and played them.

Chang argues that retrieving this materiality and the entropy inherent to it gives us "a way to reopen the closed circuits of the magic circle, the black box, and human–computer interaction" and guides "our attention to the shadowy source/sink dynamics of game-related manufacturing" and "the omission of waste, disorder, and unspectacular forms of excess from most games" (*Playing Nature* 146–47). That's precisely what is happening here—a retrieval, by way of an older videogame form that depends as much on prose as it does interactive mechanics (the point-and-click adventure), of ways of playing with machines and, yes, the conventions of realist storytelling itself.

Looking back to some of the recent definitions of realism reviewed earlier,

Chang's arguments on the unspectacular excess of videogames speaks to the ordinary profanity and social reality that Groys and Galloway describe, in which audiences are deliberately reminded of the limits of their world and their places within it through specific formal techniques of disruption and defamiliarization. Through this lens, the FASCA subplot can be read as a form of realist self-satire, with ZA/UM expressing a darkly humorous version of its everyday reality working within videogame development. During *DE*'s production, ZA/UM was an upstart game studio that, like FACSA, was working on its first game, an adventure roleplaying game heavily influenced by the designers' personal histories with TTRPGs. Furthermore, FASCA's experimental attempts to utilize radio stations to create its game can be framed as parallel to the equally innovative dialogue and progression system that ZA/UM developed for *DE*. Both were stark deviations from the standards of the genres from which they emerged, and in their ambition, both had a high chance of failure.

This reading is further underscored through the name that ZA/UM chose for FASCA's unfinished radio game: *Wirral Untethered*. This name can be read as a joking reference to *Camelot Unchained*, a notoriously unfinished open-world massive multiplayer online roleplaying game that received an enormous amount of initial funding through a Kickstarter campaign but has since spent years in slow, meandering development. Unfortunately for any potential videogame fans in the world of *DE*, FASCA fell victim to a combination of financial and technological entropy. Indeed, ZA/UM itself has begun to suffer comparable implosive processes. Although, unlike *Wirral Untethered*, *DE* was an enormous financial success, there were major internal conflicts going on within ZA/UM that resulted in the team's three creative leads being forcefully ejected from the company they had founded and losing legal control of the intellectual property they had coauthored.

Collectively, these ruinous resonances enable FASCA to function as, if not always an intentionally mixed realist reflection of ZA/UM itself, then as an element that draws the player's attention beyond the game's narrative and toward the chaotic, banal, and sometimes abusive processes of real-world videogame production. Additionally, through its deliberate grafting of artistic, computational, radio, and game histories onto a single fictional narrative, *DE* works to highlight how these seemingly disparate contexts have many unexpected interconnections. These interconnections work to demonstrate the critical potential of realist interactive narratives and their ability to reveal how we tell stories with, about, and around videogames.

The Disorienting Entropy of Videogame History

Anable's call for disorientation as a methodology proves to be productive when reflecting on *DE* and *KR0*'s messy approaches to videogame history. Through the confusing irrationality of the Pale and the entropic cracks that it creates within *DE*'s reality, we are able to peek through and find unexpected real-world counterparts to FASCA and its revolutionary yet ultimately failed game. Like the all-too-steady forces of technological obsolescence, the Pale gobbled up *Wirral Untethered,* disrupted its radio waves, interfered with the radio-based "filament cubes" it was stored on, and prevented a nascent community of game enthusiasts from sharing its art with the world.

Speculating on the Pale's dark nothingness offers further opportunities to productively apply Anable's disorienting method: "Deep in the darkness our bodies can become unmoored in time and space." Anable argues that this is a state that allows for the "productive confusion between present and past, self and other, and inside and outside" (12). While Anable is speaking primarily about the dual context of *KR0* and affect theory, *DE* achieves a comparable effect through its allusive world building and self-reflective referencing. In the dimly lit, dusty spaces of the empty FASCA studio and the dilapidated church, there are ample amounts of disorienting darkness within which to become unmoored from the game's fiction and to float within its magical and mixed realist approach to history.

Conversely, if we are to take the entropic focus of *DE* and apply it to *KR0,* there are equally significant applications for Anable's disorienting lens. I have already worked to establish a connection between the two games through their shared interest in analog and digital games as well as how they use radio and sound recording technology as a signifier for new media experimentation. However, there also are several potential connections to be identified in *KR0*'s approach to the topics of decay and obsolescence. Although it is beyond the scope of this essay to discuss every instance of these themes across *KR0*'s elaborate and ramifying narrative, significant examples are to be found just within the Hall of the Mountain King alone.

Over the course of the Xanadu subplot, the player learns that the computer became infested by and eventually formed an inexplicably symbiotic relationship with a strain of mold native to the cave. The mold reformed the game's circuitry and programming such that Xanadu became alive and could transform itself in ways that Donald and his team could not predict or account for. In this way, the mold functions as a form of productive entropy, less in the sense of biological decay and more in the way that it has been defined in physics, as a chaotic and disorganizing process. Indeed, it appears to align more with the idea of information entropy, which Chang defines as "a measurement of variability in information encoding." Chang explains that there are surprising connections between the hard sciences and the field of game studies, due to their shared preference for "tidy, bounded, and functional systems." Rather than looking at videogames as statically organized systems and instead focusing on how material entropy functions, we might see videogames "afresh as both gloriously messy and discouragingly wasteful objects" (*Playing Nature* 148).

In this context, Xanadu's mold-encrusted circuitry and its mycologically induced ability to grow are indicative of the ways that videogame history has shifted and changed over time. Xanadu is no longer "a definitive or stable entity conducive to preservation" and, likewise, when we look at the way that videogames are affected and change over time, "what we think of as simply 'a game' is in actuality spread over time, through sequels, patches, and updates, as well as across regions, platforms, and player experiences" (153). In this way, putatively outdated videogame genres like the point-and-click adventure game can tell a different story about videogames.

DE and *KR0* are spread across time in ways that are both disorienting and revelatory. Their temporal ambiguity and metaleptic narratives work to construct a magical and mixed relationship between their players and the histories of technology, art, and capitalism that precede them. Through *KR0*'s dramatic and ecological framing of *Colossal Cave Adventure*, videogame history is allegorically transformed into a firelit subterranean cavern. Within this liminal space, what falls within real videogame history and what falls outside of it become enfolded into and entangled with each other. Similarly, within the dim postindustrial space of Lula Chamberlain's *Overdubbed Nam June Paik installation*, this already disorienting approach to real-world new media art histories is linked to the obscured origins of videogame development. All of this works to distort the player's ability to accurately distinguish between the factual past and the strange surreality of *KR0*'s world building. Although *DE* relies less explicitly on factual historiography than does *KR0*, *DE*'s many sly references to actual TTRPGs and lost videogames is also an attempt to make its narrative metaleptically porous and to let the real and fractal history of videogames seep in.

In focusing so intently on the technocultural history of videogames, *KR0* and *DE* work to mix the reality of their fiction with the factuality of the past, but this narrative effect is not the only effect being achieved. By self-reflectively highlighting how videogames have been produced over the past half century, *KRO* and *DE* also function as ciphers for the realities of their creators. Donald and Lula are both creative practitioners working within the spaces of new media, videogames, and visual art—which can also be said of *KRO*'s and *DE*'s developers. The sheer density of these interlocking references and modes of self-reflective, metaleptic, and metatextual expression makes the experience of playing these games disorienting.

And this is precisely because these stories about videogames, videogame developers, and videogame players are told through the old-fashioned techniques of the point-and-click adventure game. In a paper on the literary qualities of those games, Robert P. Fletcher argues in rather melancholy fashion that "in demanding that the user take time to notice everything, especially the artifice, the adventure game may have condemned itself to museum status." Fletcher explains that the adventure game's museum-ready qualities are one of the reasons they have declined in popularity over time, and that they have thereby resigned themselves "to be appreciated by the few willing to take time to reflect on the mechanism" (261).

Although Fletcher frames this as an unfortunate limitation, I see *KRO*'s and *DE*'s deployment of the point-and-click adventure game's ludonarrative mechanics as a unique strength, presenting mixed realist museums of videogame history. These games demonstrate the potential for videogames to be used as tool to tell the history of their medium and genre by combining prose and gameplay into a cohesive, though disorienting storytelling language—a language beholden to both digital and nondigital traditions. Through their examination of the materiality and historicity of videogame production, hardware, and relations with other forms of art, literature, and technology, *DE* and *KRO* form a symbiotic web between their fictional worlds and the external reality within which they exist. There is productive confusion to be found in revealing to their players that the real history of videogames is constituted as much by entropic artifice, disorienting poetics, and messy interpersonal relationships as by the orderly forward march of technological progress. By digging into the dark, historical spaces that *DE* and *KRO* offer, the player can encounter "the shock of a failed reality test" (Groys), which allows multiple, contradictory, but undeniably real representations of the history of how we tell stories with, about, and around videogames.

WORKS CITED

Anable, Aubrey. *Playing with Feelings: Video Games and Affect.* University of Minnesota Press, 2018.

Burford, Doc. "On Virtual Realism." *Kotaku,* 4 September 2016. https://kotaku.com/on-virtual-realism-1786167520.

Caldwell-Gervais, Noah. "Notes from Along Kentucky Route Zero [Spoilers]." *YouTube,* 8 September 2020. https://youtu.be/pW3qZfF6JfI.

Chang, Alenda Y. "Games as Environmental Texts." *Qui Parle: Critical Humanities and Social Sciences,* vol. 19, no. 2, 2011, pp. 57–84.

———. *Playing Nature.* University of Minnesota Press, 2019.

Colossal Cave Adventure. William Crowther, 1976.

Denthridge, Lisa. "The Magic Realism of a Virtual Second Life." *Literature & Aesthetics,* vol. 19, no. 2, 2009, p. 278.

Disco Elysium. ZA/UM, 2019.

Dungeons and Dragons. TSR, 1974.

English, Trevor. "You Could Download Video Games from the Radio in the 1980s." *Interesting Engineering,* 8 March 2020. https://amp.interestingengineering.com/you-could-download-video-games-from-the-radio-in-the-1980s.

Felkai, Adam, Robert Kurvitz, and Aleksander Rostov. "Szórakoztató bukás és játékforradalom: No Truce with the Furies—Fejlesztői interjú [Fun Fall and Game Revolution: No Truce with the Furies—Developer Interview]," translated by Mikk Metsniit. *ZA/UM Studio,* 31 March 2017. https://zaumstudio.com/2017/03/31/the-hungarian-interview/. Originally published in Hungarian at *Geekz.444,* 30 March 2017.

Fletcher, R. P. "Of Puppets, Automatons, and Avatars: Automating the Reader-Player in Electronic Literature and Computer Games." *Playing the Past: History and Nostalgia in Video Games,* edited by Zach Whalen and Laurie N. Taylor. Vanderbilt University Press, 2011, pp. 239–64.

Friz, Anna. "The Radio of the Future Redux: Rethinking Transmission Through Experiments in Radio Art." 2011. York University, PhD dissertation.

Galloway, Alexander R.. *Gaming: Essays on Algorithmic Culture.* University of Minnesota Press, 2006.

Groys, Boris. "Towards the New Realism." *e-flux,* no. 77, November 2016. https://www.e-flux.com/journal/77/77109/towards-the-new-realism.

Hildebrandt, Magnus. "Kentucky Fried Zero—English Edition," translated by Dennis Kogel. *SuperLevel,* 21 April 2013. https://superlevel.rip/spiele/indie-spiele/kentucky-fried-zero-english-edition.

Jerz, Dennis G. "Somewhere Nearby Is Colossal Cave: Examining Will Crowther's Original 'Adventure' in Code and in Kentucky." *Digital Humanities Quarterly,* vol. 1, no. 2, 2007.

Kentucky Route Zero. Cardboard Computer, 2020.

Morton, Timothy. *Ecology Without Nature: Rethinking Environmental Aesthetics.* Harvard University Press, 2007.

Packard, Edward. *Choose Your Own Adventure.* Bantam Books, 1978–1998.

Peel, Jeremy. "The Dungeon Masters: How D&D Shaped Every Corner of PC Gaming." *PC Gamer: Annual,* vol. 6, 2022, pp. 67–73.

Sedgwick, Eve Kosofsky, and Adam Frank. "Shame in the Cybernetic Fold: Reading Silvan Tomkins." *Shame and Its Sisters: A Silvan Tomkins Reader,* edited by Eve Kosoksky Sedgewick and Adam Frank. Duke University Press, 1995, pp. 1–28.

Settlers of Catan. Catan Studio, 1995.

Skågeby, Jörgen. "The Media Archaeology of File Sharing: Broadcasting Computer Code to Swedish Homes." *Popular Communication,* vol. 13, no. 1, 2015, pp. 62–73.

Thorington, Helen. "Radio, Art, Life: New Contexts." *Tate,* 2008. http://www2.tate.org.uk/intermediaart/radio_art_text.shtm.

Veraart, Frank. "Basicode: Co-Producing a Microcomputer Esperanto." *History of Technology, Volume Twenty-Eight,* edited by Ian Inkster. Continuum, 2008, pp. 129–47.

———. "Transnational (Dis)Connection in Localizing Personal Computing in the Netherlands, 1975–1990." *Hacking Europe: From Computer Cultures to Demoscenes,* edited by Gerard Alberts and Ruth Oldenziel. Springer, 2014, pp. 25–48.

Welsh, Timothy J. *Mixed Realism: Videogames and the Violence of Fiction.* University of Minnesota Press, 2016.

Wilson, Jason. "'Participation TV': Videogame Archeology and New Media Art." *The Pleasure of Computer Gaming,* edited by Melanie Swalwell and Jason Wilson. McFarland, 2008, pp. 94–117.

Wojnowski, Konrad. "Simulational Realism—Playing as Trying to Remember." *Art History & Criticism,* vol. 14, no. 1, 2018, pp. 86–98.

Feeling Reading, Reading Feelies

A Postdigital Prehistory of the Written Culture of Videogames

CHLOE ANNA MILLIGAN

To better appreciate the stories we tell with, about, and around videogames, we must attend to the stories we told before videogames. This mission is a must, now that videogames colonize the concept of play itself (Boluk and LeMieux 8). By reading against the grain of homogenized play practices that narrowly define what "real" games do and are, a look backwards can inspire a renewed perspective on the state of videogames going forward (Consalvo and Paul; see also Starkowski in this volume). "Reading" is our operative term. As gatekeepers remind us, "real" games prioritize action, and action supposedly precludes reading. Readers, those prehistoric people of the book, needn't apply.

This rhetoric has prompted censure among both players and academics, including Alexander Galloway, who (in)famously declared that "videogames are actions" and predicated his claim upon a print metaphor that "separates games from an 'abstract rule *book*'" (Galloway 2, emphasis added). In more popular context, it informs contempt for the so-called "walking simulator" (Bohunicky and Milligan 55). Even interest in storytelling strategies over procedural components of videogames often justifies itself by acknowledging videogames' fundamental difference from all previous media, on kinetic grounds—through physical, embodied, haptic, tactile, proprioceptive action. That is the hands-on work of play that videogames have perfected.

However, this narrow perspective doesn't hold up under close scrutiny. While, as Anastasia Salter has argued, "drawing clear distinctions between games and other media, such as books and film, was at first essential to appreciating what videogames can do that other media do not so readily offer" (7), these distinctions erase both popular traditions like interactive fiction and future games that explore the "as-yet-uncharted space between game and book" (4). Yes, the distinction is significant. Astrid Ensslin notes the need to clarify differences between "playful (print) literature" and literary games while also granting a history of overlapping methods and materials (7). Ensslin concludes, "Having moved well into the second decade of the twenty-first century, it would be somewhat ill-advised . . . to presuppose a complete separation between print and digital in relation to literary gaming" (10). In fact, our postdigital culture provides us the context we need to see that there never was any separation.

Rather than insisting on the uniqueness of videogames as digital artifacts that resist reading, we would do better to understand the role of the analog in reading and/or gaming in a new way. Illya Szilak encourages us to see that "the choice is not between analog and digital forms of communication, old and new media, the 'real' and the 'virtual,' but rather how we will negotiate and release them from their binary capture." With the right lusory attitude, we can move beyond binary choices and highlight the physical and embodied, haptic, tactile, and proprioceptive modes of print and digital reading play. "The body—perhaps the most analog of all objects," says James Charlton, is the controller we play with, and it's uniquely "capable of constructing a co-constituted digital structure, thus chronologically freeing *the digital* from specific media histories" demonstrating even that "*the digital* predates the development of digital technologies" (150).

Reading is an embodied process and is just as much part of the affective experience of videogames as playing. I posit the figure of the "feelie" to secure the historical and ontological presence of the literary page in videogames, outside and alongside them as well as within them. Ian Peters defines the feelie as "a life-size reproduction of an object within the game world that players can hold in their hands and study in the physical realm exactly as a character in the virtual realm can . . . Holding them puts the player into a character's shoes, thereby expanding the game experience beyond the game's digital components while maintaining the potential to generate their own textual meaning." Feelies were popularized by the interactive fiction (IF) computer game company Infocom in the 1980s, beginning with the murder mystery *Deadline* (1982). The term comes from Aldous Huxley's *Brave New World* (1932) and his concept of tactile cinema. However, feelies take their ludonarrative method from Dennis Wheatley and J. G. Links's *Murder off Miami* (1936), a book of loose-leaf "evidence" ranging from small texts to fabrics and human hair, which fell into the hands of Infocom designers after its reprinting in 1979.

My work here is allied with the aims of "media archaeology," which Lori Emerson defines as the scholarly endeavor to read the present against the past in order "to avoid reinstating a model of media history that tends toward narratives of progress and generally ignores neglected, failed, or dead media." But beyond just the teleological and technological, I'm invested in what Emerson terms "media poetics," a practice of engaging with media in a fashion "such that poetry could be visual art as much as it could be fiction and vice versa," resulting in a "strange blurring of, even feedback loop between, reading and writing [that] signals a definitive shift in the nature and definition of literature" (xiii–xiv). Emerson provides a useful direction for how stories can be told in a fashion that promotes lusory attitudes and activity.

Recovering the history of feelies offers a new angle from which to understand the written culture of videogames. This written culture must be understood as having always been tactile, reinforcing the kinds of embodiment and materiality that some have argued is put at risk by the digital. Ultimately, the histories of such embodied reading matter more than ever to videogame culture. Indeed, I would argue that reading itself should be considered a playful activity, precisely because it can take place across print and digital media. Upon this betwixt basis, then, playful reading functions as a queering of the relationships between media that are too often assumed to be distinct, or even as an affective intervention in their purported medial conflict. By transgressing binaries between print and digital forms and methods, particularly as they concern representations and experiences of play, we can tell more interesting, more embodied stories and draw more nuanced, generatively messier conclusions that allow for a more expansive understanding of what reading, playing, and videogames can be *together*.

It's fitting to discuss feelies and their foundations in IF as a starting point for videogame history, considering how important IF is to videogames and to genres still developing today. William Crowther and Don Woods's 1976 *Colossal Cave Adventure* is typically cited as the starting point of the genre. But it wasn't the very first videogame—that would be William Higinbotham's *Tennis for Two*, in 1958, though there are earlier candidates. Indeed, I begin my (pre)history in the 1930s, the decade that saw the appearance of *Brave New World* and *Murder off Miami*, the two works that established the feelie in modern parlance and practice— and did so in dialogue with the theoretical and formal concerns of modern art.

K. Shannon Howard succinctly states, "Analog is embodied" (8). As I will demonstrate, *Brave New World* and *Murder off Miami* describe and enact, respectively, how readers with the right lusory attitude "are able to shuttle *between* the analog and digital in some ways that previous generations did not" (Howard 9). The feelie as both figure and feature embodies the surface for shuttling, connecting analog to digital in a suspended betweenness that speaks simultaneously to anxieties about the loss of literary value and the techniques that can enhance literary engagement. Indeed, like works of so-called postdigital art, "they use the space between the reality of physical space and that of media representations as a theatre in which to perform," as Josephine Bosma puts it. "This in-between space is a physical space, a technological space, and a conceptual space at once" (114). Feelies, a figure for degraded reading in Huxley's book and a method for enabling a higher degree of engaged reading for Wheatley and Links, provide the shuttle between the stories we played before videogames and the games we read today.

Feelies and the Degradation of Literary eExperience: Huxley's *Brave New World*

Brave New World is often categorized as a prophetic dystopian science fiction. However, with all its soma and feelies, it is just as much a satirical condemnation of the visual modernity of Huxley's moment and what he felt to be its addiction to excess—and its willingness to forgo the "higher" qualities of true literature. The feelies, in particular, serve as a timely, cynical response to the cinematically mediated culture of Huxley's day—another thing he found distasteful. So, before feelies were redefined by Infocom, what did Huxley imagine them to be and to say about film, technology, and most importantly, literature in 1932? To answer this question, we'll need to feel out what Abbie Garrington defines as "haptic modernism."

Garrington situates haptic modernism in the contexts of both the artistic avant-garde and ideologies of technological progress. Haptic modernism describes the ways in which the art and literature of the early twentieth century explored changing notions of touch ("haptic" meaning "relating to the sense of touch") during a time defined by advances in the sciences and technologies of embodiment. She cites, for example, Italian futurist F. T. Marinetti's *Tactilism: A Futurist Manifesto* (1921), an avant-garde call to action for the construction of "tactile theaters." For Garrington, modernist literature like Marinetti's "responds and contributes to a kind of 'hinge point' in the multi-stranded history of the haptic, drawing on" earlier "theorizations . . . to consolidate a notion of the role of touch for the perceiving subject, and therefore providing the groundwork for the many purposes to which the notion of the haptic is put . . . later" (17).

Garrington discusses the feelies from *Brave New World*, and she further connects her close reading to Marinetti's *Tactilism*. The feelies are Huxley's idea of a "cinematic entertainment that seeks not only to thrill the eye but also to stimulate the haptic responses of the human body, mediated through the grasp of the viewer's/feeler's hand" upon galvanic knobs (Garrington 33). But aside from their satirical charge, the feelies also envision a way to incorporate haptic and tactile sensation into visual sense experience through design. In this way, "cinema—with only a flat screen, and without the benefit of galvanic knobs—is able to stimulate the whole human sensorium," to treat viewers, in the words of Siegfried Kracauer, "as a 'human being with skin and hair'" (qtd. in Garrington 40). Human beings, complete with skin and hair, crave yet more sensory engagement, which Huxley imagines feelies could provide with "every hair of the bear reproduced. The most amazing tactual [sic] effects" (35). There are, however, elements of the human sensorium that film does not quite touch—which the "galvanic knobs" of videogame interfaces and the feelies of Infocom later achieve.

However, we should note that Huxley's feelies are distinct from Marinetti's enthusiastically utopian "tactile theaters," despite both being rooted as they are in "a time when cinema's technological innovations were not just observed but were truly felt" (Frost 444). Huxley's feelies are satirical warnings. They are a response to Huxley's fears about the degradation of aesthetics by way of what Tom Gunning has described as the "cinema of attractions" and its production of new frameworks for seeing and feeling. The "cinema of attractions," Gunning explains, "is a cinema that displays its visibility, willing to rupture a self-enclosed fictional world for a chance to solicit the attention of the spectator" (64). This was by no means an attraction for Huxley. But the feelies also resonate with Steven Wingate's notion of "textual screen work," which he defines as "a continuum of artistic strategies . . . that incorporate the interrogation of textuality itself into artworks" (174). So if, as I would suggest, *Brave New World* is a prototypical story about the haptic attractions of videogames, it is not an advertisement for them, though that has not been clear to all of his readers.

Laura Frost notes, "One of the cultural ironies of Huxley's fate in [contemporary] culture is the way he has been taken up by the popular culture he claims to despise (the title of his most famous novel has become a catchphrase) and in his absence from most critical discussions of modernism" (448). Huxley's feelies convey his distaste for popular culture, but what he finds distasteful about it is fascinatingly problematic, particularly when understood as a speculative narrative about a technology that did not yet exist. Anne Cranny-Francis points out that "Huxley's description of the feelies is often read as a criticism of popular culture," but this criticism needs to be understood in terms of Huxley's association of that culture with "the 'baser' human senses such as touch and smell (164). The feelies, "nothing but pure sensation" (Huxley 221), signify to Huxley and to his intended readers the idea of the popular "as degraded cultural forms, lacking the intellectual content of great art" (Cranny-Francis 164). Thus, Cranny-Francis argues, the feelies are a perfect example of a metaphor for art "that deadened [people] to the meaninglessness of their lives and . . . enhanced that dissociation from the world [through] 'pure sensation'" (164). Feelies, by their very feltness, qualify for Huxley as a *somatechnic* drug that stands in opposition to "canonical Western art" and the higher feelings and ideals it conveys.

Carly Kocurek argues that interactive fiction, as a mixed-media, interactive medium, "like the talkies and games more generally, would likely have invoked Huxley's ire. Feelies and games are together in the list of standardized amusements articulated in *Brave New World*: 'Seven and a half hours of mild, unexhausting labour, and then the soma ration and games and unrestricted copulation and the feelies.' They are together, too, . . . in the history of gaming" (296). Huxley's snobbish representation of haptically enhanced entertainment fails to account for the ways it can be used for purposes beyond merely entertainment, which is evident in the literary pretensions of Infocom's interactive fiction. But that same snobbishness also alerts us to persistent anxieties about the ways in which videogames—even videogames that aim for "higher" artistic goals—implicate our bodies. Just as the feelies of *Brave New World* became something much more than originally intended, especially in the popular imagination, the feelies Infocom made for their games left a lasting mark on videogames that was more inventive than they likely had in mind. I'll explore this in the conclusion to this essay, but to understand the nature of that legacy, we need to look to another precursor, this one less concerned with the degradation of literature by the haptic than with its enhancement.

Feelies and the Haptic Enhancement of Reading: *Murder off Miami*

Wheatley and Links's *Murder off Miami* is the ultimate and originary work of feelie literature, what Jason Scott deems "the Feelie that started it all." But it was the start of more than that. It fulfilled the sensory promise of Huxley's cinema of attractions, and it did so to enhance the experience of literature rather than distract and detract from it. Billed as "crime dossiers," *Murder off Miami* and its three sequels, *Who Killed Robert Prentice?* (1937), *The Malinsay Massacre* (1938), and *Herewith the Clues!* (1939), were hailed as a "completely original novelty" (Humphreys). Humphreys also tells us that although the particular haptic strategy of *Murder off Miami* is predated by "Baffles" by Lassiter Wren and Randall McKay ("Originators of the Detective Puzzle Form"), which appeared in the pulp detective magazine *Clues* from the late 1920s, Wheatley and Links were the first "to take the format one or more steps further."

Murder off Miami is designed to resemble a book full of loose-leaf evidence, including various documents such as cablegrams, police reports, interview transcripts, handwritten letters, and newspaper clippings. But in addition to documentary-style reading materials, *Murder off Miami* also came with other kinds of objects relating to the mystery: photographs from the scene of the crime, (real) curtain fabric stained with (fake) blood, burned matches, cigarette ends, and actual human hair.

From the perspective of production, it's hard not to "recognize this for what it is, a fulfillment nightmare" (Scott). For the 1979 reprint, according to Martin Wainwright:

> Nuns from convents all over Europe provided the vital twists of hair for the new editions (the sample the detective finds is a mixture of gold strands and black). The used matches which play a part in the affair kept the printers busy after work, when their staff each took home several books and patiently struck their contents. Finally, a special chemical mixture provided a lasting bloodstain on the piece of curtain glued in each book, after the real blood donated by a director of the printing firm faded almost at once. (Humphreys)

The first edition sold in Britain for three shillings and sixpence, making profit margins tight against the high production costs. Nevertheless, "what had been originally considered a crazy idea both by the publisher and all sane retailers ended up selling 120,000 copies in the first six months" (SelenicMartian), even against mixed critical reception. *Murder off Miami* was surprisingly and wildly popular at a time when haptic interactive experiences were quite rare. It was "shortly after the then still flipper-less pinball machines had introduced tilt detectors, and . . . *Monopoly* had hit the market" (SelenicMartian), and four decades before Edward Packard would publish *Sugarcane Island*, the proof of concept for what would become the Choose Your Own Adventure series in 1979—the same year that the new edition of *Murder off Miami* was published. Some of its runaway success is inseparable from the fact that the novelty of its form was simultaneously the appeal of its method.

But what was its method; what was a reader/player meant to do with all of this stuff? And in light of our broader concern here with the stories we tell with, about, and around videogames, what ideas are communicated about the playful reader?

Those who open the case file of this crime dossier are more than readers; they take on the role of Detective Officer Kettering, tasked with solving the mystery of who murdered Bolitho Blane. Reading is undoubtedly playing here, given how much the text asks of its audience, both in terms of the puzzle qualities we associate with mystery novels and in terms of the haptic demands of the text. They have to approach the act of reading in a novel register, with the right lusory attitude, we might say, to enact an analog form of immersion. (For discussion of comparable examples, see Starkowski in this volume.) Humphreys explains that "there is no narrative as such, the reader provides that himself, by assimilating the facts and assessing the evidence surrounding the case. The result is therefore a curious cross between a work of fiction to be read and a game to be played."

This type of betweenness is exactly where I want to situate *Murder off Miami* in terms of both the resurrection of feelies in the 1980s and the larger issue of how we understand videogames as an embodied narrative medium. This curio of a folio calls into question some of the interactive practices of videogames that it puts to the test decades before videogames—and our assumptions about what it means to tell a digital, interactive narrative. With a closer focus on the physical, embodied properties of games in the wake of Wheatley and Links's work, I consider the tangible, tactile items also included in their crime dossier just as important to "read."

I've previously written that "the way we read is changing with the way we touch" (Milligan, "The Page Is a Touchscreen" 287); in other words, our relationship to the forms and methods of reading is complicated by increased interaction with digital haptic media such as touch screens. Ironically, rather than disrupting our relationship to literature, as Huxley feared, such interaction enables a deeper appreciation of the heretofore taken-for-granted tactility of print media. *Murder off Miami* presents a compelling case for reiterating that claim—and not merely reiterating but backdating it to a moment when similar concerns about the tactility of emergent media were raising fears among cultural authorities like Huxley. Touching its various tactile surfaces, whether document facsimile or human hair, becomes another register of reading the text—in this case, reading the text through its texture. It deepens our immersion in the text precisely at the surface(s) of that text.

In her work on touch as a sensation in constant movement, Erin Manning breaks away from the model of "an active giver and a passive receptor" in favor of a more reciprocal reckoning between bodies (xii). Touch is not just something one body does to another body; it's done to both, by the logic that to touch is to be touched. Or as Manning has it, "Touch is not simply the laying of hands. Touch is the act of reaching toward, of creating space-time through the worlding that occurs when bodies move" (xiv). "Worlding" is a wonderful term for describing the playful practice of maintaining a state of engaged readerly immersion through the body. Here I would advocate that we make space(-time) for the theorization of bodies both corporeal and textual in both the readerly and the playerly relation to one another—and perhaps for understanding the particular power of stories we tell with, about, and around videogames.

If touch, as Manning writes, "invents by drawing the other into relation, thereby qualitatively altering the limits of the emerging touched-touching bodies" (vix), we can consider that invention in both a ludic and literary sense, as a way to imagine gameplay and to imagine stories about gameplay. What Wheatley and Links invent between their audience and their crime dossier is an embodied application of a lusory attitude, a narrative worlding that is intended to include us not merely as readers but as a character in the narrative. Reading is worlded in terms of the manipulation of objects and the growing recognition of the narrative that tied those objects together.

In other words, with the right attitude, we aren't just reading *about* what Kettering does; we *become* Kettering by touching what he touches. Reading is playing a game and playing as a character. And yet at the same time, "we" aren't the ones doing that—in a way, the documents with their textures and stocks and heaviness, the fabrics and hair and burned matches, do it to us when they touch us. In *Playing with Feelings: Video Games and Affect*, Aubrey Anable asks, "What does it mean when a game touches us and what does it mean when we touch a game?" (xx). If the answer to that question concerns "the embodied capacity to feel" (xix), I'm not sure we can answer that question without better understanding the embodied experience of *Murder off Miami* and other predigital haptic texts (for example, those discussed by Starkowski and by Żmuda in this volume).

Feeling the Links Between Videogames and Modernism

Just as feelies take a page from Wheatley and Links' book—almost literally, as "nearly everyone . . . who had something to do with Infocom's feelies had owned or knew of" it (Scott)—that book also participated in a broader discourse of art and embodiment. Here, I would situate *Murder off Miami* as part of the widespread modernist interest in affect, representation, and objectivity—a trend that Jason Wilson has explored with respect to the use of abstract figuration in the work of Barnett Newman, Nam June Paik, and videogame designers Nolan Bushnell and Ralph Baer. Reg Gadney, writing for *London Magazine* in 1969, draws parallels between the innovative material storytelling practice of *Murder off Miami* and Marcel Duchamp's readymades, arguing that, just as "Duchamp had already exhibited a urinal and [thus] the barriers between artifacts and reality were starting to collapse" (qtd. in Edwards), Wheatley and Links were similarly looking to collapse the lines between art and life. Humphreys elaborates on this point: "In the case of Duchamp, his real objects . . . were presented as complete object d'art but, because of their mass-produced nature, they challenged the very meaning of art itself by requiring the viewer to construct his own aesthetic. In a similar way, the dossiers challenged the meaning of fiction in that they presented the scene of crime material and various facts about the case and left the reader to construct the story."

Unfortunately, both Gadney and Humphreys treat Wheatley and Links's crime dossiers as historical curiosities. Despite their immense popularity in the 1930s, it's true that they soon after fell out of mind and out of print. However, though he could not predict their 1979 reissue or their subsequent influence on interactive fiction of the 1980s, Gadney praises the dossiers as "very much objects in their own right and, as such . . . distinctly related to Dada and certain sorts of Concrete Poetry" (qtd. in Edwards).

Though Gadney references Duchamp's more widely recognized *Fountain* (1917), his *Unhappy Readymade* (1919) can tell us more about the shared history of real objects and haptic aesthetic experience. Upon learning that his sister, Suzanne, had married artist Jean Crotti while he was away in Argentina, Duchamp sent her his instructions for an "unhappy readymade" as a wedding present. She was instructed to take a regular old geometry textbook he had mailed and hang it outside on their porch opened faceup to be slowly destroyed by the elements. Suzanne and Crotti followed those instructions, and wind tore, rain drenched, and sun bleached it. As Kristina Seekamp puts it, *"Unhappy Readymade* was made in this manner not by Duchamp, but by his sister Suzanne. She was instructed to make it through written correspondence with her brother."

Suzanne carried out the goal of this art piece by playing along with the meaning-making experience according to specific rules and with a specific object. In contrast to the paintings and installations discussed by Jason Wilson, we find here a focus on everyday objects that, through the interaction of the user, become freighted with new meaning. Duchamp's instructions transform a book into an artistic experience, just as *Murder off Miami*'s murder mystery turns a collection of documents and items into artifacts of ludic worlding. But the most significant element shared between them is the lusory attitude of the user, a willingness to play with objects and along with the fiction.

Feelies Are Dead! Long Live Feelies!

Forty-three years after the first edition of *Murder off Miami* was published, and the same year as the publication of its second edition, the most influential interactive fiction company of all time was founded. Inspired by *Adventure* and, later, by *Murder off Miami*, Marc Blank, Dave Lebling, Tim Anderson, and Bruce Daniels created what would become the first Infocom game, *Zork*, in 1977. All but Daniels went on to establish Infocom. By 1983, Infocom reigned over the computer game market, with all of its titles topping Softsel's list of best-selling games. By 1986, it was bought out by Activision, and it was shut down in 1989. Despite its short run, Infocom left an indelible mark on videogames, a mark that is all the more legible now, as text-based games have become, on one hand, popular to make and easy to share (see Anthropy) and, on the other, integral to games that involve multiple kinds of play. But their influence also materializes in the widespread presence of haptic reading—feelies in a variety of forms, many of them indiscernible to most players.

Infocom first introduced feelies with *Deadline* (1982), a game directly inspired by Wheatley's work, which designer Marc Blank acquired after the 1979 reprinting of *Murder off Miami*. Blank wanted the player to feel that they were the detective and were immersed in the story, and he included a variety of diegetic documents and a small plastic bag with three white pills, an elegant solution to the limited memory capacity of the game's floppy disks but also a way to develop haptic immersivity—to, in Jimmy Maher's words, "*really* play the detective*.*" Subsequently, feelies became something of a trademark for Infocom, most famously in "peril sensitive" (completely opaque, cardboard) sunglasses from *The Hitchhiker's Guide to the Galaxy* (1984), the decoder wheel from *A Mind Forever Voyaging* (1985), a scratch-and-sniff card from *Leather Goddesses of Phobos* (1986), and the velvet reticule from *Plundered Hearts* (1987). But we should not forget the other, readable feelies Infocom included with its games, like the issue of *Dakota* magazine, dated April 2031, packaged with *A Mind Forever Voyaging*.

In contrast to their use in *Murder off Miami* and Wheatley and Links's other portfolios, feelies here function more like what Huxley envisioned, as artifacts that paratextually extend the affective interface of the screen. In this way, Infocom's feelies embody the hybridized visual/haptic interactions that Anable identifies "at the interface—at the moment of transmission or contact—when affect gets called up into representation" (xviii), in this case not only as tactile transmediation of the interactive fiction experience but also as the only visual evidence of the otherwise entirely textual game world. The filmic origin of Huxley's feelies—minus the disdain—returns through this visual/haptic tension.

But rather than providing a totalizing sensory experience, the feelies work in terms of a kind of haptic deferral, a material disconnect between the gameplay of the computerized text and the gameplay of the objects integrated first and foremost by the reader/player's lusory attitude, an attitude built on the rejection of a strict binarization of analog and digital media. Touching the feelies puts us in touch with the IF game world without ever touching it, a performative mode of interaction that resists limiting gameplay to the digital screen. It marks the storytelling potential implicit in the "failure" to touch the digital text, to (re)produce any legible engagement that would prompt the text to respond to us. This failure may explain why some scholars have dismissed the feelies as just gimmicky. But failure may not be such a bad thing—and in fact may be the essential activity and affect that generates the stories we tell with, about, and around videogames.

Conclusion, or the Present Future of Feelies

Through an affective framing of the gap between the digital and the nondigital, we can "seek to expand our understanding of the ways video games and game studies can participate in feminist and queer interventions in digital media culture" (Anable xvii). So with feelies in hand, I nominate the failure to fully and only engage with the videogame's digital components as a postdigital practice—a story we tell *alongside* the videogame. There's a practice embedded here that echoes Jack Halberstam's notion of the "queer art of failure." Halberstam argues that failure as a queer art pushes against the heteronormative capitalist drives of cultures addicted to success and proliferation. He describes "failing, losing, forgetting, unmaking, undoing, unbecoming, not knowing" as "more creative, more cooperative, more surprising ways of being in the world" (2–3).

Though originally designed to overcome the limits of technology and to discourage piracy, the feelies' disruption of the analog/digital binarization, when situated in the longer history of digital storytelling, becomes "a way of refusing to acquiesce to dominant logics of power and discipline and as a form of critique" (Halberstam 88). In the case of feelies, those logics include constraining the history of videogames within the history of computers, constraining play solely within the interaction of player and machine, and deeming everything outside that interaction as historical curiosity or inessential supplement.

I insist, along with Anable, on analyzing "video games not as an entirely new medium or as an autonomous art form but rather as part of the historically and technologically grounded, yet emergent and evasive, shifts in the everyday conditions of our computer-mediated world," with the understanding that digital began before the digital (xiii). I'm not sure we can see the presence of the literary page persisting in contemporary videogames (not leastly those that persist in novels, poems, and the other narratives described in this volume) without acknowledging the failures—technical, narrative, economic, and otherwise—that have modeled and persisted in new kinds of videogame stories and in new ways of interacting with them that are not controlled or encompassed by the digital. Locating the descendants of feelies today can tell us much about contemporary conditions of the written and read cultures of videogames. Notwithstanding widespread reports of "digital disenchantment" and analog (re)interest, it's hard not to feel that the digital is taking over (Cramer 12). So, whither feelies?

One direction is so-called digital feelies. Michael Abbott coined the term to describe *Mass Effect 2*'s (2010) expanded Codex, a "gloriously overstuffed lore device" essential to learning every bit of background information for the *Mass Effect* trilogy. The Codex embodies what Janet Murray calls "encyclopedic writing," a form of totalizing narrative that invites "our participation by offering us many things to keep track of and by rewarding our attention with a consistency of imagination" (111). Unfortunately, the Codex doesn't *feel* like a feelie. Even in the world of *Mass Effect*, it's a digital device, basically a futuristic e-book, circa 2185. But that doesn't mean Abbott was wrong to identify the possibility of digital feelies.

Many videogames make reading essential to playing them (through menus or dialogue, for instance), or inessential but attractive (as in websites, novelizations, and so on), and deluxe collector's editions often come with diegetic collectibles that preserve at least some of the feelies' haptic legacy. But these don't quite embody what digital feelies are. I would suggest that they are the digital representation of print artifacts that readers/players interact with in the virtual game world. There are any number of examples of such texts, from the diaries, calendars, and hastily scribbled notes in *Gone Home* (2013) to the ever-proliferating identification documents of *Papers, Please* (2013) to the anomalies of *Oxenfree* (2016) to the eerie artifacts of *All the Delicate Duplicates* (2017) to the family souvenirs of *Tell Me Why* (2020) and *Ghost on the Shore* (2022). These artifacts invert the "failure" of the feelies, introducing into the digital space the texture, manipulability, and affective charge of real-life objects. Not coincidentally, many of these games are derided by gatekeepers as "not videogames."

The presence of the textured page and other textualized objects in videogames functions like a haptic oxymoron, but it points to medial shifts in reading habits that arguably parallel ontological shifts in embodied selfhood spurred by the digital and now postdigital revolutions. For hundreds of years, Western cultures have generally conceived of human subjectivity through bookish ways of making, thinking, and being. As more directly physical, haptic, tactile, and proprioceptive modes of interaction undergo yet more digital abstraction, it's no wonder that the embodied ways we conceive of self would become abstracted, too—but also would drive the (re)discovery and (re)creation of other ways of touching storyworlds and being touched by them.

I would double down here on what I've argued elsewhere, that these digital feelies may offer "perhaps the best ways to play with discovering what that networked self is, caught between paper-work and networks" (Milligan, "From Codex to Ludex" 22). Digital feelies collaborate alongside many other forms of reading and storytelling and therefore are forms that both depend on and generate a range of affectively charged interfaces on, off, and between inscribed surfaces. Anable observes that "at the interface, we get fragments that tell us something about the larger picture that cannot all be grasped at once. A videogame is such an interface for grasping a contemporary structure of feeling" (xix).

What I've argued here is that grasping a contemporary structure of feeling through videogames requires a much bigger worlding of multiple interfaces— and a recognition of the essential role that touch plays with, around, and about the videogame. I've endeavored to demonstrate that reading as playing is an embodied process with material registers and ramifications and that understanding these things is more important than ever, both in postdigital cultures and in the evolution of videogames and our understanding of their roles in our lives. But revising our interaction with and understanding of videogames isn't possible without attending to their postdigital prehistory and their tactile present future.

WORKS CITED

Abbott, Michael. "Digital Feelies." *Brainy Gamer,* 3 February 2010. https://www.brainy gamer.com/the_brainy_gamer/2010/02/digital-feelies.html.

Anable, Aubrey. *Playing with Feelings: Video Games and Affect.* University of Minnesota Press, 2018.

Anthropy, Anna. *Rise of the Videogame Zinesters.* Seven Stories Press, 2012.

Bohunicky, Kira, and Chloe Anna Milligan. "Reading, Writing, Lexigraphing: Active Passivity as Queer Play in Walking Simulators." *Press Start,* vol. 5, no. 2, 2018, pp. 51–71.

Boluk, Stephanie, and Patrick LeMieux. *Metagaming: Playing, Competing, Spectating, Cheating, Trading, Making, and Breaking Videogames.* University of Minnesota Press, 2017.

Bosma, Josephine. "Post-digital Is Post-screen: Arnheim's Visual Thinking Applied to Art in the Expanded Digital Media Field." *APRJA,* vol. 3, no. 1, 2014, pp. 106–19. https://aprja.net//article/view/116091.

Charlton, James. "On Remembering a Post-digital Future." *APRJA,* vol. 3, no. 1, 2014, pp. 144–155. https://aprja.net//article/view/116094.

Consalvo, Mia, and Christopher A. Paul. *Real Games: What's Legitimate and What's Not in Contemporary Videogames.* MIT Press, 2019.

Cramer, Florian. "What Is Post-digital?" *APRJA,* vol. 3, no. 1, 2014, pp. 10–25. https:// aprja.net//article/view/116068.

Emerson, Lori. *Reading Writing Interfaces: From the Digital to the Bookbound.* University of Minnesota Press, 2014.

Ensslin, Astrid. *Literary Gaming.* MIT Press, 2014.

Frost, Laura. "Huxley's Feelies: The Cinema of Sensation in *Brave New World.*" *Twentieth Century Literature,* vol. 52, no. 4, Winter 2006, pp. 443–73.

Galloway, Alexander R. *Gaming: Essays on Algorithmic Culture.* University of Minnesota Press, 2006.

Garrington, Abbie. *Haptic Modernism: Touch and the Tactile in Modernist Writing.* Edinburgh University Press, 2015.

Gunning, Tom. "The Cinema of Attraction: Early Cinema, Its Spectator, and the Avant-Garde." *Wide Angle*, vol. 8, no. 3, 1986, pp. 63–70.

Halberstam, Jack. *The Queer Art of Failure.* Duke University Press, 2011.

Howard, K. Shannon. *Unplugging Popular Culture: Reconsidering Analog Technology, Materiality, and the "Digital Native."* Routledge, 2018.

Humphreys, Richard. "The Crime Dossiers of Dennis Wheatley and J. G. Links," 2002. http://www.denniswheatley.info/crimedossiers.htm.

Huxley, Aldous. *Brave New World.* Harper, 1998.

Kocurek, Carly A. "The Treachery of Pixels: Reconsidering Feelies in an Era of Digital Play." *Journal of Gaming & Virtual Worlds*, vol. 5, no. 3, September 2013, pp. 295–306.

Maher, Jimmy. "The Dennis Wheatley Crime Dossiers." *Digital Antiquarian*, 8 July 2012. https://www.filfre.net/2012/07/the-dennis-wheatley-crime-dossiers.

Manning, Erin. *Politics of Touch: Sense, Movement, Sovereignty.* University of Minnesota Press, 2006.

Milligan, Chloe Anna. "From Codex to Ludex: Paper Machines, Digital Games, and Haptic Subjectivities." *Publije: e-Revue de critique littéraire*, vol. 8, no. 1, 2019, pp. 1–24. http://revues.univ-lemans.fr/index.php/publije/article/view/141/135.

———. "The Page Is a Touchscreen: Haptic Narratives and 'Novel' Media." *Paradoxa*, vol. 29, 2018, pp. 287–311.

Murray, Janet H. *Hamlet on the Holodeck: The Future of Narrative in Cyberspace.* MIT Press, 1997.

Peters, Ian M. "Peril-Sensitive Sunglasses, Superheroes in Miniature, and Pink Polka-Dot Boxers: Artifact and Collectible Video Game Feelies, Play, and the Paratextual Gaming Experience." *Transformative Works and Cultures*, vol. 16, 2014. https://journal.transformativeworks.org/index.php/twc/article/view/509/447.

Salter, Anastasia. *What Is Your Quest? From Adventure Games to Interactive Books.* University of Iowa Press, 2014.

Scott, Jason. "The Feelies." *ASCII by Jason Scott*, 22 February 2008. http://ascii.textfiles.com/archives/1321.

Seekamp, Kristina. "Unmaking the Museum: Marcel Duchamp's Readymades in Context." *Toufait.com*, 22 March 2022. https://www.toutfait.com/unmaking-the-museum-marcel-duchamps-readymades-in-context.

SelenicMartian. "Murder off Miami." *Let's Play Archive*, 12 November 2015. https://lparchive.org/Murder-off-Miami/.

Szilak, Illya. "Towards Minor Literary Forms: Digital Literature and the Art of Failure." *Electronic Book Review*, 2 August 2015. https://electronicbookreview.com/essay/towards-minor-literary-forms-digital-literature-and-the-art-of-failure.

Wheatley, Dennis, and J. G. Links. *Murder off Miami.* Hutchinson, 1936.

Wilson, Jason. "'Participation TV': Videogame Archeology and New Media Art." *The Pleasure of Computer Gaming,* edited by Melanie Swalwell and Jason Wilson. McFarland, 2008, pp. 94–117.

Wingate, Steven. "Watching Textual Screens Then and Now: Text Movies, Electronic Literature, and the Continuum of Countertextual Practice." *CounterText,* vol. 2, no. 2., 2016, pp. 172–90.

Get Ready to Read!

The Fictionalization of Videogame Worlds for Young Readers

MICHELLE SHEA

Videogames have reached an apex in the entertainment industry as stand-alone interactive media with multidimensional revenue streams. A field built upon circuits and software has multiplied into a business of books and baubles. While players dedicate hours to their favorite games, many also read comics, magazines, short stories, and novels about virtual worlds. People who play, read, and write stories about videogames can explore narratives and encounter inspiration. As Paul Bloom noted in 2010, "When we are free to do whatever we want, we retreat to the imagination—to worlds created by others, as with books, movies, videogames, and television." By connecting mediums, gamers become immersed in the vivid settings and lore of videogames as both players and readers.

In this essay, I will discuss adaptations and novelizations related to videogames. I will also address the appeal of books for consumers and marketers, while considering series and publishing trends. My theoretical goals are to analyze videogame fictionalizations as literature, assess whether genres or themes influence formatting, and determine how fictionalizations for children and teens are unique. One can assume that videogame writing should align with general publishing expectations such as page counts or topic selection, but marketing strategies will vary. My examination will begin with adaptation theory, transition to motivations for game-based texts, and then narrow to younger readers with specific series examples.

What Are Videogame Adaptations, Novelizations, and Fictionalizations?

Adaptations retell and reinterpret existing material between formats and genres. In *A Theory of Adaptation*, Linda Hutcheon notes that adapted material seeks "equivalences" between "the various elements of the story," which includes "its themes, events, world, characters, motivations, points of view, consequences, contexts, symbols, [and] imagery" (10). According to this definition, videogame adaptations should be as well written as any other prose because readability is dependent on an author's choices and literary elements. While games allow for interactive characterization, such as player-directed movement and choices, books provide a guided adventure with the possibility of expanded characterization. For example, *Halo*'s fictionalization shows the outwardly stoic Spartans having internal concerns about war.

Successful adaptations must meet certain criteria when adapting story elements. Writing with respect to adaptations of Shakespeare, Bruce Coville asserts that adapted characters and stories should be relatable, writers must become immersed into source material, the original story structure should be respected, reimagined versions can reference specific passages, and tales should be formatted for legibility (60–65). Considering these standards more generally, writers can create books that honor both the story and the medium of adapted works. For videogame novels, authors should conduct research by playing the games, reviewing publisher releases, and reading other novelizations. Additionally, publisher guides can help novelists understand writing expectations.

When an author writes a story based on a different medium, such as a show or videogame, this adaptation is called novelization. The word "novelization" is an "umbrella term" (Van Parys 288) that includes written versions of existing visual content, new stories based on ongoing worlds, and companion books. In the case of videogames, novelized books can utilize existing settings and characters, though the tales do not need to directly follow original plot and pacing. In terms of the videogame's original storyworld, novelizations can be canon if they are published with game creators, but they more often stand alone.

Thomas Van Parys points out that "novelizations follow . . . the rules of popular fiction" with few "genre-specific elements" (291), so most stories rely on dialogue and literary devices more than game affordances. However, since readers cannot usually rely on visuals (except with graphic novels), most authors will include explanations, similes, or metaphors to capture the look and feel of games. That will also depend on the intended audience and format. Texts aimed at adults may include multiple narrators and fluctuating time periods, while novelizations for youth often have short chapters and linear problem-solution plots.

Typically, fictionalization occurs when real-life individuals are incorporated into a storyline and facts are altered for a narrative, which Frank Kessler characterizes as a "process of fictionalization" that shows a "world which is similar to but also radically separated from ours" (130). For historical games like *Assassin's Creed*, real people are already part of the story; however, behaviors or dialogue are invented. Thus, in the 2010 companion book *Renaissance*, as in the game, the real Medici family is included (Bowden). In contrast, for the fictionalization of *World of Warcraft*, a fantasy game, the social roles are imagined; in *Halo*, descriptions of tactics and troops are the key; in *Minecraft*, survival skills are the focus. Videogame adaptations utilize fictionalization so that readers have a satisfying and connective experience to their game. To sum it up, videogame adaptations retell not just the story but also the feelings of play in a new format.

Why Novelize Videogames?

The first stand-alone written works about videogames were strategy guides, in which players would read 100 percent walkthroughs with game tips and hidden achievements. It wasn't until the late 1980s and early 1990s that novelizations became popular. *Final Fantasy* adaptations appeared as manga and novelizations from 1989 to 2012, with English editions rereleased up to 2020. Barry Grant and Scott Henderson note that a "publisher noticed that his readers had taken a real liking to the new videogame," so "he bought the comic book rights to *Pokémon*" (86). As a result, *Pokémon* comic books have been consistently issued from 1996 to the present, while chapter books were first published in 1999 and rereleased in 2017 by Scholastic, a mainstream curator of children's books. Game company Nintendo also published comics, for *Donkey Kong* and *Super Mario*, in the late 1990s, and more recently has released coloring books and stickers.

For other studios, publishing time frames have coincided with game releases. The main *Resident Evil* book series ran from 1998 to 2004 to overlap with the first five games; however, in the past fifteen years, reprints have been more common. Other game novelizations follow similar trends, as only popular or ongoing series are republished. Additionally, videogame novels are often written by authors with an extensive publishing history. For example, Christine Golden has written adaptations of *Assassin's Creed, World of Warcraft,* and *Starcraft.* Other authors have explored multiple formats, as Peter David has with a *Halo* novel and in short stories for *Fable.*

There is a distinct difference in how stories are told, depending on the medium. A novel "tells a story about the past . . . to the reader," while a videogame involves "writing many possible stories . . . where the player is taking an active role in choosing" what occurs (Copplestone 86). In practice, this means that videogame novelizations select narrative threads to follow, since there is no space or time to address all possible side stories. Authors typically condense plots while increasing character descriptions to stay within publication parameters. Some game-based series venture into uncharted territory by introducing original story elements in combination with familiar settings or timelines. In the 2012 *Fable* short stories, for example, antagonists and heroes are given backstories that run parallel to the games (David). *Sonic the Hedgehog, Mega Man,* and other books also follow this pattern, as readers want content for favorite characters.

A primary motivator for novelizations is multimedia marketing strategies to bolster game sales, but book publishers also see the massive profits of the videogame industry. MarketLine, an industry profiler, reported that $20.1 billion dollars was spent on games in 2020, with an anticipated rise to $25.4 billion by 2025 ("Games"). In contrast, $25.8 billion was spent on books in 2020, with predictions for slightly decreased margins ("Books"). There is some overlap in the intended audience, but videogames are expected to capture a large market share. Books based on hobbies or media draw in young readers, too. In 2020, Scholastic made $875 million dollars through the children's book sector alone ("Scholastic Corporation"). According to *How to Write and Publish a Successful Children's Book,* medium-size publishing houses "bring in between $10 million and $50 million in annual sales," while larger publishers "promote more than 500 books a year" and earn more than $50 million annually (Reeser 40–41). If revenue was added up from multiple children's publishers, the amounts would be sizable.

Since there is financial incentive to publish for young readers, publishers have released more videogame novelizations in the trade and mass market sectors. Videogame books are often sold near related materials such as key chains and coloring packs to build recognition and collectability for popular or current releases. Scholastic, as the "largest operator of . . . school-based book fairs" in

America, has a "broad portfolio" of literacy choices for children, teachers, and libraries (MarketLine, "Scholastic SWOT"). With a new CEO in 2021 and a renewed focus on "direct-to-parent marketing of books," Scholastic is focused on the "trade business" of new releases and its "entertainment and media properties" ("Scholastic Names New CEO"). This could include book trailers, movies, or alternate media tie-ins such as videogame partnerships. Based on trends, it's likely they may pivot toward e-books, digital sales, and targeted print advertising. With threats like "budgetary restraints" in education and "intense competition" from popular publishers, Scholastic plans to address target audiences in new ways (MarketLine, "Scholastic SWOT"). When publishing profits drop, media industry alliances are the next logical step.

Publishers know that young readers are usually fans of series, so there is incentive to novelize franchise-based games. With series, children transfer knowledge of characters and settings, just as they would do with videogame sequels. Even if they cannot read novels in order, they can still "move to another available part of the series" to fill "gaps in the narrative" (Newland 149). Perhaps not coincidentally, many videogames are initially published in a chronologically scattered order. For example, in the *Legend of Zelda* series, *Skyward Sword* is positioned near the world's starting timeline, even though it was released decades after the first game. While most books are published sequentially, those written about videogames break the mold, as popular games are novelized first. Gamers are accustomed to constantly updating continuity, so they aren't dissuaded from reading if a few titles are not immediately published.

Another reason for videogame novelizations is that videogames teach useful and transferable literacy skills. Catherine Compton-Lilly points out that adolescents often form a "projective identity" as readers and as gamers, which impacts self-confidence. If youth relate to characters, themes, or plots in games, they may positively identify with similar aspects within books. Additionally, game novelizations can promote regular reading practice, since children understand books better when they self-select source material (720–21). John Alberti observed in 2008 that novelizations inspire an "interest and enthusiasm in reading and writing" for the "gaming discourse community," which results in "artistic and cultural development" for youth (260). Reading about videogames can ignite creative thoughts, lead to writing about established characters or worlds, and promote social engagement.

When books and games overlap, there is opportunity for cross-media promotion. Thomas Apperley and Christopher Walsh argue that texts and videogames mutually contribute to information seeking and entertainment, based on shared "action, design, situation[s], and systems" (117). These concepts are explored through in-game text, guides, full-length books, or graphic novels. Visual media like videos and artwork can also contribute to reading proficiency, as secondary sources amplify virtual worlds. For example, YouTube clips for battle royale games like *Overwatch* build characters and story arcs that are not fully explained in-game. In this context, gaming literacy involves players' reading selections, collaborative or cultural gaming experiences, and underlying expectations for formats. Essentially, varied modalities of writing, watching, and listening create a context of cross-media literacy. By reading in-game text, checking out game novelizations, and watching captioned videos, players can increase peer engagement and enjoyment.

How Do Videogame Novels Appeal to Young Readers?

Research has shown that youth who see texts as "important and personally beneficial" are more likely to read (Codling 91). Children often revisit and reflect on material that they find helpful. In the 2009 book *Reading Japan Cool*, a young boy reports that he "was interested in videogames and read the related manga" because that "information was useful for [his] game," to the point that he "read almost everything . . . many times" (Ingulsrud and Allen 143). The child reread to capture bits of data, compare it to his game, and evaluate whether his perception changed.

Videogame novels also appeal to reluctant readers who may have the misconception that comics or magazines don't count. Graphic novels, short stories, and fan fiction are all formats that fascinate young readers, as these texts use illustrations, brevity, and vivid descriptions to be approachable. For example, the 2018 short story collection *Sonic and the Tales of Deception* has pictures of robot bees and short lines like "The speedy hedgehog was poised to strike" (Black 9), which is readable for children in second or third grade. Videogame novelizations further bridge the gap by adapting interactive, story-based elements. As Stephanie Altchuler and Hannah Chai reported in 2019, books that encourage imagination and predictions of future actions enhance enjoyment, improve memory, and lead to thoughtful reading. When children dynamically interact with books, they experience better self-perceptions, too.

Although boys are not the only gamers, they are more likely to read under specific circumstances. As described by Katya Henry, Anna Lagos, and Frances

Berndt, male readers tend to want books with action, competition, purpose, and topics of personal interest. And while playthrough guides address utilitarian needs for strategizing, game-based novelizations fulfill readers' desire for creativity. These literary texts generally use fast-paced storylines and develop characters' motivations. In early *Pokémon* games, for example, the main character, Red, is competitive with his neighbor, Blue. For the printed *Pokémon Adventures*, these characters are renamed Ash and Gary and are given detailed backstories.

Players who are passionate about a series may delve deeper, especially when they can discuss with peers. Illustrated or electronic books tend to be particularly attractive to boys. As researchers Maria Rasmusson and Lisbeth Åberg-Bengtsson observed in 2015, boys have better literacy outcomes when texts are digital, due to device proficiency and the "additional visual-spatial skills . . . enhanced by playing computer games" (705). Male youth may enjoy print books about videogames when visuals are incorporated; however, longer works, such as novels, can also be more readable as e-books. Some notable series with digital texts are *Tekken, God of War, The Last of Us,* and *Uncharted.*

In contrast, for girls, interest in game-based reading typically depends on the story elements. In *Ethnographies of the Videogame,* Helen Thornham notes that a female player's enjoyment of videogames tended to be based on the "emphasis she places on the romance narrative" above other types, such as "revenge, rescue, friendship, and teenage angst," although those themes are also popular (62). A few thematically similar game novelizations are *Final Fantasy, Tomb Raider,* and *Kingdom Hearts.* Of course, gender-based analyses often rely on generalities, so individual children may exhibit alternate preferences. Regardless, publishers must consider where children are in their lives and include diverse and relatable characters and details.

Graphic Novels, Manga, and Comics: Visual Literacy and Reading

When selecting books, students tend to favor specific formats. Dawnelle Henretty and John McEneaney report that reading involves "cues anchored in the text," which are "combined with reader-based sources of information in meaning making" (185). Essentially, readers use prior knowledge, printed text, and associated images to understand story events. For videogame novels, background understanding usually comes from playing games, as preexisting awareness of problems or settings can create interest and facilitate reading efforts.

Further, as Pamela Mason and Jacy Ippolito affirm, young readers benefit from "individual reading plans that include both traditional and nontraditional texts," such as the electronic formats previously noted, as well as "graphic novels, videogame magazines, [and] manga" (325). Often, image-heavy books include supplemental nonfiction notes, like author or illustrator interviews and sketch art, to give insight into the creative process. When combined, fictional, graphic, and nonfiction texts attract gaming readers to enhance the multimedia experience.

The distinguishing features of graphic novels are full-color pages, overlapping or sequential stories, and complete story arcs. These adapt not just narrative content but also visual style from games and shows for cross-media storytelling. Jessica Abel notes that the graphic novel format consists of a "larger proportion of science fiction and adventures stories," which can be "put on lower shelves" when "aimed at young readers" (19–20). That would seem to be the case with videogame adaptations as well. As mentioned, the *Pokémon* series has published multiple comic and graphic novels over two decades, such as *Battle with the Ultra Beast* and *Grand Trial Showdown*, both written by author Simcha Whitehill in 2019 for Scholastic. Notable features of the *Pokémon* books include 128-page formats and frequent exclamatory text. Word balloons for dialogue and descriptive panels have one or two sentences each, which orients reading toward children in lower elementary grades (Whitehill, *Battle*). Additionally, themes of friendship and courage are threaded into the adventure narrative, as seen in Ash Ketchum's teamwork and challenging fights.

Children read these for entertainment, of course, but also as fans of the games, anime, or individual Pokémon. Over time, they'll likely read others they find nearby—graphic novel sales tend to improve when similar materials are shelved together. *Pokémon* and other graphic novels are organized by topic or format and are strategically promoted with posters, outward-facing covers, and accessible sections to improve interest and sales. This practice, undertaken by book fairs, catalogs, and libraries, can increase interest in their wares.

One graphic format that is growing in popularity is manga, which is oriented in a right-to-left reading format. These translated videogame adaptations from Japan are increasingly common and have expanded to international audiences. Viz Media, a purveyor of manga, regularly features main heroes, allies, and antagonists on covers. Generally, manga also incorporates bright colors and large images to grab attention, as seen in *Splatoon* and *Kingdom Hearts*. A typical example of manga would be Nintendo's *Legend of Zelda*. Though originally sold as separate volumes that ended with cliffhangers, subsequent versions were compiled into "legendary editions." *The Legend of Zelda: Ocarina of Time*, published in 2016, is organized with a table of contents to add structure to its 350-page length. Most story iterations involve Link, the series' heroic youth, saving Zelda, the princess of Hyrule, from Ganondorf—the same story as most of the original videogames. This is true of the themes, too: coming of age, good versus evil, and persistence, as represented by Link's journey. While color printing in the first chapter is designed to engage readers new to manga, the text transitions to a black-and-white format in subsequent sections to save on printing costs (Himekawa). Panels of varying sizes create visual contrast to draw eyes from top to bottom, and some images even layer to produce a three-dimensional effect. Settings such as the Lost Woods and Death Mountain are also shared between the games and manga. While manga are read by people of all ages, adaptations oriented for children in late elementary or middle school often duplicate plotlines in an effort to build context for uncommon words.

The third and final form of graphic adaptation is comics, which visually duplicate action while telling stories about interactions beyond the original game, including flashbacks. With the first *Overwatch: Anthology* volume in 2017, for example, twelve brief comics by various authors and artists highlight the personalities, traits, and abilities of these iconic but narratively thin battle royale fighters. Explosions expert Junkrat is talkative and impulsive, while his partner, Roadhog, is quiet but forceful (Brooks et al.). *Overwatch* fighters are located across the planet, so settings such as Brazil, Egypt, and Sweden are featured alongside tiny towns, traveling trains, and combat zones. Each location contributes to storytelling about motivations, as seen with Symmetra, who has perfectionist tendencies and grew up poor, but they also allow for visual adaptation of specific character movement characteristics that would be familiar to players. For many characters, challenges are revealed through internal or conversational dialogue. *Overwatch* is marketed to all ages, although its mild and implied comic violence is better suited for middle-grade youth. Notably, not every playable character is included in the comics, due to updated seasonal rosters.

Short Stories: Tiny Tales with Emotion

Like novelizations, short story adaptations incorporate existing characters or settings into scenarios with a clear beginning, middle, and end. Further, as described by Charles Barrett, short story length is not based on "some arbitrary word limit" but rather on "the theme with which it deals" (14). Videogame short stories center on one or two core conflicts that are resolved within the tale, so character development is rounded and reader comprehension is enabled. We also see world building that is familiar to fans. For example, in *World of Warcraft's* digital comics, readers learn about political activities, secondary characters, and new arcs.

The short story adaptations of *Sonic the Hedgehog* are written for children and emphasize new adventures with friends. There are currently two compilations from 2018, *Sonic and the Tales of Deception* and *Sonic and the Tales of Terror*. Although the *Sonic* universe is commonly represented in comics, this foray into short stories shows demand for multiple formats. For developing readers, these short tales bridge the gap between early readers and chapter books and feature stories distinct from the games. Each compilation has three original narratives, at about twenty pages each, which center on battles between the heroes and Dr. Eggman, Shadow, and other villains. To further appeal to children, Penguin Young Readers published the illustrations, headings, and transitions in steel blue and cobalt, while the main text utilizes black font—a visual design that is functional and attractive for beginning readers. To further accommodate those readers, illustrations embedded in the text directly relate to what is occurring in the prose, and the writing focuses on dialogue, urgent exclamations, and action. In line with Barrett's observation, stories are organized by theme and conflict. Here, as in the games, the focus is teamwork and strategizing to solve challenges. When Sonic and his friends are separated, they need to rescue each other and fight past nemeses. While villains have dastardly intentions, children familiar with the games know that the heroes will prevail, so they can enjoy the story without worry.

As readers age, they tend to expect and enjoy more narrative complexity, including ambiguous endings and unreliable narrators. For the *Five Nights at Freddy's* (*FNAF*) survival horror series, which incorporates terror and mystery, there are currently twelve books in the Fazbear Frights collection, published by Scholastic. Each book is named after one of three spooky short stories contained within. Many of the stories deal with youth who are lonely, in trouble, or dealing with childhood dilemmas, while a few tales focus on adults with less-than-perfect lives. Each self-contained story is about sixty to eighty pages. These ranges are lengthy for a short story, since that page count approaches the limits of a novella, but I have observed while teaching that children will read if a tale has good pacing and evokes emotions. The additional length also allows suspense to build, which is important for a series based on ominous animatronics and jump scares.

As is the case with many fictionalizations, these stories occasionally adapt gameplay mechanics, as seen in "Room for One More," with its night guard carrying a flashlight (Cawthorn et al., 1:35 A.M.), and "Bunny Call," with its randomly appearing animatronic and six a.m. reprieve from terror (Cawthorn et al., *Bunny Call*). The tales are linked both by frightening antagonists and world building, with readers often seeking out clues about the overall *FNAF* narrative. New animatronic personalities, like Fetch, are introduced, but most creepy characters are variations of the ones in-game, including Funtime Freddy, Foxy, and Ballora. Videogame novelizations should reward readers with new lore or characters while also respecting existing plotlines, and this is particularly true of the *FNAF* series, as it is designed for an older youth audience. Accordingly, *Five Nights at Freddy's* is a strong example of short story series publishing.

Short story game adaptations capitalize on prior knowledge, build on narrative continuity, and manage pacing to maintain suspense in a fashion that accords with the source game. Unlike novelizations, though, short stories have a strong emphasis on theme and a bolder emphasis on conflict and conflict resolution. Thus, even though short stories are less common for game novelizations, there are readers who dedicate their time to them.

Novels: Crafting a World Beyond the Games

Full-length, single-narrative books are the most standardized format, since publishing conventions and the market are well established. Reeser has observed that "fantasy, adventure, humor, horror, and family-oriented stories and sagas" tend to appeal to middle-grade readers, who want stories "about the world around them" (32). Thus, for videogame adaptations, publishers tend to choose themes, character types, and genre conventions that align clearly with those expectations and with the games they adapt. These will typically include stories about family or friends that have clear and resolvable conflicts or that integrate comedy. Videogame novels may be printed or digital, have game-based plotting, include illustrations, and represent characters who can sustain emotional engagement. A full survey of published gaming novels is impossible, but the examples here will provide some sense of the market for late elementary to middle school audiences.

For fans of *Minecraft*, a sandbox game that has no particular plot or world building, the novels shift focus toward narrative and in-game mechanics, such as crafting stones. At least twelve official novels have been released as of 2022. The first one, *Minecraft: The Island*, appeared in 2017 and was written by Max Brooks, the author of *World War Z*. The premise is that the protagonist has awoken in-game, and everything, including the sun and clouds, is block-shaped. He subsequently collects items with punches, runs from creepers, crafts houses, and explores the expanse of the island. As the book progresses, the main character learns how to farm, mine, hunt, fish, and care for himself, while discovering new terrain, materials, and the larger world of adventure.

The comedy-horror writing will thrill both seasoned gamers and those who have never played, as the protagonist's adventures serve as a kind of tutorial. Most chapters run between ten to fifteen pages and have advisory titles. A directory of tips, such as "Conserve your resources" and "It's not failure that matters, but how you recover," is included in final pages (Brooks 267–70). While later *Minecraft* novels focus on storylines over mechanics, the whole collection encourages the same kind of sandbox creativity and continuity from book to book. For teachers who want high-interest classroom novels, books like these provide children with simultaneous game tutorials, life lessons, and literacy skills.

Not all readers who want novel-style narratives are ready for long chapter books. Illustrated novels enable younger readers to visualize action, detect context clues, and transition from comics to conventional books. These novels are also shrewd marketing opportunities. For example, the novels for *Spyro the Dragon* were published after developer Activision released a new *Skylanders* arc in 2012. The books reflect the *Skylanders* narrative and its particular brand of interactive gameplay. In the eight-volume Mask of Power series from 2013 to 2016, Spyro faces elementally powered monsters that seek magical Skylands, mirroring the overall plot of the new *Skylanders* arc. Most paragraphs contain a mix of simple and complex sentences, such as, "Magic courses through every rock, plant, and animal—even the sheep" (Beakman 1).

While working with fourth- and fifth-grade readers, I found that humor and relatable dialogue were preferred, and these books fill the bill with parenthetical asides, jokes, and casual language. Some strategic marketing choices can also be seen, such as the childlike ghostwriter pseudonym, prominent *Skylanders: Universe* branding, and hero names featured in book titles. Since the *Skylanders* and *Spyro* games are action oriented, these books capitalize on character posing, flashy entrances, and combat sequences. At times, the fictionalization shifts from Spyro, but this strategy aligns with Activision's character expansion plan. Children enjoy media crossovers and physical items, as evidenced by total sales, so other toys-to-life games and products may be adapted into novels eventually.

Teenage gamers also have options for adapted novels. The *Assassins Creed* stealth series was previously novelized by Penguin Books, but now game studio Ubisoft has a publishing imprint. The premise of the narrative is that a secret society in the present uses a machine called the Animus to reenact memories of bloodline predecessors, who are members of that same secret organization. These ancestors are from sixteenth-century Italy, eighteenth-century London, and other eras, yet they have shared abilities, such as eagle vision, hidden blade wielding, and leaps of faith. The texts typically emphasize characters, relationships, and lore from the games, so the novels are probably better read after playing. Most of the books focus on the ancestors rather than their modern-day counterparts; however, *Assassins Creed: Heresy* covers both perspectives. In that book, one of the Animus researchers wants to relive Joan of Arc's history in order to repair an artifact.

With eight- to nine-page chapters, this roughly three-hundred-page book moves speedily between past and future events. A 2016 spin-off series called *Last Descendants*, written for middle schoolers, has a distinct visual style and narrative premise that differs from the games, with variations such as adolescents who encounter an Animus at school. With only a slightly shorter length, at around 250 pages, readers of *Last Descendants* still get gamelike storylines, as the books merge historical and science fiction genres with literary themes such as survival, identity, revenge, and regret. Young players can use books like these to connect with real-life concerns such as strained friendships or feelings of displacement.

Fan Fiction: Writing from the Web

Fan fiction, which is primarily a digital phenomenon, has broad applications as a less-regulated avenue for novelizations. In general, fan fiction sites cover diverse narrative media, including television series, anime, movies, books, musicals, and games. The largest portal is FanFiction.net, a free-to-publish website with thousands of stories. As noted by Cecilia Aragon, fan fiction assists writers in "finding community, establishing identity, and exploring new trends that have not yet found mainstream acceptance." For gamers, writing might include personalized narratives or reinvented interactions. Aragon, who looked at multiple fandoms and interviewed multiple authors, discovered that the average age of fan fiction writers was about fifteen and a half, and those writers explored themes and characters that often were underrepresented in the texts they adapted. Aragon also notes that writers regularly mentor each other, and it's likely that these responsive online communities generate a feedback cycle for improved reading and writing, although writers will still need to sift through constructive comments. Similarly, we can imagine writers replaying games and discovering new perspectives while writing for fun.

Currently, the most novelized game is *Pokémon*, which has almost eighty thousand fan stories in many languages. Around one hundred other games, including *Final Fantasy* and *Fire Emblem*, have at least one thousand fan fictions. In schools, fan fiction is written with media-based characters, settings, and events that both avid and reluctant readers can outline on story maps. On fan fiction sites, young creators can rate work as appropriate for kids or teens and assign a genre. Prospective readers can see a story summary, word count, and any reviews, favorites, or follows. While small printers may release unofficial novels, like those for *Fortnite,* many prospective authors publish independently, since fan fiction can be a unique testing ground for unproven writers to hone their skills. For readers, there are virtually endless possibilities for new adaptations of their favorite games.

Publishing Trends: What Have We Learned?

Gamers have literary choices across genres and formats; however, there are patterns. Currently, action-adventure, multiplayer, and role playing are the most popular genres to adapt. While there are some strategy and platformer novelizations, such as *Super Mario,* those mostly originated before 2000. Fewer novelized games can be found for combat, rhythm, simulations, or sports, probably because strong storylines are easier to adapt than open-concept or sandbox entries. It's also likely that the popularity of specific literary genres plays a role in book selection. Neal Wyatt and Joyce Saricks observe that "literary fiction authors are eager adopters" of "[science fiction]–infused Horror, Mystery, and Adventure" (109), which is evident in genre crossovers like *Bioshock, Assassin's Creed,* and *Halo.* Other titles, like *Sonic the Hedgehog* and *Pokémon,* also bridge science fiction and adventure by incorporating technology such as robots and Poké Balls, into their playful worlds. Additionally, "there is a natural connection . . . between Fantasy books and Fantasy videogames" due to imaginative world building (Wyatt and Saricks 144). This is the case with *The Legend of Zelda, Spyro the Dragon, World of Warcraft,* and *Final Fantasy.*

Literary game adaptations explore a wide range of themes, such as fate, heroism, power struggles, growing up, friendship, isolation, betrayal, and truth. However, the plots tend to be less varied, with multiple protagonists working together toward a common goal or against a malevolent force. Most adaptations follow the "hero's journey" model that has persisted since early mythological tales, although exceptions do exist. Regardless, young readers can find something interesting to read, even if their preferred genres, such as romance or mystery, are only featured in side plots or short stories.

Book formatting details demonstrate what children can comfortably read at different levels, but they also determine the feel of varied novelizations. Graphic novels are commonly between 200 and 350 pages, include unpredictable word counts, and use images as needed, while comics are often released as scheduled serials or anthology paperbacks. Short tales usually range from thirty to forty pages and are packaged in sets of three or more (unless they are electronic versions) to meet editing standards. Full novels, the most conventional format, typically are 150 to 300 pages for children and 300 to 400 pages for young adults. Finally, as an outlier that relies on free digital posting or small publishers, fan fiction has the fewest rules when it comes to formatting, as seen in the generous word count limits, variable quality, and unique challenges of the stories published on FanFiction.net. In sum, gamers have a wide range of choices based on interest, formatting, or other personal factors.

Conclusions: Are Players Ready to Read?

As an overview of the videogame literature market, I've explored an equitable number of graphic books, short stories, and novels. However, publishing rates and accessibility for readers may fluctuate based on demand. Books can be sourced through libraries, Amazon, and publisher websites. Physical comics and whole novels are easier to locate than short stories, which are often relegated to digital mediums. Outside of regular publishing, fan fiction has limitless potential, though built-in audiences tend to be dependent on game popularity and access to digital content. Quickly produced writing can tie in with game releases, since many series have a one- to two-year gap between books.

I could not represent every game adaptation, but the examples here are reliable guideposts for most published genres and formats. They clearly indicate that playing videogames and reading their adaptations can be complementary activities for children and teens, enabling them to build literacy skills while learning about favorite characters and worlds. As new, plot-driven games are released, a rise in related publications is likely, since publishers can capitalize on the consistently healthy profit margins, cross-industry collaborations, and built-in audiences. For this form of videogame literature, children and young adults are quickly discovering that the "reader" and "gamer" tags are not mutually exclusive. The mission is clear: Get ready to read!

WORKS CITED

Primary Sources

Beakman, Onk. *The Mask of Power: Spyro Versus the Mega Monsters,* illustrated by Tino Santanach. Grosset & Dunlap, 2013.

Black, Jake. *Sonic and the Tales of Deception,* illustrated by Ian McGinty. Penguin Young Readers, 2018.

Bowden, Oliver. *Assassin's Creed: Renaissance.* Ace, 2010.

Brooks, Max. *Minecraft: The Island.* Del Rey, 2017.

Brooks, Robert, Matt Burns, Michael Chu, Micky Neilson, Andrew Robinson, and James Waugh. *Overwatch: Anthology,* vol. 1, illustrated by Bengal, Jeffrey Cruz, Espen Grundetjern, Miki Montllo, Nesskain, Joe Ng, and Gray Shuko. Dark Horse Comics, 2017.

Cawthorn, Scott, Elley Cooper, and Andrea Waggener. *1:35 A.M.* Fazbear Frights 3. Scholastic, 2020.

———. *Bunny Call.* Fazbear Frights 5. Scholastic, 2020.

David, Peter. *Fable: Reaver.* Del Rey, 2012.

Golden, Christine. *Assassin's Creed: Heresy.* Ubisoft, 2016.

Himekawa, Akira. *The Legend of Zelda: Ocarina of Time.* Viz Media, 2016.

Kirby, Matthew. *Last Descendants: An Assassin's Creed Novel Series.* Scholastic, 2016.

Phegley, Kiel. *Sonic and the Tales of Terror,* illustrated by Patrick Spaziante. Penguin Young Readers, 2018.

Whitehill, Simcha. *Battle with the Ultra Beast.* New York: Scholastic, 2019.

———. *Grand Trial Showdown.* New York: Scholastic, 2019.

Secondary Sources

Abel, Jessica. "The Art of Selling Graphic Novels." *Publishers Weekly,* vol. 248, no. 26, June 2001, pp. 18–20.

Alberti, John. "The Game of Reading and Writing: How Video Games Reframe Our Understanding of Literacy." *Computers & Composition,* vol. 25, no. 3, September 2008, pp. 258–69.

Altchuler, Stephanie, and Hannah Chai. "'Getting Unstuck': Reluctant Readers and the Impact of Visualization Strategies." *Reading Improvement,* vol. 56, no. 4, Winter 2019, pp. 197–207.

Apperley, Thomas, and Christopher Walsh. "What Digital Games and Literacy Have in Common: A Heuristic for Understanding Pupils' Gaming Literacy." *Literacy,* vol. 46, no. 3, November 2012, pp. 115–22.

Aragon, Cecilia. "What I Learned From Studying Billions of Words of Online Fan Fiction." *Technology Review,* December 2019.

Barrett, Charles Raymond. *Short Story Writing: A Practical Treatise on the Art of the Short Story.* Floating Press, 2009.

Bloom, Paul. "The Pleasure of Imagination." *Chronicle of Higher Education Review,* May 2010.

Codling, Rose Marie. "Creating an Optimal Learning Environment for Struggling Readers." *Advanced Literacy Practices: From the Clinic to the Classroom,* edited by Evan Ortlieb and Earl H. Cheek. Emerald Group, 2013, pp. 87–113.

Compton-Lilly, Catherine. "What Can Video Games Teach Us About Teaching Reading?" *Reading Teacher,* vol. 60, no. 8, May 2007, pp. 718–27.

Copplestone, Tara Jane. "Designing and Developing a Playful Past in Videogames." *The Interactive Past: Archaeology, Heritage & and Videogames,* edited by Angus A. A. Mol, Csilla E. Ariese-Vandemeulebroucke, Krijn H. J. Boom, and Aris Politopoulos. Sidestone Press, 2017, pp. 85–97.

Coville, Bruce. "Nutshells and Infinite Space: Stage of Adaptation." *Reimagining Shakespeare for Children and Young Adults,* edited by Naomi Miller. Routledge, 2013, pp. 56–66.

Grant, Barry Keith, and Scott Henderson. *Comics and Pop Culture: Adaptation from Panel to Frame.* University of Texas Press, 2019.

Henretty, Dawnelle J., and John E. McEneaney. "Bottom-Up and Top-Down Cues in a Comics Reading Task." *Reading Psychology,* vol. 41, no. 3, April 2020, pp. 183–204.

Henry, Katya, Anna Lagos, and Frances Berndt. "Bridging the Literacy Gap Between Boys and Girls: An Opportunity for the National Year of Reading 2012." *Australian Library Journal,* vol. 61, no. 2, May 2012, pp. 143–50.

Hutcheon, Linda. *A Theory of Adaptation.* 2nd ed., Routledge, 2012.

Ingulsrud, John E., and Kate Allen. *Reading Japan Cool: Patterns of Manga Literacy and Discourse.* Lexington Books, 2009.

Kessler, Frank. "'Spellbound in Darkness': Narrative Absorption Discussed by Film Theory." *Narrative Absorption,* edited by Frank Hakemulder, Moniek M. Kuijpers, Ed S. Tan, Katalin Bálint, and Miruna M. Doicaru. John Benjamins, 2017, pp. 119–31.

MarketLine. "Books in the United States." *MarketLine Industry Profile,* 2021, pp. 1–31.

———. "Games Software in the United States." *MarketLine Industry Profile,* 2021, pp. 1–47.

———. "Scholastic Corporation." *MarketLine Company Profile,* 2021, pp. 1–31.

———. "Scholastic SWOT Analysis." *MarketLine Company Profile,* 2021, pp. 1–7.

Mason, Pamela A., and Jacy Ippolito. "What Is the Role of the Reading Specialist in Promoting Adolescent Literature?" *Essential Questions in Adolescent Literacy: Teachers and Researchers Describe What Works in Classrooms,* edited by Jill Lewis. Guilford Press, 2009, pp. 312–36.

Newland, Jane. "Surfing the Series: A Rhizomic Reading of Series Fiction." *Children's Literature and Culture,* edited by Harry Edwin Eiss. Cambridge Scholars, 2007, pp. 147–56.

Rasmusson, Maria, and Lisbeth Åberg-Bengtsson. "Does Performance in Digital Reading Relate to Computer Game Playing? A Study of Factor Structure and Gender Patterns in 15-Year-Olds' Reading Literacy Performance." *Scandinavian Journal of Educational Research,* vol. 59, no. 6, December 2015, pp. 691–709.

Reeser, Cynthia. "Children's Publishing Market Assessment." *How to Write and Publish a Successful Children's Book: Everything You Need to Know Explained Simply.* Atlantic, 2010, pp. 23–46.

"Scholastic Names New CEO, Expects Improvement in Fiscal 2022." *Publishers Weekly,* vol. 268, no. 30, July 2021, p. 5.

Thornham, Helen. *Ethnographies of the Videogame: Gender, Narrative and Praxis.* Ashgate, 2011.

Van Parys, Thomas. "A Fantastic Voyage into Inner Space: Description in Science-Fiction Novelizations." *Science Fiction Studies,* vol. 38, no. 2, July 2011, pp. 288–303.

Wyatt, Neal, and Joyce G. Saricks. *The Readers' Advisory Guide to Genre Fiction.* 3rd ed., ALA Editions, 2019.

Nonsense Games

Cultures of Play Since *Alice's Adventures in Wonderland*

KRISTEN STARKOWSKI

Inspired by Lewis Carroll's *Alice's Adventures in Wonderland* and *Through the Looking-Glass: And What Alice Found There*, Cortopia Studio's *Down the Rabbit Hole* (2020) virtual reality (VR) adventure takes players into Wonderland to solve puzzles and find invitations that unlock access to new locations in this re-mediated version of Alice and her topsy-turvy world. Premised upon the famil-iar trope of "falling down the rabbit hole," the game's developers invite players to "determine the fate of an unnamed girl [who] has accidentally wandered" far from home. Indeed, like Carroll's protagonist, the player of *Down the Rabbit Hole* slips while climbing down a ladder and experiences an "endless fall" as the game begins.

The game's central premise will be familiar to most players, since Carroll's novels have been adapted again and again since the nineteenth century. Indeed, both books have been translated into over forty-seven languages, and for more than 150 years the phrase "Down the rabbit hole" has been used figuratively in media, literature, economics, and politics to indicate entry into a disorienting alternate reality. Additionally, the books have been turned into films, music videos, brainteasers, decks of cards, amusement park rides, and videogames. The *Down the Rabbit Hole* VR thus registers a double legacy: first, in terms of the original text's history of cultural remediation, and second, in terms of Car-roll's history of linking games to narrative by inviting readers to participate in fantastical worlds that are full of puzzles. The *Alice* stories are ideally suited to digital games and to virtual reality because videogames—even more so than the gameful tropes that Carroll integrates into the language and structure of his stories—directly engage the audience in generating the narrative by revising sensorimotor expectations in ways that cause players to dissociate from their everyday body schemas.

How is it that Alice's adventures have emerged as an exemplar of remediation through virtual reality? I argue that the double legacy of the *Alice* books and the success of these videogame adaptations stems from the fact that Carroll was already actively experimenting with language, time and space, size and proportion, and reality and fantasy through textual gameplay. For example, when Alice first meets the Mad Hatter and the March Hare at a tea party in *Alice's Adventures in Wonderland*, they immediately present riddles that both Alice and the reader are encouraged to answer, a practice that Victorian readers would be quite familiar with because word scrambling games or charades were popular pastimes. As such, Carroll's desire to get readers thinking about the materiality of language preceded videogames, and contemporary games that rely on Alice's story—such as *American McGee's Alice* (2000), *Madness Returns* (2011), *Alice VR* (2016), and *Down the Rabbit Hole* (2020)—are successful as adaptations in part because Carroll was already experimenting with gamified text.

In much the same way, contemporary VR adaptations of Carroll's work collapse the real and the augmented worlds by inviting players to create their own narratives through nonlinear gameplay once they emerge from the virtual rabbit hole. Thus, adaptations of Carroll's work are adaptations not just of narratives but also of the ludic mechanisms of his writing. Scholars therefore need to be aware of the longer historical and broader ludological character of videogame literature, which can be traced back to the *Alice* books.

Writing about adaptation as a cultural process, Linda Hutcheon compares adaptations to flexible translation: "Just as there is no such thing as a literal translation, there can be no literal adaptation" (16). Hutcheon's definition of "adaptation" as the telling and retelling of a story in different ways across various media—often through means that invite different kinds of interaction—offers a theoretical foundation for my consideration of recent VR adventures based on Carroll's novels. Indeed, as Deborah Cartmell and Imelda Whelehan have observed, the central appeal of moving from text to screen (whether a film or videogame) is "the more enhanced representation of reality—the speed by which mood and action can be communicated" (5). Kevin Flanagan offers a similar reading of videogame adaptation, noting that "videogames provide a logical nexus for adaptation studies because they depend on making older narrative sources more dynamic" (441). Flanagan identifies forms of adaptation that encourage interactivity in this way, particularly porting a game to a new operating system or modding, which is when players modify a game. Video-games allow both producers and players to shape the narrative at all stages of the process, whether at the moment of creation or of reception.

It is generally recognized that texts invite readers to participate in the creation of narrative through interpretation, but I'm interested in the ways in which the ludic qualities of nondigital games and of Victorian literature more generally can be detected in contemporary digital adaptations, my focus here being on Carroll's two *Alice* novels. The success of a videogame based on a novel or movie depends not only on fealty to the narrative but also on the developer's ability to translate between the specific modes of interactivity native to these forms of media. People often assume that novels and films are passive, nonparticipatory genres, but they are, as Marcus Schulzke argues, "by no means static artifacts: these media encourage audiences to imaginatively fill in missing information, to judge characters and their motives, and to discover the meaning of the texts" (71). A book's or film's success as a videogame requires offering players new interpretive challenges and requiring player input in ways that allow the person to affect the game world while also remaining true to the interpretive challenges of the original. Through the wordplay and logic games in the *Alice* books and its VR adaptations, player-readers are direct participants in the meaning-making process, but the ludic nature of the participation was already part of the original texts.

Critics have identified several aspects of the *Alice* books that make them a promising source for videogame adaptation. First, as Cathlena Martin has observed, *Alice* is successful in game form because the book series already employs the "basic narrative criteria" that is also needed for games, such as a hero who collaborates with outsiders to save someone in need or to escape from a villain (134). Second, children's stories like *Alice's Adventures in Wonderland* and *Peter Pan* are "easily adapted as [videogame] narratives . . . because these stories also exist within a multitude of revisions . . . making the stories part of cultural knowledge" (Martin 134). Most players will not need to have read Carroll to be familiar with the narrative.

For Linda Hutcheon, children's stories are often turned into videogames because they already encourage exploratory play—children's stories and role-playing games share a central purpose and investment in interactivity. Hutcheon describes one of the earliest digital remediations of the *Alice* books, Atomic Antelope's *Alice's Adventures in Wonderland* iBook, which, like the VR experiences I describe here, encourages player-readers to manipulate the text and the objects that appear on the screen: "This application supplemented the text with dynamic elements in the color illustrations that respond via the touch screen interface to the tapping and swiping of objects such as the Drink Me bottle, and the comfits awarded after the Caucus Race" (200). Even though *Alice VR* would not be released for another six years and *Down the Rabbit Hole* would not appear for another ten, the iPad application's designers had already experienced the success of adapting the original's gamelike structures in previous iterations. However, Atomic Antelope's *Alice* iBook was more than a simple platform port; it expanded the materiality of play, encouraging exploration through video, sound, color, animation, and a touch screen interface, setting the standard for the interactive use of screen space. What contemporary VR adaptations appear to do better than their two-dimensional kin is to channel that exploratory and interactive urge, to enable the player to influence the narrative rather than merely witness it.

Alice VR and *Down the Rabbit Hole* offer new, dynamic ways of encountering the Wonderland narrative. Both VR adventures supplement the storyline we already know well, allowing players to experience Alice's adventures for themselves, in a similar but changed setting, through VR headsets. *Down the Rabbit Hole* lets the reader choose from several scripts at different moments in the VR adventure. In *Alice VR*, solving puzzles and completing tasks (or failing to do so) causes players to embody the Alice avatar in different ways, depending on the player's success at each point in the mission. For example, at the end of the game, the player enters an evacuated but gas-filled mine; inhaling too many fumes causes the player to black out or even to turn into a caterpillar. These outcomes "create unique new viewable and executable worlds through which the player can examine and reinterpret the traditional tales" (Martin 134). Thus, these adaptations allow users to experience the narrative as Alice, through touch, vision, proprioception, and other sensory elements of body movement and body position in virtual space.

Many of the other essays in the present anthology explore the role of literature in shaping how we think about videogames, particularly about their participatory demands. In contrast to these essays, however, I argue that *Alice VR* and *Down the Rabbit Hole* manipulate the gameplay experience in ways that are distinctly literary. These games experiment with time, space, and proportion through language while also evoking nineteenth-century cultures of textual play. This suggests a much broader idea: Carroll and his fellow Victorian writers established the basic groundwork for what we now consider a "playful" narrative, suggesting that scholars should consider playful and nonsense literature as early examples of "videogame literature."

Victorian Cultures of Play

When Lewis Carroll was penning *Alice's Adventures in Wonderland* and *Through the Looking-Glass*, participatory puzzles, riddles, and verbal play were essential to Victorian culture, especially among the British middle and upper classes. Patrick Beaver has called the Victorian period the golden age of logic and word-play games. Known as parlor games because they were linked to high society and to a particular domestic space—the parlor—indoor activities like charades, the minister's cat, tableau vivant, and blindman's buff were played by Victorian youth and adults alike. Indeed, for many Victorians, parlor games were part of an intertwined program of daily entertainment that included dancing, singing, piano playing, and storytelling. These playful activities were understood as preparation for real-life situations: "Games in which the individual pits his wits against other individuals [were] only a reflection of the struggle to live and better oneself in the world of reality" (Beaver 13). Many Victorian parlor games remain popular today in altered forms, including charades, collective storytelling games that resemble the Endless Story, and Dictionary, which has been adapted into *Balderdash*.

Drawing on the popularity of nineteenth-century cultures of play, many English novelists incorporated verbal play into their fictions. In Jane Austen's *Emma* (1815), for example, Frank Churchill and Jane Fairfax engage in a word scrambling game, and Emma and Harriet collect riddles in a scrapbook. In Charlotte Brontë's *Jane Eyre* (1847), Jane watches Rochester and Blanche play charades. When the word turns out to be "Bridewell," Jane mistakenly comes to believe that Rochester and Blanche may soon be married (214). In William Makepeace Thackeray's *Vanity Fair* (1847), Becky and the others at Gaunt House play charades, which, as the narrator warns readers, "may or may not puzzle the reader" (595). Verbal play is never merely passive entertainment in Victorian fiction; it is a participatory form of entertainment that is treated with moral seriousness throughout the period's fictions. Victorian authors used scenes of play to generate new plot points and to reveal characters' inner thoughts while also appealing to audiences' familiarity with these games and the situations they might generate.

Literary critics have also commented on the participatory nature of what has been called the literary nonsense genre. As Jean-Jacques Lecercle has written, "Literary nonsense is a Chomskyan game," one full of syntactical inversions. For an example of such inversions in *Alice's Adventures in Wonderland*, we need only look to the Hatter's comment that "'I see what I eat' is the same thing as 'I eat what I see'" (61). Examples from *Through the Looking-Glass* include Humpty Dumpty's references to "un-birthday presents" (190) and the king's direction to pronounce the name of the messenger "Haigha" so that it rhymes with the word "mayor" (200).

Critics such as Elizabeth Bruss show that nonsense literature is uniquely interactive. Player-readers encounter puzzles, ponder riddles, and choose between "incompatible alternatives," which "turns the projected activity of the reader into a series of [seemingly arbitrary] 'moves'" that only later generate a coherent tale (Bruss 158). Narrative matrices of logic, language, and verbal play close the gap between the narrator and the reader, inviting the reader to work through the puzzles in the real world, as is the case in the *Alice* books. Both *Alice VR* and *Down the Rabbit Hole* link language to game components through puzzles, riddles, and heads-up displays in ways that promote the player's cognitive interaction with the game. These digital adaptations uniquely manipulate sensorimotor and spatial expectations, in addition to spatial puns and riddles, to draw the player deeper into Wonderland. But those strategies were already part of the original stories.

Structures of Time, Space, and Disorientation in the *Alice* Books and *Alice VR*

Virtual reality brings new possibilities to the interactive legacies of Carroll's books. While we play as Alice in both games, completing objectives requires altering our character's size and shape throughout the journey. As a result, the spatial reality of Wonderland becomes disorienting, requiring users to interact with objects in the game space in unexpected ways. However, these embodied aspects of VR games can be traced back to *Alice's Adventures in Wonderland* and *Through the Looking-Glass*. After descending into Wonderland and, later, the Looking-Glass world, Alice tries her best to understand the nonsense that the characters spew, hoping it will help her to escape. These characters speak in riddles, pose philosophical questions, and play logic games, and solving these puzzles proves essential to Alice's ability to survive in these realms, which also integrate games of cards, croquet, and chess into the journey.

Carroll organizes his books according to intricate structures of play, which transforms language into game components by playing with space, proportion, and especially time. For example, before Alice falls down the rabbit hole, the game-based structure of *Alice's Adventures in Wonderland* is apparent through Carroll's framing of time. Just as Alice grows weary of her sister, the White Rabbit appears and takes out a watch, mumbling, "Oh dear! I shall be too late" (9). In an increasingly industrialized society characterized by the birth of the railroad and debates over working hours, time was frequently on the minds of most Victorians, and Lewis Carroll was playing with Victorians' perceptions of it—time and space become increasingly fluid as the narrative progresses. Time was also essential to Victorian recreation, and serious players of Victorian parlor games often only had a few seconds to guess a riddle or unscramble a word. Even Alice herself, who runs across the field after the White Rabbit, is just in time to see the creature fall down the rabbit hole. Throughout her adventures, Alice makes several narrow escapes, and time is essential to the progress of Carroll's narratives, just as it is essential to gaming, particularly in sports and videogames.

In both *Alice VR* and *Down the Rabbit Hole*, players must complete tasks within a certain period to advance, but they may also lose a sense of real-world time as they do so. In much the same way, readers of Carroll's narratives may find themselves breezing through certain word games that Alice encounters but pausing at others. After all, a reader's engagement with the story may not always be linear, confirming literary critic Paul Ricoeur's instinct that even the "simplest stor[ies] also [escape] the ordinary notion of time" (174). Just as Alice falsely senses that she has progressed through thick, mysterious forests or spaces on a chessboard, only to find herself back where she began, readers repeatedly find themselves backtracking to make sense of riddles or to form connections between the disparate but interconnected scenes composing Carroll's narratives.

In addition to time, Carroll actively experiments with size and proportion in *Alice's Adventures in Wonderland*. Alice soon realizes that she has entered a changed world where nothing is the same, starting with her own body. Alice finds herself in a "long, low hall" surrounded by locked doors. She is never the right size to fit into the spaces she hopes to explore. For example, after Alice escapes the long passageway, she finds herself in a smaller passageway, which requires that she "shut herself up like a telescope" (13). Alice discovers that she is only ten inches tall, and when she enters a nearby garden, she has trouble reaching items.

Similarly, as Alice surveys the country by rail in the chapter "Looking-Glass Insects," she finds that nothing is the size she expects. Bees are elephants, and passengers hold out train tickets that are just as large as they are. The ticket guard reinforces this theme as he examines Alice through many different lenses, "looking at her first through a telescope, then through a microscope, and then through an opera-glass" (150). These views present different pictures of the same object.

These struggles persist throughout Alice's adventures, extending even to the page itself. For example, in *Through the Looking-Glass*, when Alice speaks to the Gnat, a fellow train passenger, the size of the text on the page shrinks, resembling the creature's "extremely small voice" (150). And we find representations of Alice's physical actions through the use of asterisks representing her leaps and bounds. In sum, Carroll plays with size and proportion, an approach to both diegetic space and the space of the medium itself (the page) that makes it immediately adaptable to videogames, which specialize precisely in the gamification of space and the objects in it.

Carroll's manipulations of the space of the page recall his experiments with proportion in *Alice's Adventures in Wonderland*, most memorably as Alice consumes everything from cake to mushrooms to fit into the various worlds within that world—with different degrees of success. These changes in size prove important to Alice's adventures, for, as Harry Levin notes, "Her shrinkages [teach] her to look at matters from . . . the animals' vantage point" (601). Carroll's experiments with font and form to create an interactive textual experience are intended to close a similar perspectival gap between Alice and her readers. Espen Aarseth's distinction between "cognitive" and "interactive" gameplay proves useful here. For Aarseth, the rewards of gameplay are highly kinesthetic: "Your skills are rewarded, your mistakes punished. . . . Pleasure follows function" (7). The linguistic objectives that we find in the *Alice* books suggest an active, puzzle-oriented cognitive interactivity that translates to the ergodic interactivity of the series' VR adaptations. As with the best videogames, the challenges of play are a synthesis of form and function.

This is quite literally an adaptation of game mechanics. Carroll's fantastic narrative and experiments with size and proportion exist against the backdrop of the much more structured space and play of a chessboard. Alice's movements in the Looking-Glass world resemble those that a player might make in a game of chess. For example, by traveling via railway, Alice skips a square, paralleling the moves that pawns make at the beginning of a game of chess: "A pawn goes two squares in its first move, you know. So you'll go very quickly through the Third Square—by railway" (146). Carroll even offers readers a diagram of Alice's progress throughout the text in the table of contents, which reads as a map of Alice's movements, and in the preface to the 1897 edition of *Through the Looking-Glass*, Carroll encourages readers to re-create the moves on an actual chessboard: "The 'check' of the White King at move 6, the capture of the Red Knight at move 7, and the final 'checkmate' of the Red King, will be found, by any one who will take the trouble to set the pieces and play the moves as directed." Carroll's preface also gives directions that enable readers to interact more effectively with the text: "Pronounce 'slithy' as if it were the two words 'sly, the': make the 'g' hard in 'gyre' and 'gimble'" (118). While these instructions arguably take away some of the fun and confusion inherent in wordplay, they also encourage readers to fully inhabit the language of the text—as Alice does.

These directions aside, the result of such manipulations of time, space, and language is often a heightened sense of disorientation for both Alice and readers. The world on the other side of Looking-Glass House operates backwards. Books are read in reverse, time moves the wrong way, and objects appear farther away as Alice approaches them. Turn after turn, Alice finds that she always ends up in the same place, so she resolves that she will only get somewhere if she speeds up. But while attempting to pick up the pace, Alice exhausts herself. Afterwards, she learns from the queen that "it takes all the running you can do, to keep in the same place" (145). Again, it is no surprise that Carroll's experimentation with space and pace in *Through the Looking-Glass* remain popular material for videogame developers; twisting staircases, gardens, and passageways characterize the player experience in both *Alice VR* and *Down the Rabbit Hole*.

The ludic nature of Alice's world becomes further evident in the fact that to survive in Wonderland and Looking-Glass world, Alice must make frequent adjustments, both literally and figuratively, in terms of size as well as language. Alice finds that none of the lessons she learned in school apply, so she must now learn "new rules of battle" (210). When trying out multiplication, for example, Alice finds that the multiplication table no longer signifies. Turning instead to geography, Alice says, "London is the capital of Paris, and Paris is the capital of Rome" (19). Alice can no longer apply the knowledge that she has acquired in the real world to make sense of her new surroundings. She struggles to integrate into Wonderland at first, in part, because she does not make the adjustments required to succeed. Alice repeats the same errors over and over again. When speaking with the Mouse, who she believes does not understand English, she says, "Ou est ma chatte?" because this was the first lesson in her French book. Alice realizes she has offended the creature, but she makes the same mistake only pages later.

Hence, Alice's first challenge in Wonderland is that she does not always make the adjustments necessary to immerse herself in the new narrative world because she is acting based on real-world rules of play. To return to an earlier point, we see that Alice is playing a role that is familiar to many videogame players: participating in a narrative by revising sensorimotor expectations in ways that cause them to dissociate from their everyday body schemas in order to fully interact with the storyworld.

Requiring similar revisions of thought and perception, structured gameplay is central to Alice's progress through Wonderland. After stumbling upon Wonderland's garden, for example, Alice encounters playing cards painting a rose tree. These playing cards are gardeners. As the gardeners have the habit of lying down when the Queen of Hearts approaches, "the pattern on their backs was the same as the rest of the pack" (72). Alice struggles to distinguish between the roles that players assume in this mock game of cards. Nonetheless, her interaction with the gardeners eventually leads her to a croquet match. The Wonderland croquet field is even more chaotic, and Alice cannot discern the rules of the game. Managing her game piece—the flamingo mallet—is Alice's first challenge, because every time she positions its head downward, the flamingo unravels itself. More difficult, though, is the fact that everyone plays at once.

A reader's familiarity with the rules and mechanics of these games—familiarity that Carroll could depend on, given the games' popularity—enables them to vividly imagine themselves into the challenges Alice faces. In this way, readers become what Colleen Rua has called "spect-characters," an ambiguous positionality in which what is happening to the character is also happening to the reader or audience. This unique position within the narrative occurs as readers immerse themselves in the play of the text, creating "multilayered identities for participating individuals who [move] beyond spectators" or readers in a dynamic fictional universe (151). In this way, Carroll troubles the divide between the spectator and participant by compelling readers to embody Alice's point of view during the croquet match—a compulsion enabled by the reader's assumed knowledge and experience of the game. Again we see how Carroll's novels provide such fruitful resources for videogame and VR adaptations. Not only do videogames excel at providing interactive, rules-based experiences, but they often depend on discrete episodes of gameplay—what videogame players commonly refer to as "minigames."

Logics of Play in the *Alice* Videogame Series and *Down the Rabbit Hole*

Videogame adaptations of the *Alice* stories have been popular since 2000, when *American McGee's Alice* (2000) and its sequel, *Madness Returns* (2009), offered psychologically thrilling remediations of the popular children's novels. More recently, though, Alice's experiences in Wonderland and Looking-Glass world have been adapted for virtual reality platforms. *Alice VR*, which was released by Carbon Studio in 2016, was the first VR adventure based on Carroll's books, though its storyworld is in some ways quite different from Carroll's. Set on a barren planet after the crash of a spaceship, the player must solve puzzles to retrieve fuel for the ship by finding their way to the fictional city of Mirabilis. Players complete numerous tasks to gather the graphene needed to refuel the spaceship, tasks that closely resemble the kinds of linguistic, logical, and spatio-temporal challenges that Alice faces as she makes her way through Wonderland and Looking-Glass world.

For instance, because there is a malfunction in the power system, the player must find the engine room and activate an auxiliary generator. However, the character has memory loss, so finding the engine room is not easy. Further-more, blocked pathways require the player to return to higher levels and use the elevators to navigate the ship; however, at least early in the game, the elevators are inoperable. As the player navigates the powerless ship, they are presented with a series of puzzles, such as finding locked tiles and using them to lead a robot to the repair distribution center, or arranging the conductor's controls. Successful completion of these puzzles allows the player to explore the mystery planet outside of the spaceship.

Despite the drastically different settings, there are clear similarities be-tween the *Alice* books and *Alice VR*, particularly in terms of how the game ma-nipulates space. When the player first steps outside of the spaceship *Red Queen*, they are greeted by familiar signs that read "Drink" and "Eat Me." There is even a sign labeled "Rabbit Hole," and in order to descend down the rabbit hole, the player must find drinking cups. These cups allow the player to consume substances that cause them to shrink to the appropriate size. Much like Alice's adventures in the books, the ability to explore Planet Speculo depends on the successful completion of puzzles that require a combination of verbal, haptic, and exploratory skills. Though they are adapted to an entirely different fictional universe, these puzzles will be familiar to readers of Carroll's *Alice* novels, whether due to explicit references like the sign pointing to the rabbit hole or to similar puzzle logics and mechanics.

As is true for Alice, as the player completes the challenges associated with the mission, disorientation is always a threat. In the beginning of the game, the player is tasked with finding a way to get inside a closed mine. However, the mine is also full of toxins. Inhaling too many toxins will turn the player into a caterpillar and jeopardize the mission. Other examples of sensory disorientation include flying chests, which make the player feel like they are spinning, and items that reflect the sun, making it difficult to see what lies ahead. Additionally, the game alters players' sense of reachable space, since Alice's size, shape, and positionality constantly change throughout the adventure. Another way that the game guides players' sense of self-location and bodily agency is by generating feelings of movement even while Alice is standing still. Such instances of bodily and spatial disorientation engage players in intensive, participatory VR experiences that are also highly textual and reminiscent of the puzzles and language games that Caroll's Alice encounters.

However, to comprehend the particular adaptive relationship between Carroll's books and these videogame adaptations, we need to take a closer look at the way Carroll plays with language and its relationship to the world. In both the books and the games, the Alice character learns the logic of language for the first time, and does so by playing games. For example, Alice's lesson in the chapter "A Mad Tea-Party" in *Alice's Adventures in Wonderland* is that saying what one means is not the same thing as meaning what one says, a lesson Alice learns after being presented with a series of riddles. The Hatter's most memorable riddle, "Why is a raven like a writing-desk?" continues to spark debate today, even though the riddle has no answer in the book—and it provides insight into the complexity of the games Carroll created for his readers. In 1886, he gave readers an answer: "Because it can produce a few notes, though they are *very* flat; and it is nevar put with the wrong end in front!" (Susina 52).

In Carroll's solution to the riddle, "nevar" is spelled as the reverse of the word "raven." Jean-Jacques Lecercle has written about Carroll's love for "portmanteau-words, words read in a mirror, [and] anagrams" (11). Other critics have noted that the name Lewis Carroll is itself a construct: "He created his pseudonym by Latinizing his first and middle names and reversing their order" (Susina

49). This is an experience shared by reader and protagonist alike. The Mad Hatter's tea party is Alice's introduction to wordplay of this nature—and to the way words can affect a person's relationship to the broader logics of social life. When she later speaks to the Gryphon and Mock Turtle, for instance, the Gryphon explains that the point of school lessons is that they *lessen*. Semantic play also characterizes her encounter with Humpty Dumpty in chapter 6 of *Through the Looking-Glass*. Alice and Humpty Dumpty are debating what names signify, and when Humpty Dumpty asks Alice what her name means, she replies, "Must a name mean something?" Humpty Dumpty answers, "My name means the shape that I am" (186). Each exchange with Humpty Dumpty presents a new riddle, and the two debate everything from birthdays to belts to cravats.

Alice's interactions in the Looking-Glass world challenge her assumptions about how language and logic operate through play. Indeed, as Alice maneuvers through the world, she becomes something of a "gamer." Both game players and our protagonist require a range of skills, from planning to adaptability to problem solving.

The notion of Alice as a gamer is made explicity by the developers at Cortopia Studios. *Down the Rabbit Hole* follows a young girl who enters Wonderland looking for her lost pet, Patches. Humpty Dumpty's lesson about the mutable relationship between words and referents is immediately apparent when the player character must decide what kind of pet Patches is: a cat, a lizard, or a turtle. What's most noteworthy here, though, is not the player's choice of a specific type of pet but the materialized textuality of this VR adventure, which is very much in the spirit of Carroll's materialization of language. Throughout the game, heads-up displays and opportunities to shape the narrative emerge in the form of playing cards and puzzles on parchment rolls, all of which are written in fonts that resemble the text of Carroll's narratives themselves. As the player falls down the rabbit hole, playing cards and other objects swirl around Alice. The environment is dark and disorienting, but also quite textual.

When the player finally stops falling, the player is invited to ask the White Rabbit one of three questions: *Where am I?*, *There's a murdering queen?*, or *How are you talking?* This is one of many examples of heads-up displays that allow the player to participate in the narrative by manipulating printed text in a manner reminiscent of Victorian text-based games, while also allowing the player to control the game's script in a way that would make the Mad Hatter and Humpty Dumpty proud. By asking players to assume the identity of Alice when collecting letters, *Down the Rabbit Hole* encourages readers to participate in the development the narrative and to do so by playing with the relationship of words and world.

As the player navigates Wonderland, he or she must complete various puzzles to unlock different chambers of the game space. Early in *Down the Rabbit Hole*, the player hears a voice say "I'm hungry" and must set the clock to lunchtime. The player's first objective is to figure out when lunchtime is by using a scheduling chart, and then to change the time of the clock to reflect this information. Very much in the spirit of Humpty Dumpty's nonsensical assertion that "My name means the shape that I am," players discover that the actions they take reshape the world around them, orienting that world to the overall logic of the game's puzzle narrative. Throughout the game, players must do things like ring bells in a specific order, navigate mazelike gardens, find hidden bookcase doors, and skip among teacups and saucers. All of these tasks and puzzles are logically connected objectives that lead to new parts of Wonderland and that, taken together, open the path for Alice to arrive at the queen's castle.

But if these tasks are difficult enough in terms of their internal puzzle logic, they are complicated by a distinctly Carroll-like play with shifting size, space, and time, making the completion of these objectives all the more challenging. The same sense of disorientation that Alice experiences in the books and that players experience in *Alice VR* also characterizes the player experience in *Down the Rabbit Hole*. The avatar cannot reach certain objects, such as the clocks, and time runs backwards. Players often experience reflections in water that flip reality, or shadows from familiar creatures such as the Mad Hatter and Caterpillar that alter their sense of what lies around the corner. But *Down the Rabbit Hole* takes the embodied disorientation a step further by putting the player in first-person perspective. Whereas the third-person perspective of earlier *Alice* digital adaptations positioned the player as a mere observer of the character's actions, *Down the Rabbit Hole* pulls players deep into Wonderland, intensifying the player's cognitive and ergodic disorientation as they learn to interact with the text and ultimately gain some sense of mastery of its ludic logic.

From Textual Play to Virtual Reality

The strength of *Down the Rabbit Hole* as an Alice adaptation lies in the way that it invites the player to shape the progress of the game through interaction with the logic of storytelling, puzzles, and the virtual space. The game's manipulations of embodiment within virtual reality—allowing players to adopt a first-person perspective, reversing temporal and spatial expectations, and altering the player's sensorimotor expectations by introducing audio and visual effects—not only introduces a higher degree of challenge for solving puzzles but also successfully embodies Lewis Carroll's most far-reaching experiments with the logics of games and the playful interactivity of reading.

From card games to comics to classical operas, the list of popular adaptations of the *Alice* stories continues to grow. Virtual Reality adventures for Steam, Oculus Rift, and PlayStation VR, such as *Alice VR* and *Down the Rabbit Hole,* are the newest additions to this list. The most recent of these, *Alice VR* and *Down the Rabbit Hole,* adapt not merely the narrative and nonsensical tone of Carroll's novels but also his playful approach to the material, logical, and textual components of storytelling itself. But there is a broader historical implication to the virtual reality adaptations. The double legacy of the *Alice* books is due in large part to the fact that Carroll was already actively adapting and remediating games through time, space, and language in the narratives. Through the novels, Carroll reimagined children's literature in ways that continue to resonate in art, film, music, and digital games.

Replacing eighteenth-century morality stories set in realistic locations, Carroll's narratives of a curious young character launched what has colloquially been called "the Age of Alice" (Patkus), an era of fantasy adventure novels for children, which included George MacDonald's *The Princess and the Goblin* (1872) and *The Princess and the Curdie* (1883). But the Age of Alice is arguably about far more than fantasy and adventure. The embodied, puzzle-oriented, world-changing interactivity of the *Alice* books that is most evident in these VR adaptations reveals a previously hidden genealogy of videogames. Indeed, they demonstrate to scholars of videogames that the history of videogames is not to be found only in computers and code but also in the playful logic of an anthropomorphic egg insisting "My name means the shape that I am."

WORKS CITED

Aarseth, Espen. "Genre Trouble." *Electronic Book Review,* 2004, pp. 1–12.
Alice: Madness Returns. Electronic Arts, 2011.
Alice VR. Carbon Studio, 2016.
American McGee's Alice. Electronic Arts, 2000.
Beaver, Patrick. *Victorian Parlor Games.* T. Nelson, 1978.
Brontë, Charlotte. *Jane Eyre.* Penguin, 2006.

Bruss, Elizabeth W. "The Game of Literature and Some Literary Games." *New Literary History*, vol. 9, no. 1, 1977, pp. 153–72.

Carroll, Lewis. *Alice's Adventures in Wonderland and Through the Looking-Glass*. Oxford University Press, 2009.

Cartmell, Deborah, and Imelda Whelehan. *Adaptations: From Text to Screen, Screen to Text*. Routledge, 1999.

Down the Rabbit Hole. Cortopia Studios, 2020.

Flanagan, Kevin M. "Videogame Adaptation." *The Oxford Handbook of Adaptation Studies*, edited by Thomas Leitch. Oxford University Press, 2017, pp. 441–58.

Flanders, Judith. *Inside the Victorian Home: A Portrait of Domestic Life in Victorian England*. W. W. Norton, 2004.

Greenaway, Kate. *Book of Games*. Michael O'Mara, 1987.

Hutcheon, Linda. *A Theory of Adaptation*. Routledge, 2013.

Jerz, Dennis G. "Puzzles in Interactive Fiction." *Jerz's Literacy Weblog*, 2 May 2000. https://jerz.setonhill.edu/if/Puzzles.htm.

Lecercle, Jean-Jacques. *Philosophy of Nonsense: The Intuitions of Victorian Nonsense Literature*. Routledge, 1994.

Levin, Harry. "Wonderland Revisited." *Kenyon Review*, vol. 47, no. 4, 1965, pp. 591–616.

Martin, Cathlena. "'Wonderland's Become Quite Strange': From Lewis Carroll's *Alice* to American McGee's *Alice*." *Beyond Adaptation: Essays on Radical Transformations of Original Works*, edited by Phyllis Frus and Christy Williams. McFarland, 2010, pp. 133–43.

Mitchell, Sally. *Daily Life in Victorian England*. 2nd ed., Greenwood, 2009.

"Parlor Games." *Encyclopedia of Play in Today's Society*, edited by Rodney Carlisle. Sage, 2009.

Patkus, Ronald. "The Age of Alice: Fairy Tales, Fantasy, and Nonsense in Victorian England." Archives & Special Collections Library, Vassar College. https://specialcollections.vassar.edu/exhibit-highlights/2011-2015/age-of-alice/fairy-tales-fantasy-nonsense.html.

Ricoeur, Paul. "Narrative Time." *Critical Inquiry*, vol. 7, no. 1, 1980, pp. 169–90.

Rua, Colleen. "Navigating Neverland and Wonderland: Audience as Spect-Character." *Theatre History Studies*, vol. 38, 2019, pp. 149–65.

Schulzke, Marcus. "Translation Between Different Forms of Interactivity: How to Build the Better Adaptation." *Game On, Hollywood! Essays on the Intersection of Videogames and Cinema*, edited by Gretchen Papazian and Joseph Michael Sommers. McFarland, 2013, pp. 70–85.

Short, Emily. *Counterfeit Monkey*. Interactive Fiction Database, 2012. https://ifdb.tads.org/viewgame?id=aearuuxv83plclpl.

Susina, Jan. *The Place of Lewis Carroll in Children's Literature*. Routledge, 2010.

Thackeray, William Makepeace. *Vanity Fair: A Novel Without a Hero*. Penguin, 2003.

Games at the Threshold

Paratexts and Storyworld Creation in Digital Games

MICHAŁ DAWID ŻMUDA

From 1984 to 1985, Brøderbund Software released three games: *Mindwheel* (1984), *Essex* (1985), and *Brimstone: The Dream of Gawain* (1985). The publisher marketed these as literary artifacts, each labeled as an "electronic novel." I find this justified because they are text-based adventures that rely heavily on prosaic narration and use literary conventions to present most of the information. In addition, Robert Pinsky, an esteemed poet and literary critic, wrote *Mindwheel*, and James Paul, also a poet, wrote *Brimstone*. This strategy of pairing literature with electronic entertainment is made even more evident by the way the games are packaged. The floppy disks are inserted into hardcover books, some more than one hundred pages long. The books are prose texts that expand the narration presented by the game software, and they possess all the characteristic traits of books: dust jackets, blurbs, title pages, edition notices, tables of contents.

But what does the term "electronic novel" refer to? Is it an electronic game that is sold as a novel thanks to the materiality of the accompanying book? Is it a novel that is expanded into an electronic creation thanks to the presence of the software? Is it a new kind of literary medium? Or maybe it is just an elaborate attempt to expand the gaming market so that the software is bought by more people.

Most digital games, if published in a physical form, are surrounded by printed materials that comment on or expand the software. In the 1980s, most games came with instruction manuals, and many with story booklets. Such artifacts have been replaced in recent years by digital counterparts: in-game tutorials, movie-like introductions, and narrative sequences. Yet such print materials are crucial for our understanding of the history of gaming. Certain ancillary artifacts are almost synonymous with particular publishers, platforms, and genres. In fact, the success of Infocom, the leader in the interactive fiction market in the 1980s, was arguably due to the so-called feelies packaged with their software. Similarly, the design of the Intellivision console required publishers to ship their games with printed overlays to be put onto controllers.

Despite the move to an all-digital market, these kinds of artifacts are still a significant facet of gaming culture (see Milligan in this volume). Many companies use supplementary materials as components of premium editions. For example, a huge figurine of the Witcher battling a monster is available only in *The Witcher 3: Wild Hunt* Collector's Edition (2015), and independent publishers like XSEED Games have revived the art of the game manual to appeal to their nostalgic customers. While these artifacts have become far less common, they have gained more value, enticing players to buy a more expensive version of a game. In this essay, I aim to inspect how the printed materials included with digital games supplement the narrativity and mediality of games.

Secondary Signals

Gérard Genette's concept of paratextuality provides tools for the inspection of auxiliary artifacts that might affect or control the players' experience and interpretation of games. Genette introduced the concept of paratext in *Palimpsests: Literature in the Second Degree* and later expanded on it in *Paratexts: Thresholds of Interpretation*. He aimed to describe all possible instances of transtextuality— "the textual transcendence of the text" (*Palimpsests* 1)—and the different relations that can take place between the text and genre norms, critical commentary, other texts, and supplementary materials. The category of paratextuality covers the relation between the primary text and its supplementary materials. According to Genette, this relationship is "less explicit and more distant" than other transtextual categories, yet it "binds the text properly speaking" with other artifacts that support or dictate the interpretation of the text. Paratexts can include titles, covers, prefaces, illustrations, blurbs, and epigraphs, to name just a few examples (*Palimpsests* 3). I argue here that they also include ancillary materials that come with games.

From one perspective, paratexts are both of the text and separate from the text; from another, they are somewhere between being inside the text and outside the text. The phenomenon is, Genette explains, "more than a boundary or a sealed border." It is an "undefined zone" because the relation is ambiguous

(*Paratexts* 1–2). Paratextual elements form the text (it is difficult to talk about a book without mentioning its title, for instance, or to read a book without interacting with its cover), but also remain distinct (an epigraph may come from another work, or the cover may change between editions). The paratexts that are part of "electronic novels" have a distinct and intriguing shape: that of a book. The materiality of the codex clearly signals that the games are far from ordinary digital software.

By way of illustration, the box covers of games published for Atari systems at that time usually classified the products with terms like "video game cartridge," "video computer system," or "game program." The last two were trademarks, officially labeling digital games as a category distinct from other media. The "electronic novel" trademark is a direct response to such an approach. Instead of branding the games as "text adventures" and thus connecting them with a popular genre of digital entertainment, the publishers aimed to convince the public that their games had more in common with literature. This strategy differentiates Brøderbund's productions, taking them out of gaming shops and onto the shelves of bookstores.

The bookish materials supplied with electronic novels act as what Genette describes as a "foyer," which lets the readers enter and exit the main text, the software of the electronic novel. Genette's foyer metaphor imagines a "zone of transition" through which text reaches the public. Paratexts "ensure the text's presence in the world, its 'reception' and consumption." They embody a kind of authorial power, attempting to guide readers so their understanding of the text is in line with the intentions of those involved in its production. As such, the zone of transition is also a zone of transaction, where the text becomes prepackaged and offered to the public (*Paratexts* 1–2, 8–9). This prepackaging can be understood literally—many paratexts work within the boundaries of the product's package—and it primarily manages communication, outlining interpretations, understandings, and visions about the text. In the case of electronic novels and other videogames, paratexts, in both their content and their form, signal how the people involved in the game's creation and distribution want it to be interpreted and handled by the users.

A Plethora of Forms

Most digital game paratexts configure the reception and consumption of digital games in relation to the printed word in some fashion. Electronic novels are one of many instances in which paratexts augment games with literary methods of communication. The original edition of *7th Guest* (1993), for example, comes with a booklet, *The Stauf Files*, which purports to be an authentic object from the American Press Association. It contains newspaper clippings, fragments from novels, a medical report, a news clipping, and a biography of the primary nonplayer character. All of these materials highlight strange happenings around and in the mansion of Henry Stauf. *7th Guest* requires the user to explore this place and uncover its mysteries. Players should read the fictional resources if they want to fully understand the game's narrative and solve the puzzles encountered during the gameplay. Similarly, Nintendo's *StarTropics* (1990) and Infocom's *Wishbringer* (1985) are supplemented with letters that, while addressed to diegetic protagonists, invite the players to enter the game world. Other diegetic paratexts include bureaucratic documents (*Bureaucracy*, 1987), popular historical texts (*Age of Empires*, 1997), fictional diaries (*Zork Nemesis*, 1996), cardboard maps (*Suspended*, 1983), comic books (*Metal Gear Solid 2*, 2001), and short novellas (*Beyond Divinity* 2004).

Publishers often mixed diegesis and instructions, as with *Ultima VII: The Black Gate* (1992). The game box includes a cloth map of Britannia (the fictional land the game is set in), a medallion, and a manual about the game's diegesis and play systems, written in the form of a fictional guide. *Birds of Prey* (1992), an action-oriented flight simulator, also mixes diegetic information with nondiegetic functions. The booklet in the game box provides a detailed overview of the game systems but also a chapter on military tactics and an encyclopedia with data about aircraft that may be encountered in the game. *Baldur's Gate* (1998) and *Baldur's Gate II* (2000) pursue a comparable strategy; they too contain printed maps and manuals written from the perspective of a diegetic character.

This plethora of paratexts challenges Genette's framework, which is concerned primarily with books. While he suggests that paratexts can take different media forms (*Paratexts* 2), he does not pay much attention to this aspect of the phenomenon. In "Texts and Paratexts in Media," Georg Stanitzek argues that paratextual theory not only can but should be transferred from literary theory to other media fields. He notes that Genette's shortcoming "is that he is not willing to risk the category of the text as book (or the work) itself" (35). Stanitzek maintains that this problem can be solved by borrowing the terminology of communication theory. He proposes to treat paratexts simply as organizers of communication. And though Stanitzek's article does not provide a full framework, his observation recognizes the phenomenon of paratextuality as something that is not contained within the book form. This thesis has been confirmed by many researchers of audiovisual media (see Birke & Christ; Desrochers & Apollon; Gray; Klecker; Rockenberger, "Video Game Framings," "Paratext"; Wolf & Bernhart) and videogames (see Consalvo; Dunne; Karhulahti; Kocurek; Rockenberger, "Video Game Framings," "Paratext"; Švelch). Many of these reinterpret Genette's theory; however, many of them remain mutually exclusive in theoretical and analytic terms.

Andrzej Gwóźdź has modified Genette's definition to include all the paratextual relations that happen around audiovisual artifacts. Gwóźdź sees paratexts as "clusters of discursive practices" that take many shapes and enable the audiovisual text (or the medium itself) to exist "outside" its material limitations. Thanks to these clusters, the text can reach the audience in a variety of ways (36). According to Gwóźdź, paratextuality encompasses media forms and avenues of communication that go beyond the boundaries of book design. For my purposes, this would include the manuals, story booklets, guides, encyclopedias, journals, and other tangible objects that I've discussed so far.

Supplementation and Extension

While we can identify these objects as paratexts, their functions are highly varied. What follows is a detailed mapping of the paratextual function in digital games, specifically, paratextuality as authorial supplementation (controlling the reception of a game) and paratextuality as a media extension (providing a game with additional forms of communication). Many paratextual objects function as materials that allow players to learn about the game's world and narrative at their own leisure. Narrative paratexts typically expand both, presenting plot threads and characters or facts about the game world. They provide additional "global mental representations" that enable "interpreters to frame inferences about the situations, characters, and occurrences either explicitly mentioned in or implied by a narrative text or discourse" (Herman, 72–73). In terms of the storyworld, both the game software and their paratexts work together to "provide blueprints" (73) that configure the players' vision of that storyworld and therefore how they play in that world. However, while all the paratexts that I discuss here share that function, their materiality and form influence how they carry it out.

The paratextual supplementation of storyworlds is most evident in travel guides and encyclopedias. The booklet added to *Ultima VII* contains sections on Britannia's geography, trade, writing system, history, culture, fauna, magic, and cosmology. The paratext directs the players' attention to certain facts and categorizes the diegetic elements, giving special significance to select aspects of the storyworld. For instance, the booklet does not elaborate on the social structure of the world, focusing instead on the adventuring archetypes that players may choose. It thus prescribes the "proper" interpretation of the diegesis, showing it through the lens of the heroic fantasy genre. Likewise, the encyclopedic portion of the *Birds of Prey* manual showcases the machines piloted by the players, omitting most of the sociohistorical context of the storyworld. What context is detailed emphasizes the militaristic view of the conflicts represented by the game, implying that the players do not have to worry about the political and moral implications of the actions simulated by the program.

However, there is something odd about these particular paratexts: though players *can* use the paratextual data while playing the game, the games do not *require* users to familiarize themselves with that data in order to play. Instead, the paratexts allow them to imaginatively customize their experience and discover or ignore chosen aspects of the storyworld. The execution of the narrative function is left to the players' discretion. This fact would seem to contradict Genette's theory. If paratexts are supposed to control the reception, can they be optional? Again, we need to consider a non-codex-focused understanding of the paratext.

As Gwóźdź noted, Genette's concept of paratexts understands them as functioning "next to" the product, acting as additions, working in its service (38). However, it is inconsequential whether all attempts at authorial control are successful—which is particularly true of videogames. The players of *Ultima VII* are aware of the paratexts supplied with their copy of the game but are not required to consult them. These materials are close to the product but in the background of the gameplay, ready to be used. It is no accident that Genette imagines paratextuality as a foyer, which connotes a movement from one position to another. But the distance between a paratext and a game is not permanent and can change depending on different factors—something that publishers understand. A comparison of two examples should demonstrate this.

Because paratextuality is fluid, the publishers of *Essex* encourage players to experience the supplementary materials. First, the team at Brøderbund Software enclosed the disks inside the book, making the materials difficult (but not impossible) to ignore, and they contain crucial information that is absent from the software's narrative. The novel introduces the science fiction conventions of the program and gives players all the backstory necessary for the understanding of the initial narrative in the game and for solving certain puzzles. The events depicted in the book are continued in the software. When the main character arrives at the titular spaceship, the narrative focalization suddenly changes, and the player is transformed from a reader to an actor on the stage: "In a few moments the adventure of your lifetime will begin. . . . In this play you will have the leading part. The curtain is about to rise—inside the *Essex*" (*Essex* novel 46). The narrative stakes are set and the players are invited to participate in the interactive story.

In the case of *The Witcher 3* and the collectible model of the protagonist, paratextuality works quite differently. The figurine from the deluxe version of the game influences the economic value of the digital product. The standard package lacks the object, so the paratextual process associated with it does not transpire (and the price is lower). What is more, the process will not happen even if a player buys a used figurine from a third-party vendor. While this figurine might be identical with the one prepackaged in the deluxe box, the original paratextuality only develops as part of the specific market situation—the figurine is supposed to sell the special edition.

This may suggest that the figurine is not that important for the *Witcher 3* experience. However, the model (even if bought from a third party) can still supplement the game, if only by encouraging a stronger emotional attachment with the protagonist. As such, the paratext can easily change its role: from being a collectible bonus to strengthening the storyworld creation. And this also can be true of the objects packaged with *Essex*: once the player has read the materials, subsequent playthroughs make them optional.

This comparison shows that the degree of paratextual proximity with a game can vary, and so can the dynamics of that relation. This ambiguity is at the core of Genette's concept. The relation between the text and its paratexts can be so close that it is hard to make a clear distinction between where the main text ends and its paratext begins. Paratexts are and are not part of the text, at the same time. Nonetheless, overlooked or not, essential or not, supplemental materials should be understood as part of the text and of players' understanding of the software. Ignoring the guide in *Ultima VII*, for example, may dramatically limit the user's vision of the storyworld, while reading it might enrich the user's exploration. And it may not matter at all when they replay it.

Ellen McCracken interprets this paratextual ambiguity as a process that can direct the readers both into and out of the text. She explains that "outward and inward pathways of semiotic engagement lead readers in various ways to the exterior and interior" (106). According to her, paratextuality can have two vectors: centripetal and centrifugal. Centripetal paratexts point the readers toward the text and its content. Centrifugal paratexts draw readers "outside the text proper," so the text can stay in the background while the reader engages with other materials (106–7). More importantly, one paratext can point in both directions. The paratextual relation is not a matter of a precise position, as Genette insisted (*Paratexts* 4), but rather a matter of scale and tendency. This paratextual uncertainty is especially evident in artifacts that function as extensions of a digital storyworld and the market forces surrounding them. Let's consider several of these artifacts and how they exemplify the centrifugal and centripetal qualities of paratexts.

It is not unusual for paratexts to extend the game into the real world of the player. For example, *Zork Nemesis* comes with a book that pretends to be a text from the game world, a document from the fictional Frobozz National Archive, written by Agent L. Bivotar and chronicling his investigation into the disappearances that take place in the game's setting. The manual for *7th Guest* also purports to be a real object from a fictional world; in this case, a book of files collected by a reporter. Both objects meticulously re-create the material aspects of physical books, including papers pasted onto pages, handwriting, signatures, and stamps that connote official documents.

Sometimes this strategy goes beyond the print form. The physical trinket that comes with *Ultima VII* is the Fellowship Medallion. In the storyworld, this accessory is worn by members of the Fellowship, a mischievous group that players are trying to stop. Similarly, the box of Infocom's *Wishbringer* includes a stone, the titular Wishbringer, a magical artifact with the power to grant wishes. The game's protagonist uses this stone to deal with obstacles that he encounters during his adventures.

These artifacts exemplify McCracken's notion of centripetal paratexts. The main goal of these is to move the players physically closer to the storyworld. The fictional universe is not only represented digitally but also exists outside the screen. In this case, paratextuality creates an illusion of physical continuity between the storyworld and the players' environment, allowing users to sensually experience parts of the diegesis. Veli-Matti Karhulahti argues that such objects trigger or intensify the feeling of immersion, augmenting the players' identification with the avatar and attachment with the diegesis (7). They make it easier for players to imagine that they are materially connected to or involved with the diegesis. The act of holding the physical Wishbringer corresponds with the protagonist's actions in the game. The ability to read Bivotar's notes eases the players into the case they are supposed to solve. This quality strengthens the representational practices of the games and influences not only how the players interpret the storyworld but also how they emotionally respond to it. In this sense, paratextuality can be a technique for affective control.

It is precisely the material difference between the artifact and the digital game that establishes the process of storyworld extension. Because they are medially dissimilar, paratexts engage players in ways that are not available in the digital medium. When compared to digital games, paratexts like those I've discussed here distinguish themselves because they are tangible materials. Yes, they can reward players with contextual data about the storyworld, enable further progress in the game, or afford a better immersion, but at the same time they demand to be physically handled outside of the digital medium. As such, the centripetal (inward) and the centrifugal (outward) vectors work simultaneously. To design meaningful physical interactions with representations of the storyworld, designers must lead players' attention away from the screen, away from the software, and away from the controller.

Two especially interesting examples should clarify how the combined centripetal/centrifugal dynamic of artifact-based paratextuality operates. In *Star-Tropics*, players must not only read the letter that comes with the software but also immerse the document in water so that it reveals a hidden code needed to advance the gameplay. It's hard to imagine a more centrifugal activity than this, given the kind of damage that can be caused to a computer by water. In Infocom's *Suspended*, players control six robots and guide them through a large, labyrinthian facility. Yet the descriptions presented by the software lack any indications of doors that lead into and out of rooms. To identify these, players must interact with a printed map that represents the facility and with tokens representing the robots to plot and mark their exploration of the environment.

These paratexts, like the others I've discussed, expand the limited representational methods of the software, introducing palpability to the experience. The users of both games are required to suspend their interaction with the computer, take the letter or the map, enact specific activities to physically transform or engage with the paratexts, and then return to the computer. As McCracken might suggest, this mode of paratextuality changes games into a backdrop for the physical actions that take place outside of the software.

Regardless, all of these paratexts build toward one main goal: they configure the players' experience of the storyworld. They are indeed "conveyors" of authorial clarifications that regulate the public's interpretation of and response to the text. However, unlike a book's typical conveyors, they both support the storytelling practices in the software and bring the storyworlds outside the games. Publishers and developers try to ensure that players will not stray too far in the wrong direction and will remain close to the software. The creators either make possible or ensure that the users refer to the "correct" data about the storyworlds. Paratexts attempt to shape the interpretative process by providing canonical information, so the interpretation and the whole experience remain close to the authorial visions.

Media Combination

In addition to dealing with respective storyworlds, the surveyed paratexts help define the mediality of each game. The examples analyzed here supply additional media to either enhance the digital narration or counter the technical limitations of the software. The *7th Guest*'s paratext exhibits different media not available in the software, while the written guide in *Ultima VII* could not be implemented within the game, as all the information would take up expensive memory space on the floppy disks. Such examples indicate that paratexts should be taken into consideration in analysis of media specifity of games.

Unfortunately, Genette's theory does not provide any tools to tackle the problem at hand, and Gwóźdź's and Stanitzek's conceptualizations lack any mention of paratexts as media extensions, let alone the kind of complex, diverse centripetal and centrifugal storyworld dynamics that I've discussed. I propose to explain this relation through Irina O. Rajewsky's understanding of intermediality as a combination of media.

Intermediality encompasses "any transgression of boundaries between conventionally distinct media of communication" that "can occur . . . as a consequence of relations or comparisons between different works or semiotic complexes" (Wolf 136). Rajewsky explains that these boundary transgressions can function as "medial configurations." In the case of videogames, such configurations are typically "the result or the very process of combining at least two conventionally distinct media" and work toward a specific construction of storyworld and player interaction with media. Each element of the overall textual package is "present in their own materiality and contribute[s] to the constitution and signification of the entire product in their own specific way" (51–52). Rajewsky emphasizes that media combination can cover a spectrum of relations, starting from contiguity between media and ending with complete integration of disparate elements.

A quick glance at the contents of *Essex*'s box reveals one such configuration. The novel, manuals, booklets, and software disks compose the entire product, but the relationship among the parts combines both paratextuality and inter-mediality. In a conventional novel, a foreword supplements the main text, and while both are written texts, we easily distinguish how one differs from the other and yet see them as belonging together. The same relation develops in *Essex*, but this time the novel functions as a paratextual supplement to the software. The book is materially distinct from the software published on disks and executed on a computer. However, the publisher indicates on the back cover of the book that the book is supposed to be read in the context of the game—providing what might be called a "configurative instruction" to the reader/player. The prose in the *Essex* novel corresponds to the prose used in the software, both themati-cally and stylistically, but they differ in terms of how the users operate them.

Recently, scholars have recognized that videogames combine multiple media (see Duret and Pons; Fuchs and Thoss; Ivănescu; Jørgensen; Melnic). However, what is missing from this discussion are the media configurations that happen at the threshold of software, screen, and controller. The paratex-tual artifacts and particular configurations of media that we see in the games I've discussed carry through on the general paratextual goal of authorial con-trol. But lest we forget, books are not videogames. So what exactly do the game makers want to regulate? In sum, they want to control not only how the texts are interpreted but also how players define and interact with them.

Media Definition

Paratextual objects allow producers to imply or outright state how they intend their game to be experienced as a medium—a crucial form of guidance, particu-larly for consumers who might encounter the game in an unusual setting or are unfamiliar with gaming media. The most common realization of this function can be observed in instruction manuals, which typically clarify how to operate the software. For instance, all the manuals of the electronic novels contain a chapter on how to "talk to" the game. The section begins with a very straight-forward description of what the game in question is: "YOU ENTER THE WORLD

OF ESSEX . . . by typing on your computer keyboard. You can type whenever text appears on the screen and you are ready to respond" (*Essex* novel 89). Then the manual clarifies especially significant keyboard commands as well as the time, space, and dialogue systems at work in the software. This instruction provides essential information about the game rules, identifying methods to operate the software and suggesting specific gameplay styles.

But just as importantly, the manual also endorses the producers' perception of their game as a medium. The introduction "YOU ENTER THE WORLD OF" paints the software as a storytelling and immersive experience. The process of media definition is not restricted to instruction booklets—indeed, it might be considered an essential function of a paratext in a context in which videogames take increasingly diverse forms for an equally diverse audience.

Paratextual media combination also plays a role, because as I've discussed, the materiality and form of a paratext can shape the experience and understanding of play. The narrative in the books could have been effortlessly presented in the text-based software, but the designers decided to support the software with other objects. Thus, the books are not only narrative tools; they also represent themselves as a separate media with a specific, distinctly "literary" relationship to the software. The blurbs on the back covers advise the players to experience the products in a remarkably concrete manner: "You start . . . by reading the first chapters of the story in this book and then go directly to the screen of your home computer. The interactive adventure picks up on the diskette." This text encourages a specific reception strategy. Players are supposed to compare two media (the book and the software) so they can notice the differences and similarities between the narrative methods these media employ.

It is precisely this performance of comparison that influences how the players understand what the game is. André Gaudreault and Philippe Marion explain, "A good understanding of a medium . . . entails understanding its relationship to other media: it is through intermediality, through a concern with the intermedial, that a medium is understood" (15). Simply put, a medium can only be defined in reference to another medium. But unlike Jay David Bolter and Richard Grusin's argument that media generally do this indirectly, through a kind of tacit invitation to compare and contrast them (55), *Essex* does this in a fashion that is quite explicit: read the book, then play the game, and thus experience the game in comparison to the book. The media combination in these electronic novels makes the users aware of the medialities at work. The players are directed not only toward the storyworld but also toward the technical devices at their disposal, which construct it and their interaction with it. "An electronic novel picks up where the printed word leaves off," the blurb reads.

Let's consider this "picking up" in more detail. The highlighted relation between the game and the printed materials accomplishes two goals. First, the broader paratextual dynamic intends that the game medium is comparable with or identical to any other medium, but it does so in a fashion that enables the player to identify the core elements of the narrative and the interaction. The blurb on the box describes *Ultima VII* as "the first chapter in the third book of the award-winning Ultima saga," suggesting an epic quality to the game. This paratextual quality has a distinct effect on reader reception, from the fairy tale that accompanies *Wishbringer* to the bureaucratic forms and files added to *Bureaucracy*, the latter revealing the reasoning behind the construction of puzzles in the game.

Second, paratextuality defines the game as a "new" medium, differentiating it from the paratextual medium to which it is being compared. The two stages of reception encouraged by electronic novels (first read the book, then play the software) identify the features that the game offers as innovative in relation to the "older" medium. Again, we see this in various forms. In *Baldur's Gate* and *Ultima VII*, the comparison between a computer roleplaying game and a travel guide brings the exploratory aspects of the software to the player's attention. The supplementary materials highlight that roleplaying games transform the genre of travel literature into a digital simulation.

In sum, the paratexts of digital games can and often do illuminate the nature of the software (particularly if audiences are unfamiliar with the game's particular affordances), deploying similarity and difference to accomplish that goal. Of course, all media are entangled in systems of relations and references. The representative potential of a given medium can be revealed only in confrontation with other methods of representation (Bolter and Grusin 65–68). But this function of paratextuality has a relatively unique role in digital games because games require a player to perform. Thus, it is vital that the media features and affordances of a given game are brought to the fore so that the player can focus simultaneously on the game's mediality and its storyworld.

The Double Logic of Videogame Paratextuality

As the examples I've explored here demonstrate, the paratextual process in digital games constantly oscillates between the textual components packaged with the text and those that are not but are implied. Further, a single paratext might perform many different tasks. A simple booklet in *Zork Nemesis* (the journal written by Bivotar) supplements the storyworld with authorized data, expands the diegesis out of the computer and into the player's hands, provides the game with additional media forms, and defines what the game medium is in order to suggest both its familiarity and its difference. So is it possible to derive an overall theory of videogame paratextuality?

I think the understanding of the phenomenon can be deepened with notions of media transparency and opacity. As shown by Bolter and Grusin (21–44), relations between media always operate within a double logic of immediacy and hypermediacy. The first logic aims for the transparency of the medium, hiding its artificiality, so we immerse ourselves in the representation it establishes and more or less forget how the medium works. For example, when a player has practiced a set of commands enough, they will be able to perform them without thinking. The second logic does the opposite, seeking to expose the multiplicity of semiotic systems of the medium so we become aware of its inner workings and are conscious of its particular representational affordances. For example, a player must learn to be aware of the different representational elements, such as the elements of the user interface and their meanings.

Both immediacy and hypermediacy act simultaneously, because both aim to create an engaging experience—the first by producing a convincing representation, the second by producing a functional mediation—and this double logic can be found in the centripetal and centrifugal vectors of videogame paratextuality. The centripetal conforms to the logic of immediacy; the centrifugal, out of the text, conforms to the logic of hypermediacy. The centripetal strengthens the game's representational practices and enables the player to achieve haptic fluency; the centrifugal brings to light the game's particular mediality, highlighting the representational and performative elements of which the player must be aware.

Another way to think about the double logic of videogame paratextuality is through the storyworld function and the media function (see table). The storyworld function works in accordance with the logic of immediacy. The act of mediation becomes less visible, if not entirely invisible, and as a consequence the player can focus on the representation created by the game and its paratexts. The media function conforms to the logic of hypermediacy. The materials bring the mediality of the paratextual relation to the attention of the player. Usually, this process centers on the technicalities of the software, exposing the particular media dimensions of the game and its paratext. This function is not concerned with representation but with mediation. It detaches the player from the game's narrativity so they can notice and ponder how this narrativity works on a technical level. Ultimately, the double logic of videogame paratextuality bridges the gap between the diegetic and nondiegetic, the inside and outside, the storyworld as an authored representation and the storyworld as a mediated artifact.

The Double Logic of Paratextuality

STORYWORLD FUNCTION	MEDIA FUNCTION
Immediacy	Hypermediacy
Representation	Mediation
Immersion	Detachment
Centripetal	Centrifugal
Storyworld creation	Media definition

I thank Nick Montfort for introducing me to the phenomenon of media materiality and giving me access to the collection of gaming artifacts at the MIT Trope Tank.

WORKS CITED

Birke, Dorothee, and Birte Christ. "Paratext and Digitized Narrative: Mapping the Field." *Narrative,* vol. 21, no. 1, 2013, pp. 65–87.

Bolter, Jay David, and Richard Grusin. *Remediation: Understanding New Media.* MIT Press, 2000.

Consalvo, Mia. *Cheating: Gaining Advantage in Videogames.* MIT Press, 2007.

Desrochers, Nadine, and Daniel Apollon, eds. *Examining Paratextual Theory and Its Applications in Digital Culture.* IGI Global, 2014.

Dunne, Daniel. "Paratext: The In-Between of Structure and Play." *Contemporary Research on Intertextuality in Video Games,* edited by Christophe Duret and Christian-Marie Pons. IGI Global, 2016, pp. 274–96.

Duret, Christophe, and Christian-Marie Pons, eds. *Contemporary Research on Intertextuality in Video Games.* IGI Global, 2016.

Flanagan, Kevin M. "Introduction—Videogame Adaptation: Some Experiments in Method." *Wide Screen,* vol. 6, no. 1, September 2016, special issue. https://widescreenjournal .org/archives/145-2.

Fuchs, Michael, and Jeff Thoss, eds. *Intermedia Games—Games Inter Media. Video Games and Intermediality.* Bloomsbury Academic, 2019.

Galloway, Alexander R. *The Interface Effect.* Polity, 2012.

Gaudreault, André, and Philippe Marion. "The Cinema as a Model for the Genealogy of Media." *Convergence*, vol. 8, no. 4, 2002, pp. 12–18.

Genette, Gérard. *Palimpsests: Literature in the Second Degree*, translated by Channa Newman and Claude Doubinsky. University of Nebraska Press, 1997.

———. *Paratexts: Thresholds of Interpretation*, translated by Jane E. Lewin. Cambridge University Press, 1997.

Gray, Jonathan. *Show Sold Separately: Promos, Spoilers, and Other Media Paratexts*. New York University Press, 2010.

Gwóźdź, Andrzej. *Obok Filmu. Między Mediami* [Next to the Movie. Between Media]. *Pogranicza Audiowizualności. Parateksty Kina, Telewizji i Nowych Mediów* [Borders of Audiovisuality. Paratexts of Cinema, Television and New Media], edited by Andrzej Gwóźdź. Universitas, 2010. [In Polish.]

Herman, David. "Narrative Ways of Worldmaking." *Narratology in the Age of Cross-Disciplinary Narrative Research*, edited by Sandra Heinen and Roy Sommer. Walter De Gruyter, 2009, pp. 71–87.

Ivănescu, Andra. *Popular Music in the Nostalgia Video Game: The Way It Never Sounded.* Palgrave Macmillan, 2019.

Jørgensen, Ida Kathrine Hammeleff. "Media and Games: An Intermedial Framework," 2018. https://pure.itu.dk/portal/files/83586834/Media_and_games_post_print.pdf.

Karhulahti, Veli-Matti. "*Feelies*: The Lost Art of Immersing the Narrative." *Proceedings of DiGRA Nordic '12 Conference: Local and Global—Games in Culture and Society*, 2012. http://www.digra.org/wp-content/uploads/digital-library/12168.03111.pdf.

Klecker, Cornelia. "The Other Kind of Film Frames: A Research Report on Paratexts in Film." *Word & Image*, vol. 31, no. 4, 2015, pp. 402–13.

Kocurek, Carly A. "The Treachery of Pixels: Reconsidering Feelies in an Era of Digital Play." *Journal of Gaming & Virtual Worlds*, vol. 5, no. 3, 2013, pp. 295–306.

McCracken, Ellen. "Expanding Genette's Epitext/Peritext Model for Transitional Electronic Literature: Centrifugal and Centripetal Vectors on Kindles and iPads." *Narrative*, vol. 21, no. 1, 2013, pp. 105–24.

Melnic, Vlad. "The Remediation of the Epic in Digital Games: *The Elder Scrolls V: Skyrim*." *American, British and Canadian Studies*, vol. 30, no. 1, 2018, pp. 153–70.

Rajewsky, Iryna O. "Intermediality, Intertextuality, and Remediation: A Literary Perspective on Intermediality." *Intermédialités*, vol. 6, 2005, pp. 43–64.

Rockenberger, Annika. "'Paratext' und Neue Medien: Probleme und Perspektiven eines Begriffstransfers." *Philologie im Netz*, vol. 76, 2016. http://web.fu-berlin.de/phin/phin76/p76t2.htm. [In German.]

———. "Video Game Framings." *Examining Paratextual Theory and Its Applications in Digital Culture*, edited by Nadine Desrochers and Daniel Apollon. IGI Global, 2014, pp. 252–86.

Stanitzek, Georg. "Texts and Paratexts in Media." *Critical Inquiry*, vol. 32, no. 1, 2005, pp. 27–42.

Švelch, Jan. *Paratexts to Non-Linear Media Texts: Paratextuality in Video Games Culture.* 2017. Charles University, Prague, PhD dissertation.

Wolf, Werner. "Relations Between Literature and Music in the Context of a General Typology of Intermediality." *Comparative Literature: Sharing Knowledge for Preserving Cultural Diversity,* vol. 1, edited by Lisa Block de Behar, Paola Mildonian, Jean-Michel Djian, Djelal Kadir, Alfons Knauth, Dolores Romero Lopez, and Marcio Seligmann Silva. Eolls/UNESCO, 2009, pp. 133–55.

Wolf, Werner, and Walter Bernhart, eds. *Framing Borders in Literature and Other Media.* Rodopi, 2006.

VIDEOGAME REFERENCES

7th Guest. Virgin Interactive, 1993.

Age of Empires. Microsoft, 1997.

Baldur's Gate. Interplay Entertainment and CD Projekt, 1998.

Baldur's Gate II: Shadows of Amn. Interplay Entertainment and CD Projekt, 2000.

Beyond Divinity. Digital Jesters, 2004.

Birds of Prey. Electronic Arts, 1992.

Brimstone: The Dream of Gawain. Brøderbund, 1985.

Bureaucracy. Infocom, 1987.

Essex. Brøderbund, 1985.

Grand Theft Auto III. Rockstar, 2002.

Metal Gear Solid 2: Sons of Liverty. Konami, 2001.

Mindwheel. Brøderbund, 1984.

StarTropics. Nintendo, 1990.

Suspended. Infocom, 1983.

The Witcher. Atari and CD Projekt, 2007.

The Witcher 3: Wild Hunt Collector's Edition. CD Projekt, 2015.

Ultima VII: The Black Gate. Origin Systems, 1992.

Wishbringer. Infocom, 1985.

Zork Nemesis: The Forbidden Lands. Activision, 1996.

CONTRIBUTORS

ANDREW BAILEY teaches game studies and new media art history in the Faculty of Arts and Sciences at Ontario College Art & Design University. His PhD dissertation within the art history program at York University focuses on how formalism and medium specificity function within videogame art history. He is currently researching Canadian media-focused artist-run centers and how their curatorial and educational programming is influenced by the platformization of game development. He is an editor for *First Person Scholar* and *Press Start Journal*.

JOSÉ BLÁZQUEZ is a media practitioner and a lecturer in media production at Bournemouth University. He has been involved in the production of multiple projects and events, such as films, documentaries, and festivals. His research revolves around the study of audience participation in cultural production processes and the use of immersive media technologies in education and entertainment. He is the author of *Participatory Worlds: The Limits of Audience Participation* and *Press Start: The Use of Videogame Assets in Audience Creative Practices*.

JESIKA BROOKS has a bachelor's degree in English from Columbia College and a master of library and information science degree from the University of South Carolina. She works as the educational technology librarian at Columbia College, where she instructs faculty, students, and staff on edtech and creates technical documentation—though she typically writes about fighting software bugs rather than fighting Ganon! Her research stems from a lifelong interest in games and writing as well as in the way that stories are constructed and shared.

FRANCIS BUTTERWORTH-PARR is a PhD student in English literature at the Scottish Graduate School of the Arts and Humanities, University of Glasgow.

He is currently researching the deployment of videogames as metaphor in contemporary literary culture.

CRAIG CAREY is associate professor of English at the University of Southern Mississippi, where he also serves as faculty advisor of the USM Game Studies Group, an organization of students, faculty, and alumni interested in the critical and creative affordances of videogames. His current book project, *Realism Redux: Authors, Archives, and Literary Invention,* explores the relationship between technologies of inscription, archival media, and literary style in the age of Edison. He also contributed a chapter on close reading and critical play to the forthcoming volume *Teaching Games and Game Studies in the Literature Classroom.*

MEGAN AMBER CONDIS is assistant professor in the Department of Communication Studies at Texas Tech University. She is the author of *Gaming Masculinities: Trolls, Fake Geeks, and the Gendered Battle for Online Culture* (2018) and serves as assistant editor for *Analog Game Studies.*

JARREL DE MATAS holds a master's degree in English literature from the University of the West Indies and is presently a PhD English candidate and teaching associate at the University of Massachusetts, Amherst. His research explores the connections between Caribbean science fiction and posthuman studies. He has published in the *Journal of West Indian Literature, Caribbean Journal of Cultural Studies, Criterion,* and *The Researcher.* He is also the producer of the Caribbean Science Fiction Network.

ROB GALLAGHER is a lecturer in film and media in the Department of English at Manchester Metropolitan University. His research considers how videogames and other digital media forms reflect and shape popular conceptions of identity, subjectivity, and embodiment. His current book project explores the relationship between digital gaming and life-writing, addressing auto/biographical videogames alongside firsthand accounts of digital gameplay. He is the author of *Videogames, Identity and Digital Subjectivity.*

AARON HEINRICH is currently pursuing his PhD in literature and criticism at Indiana University of Pennsylvania. His research focuses, in part, on fostering game studies literacy in East African classrooms and beyond.

CHRISTOPHER LOVINS is assistant professor of Korean history and civilization at the Ulsan National Institute of Science and Technology. His publications include *King Chŏngjo: An Enlightened Despot in Early Modern Korea* and, most recently, "A Ghost in the Replicant? Questions of Humanity and Technological Integration in *Blade Runner* and *Ghost in the Shell*." He has also published on legitimacy, evolutionary approaches to the humanities, historical film, and science fiction.

RIZIKI MILLANZI is a doctoral researcher at the Sussex Centre for American Studies, University of Sussex. Her research examines the representation of Black women in literature, film, and popular culture, exploring how representation within media, such as videogames and videogame literature, becomes a microcosm through which we can examine representational practices and issues within wider society. Millanzi has been an avid gamer for as long as she can remember, but these days she prefers *Dead by Daylight* and *Animal Crossing* over *Sabrina the Teenage Witch* and *Spyro*.

CHLOE ANNA MILLIGAN is assistant professor of digital humanities in the Writing and Digital Media Program at Pennsylvania State University, Berks. She teaches, researches, and publishes primarily about topics in electronic literature and game studies, with emphases on embodied affect and queer materiality in both analog and digital contexts. Her work has appeared in journals such as *ROMchip*, *Press Start*, *Publije*, and *Computers and Composition Online*. Her book *Novel Media: Post-digital Literature Beyond the Book* is forthcoming as part of Cambridge University Press's new Elements in Digital Fictions series.

HOLLY PARKER is an associate lecturer and PhD researcher at the University of Lincoln. She also works as a guest editor for *Alluvium*. Her current research focuses on affect and performance in twenty-first-century fiction, an interdisciplinary study across affect theory and performance studies that rests on the cultural backdrop of neoliberalism and postmillennial digital culture.

MIKE SELL is professor of English at Indiana University of Pennsylvania, where he teaches Black American literature and culture, critical theory, and playful literatures. He is the coauthor, with Michael M. Chemers, of *Systemic Dramaturgy: A Handbook for the Digital Age*; author of *The Avant-Garde: Race Religion War*; and editor of *Modern American Drama: Playwriting in the 1960s*. He is the founder and coleader of the Digital Storytelling Project, which supports K-12 teachers in the integration of creative coding, design thinking, and ethical decision-making into standards-based curricula.

MICHELLE SHEA is an education librarian and the co-head of public services at Texas A&M University–Central Texas. As a former teacher and current librarian, she enjoys making book recommendations and building the children's and young adult collection for students and community members. Her passion is in writing about literacy, librarianship, programming, and services for patrons of all ages.

KRISTEN STARKOWSKI is a preceptor in expository writing at Harvard College. She completed her PhD in English at Princeton University. Her current writing project focuses on minor characters in the Victorian novel and proposes a new methodology of reading for the various networks of survival and subsistence in the nineteenth-century social and economic world. Her work has appeared in *NOVEL*, *Victorian Review*, and *Journal of Literary and Cultural Disability Studies*. Her other research interests include writing pedagogy, digital humanities, disability studies, and Latinx studies.

NIELS 'T HOOFT is an entrepreneur and writer living in Utrecht, the Netherlands. He has written several novels as well as stories for videogames, including *Rive* and *Toki Tori 2+*. He is the founder of various Dutch gaming media, including websites and magazines, and also worked as a journalist, writing about games for the daily newspaper *NRC* and other publications. He is a past committee member of the advisory board of the Dutch Foundation for Literature, current committee member of the Flanders Audiovisual Fund's games department, and cofounder and CEO of the reading startup Immer. He is presently writing a short story collection and developing small games in his spare time.

MICHAŁ DAWID ŻMUDA is assistant professor in the College of Humanities at the University of Rzeszów. He is a Fulbright graduate and has been a research assistant in the Comparative Media/Writing Department at the Massachusetts Institute of Technology and in the Center for Computer Games Research at the IT University of Copenhagen. Currently, he researches the media archeology of skeuomorphic graphical user interfaces and the discourse networks and formations (the substances, electrons, information, and subjects) behind technologies of flowing.

INDEX

VIDEOGAMES